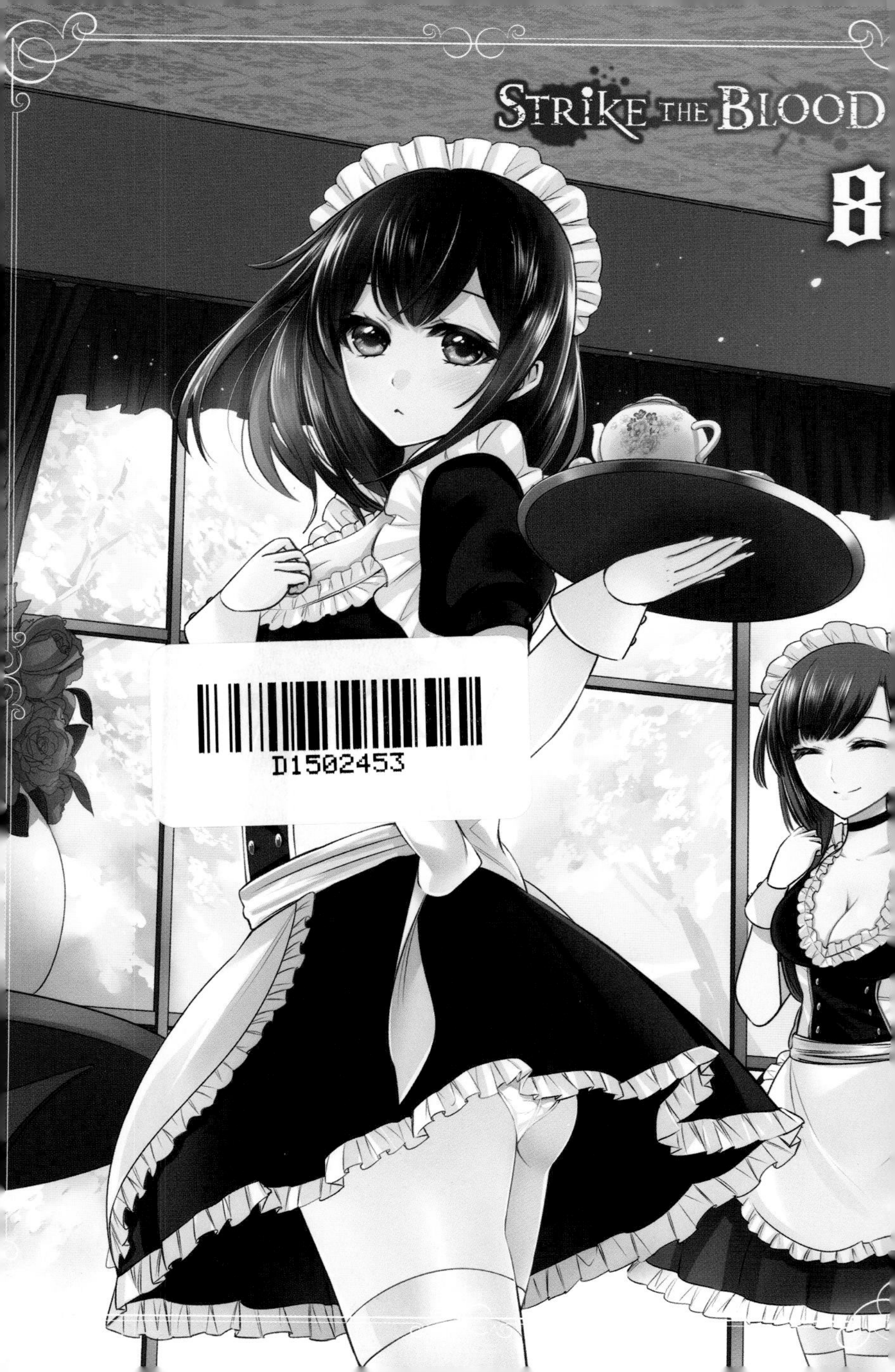
STRIKE THE BLOOD
8

STRIKE THE BLOOD

The Fourth Primogenitor is immortal and indestructible. Rejecting his vampiric brethren, he does not desire domination, but only the service of the twelve Beast Vassals that are disaster incarnate, the sipping of blood, carnage, and destruction. The vampire is said to be ruthless and heartless, completely beyond the doctrines of the world; a monster who had laid waste to many cities in the past.

CONTENTS

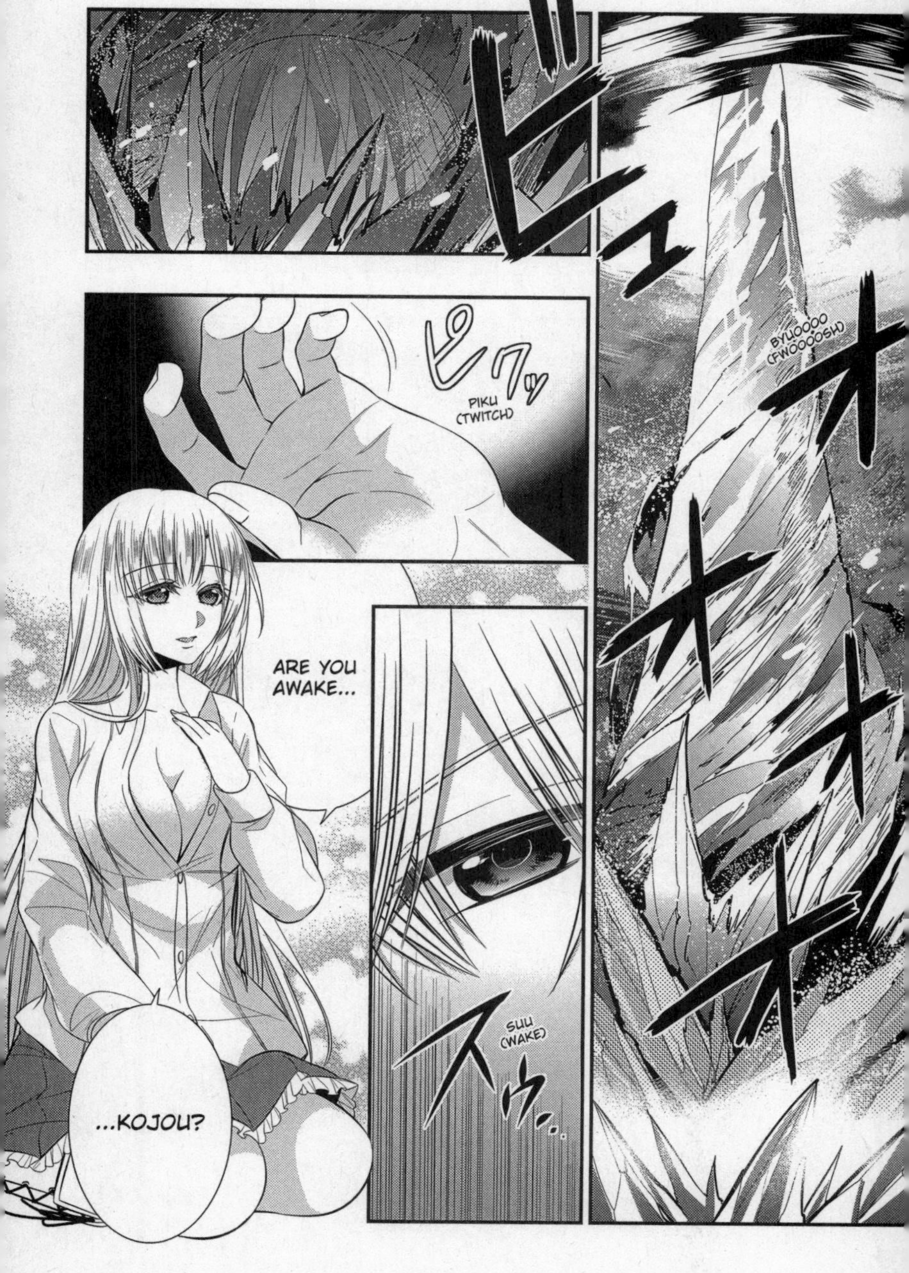
BYUOOOO
(FWOOOOSH)
PIKU
(TWITCH)
SUU
(WAKE)
ARE YOU AWAKE...
...KOJOU?

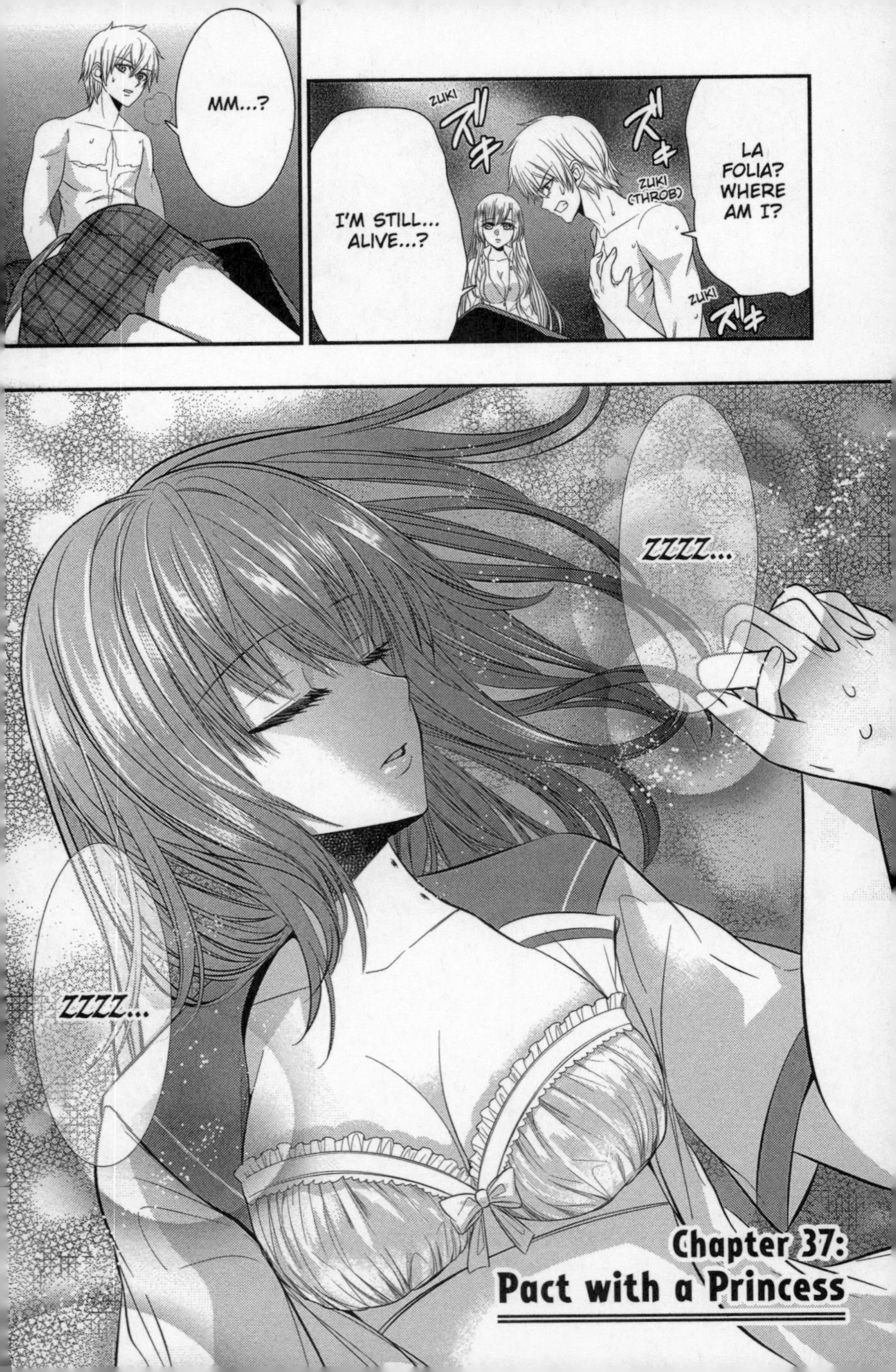
LA FOLIA? WHERE AM I?
ズキ ZUKI
ズキ ZUKI (THROB)
ズキ ZUKI
I'M STILL... ALIVE...?
MM...?
ZZZZ...
ZZZZ...
Chapter 37: Pact with a Princess

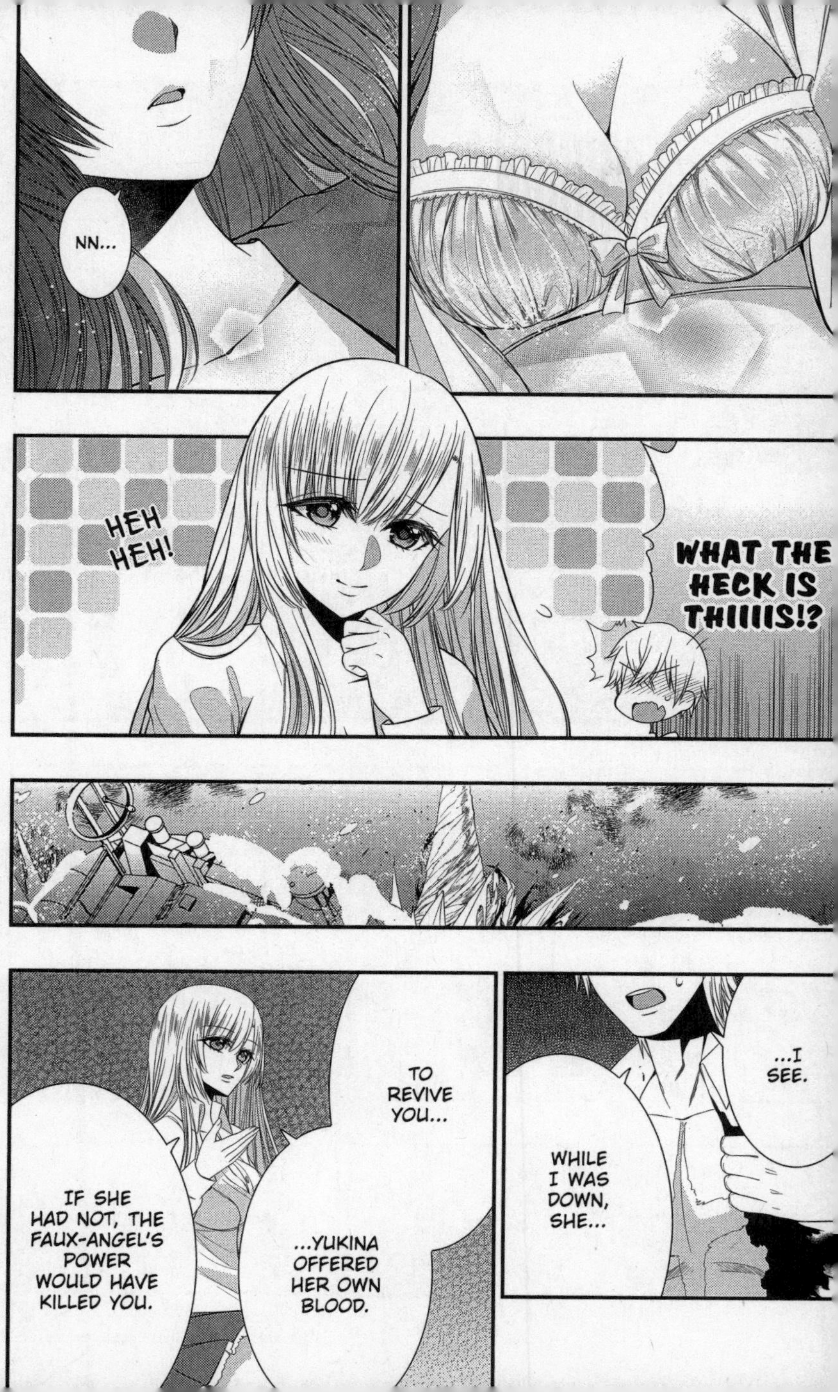
NN...
WHAT THE HECK IS THIIIIS!?
HEH HEH!
...I SEE.
WHILE I WAS DOWN, SHE...
TO REVIVE YOU...
...YUKINA OFFERED HER OWN BLOOD.
IF SHE HAD NOT, THE FAUX-ANGEL'S POWER WOULD HAVE KILLED YOU.

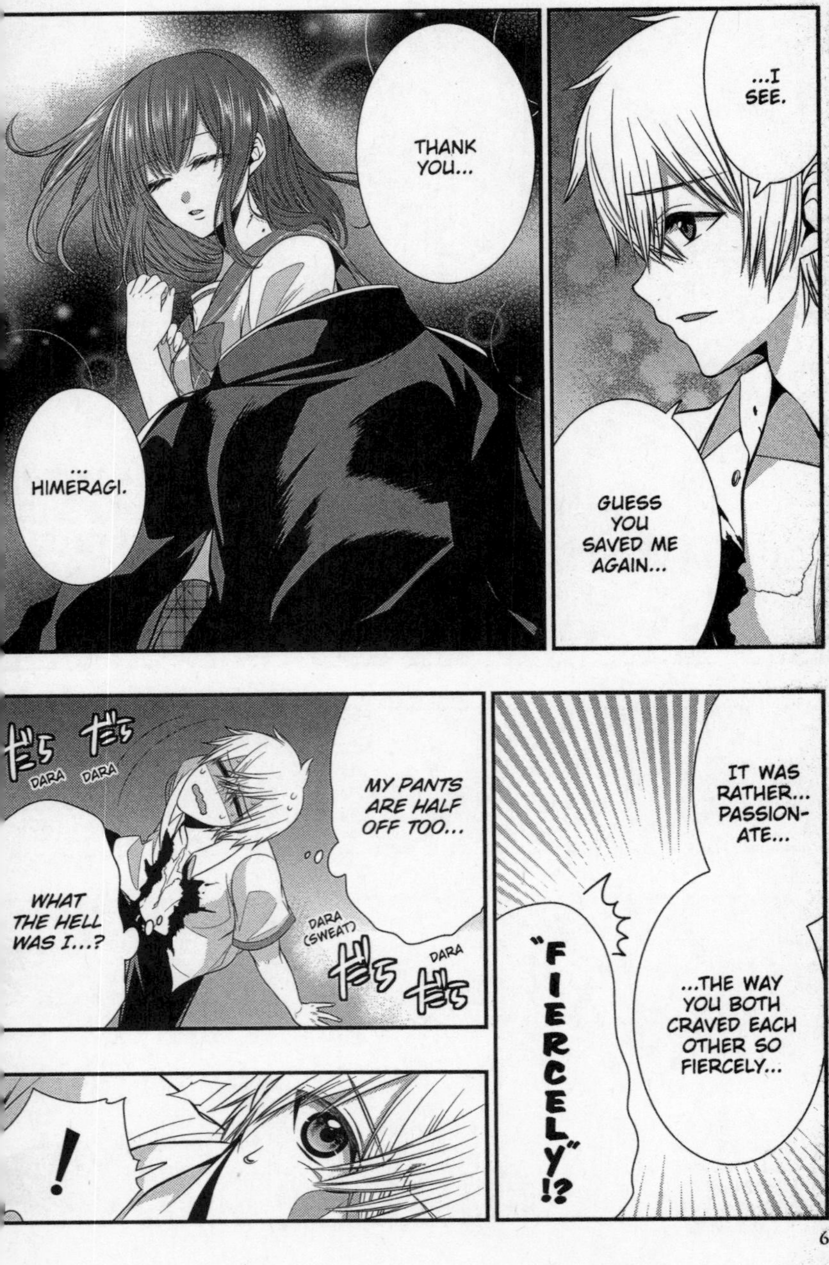
...I SEE.
GUESS YOU SAVED ME AGAIN...
THANK YOU...
... HIMERAGI.
IT WAS RATHER... PASSION-ATE...
...THE WAY YOU BOTH CRAVED EACH OTHER SO FIERCELY...
"FIERCELY"!?
MY PANTS ARE HALF OFF TOO...
DARA DARA
WHAT THE HELL WAS I...?
DARA (SWEAT)
DARA
!

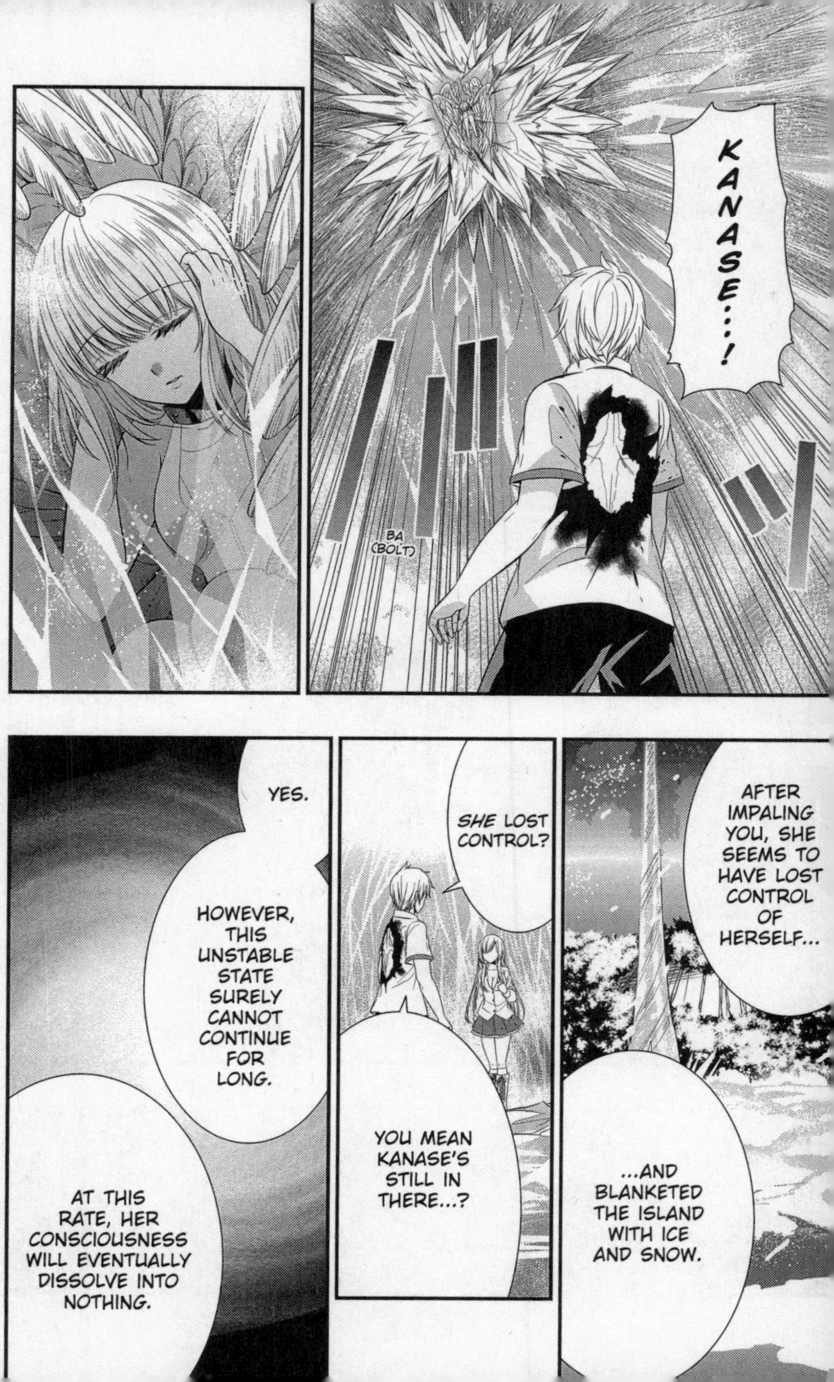
KANASE...!
BA (BOLT)
AFTER IMPALING YOU, SHE SEEMS TO HAVE LOST CONTROL OF HERSELF...
...AND BLANKETED THE ISLAND WITH ICE AND SNOW.
SHE LOST CONTROL?
YOU MEAN KANASE'S STILL IN THERE...?
YES.
HOWEVER, THIS UNSTABLE STATE SURELY CANNOT CONTINUE FOR LONG.
AT THIS RATE, HER CONSCIOUSNESS WILL EVENTUALLY DISSOLVE INTO NOTHING.

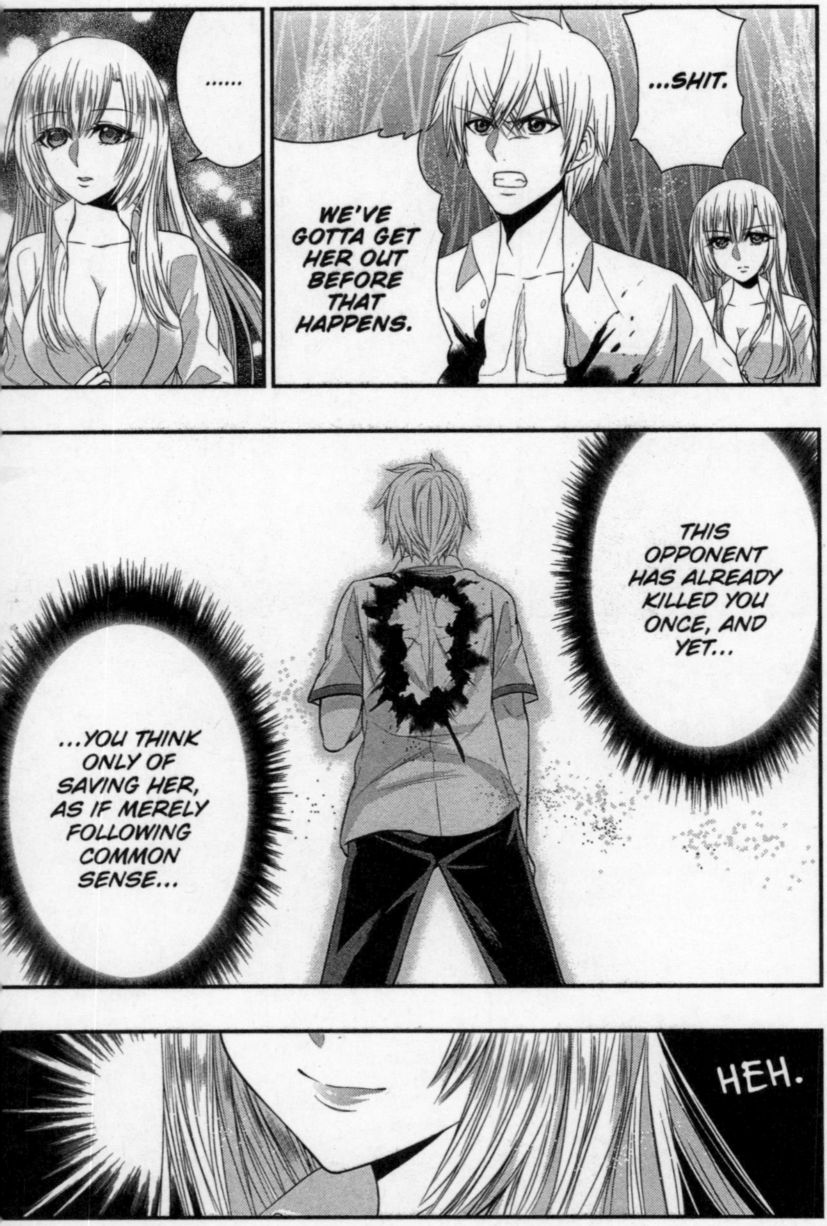
...SHIT.
WE'VE GOTTA GET HER OUT BEFORE THAT HAPPENS.
......
THIS OPPONENT HAS ALREADY KILLED YOU ONCE, AND YET...
...YOU THINK ONLY OF SAVING HER, AS IF MERELY FOLLOWING COMMON SENSE...
HEH.

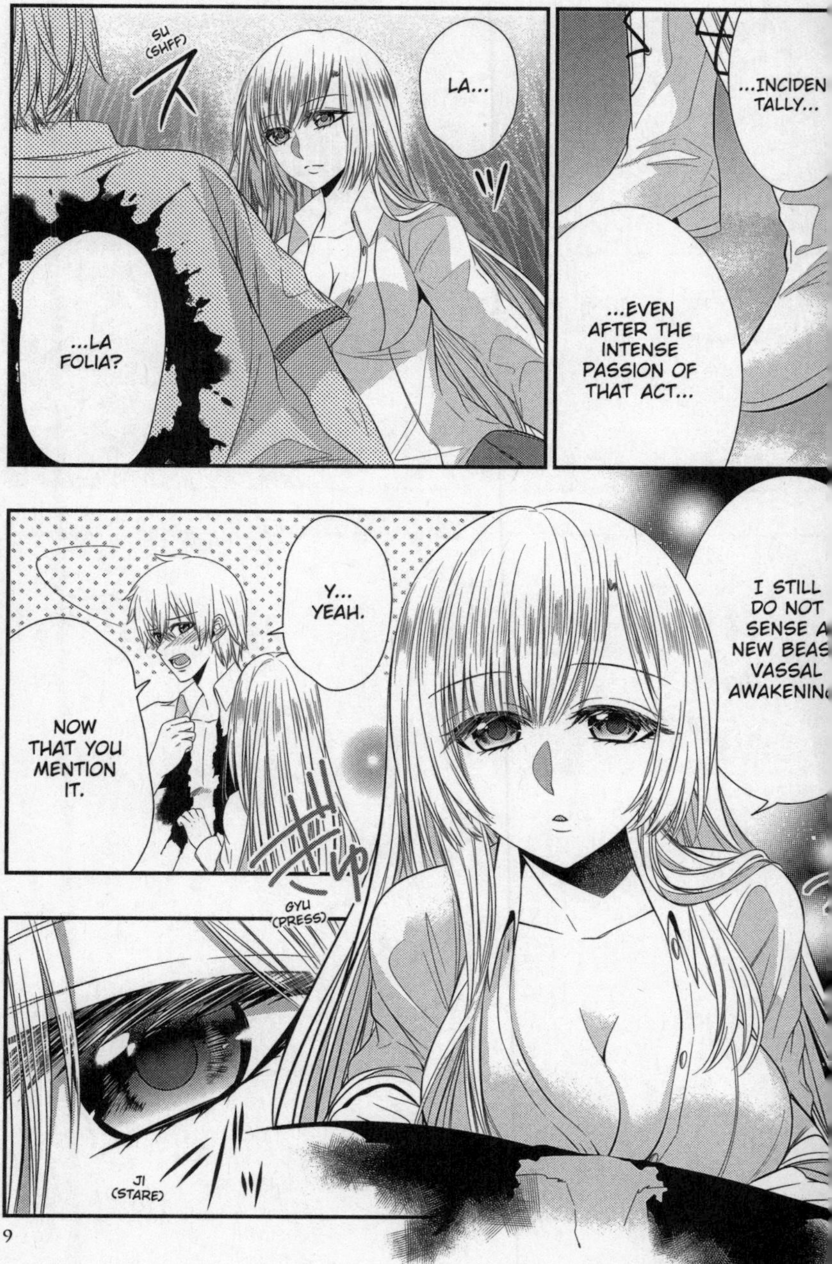
...INCIDENTALLY...
...EVEN AFTER THE INTENSE PASSION OF THAT ACT...
LA...
SU (SHFF)
...LA FOLIA?
I STILL DO NOT SENSE A NEW BEAS VASSAL AWAKENIN
Y... YEAH.
NOW THAT YOU MENTION IT.
GYU (PRESS)
JI (STARE)

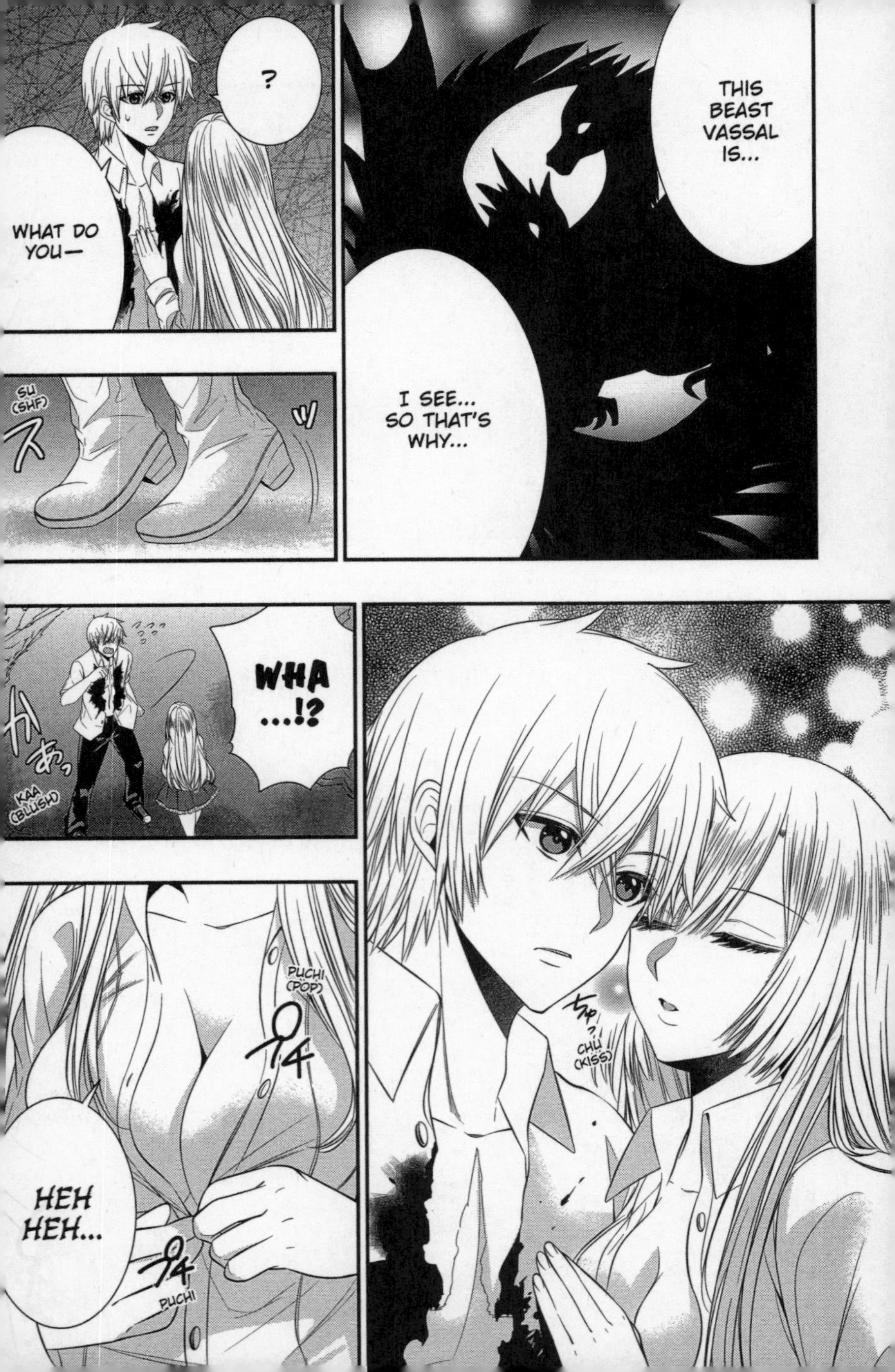

THIS BEAST VASSAL IS...
I SEE... SO THAT'S WHY...
?
WHAT DO YOU—
SU (SHF)
CHU (KISS)
WHA ...!?
KAA (BLUSH)
PUCHI (POP)
HEH HEH...
PUCHI

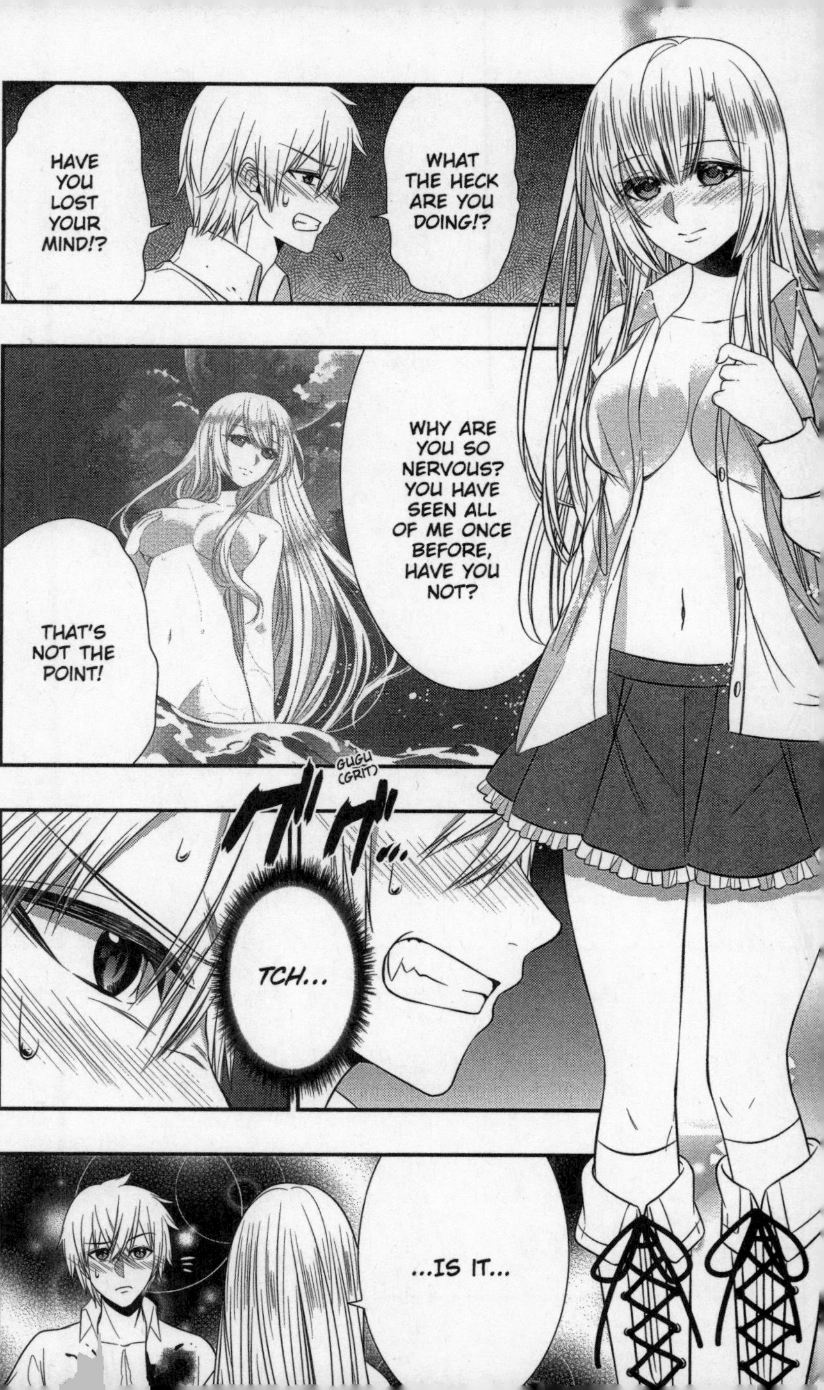
WHAT THE HECK ARE YOU DOING!?
HAVE YOU LOST YOUR MIND!?
WHY ARE YOU SO NERVOUS? YOU HAVE SEEN ALL OF ME ONCE BEFORE, HAVE YOU NOT?
THAT'S NOT THE POINT!
GUGU (GRIT)
TCH...
...IS IT...

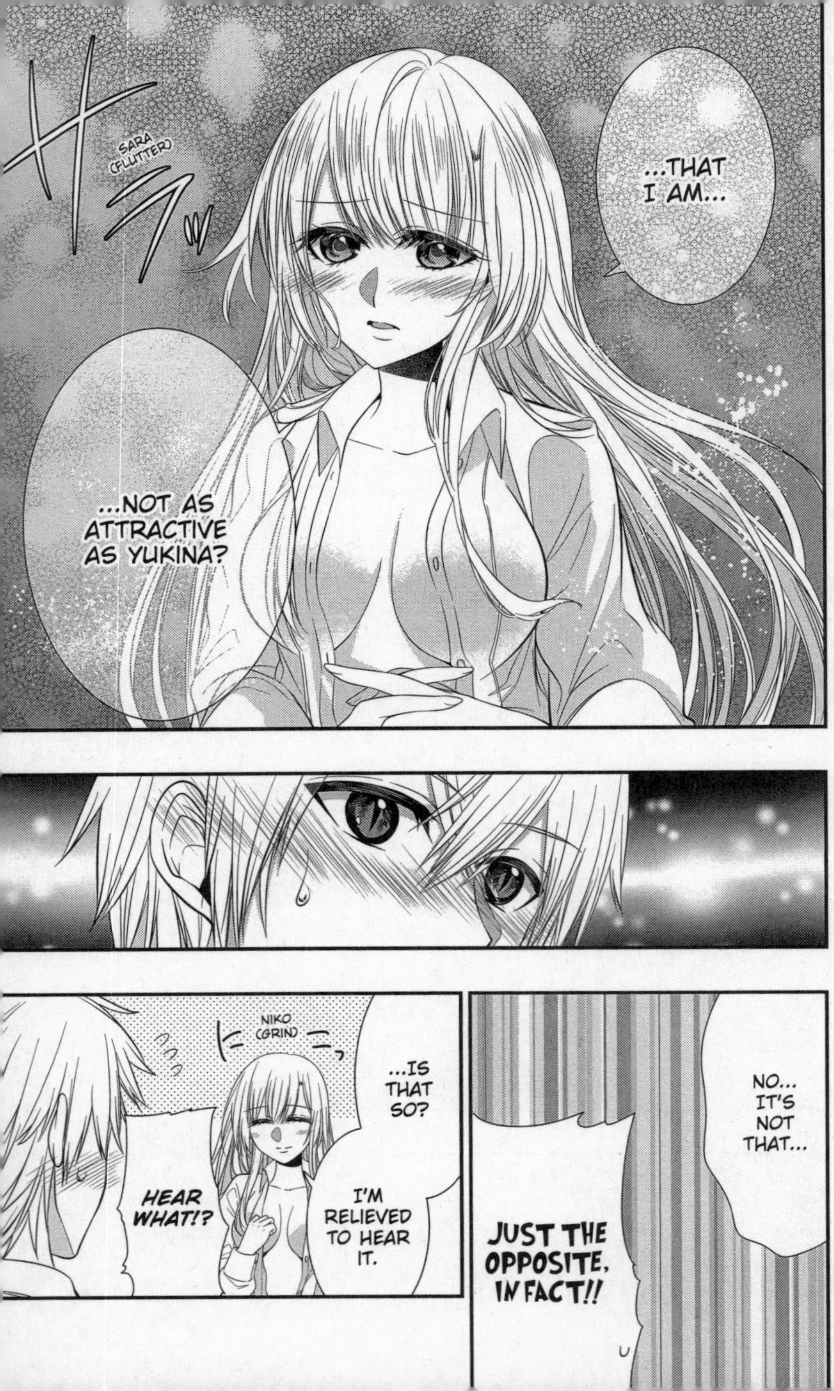
...THAT I AM...
SARA (FLUTTER)
...NOT AS ATTRACTIVE AS YUKINA?
NO... IT'S NOT THAT...
JUST THE OPPOSITE, IN FACT!!
...IS THAT SO?
NIKO (GRIND)
I'M RELIEVED TO HEAR IT.
HEAR WHAT!?

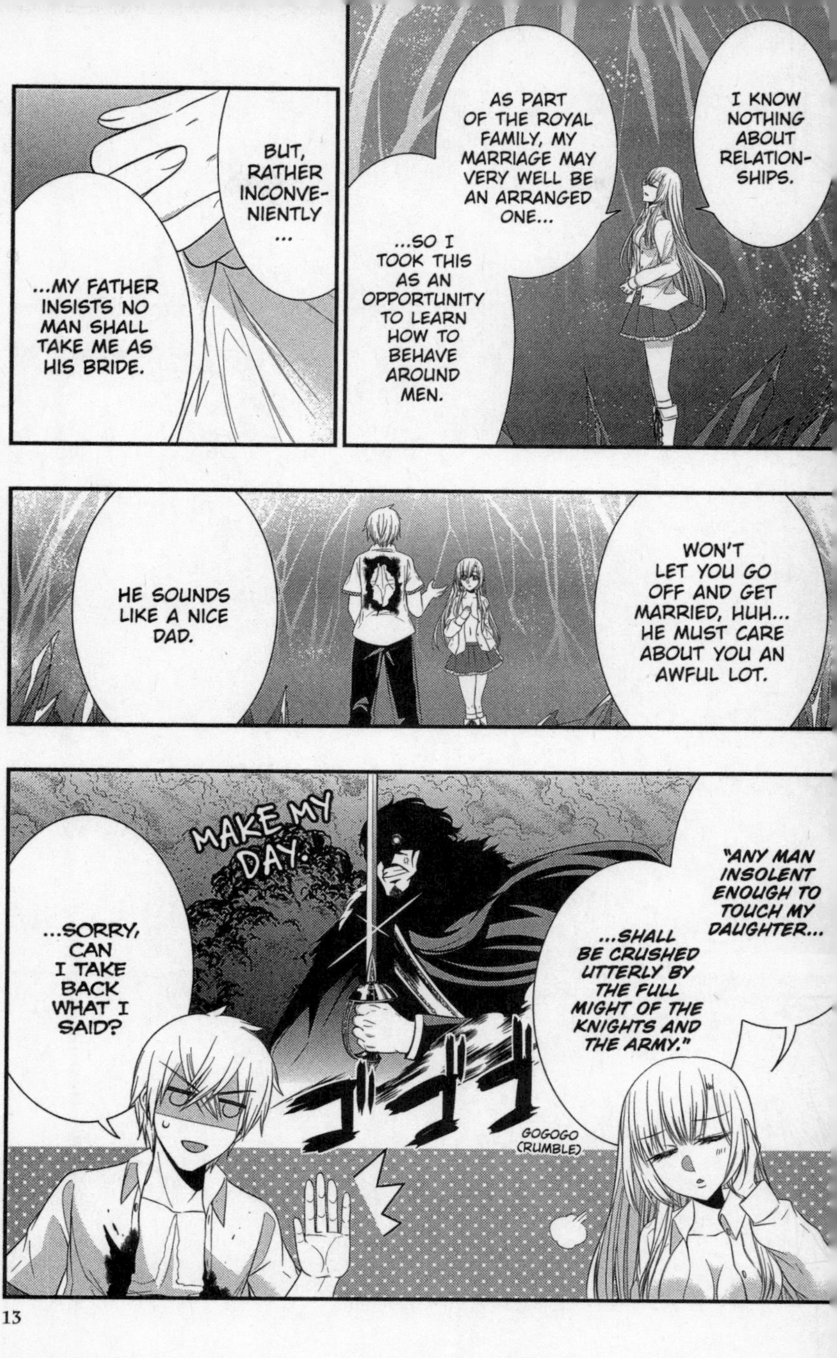
I KNOW NOTHING ABOUT RELATIONSHIPS.
AS PART OF THE ROYAL FAMILY, MY MARRIAGE MAY VERY WELL BE AN ARRANGED ONE...
...SO I TOOK THIS AS AN OPPORTUNITY TO LEARN HOW TO BEHAVE AROUND MEN.
BUT, RATHER INCONVENIENTLY...
...MY FATHER INSISTS NO MAN SHALL TAKE ME AS HIS BRIDE.
WON'T LET YOU GO OFF AND GET MARRIED, HUH... HE MUST CARE ABOUT YOU AN AWFUL LOT.
HE SOUNDS LIKE A NICE DAD.
"ANY MAN INSOLENT ENOUGH TO TOUCH MY DAUGHTER...
...SHALL BE CRUSHED UTTERLY BY THE FULL MIGHT OF THE KNIGHTS AND THE ARMY."
MAKE MY DAY.
GOGOGO (RUMBLE)
...SORRY, CAN I TAKE BACK WHAT I SAID?

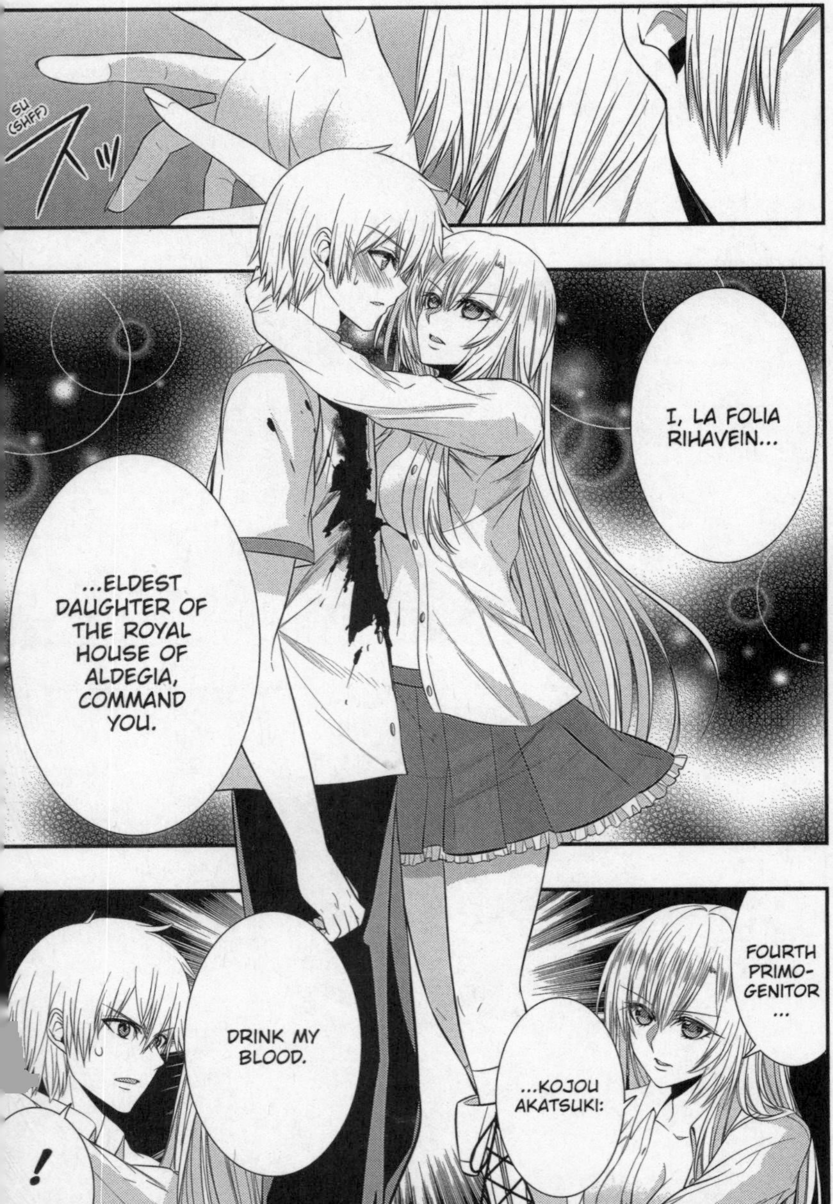
SU (SHFF)
スッ
I, LA FOLIA RIHAVEIN...
...ELDEST DAUGHTER OF THE ROYAL HOUSE OF ALDEGIA, COMMAND YOU.
FOURTH PRIMO-GENITOR ...
...KOJOU AKATSUKI:
DRINK MY BLOOD.
!

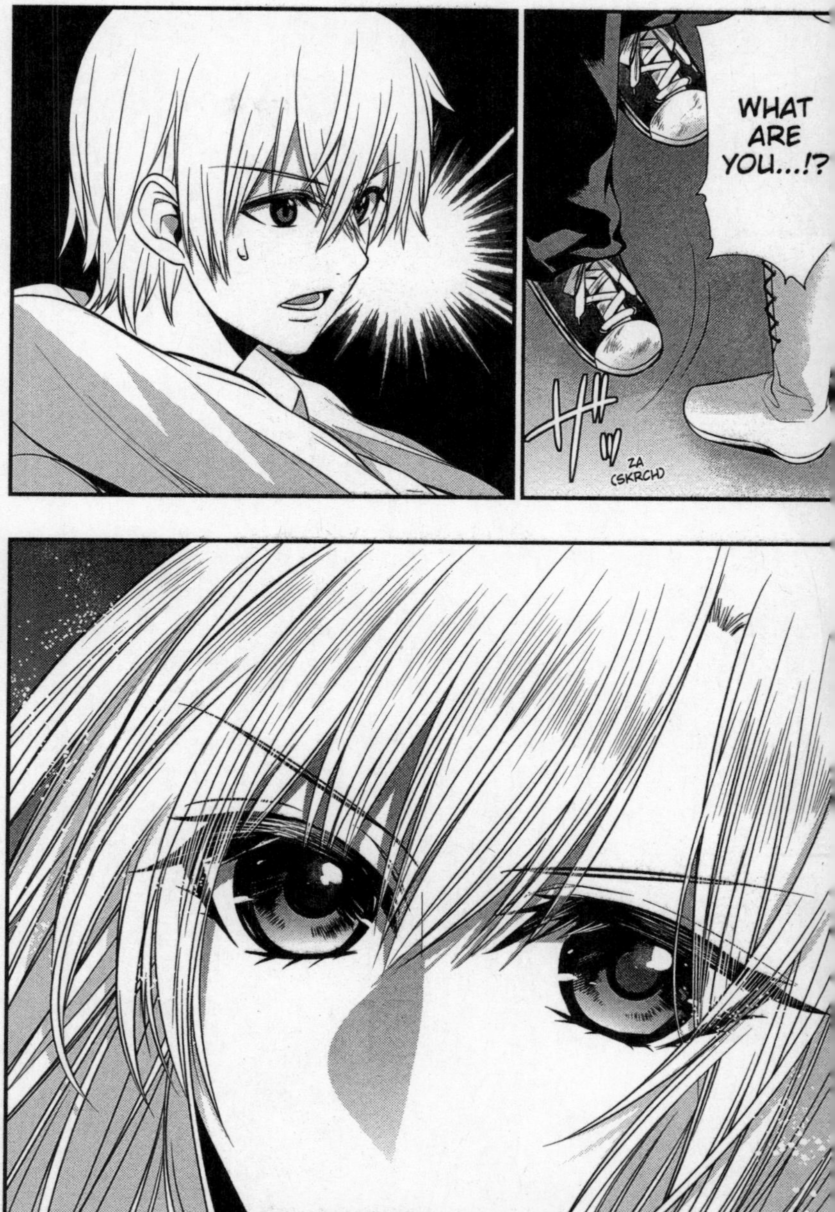
WHAT ARE YOU...!?
ZA (SKRCH)

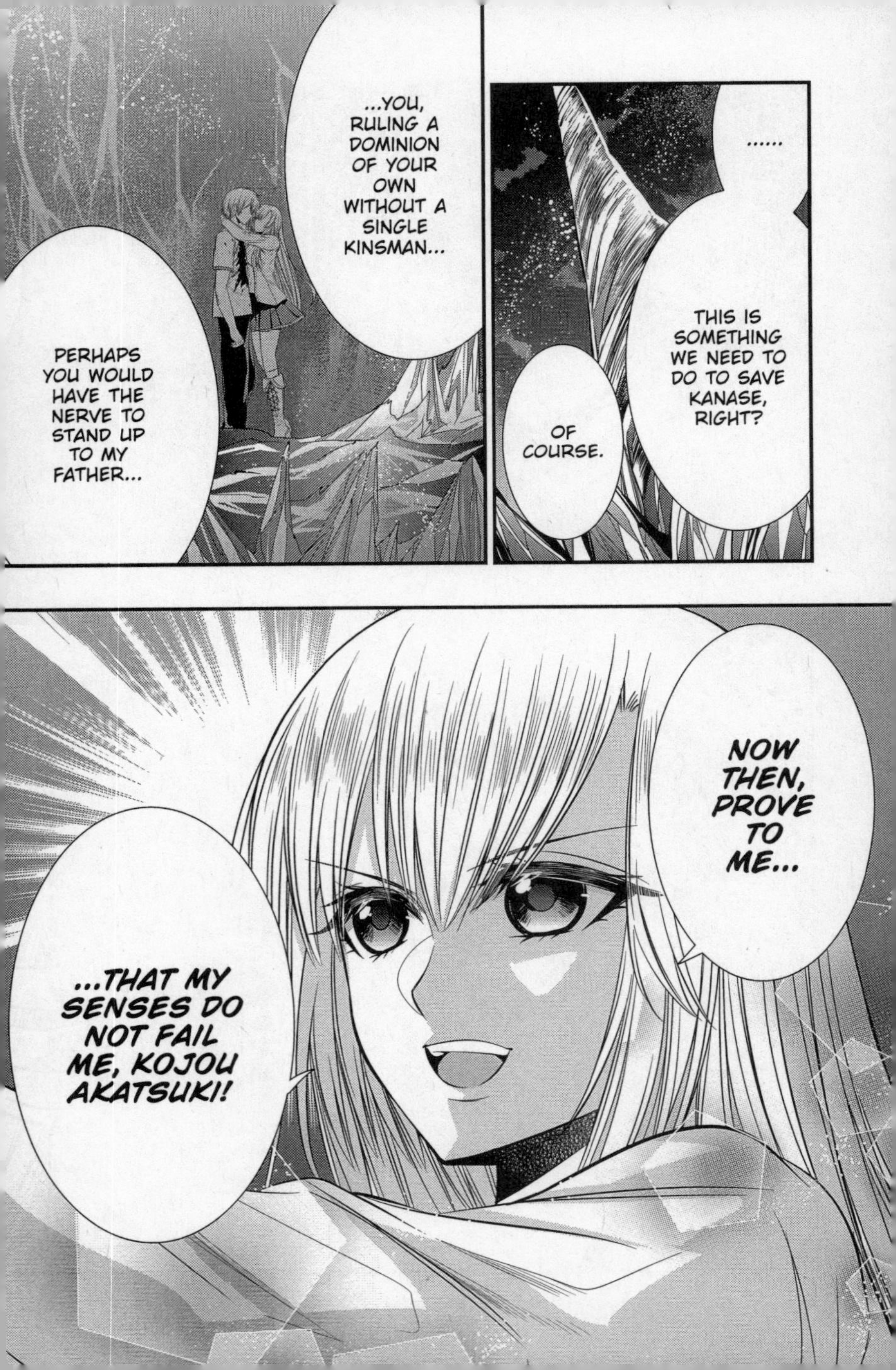
......
THIS IS SOMETHING WE NEED TO DO TO SAVE KANASE, RIGHT?
OF COURSE.
...YOU, RULING A DOMINION OF YOUR OWN WITHOUT A SINGLE KINSMAN...
PERHAPS YOU WOULD HAVE THE NERVE TO STAND UP TO MY FATHER...
NOW THEN, PROVE TO ME...
...THAT MY SENSES DO NOT FAIL ME, KOJOU AKATSUKI!

SAAAA
(FSHHH)

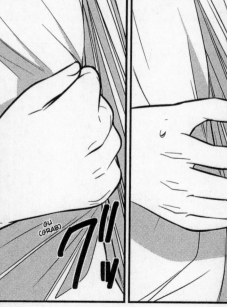

......

ALL
RIGHT,
THEN...

GU
(GRAB)

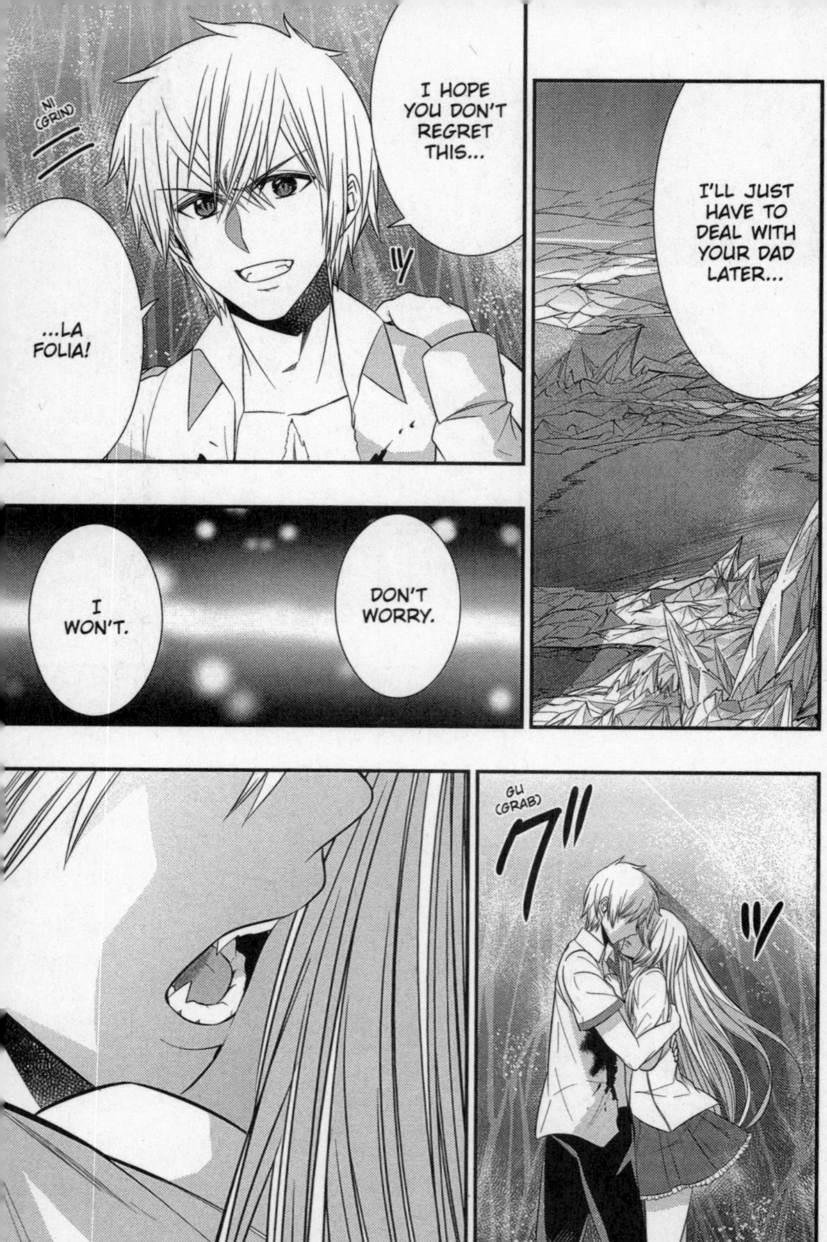
I'LL JUST HAVE TO DEAL WITH YOUR DAD LATER...
I HOPE YOU DON'T REGRET THIS...
NI (GRIND)
...LA FOLIA!
DON'T WORRY.
I WON'T.
GU (GRAB)

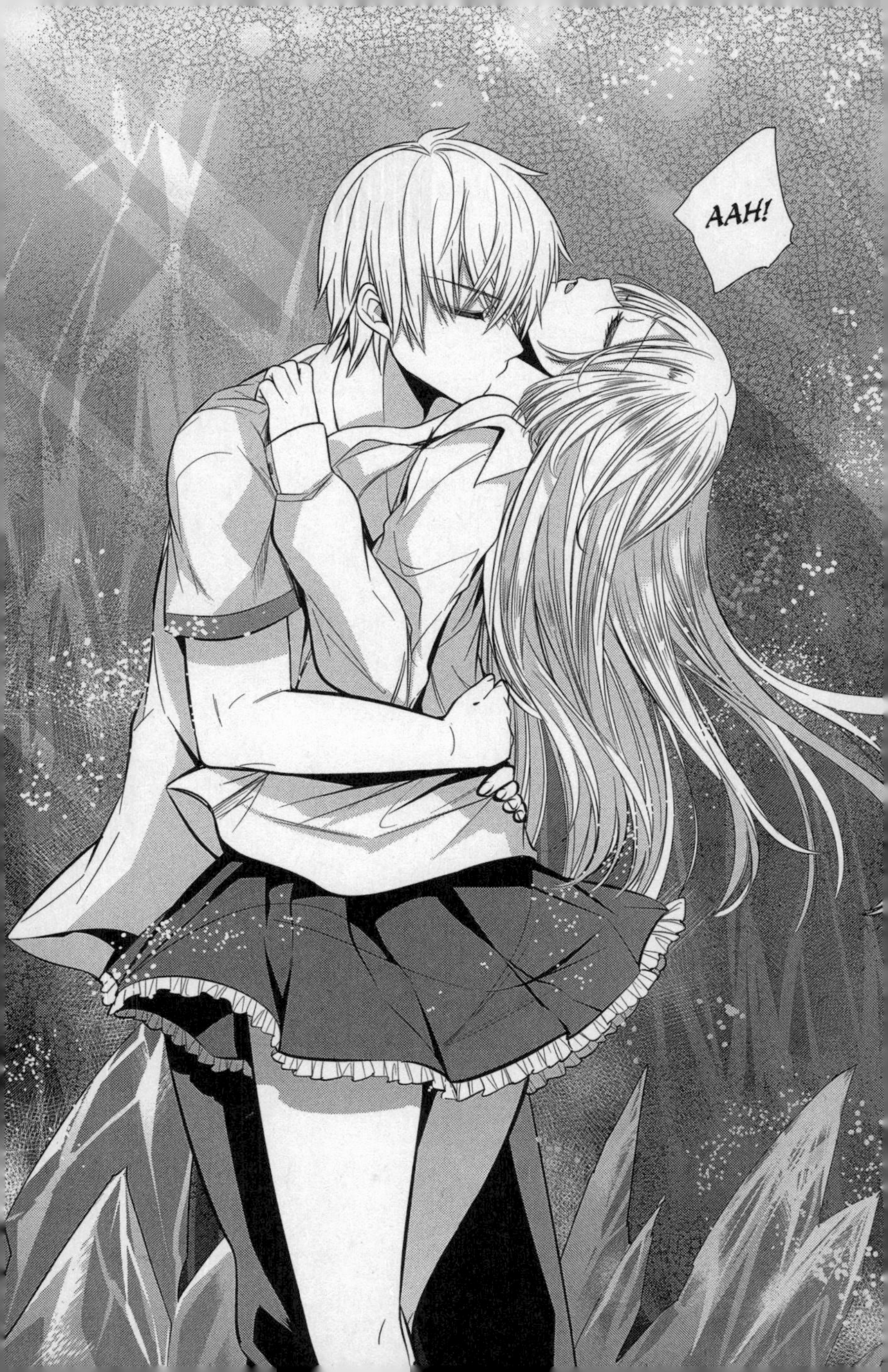
AAH!

STRIKE THE BLOOD

DEFINITION

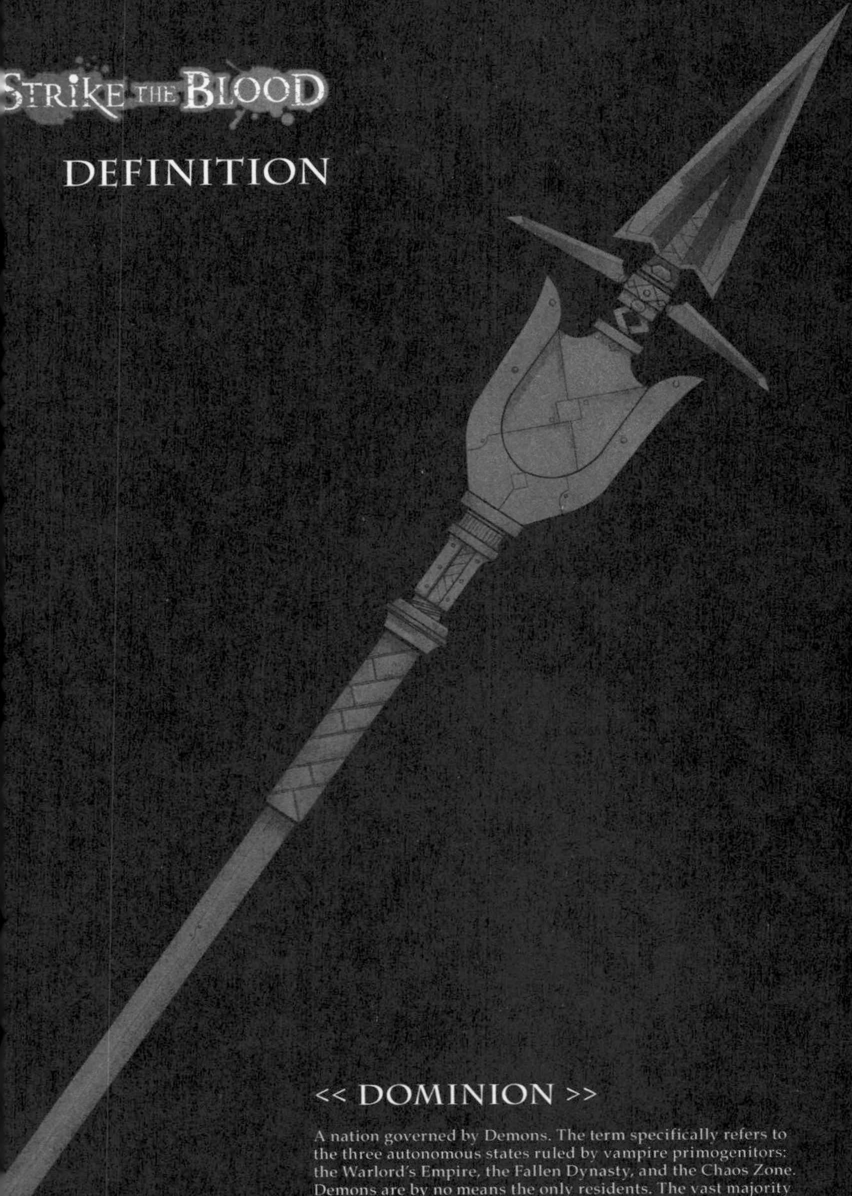

<< DOMINION >>

A nation governed by Demons. The term specifically refers to the three autonomous states ruled by vampire primogenitors: the Warlord's Empire, the Fallen Dynasty, and the Chaos Zone. Demons are by no means the only residents. The vast majority of their populations are ordinary human beings. However, the rights of citizens vary greatly depending upon the Dominion.

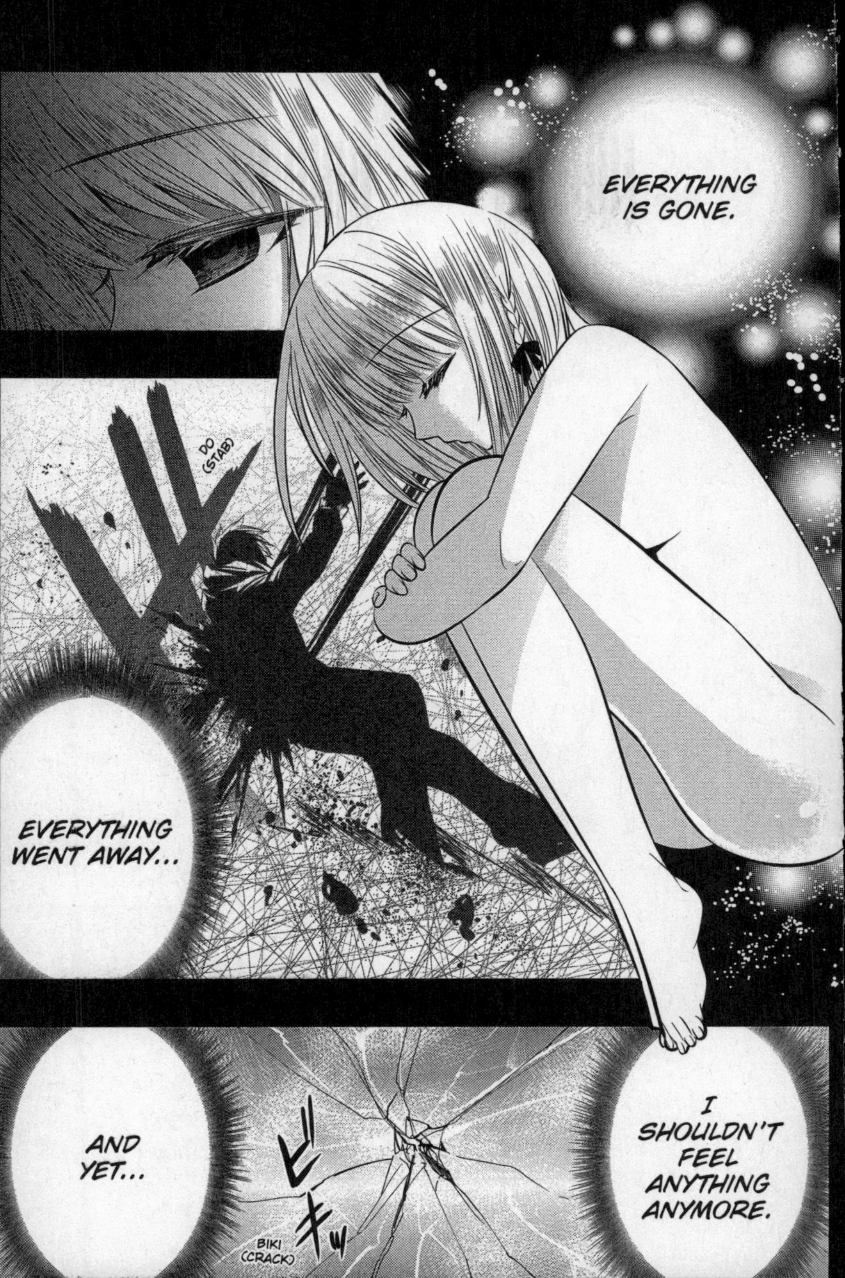
EVERYTHING IS GONE.
DO (STAB)
EVERYTHING WENT AWAY...
I SHOULDN'T FEEL ANYTHING ANYMORE.
AND YET...
BIKI (CRACK)

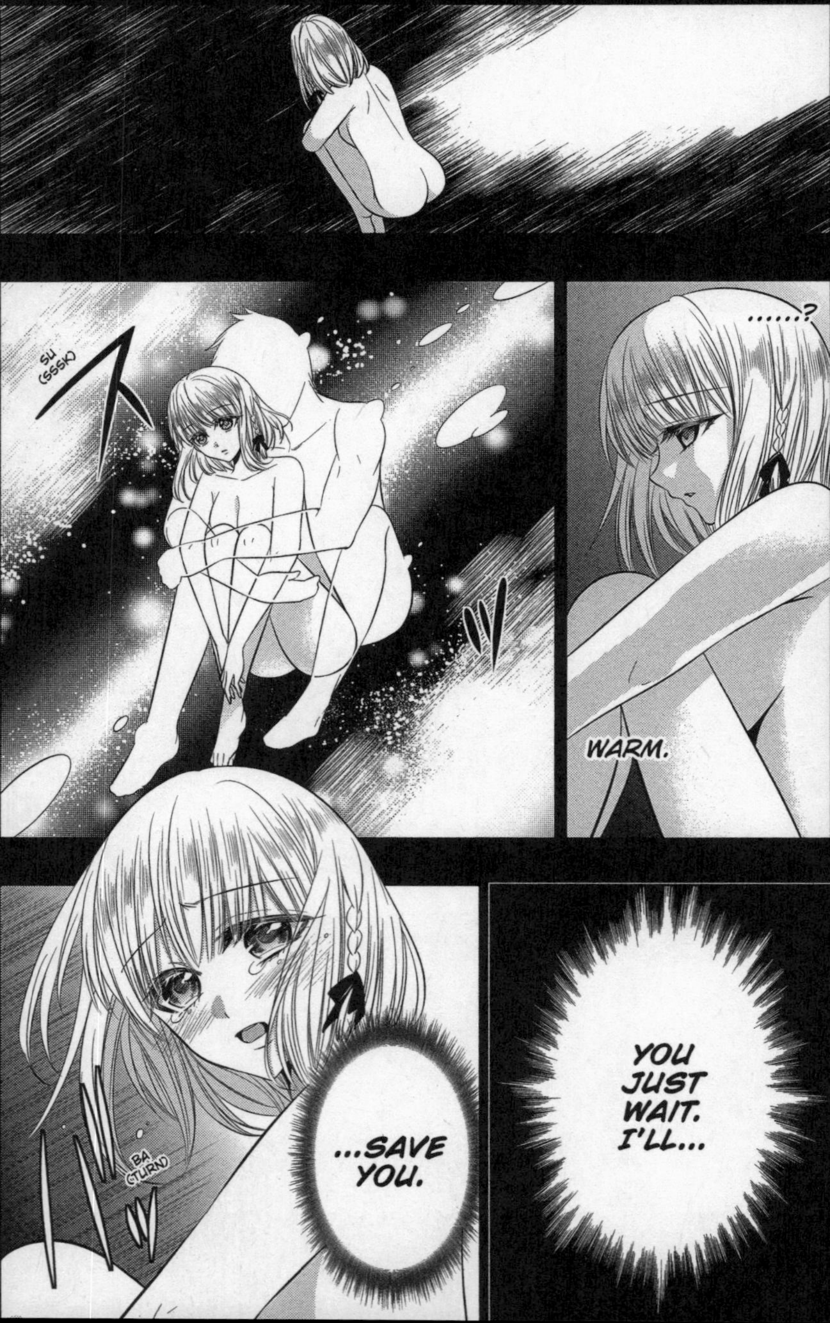

......?
WARM.
SU (SSSK)
YOU JUST WAIT. I'LL...
...SAVE YOU.
BA (TURN)

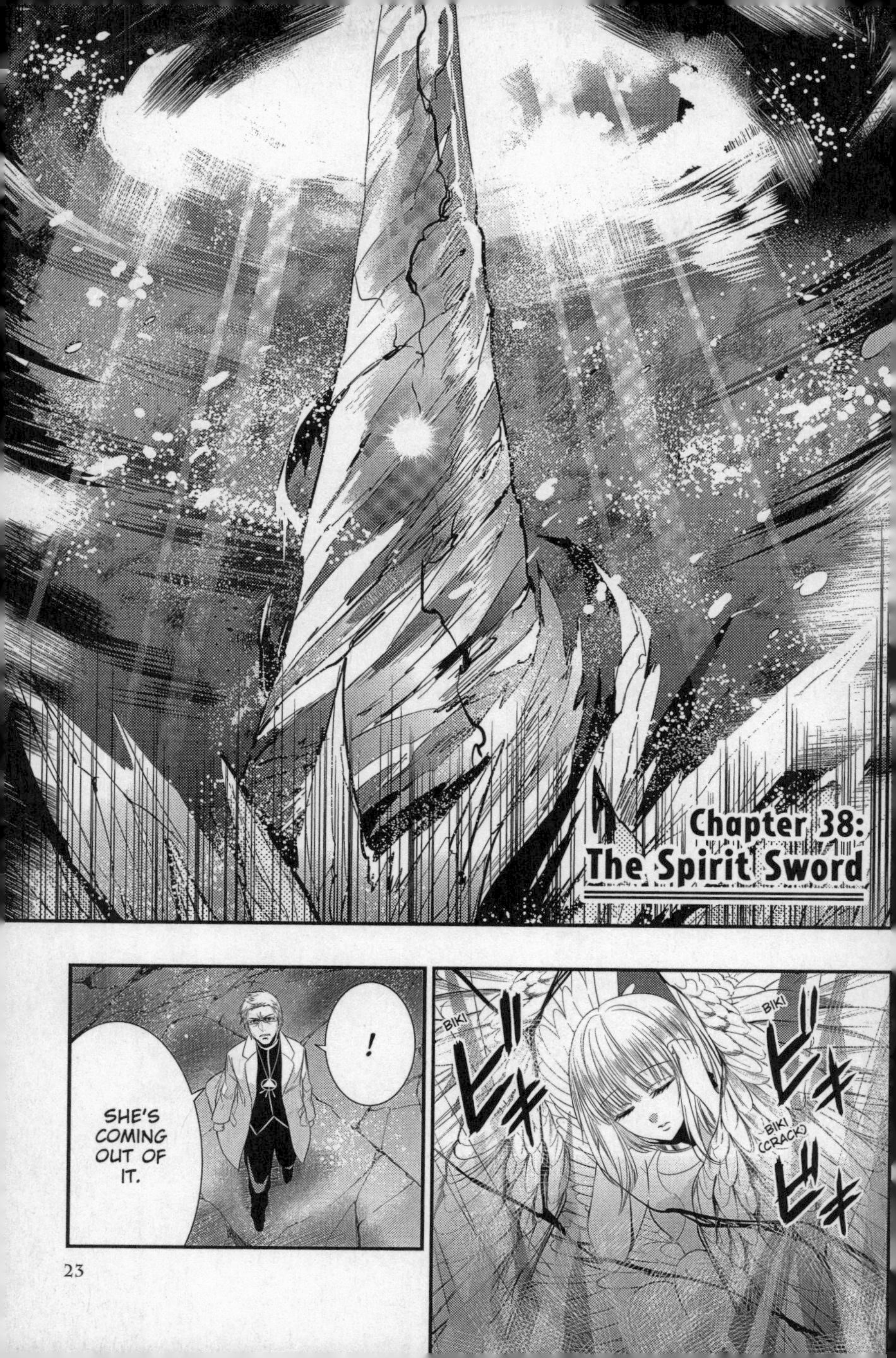
Chapter 38:
The Spirit Sword
BIKI
BIKI
BIKI (CRACK)
!
SHE'S COMING OUT OF IT.

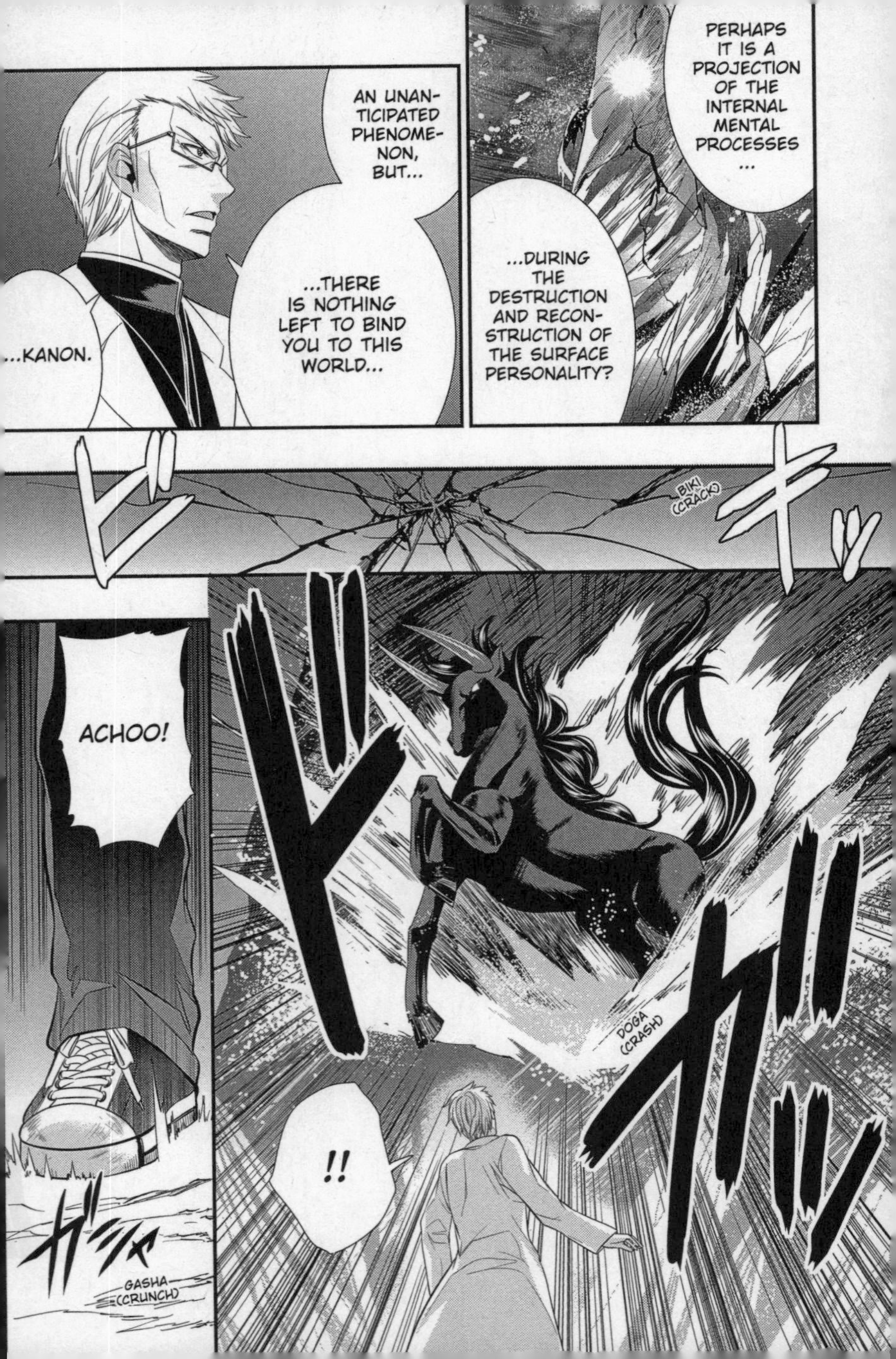
PERHAPS IT IS A PROJECTION OF THE INTERNAL MENTAL PROCESSES ...
...DURING THE DESTRUCTION AND RECONSTRUCTION OF THE SURFACE PERSONALITY?
AN UNANTICIPATED PHENOMENON, BUT...
...THERE IS NOTHING LEFT TO BIND YOU TO THIS WORLD...
...KANON.
BIKI (CRACK)
DOGA (CRASH)
!!
ACHOO!
GASHA (CRUNCH)

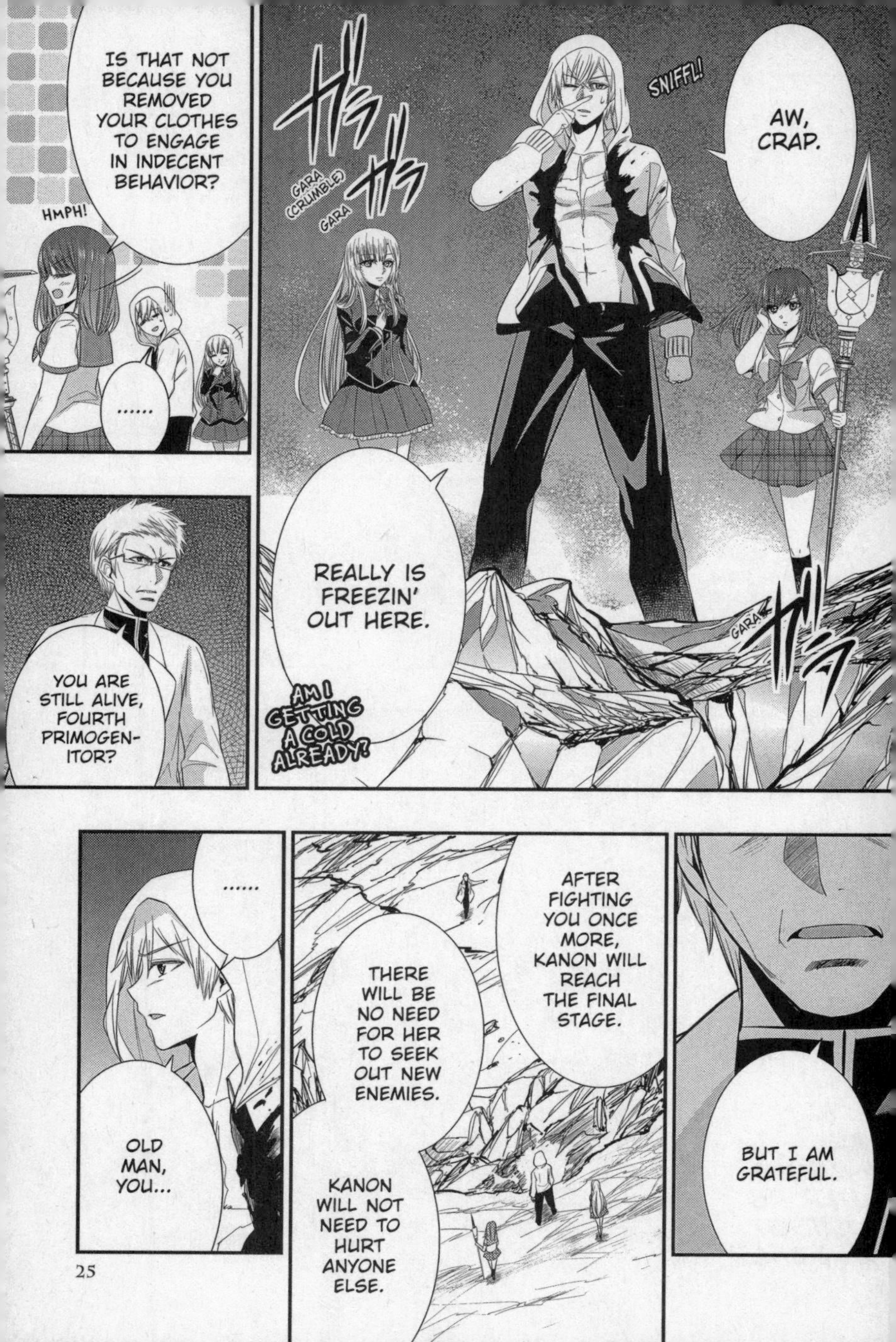
SNIFFL!
AW, CRAP.
GARA (CRUMBLE) GARA
REALLY IS FREEZIN' OUT HERE.
AM I GETTING A COLD ALREADY?
GARA
IS THAT NOT BECAUSE YOU REMOVED YOUR CLOTHES TO ENGAGE IN INDECENT BEHAVIOR?
HMPH!
......
YOU ARE STILL ALIVE, FOURTH PRIMOGEN-ITOR?
BUT I AM GRATEFUL.
AFTER FIGHTING YOU ONCE MORE, KANON WILL REACH THE FINAL STAGE.
THERE WILL BE NO NEED FOR HER TO SEEK OUT NEW ENEMIES.
KANON WILL NOT NEED TO HURT ANYONE ELSE.
......
OLD MAN, YOU...

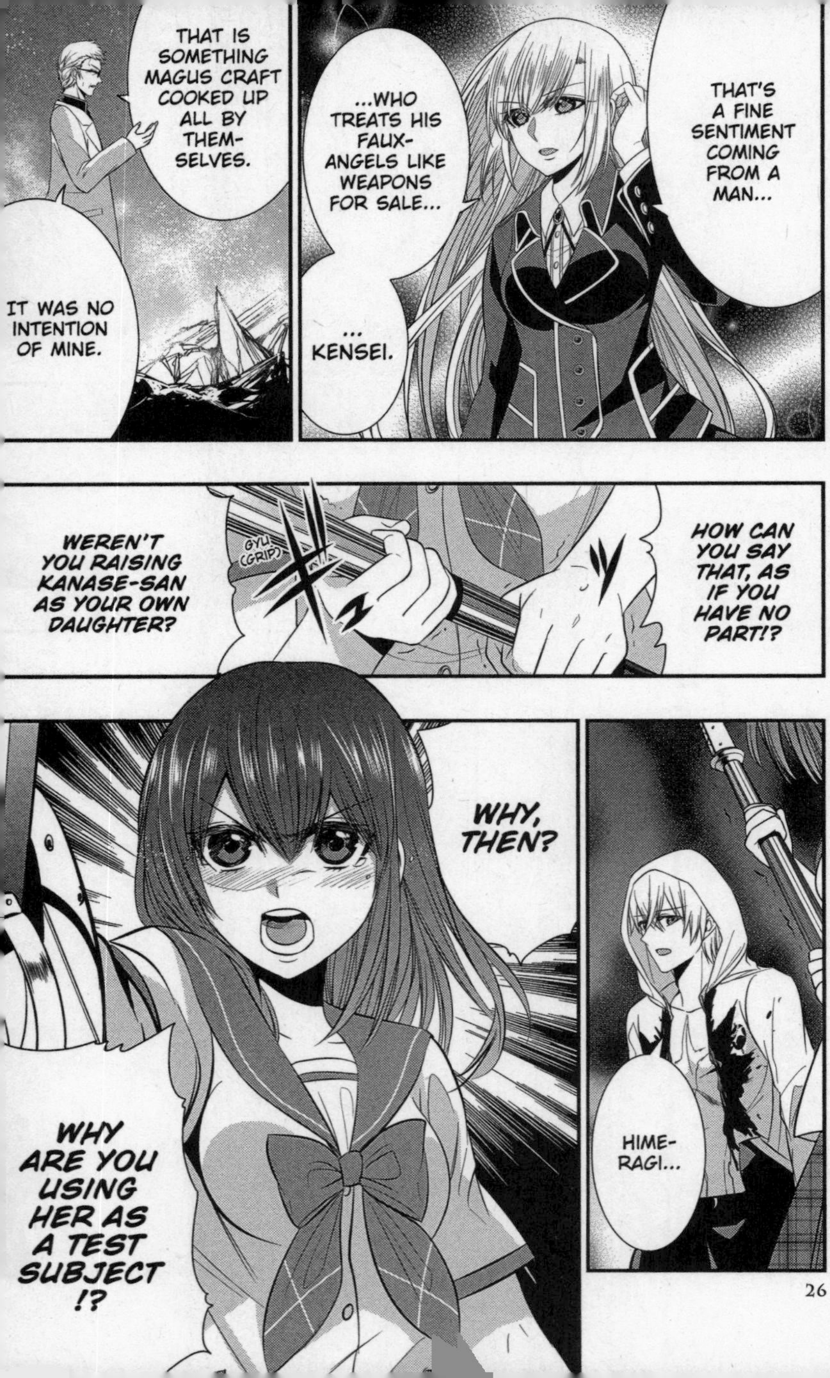
THAT'S A FINE SENTIMENT COMING FROM A MAN...
...WHO TREATS HIS FAUX-ANGELS LIKE WEAPONS FOR SALE...
... KENSEI.
THAT IS SOMETHING MAGUS CRAFT COOKED UP ALL BY THEM-SELVES.
IT WAS NO INTENTION OF MINE.
HOW CAN YOU SAY THAT, AS IF YOU HAVE NO PART!?
GYU (GRIP)
WEREN'T YOU RAISING KANASE-SAN AS YOUR OWN DAUGHTER?
HIME-RAGI...
WHY, THEN?
WHY ARE YOU USING HER AS A TEST SUBJECT !?

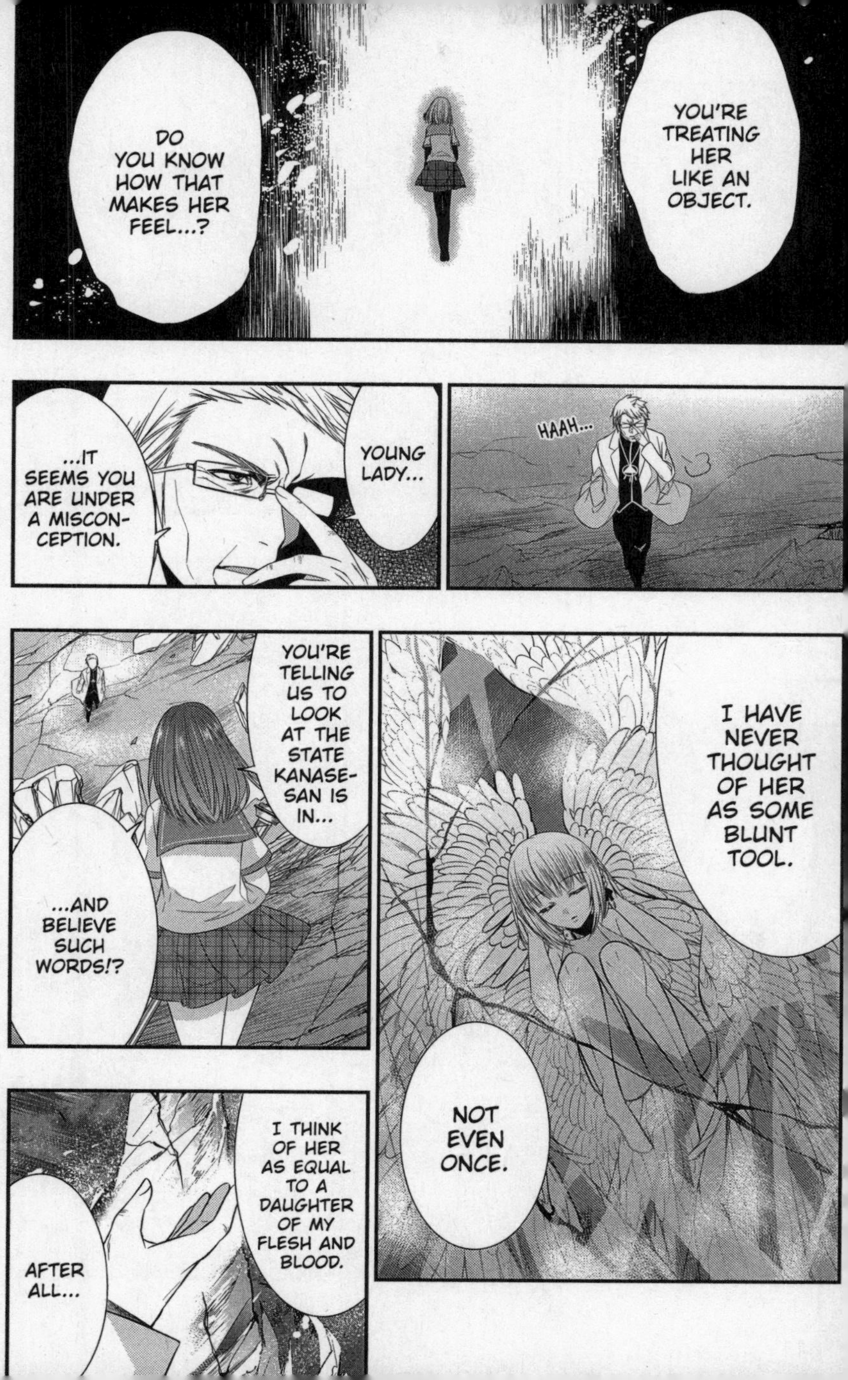

YOU'RE TREATING HER LIKE AN OBJECT.
DO YOU KNOW HOW THAT MAKES HER FEEL...?
HAAH...
YOUNG LADY...
...IT SEEMS YOU ARE UNDER A MISCONCEPTION.
I HAVE NEVER THOUGHT OF HER AS SOME BLUNT TOOL.
NOT EVEN ONCE.
YOU'RE TELLING US TO LOOK AT THE STATE KANASE-SAN IS IN...
...AND BELIEVE SUCH WORDS!?
I THINK OF HER AS EQUAL TO A DAUGHTER OF MY FLESH AND BLOOD.
AFTER ALL...

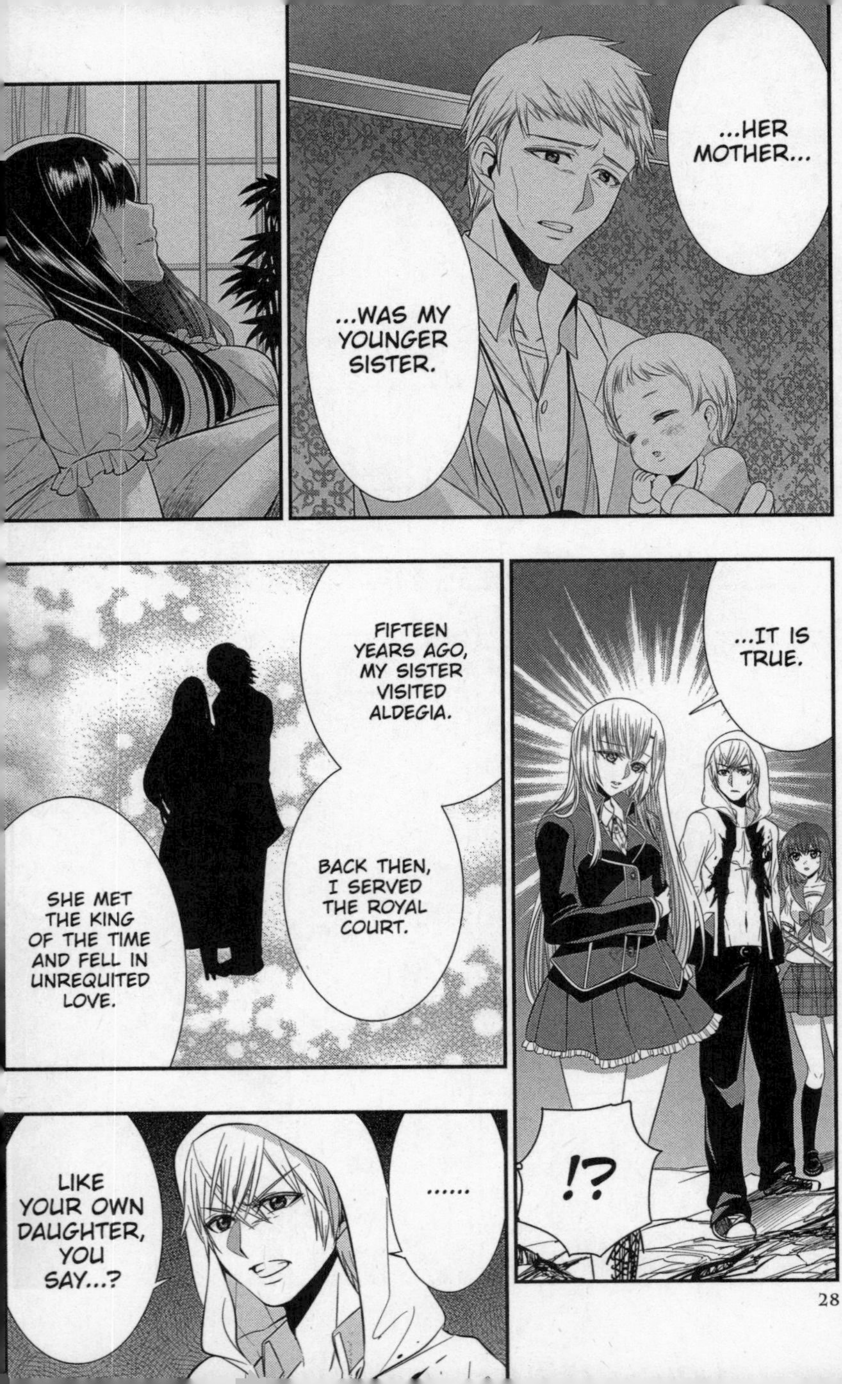
...HER MOTHER...
...WAS MY YOUNGER SISTER.
...IT IS TRUE.
!?
FIFTEEN YEARS AGO, MY SISTER VISITED ALDEGIA.
BACK THEN, I SERVED THE ROYAL COURT.
SHE MET THE KING OF THE TIME AND FELL IN UNREQUITED LOVE.
......
LIKE YOUR OWN DAUGHTER, YOU SAY...?

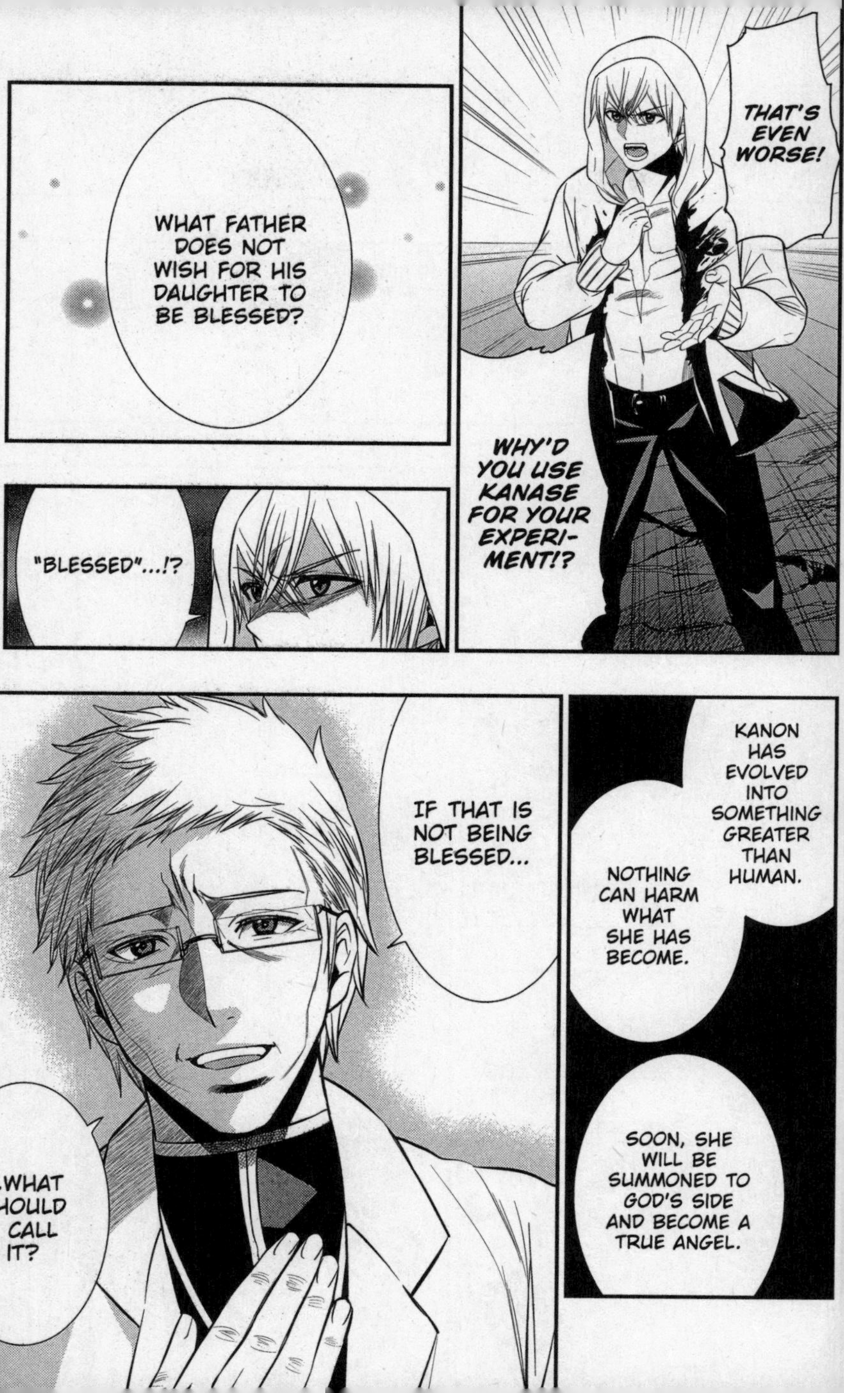
THAT'S EVEN WORSE!
WHY'D YOU USE KANASE FOR YOUR EXPERIMENT!?
WHAT FATHER DOES NOT WISH FOR HIS DAUGHTER TO BE BLESSED?
"BLESSED"...!?
KANON HAS EVOLVED INTO SOMETHING GREATER THAN HUMAN.
NOTHING CAN HARM WHAT SHE HAS BECOME.
SOON, SHE WILL BE SUMMONED TO GOD'S SIDE AND BECOME A TRUE ANGEL.
IF THAT IS NOT BEING BLESSED...
...WHAT SHOULD I CALL IT?

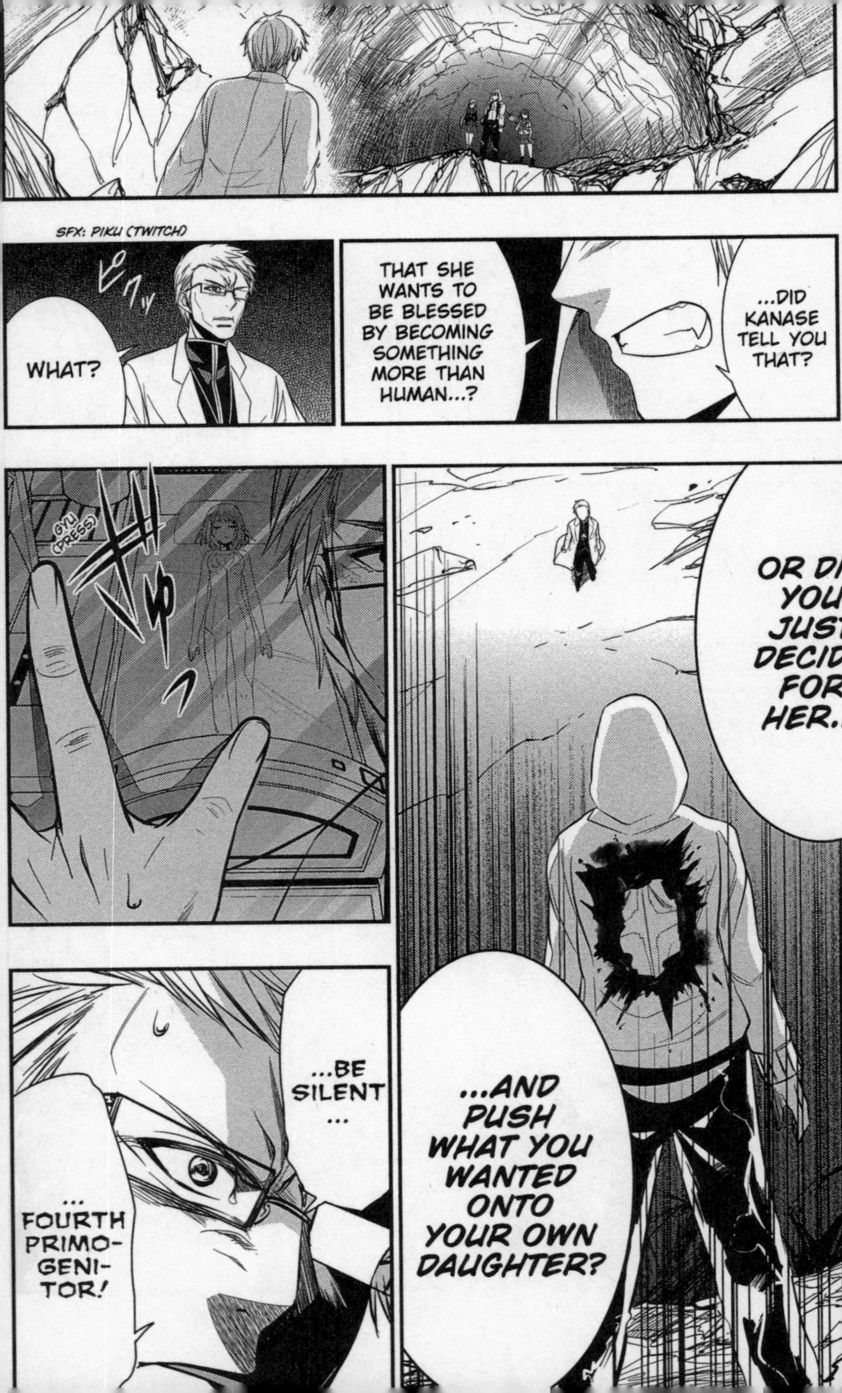
THAT SHE WANTS TO BE BLESSED BY BECOMING SOMETHING MORE THAN HUMAN...?
...DID KANASE TELL YOU THAT?
SFX: PIKU (TWITCH)
ピクッ
WHAT?
OR DID YOU JUST DECIDE FOR HER...
...AND PUSH WHAT YOU WANTED ONTO YOUR OWN DAUGHTER?
GYU (PRESS)
ギュッ
...BE SILENT...
...FOURTH PRIMO-GENI-TOR!

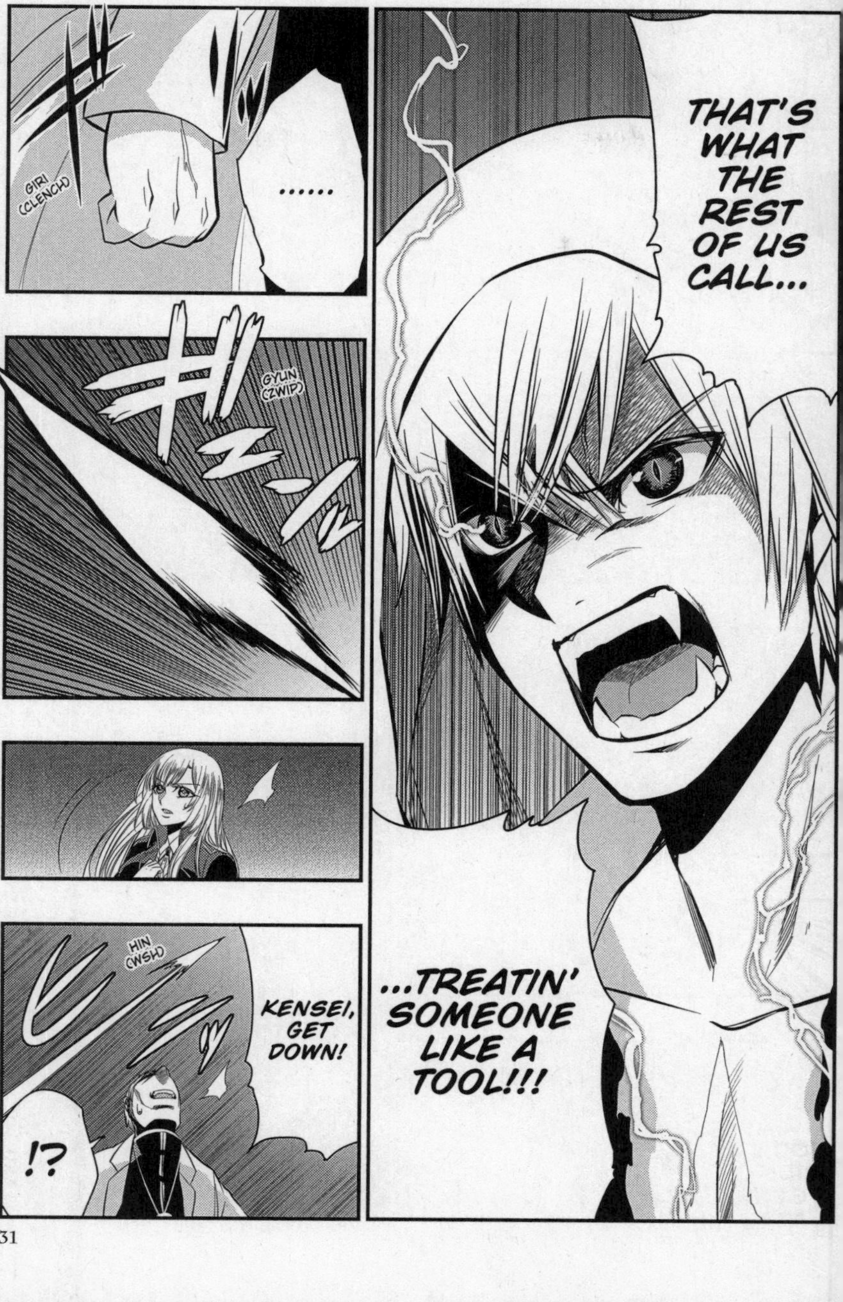
THAT'S WHAT THE REST OF US CALL...
...TREATIN' SOMEONE LIKE A TOOL!!!
......
GIRI (CLENCH)
GYLIN (ZWIP)
HIN (WSH)
KENSEI, GET DOWN!
!?

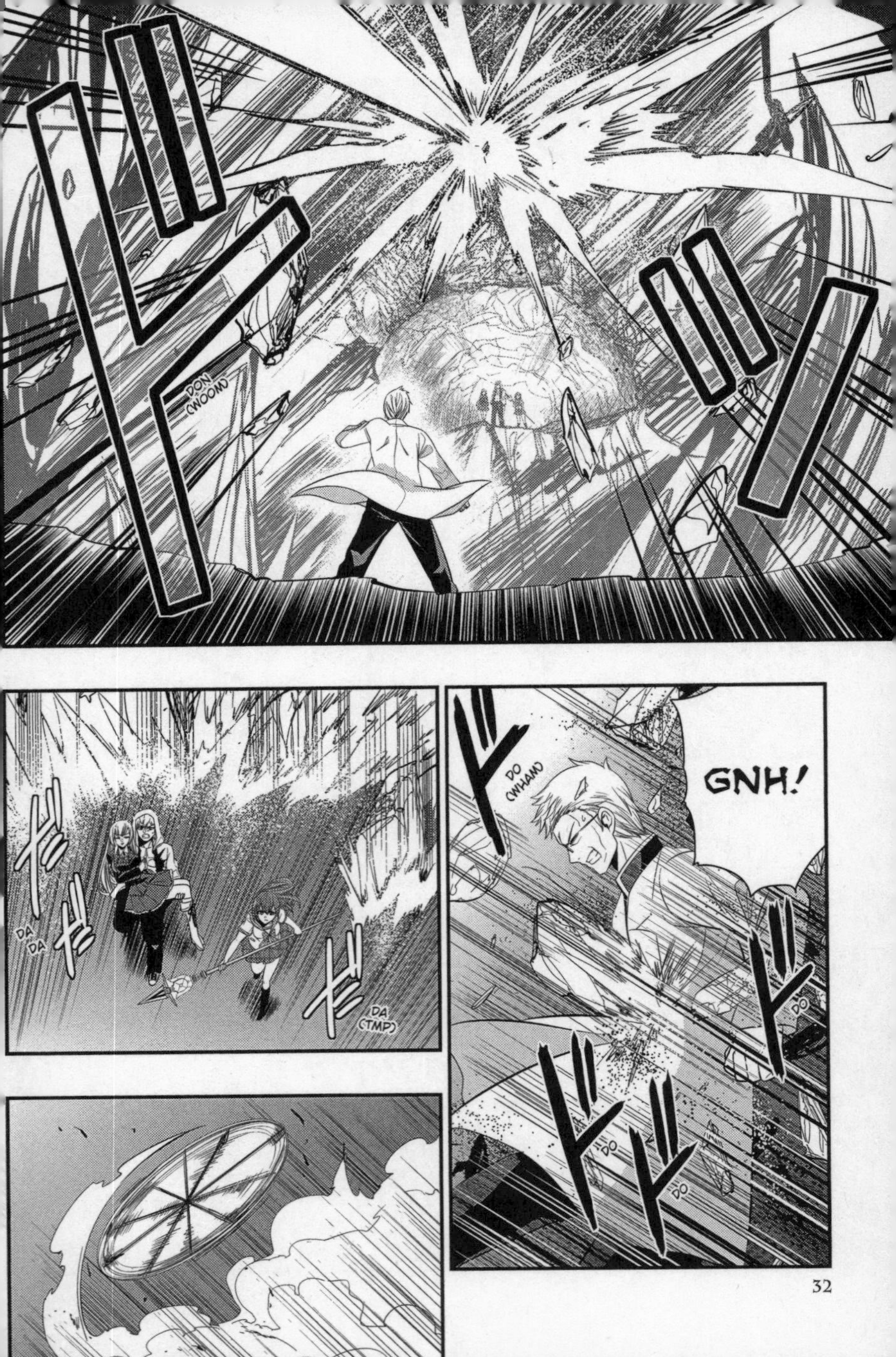
DON (WOOM)
DO (WHAM)
GNH!
DO
DO
DO
DA DA
DA (TMP)

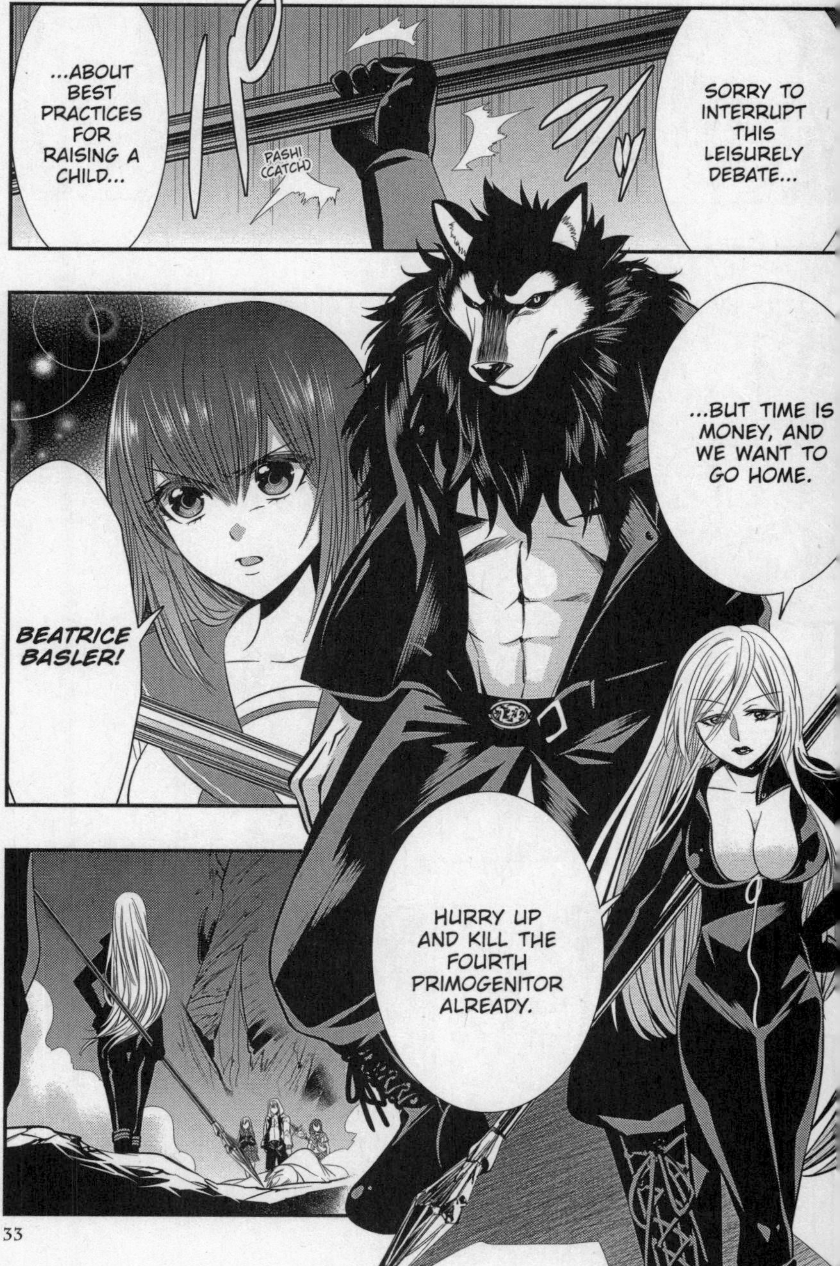
SORRY TO INTERRUPT THIS LEISURELY DEBATE...
PASHI (CATCH)
...ABOUT BEST PRACTICES FOR RAISING A CHILD...
...BUT TIME IS MONEY, AND WE WANT TO GO HOME.
BEATRICE BASLER!
HURRY UP AND KILL THE FOURTH PRIMOGENITOR ALREADY.

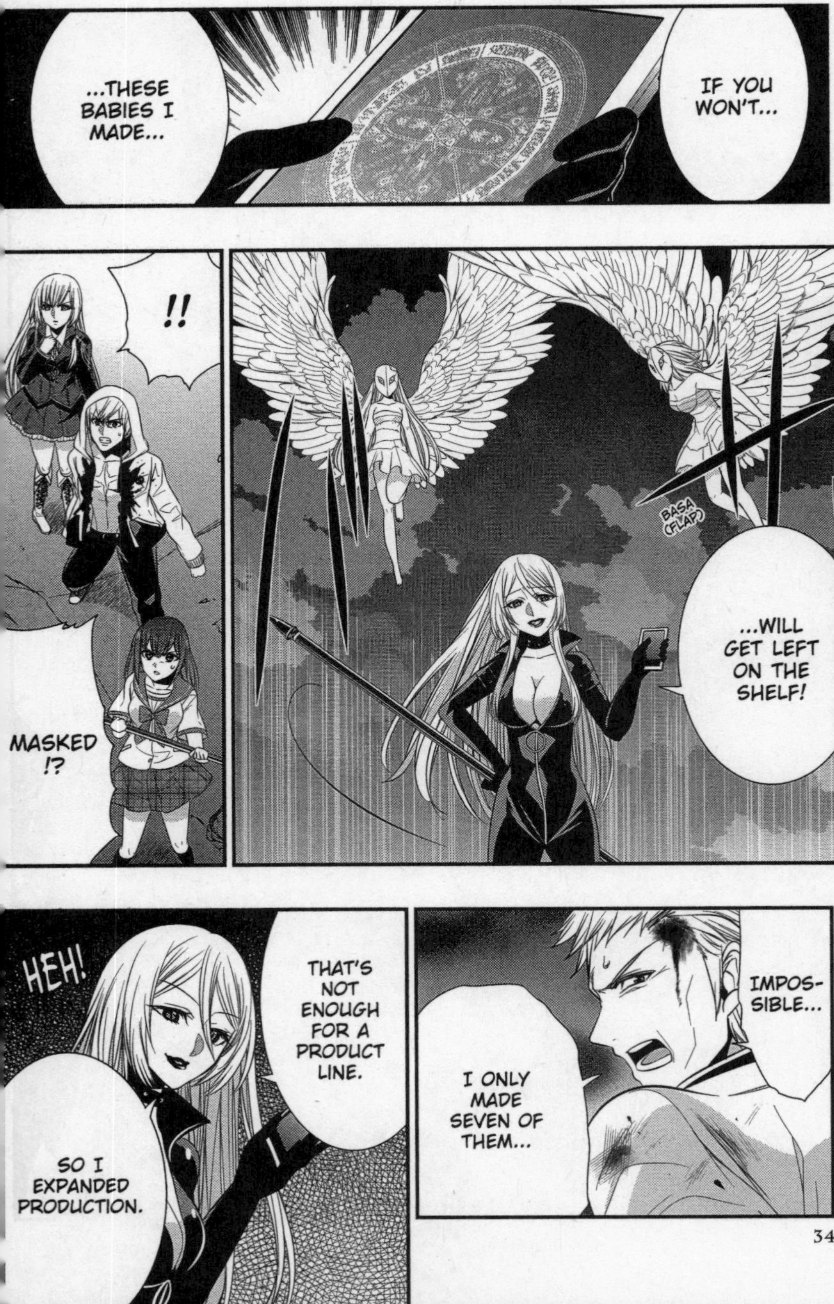

IF YOU WON'T...
...THESE BABIES I MADE...
BASA (FLAP)
...WILL GET LEFT ON THE SHELF!
!!
MASKED !?
IMPOS-SIBLE...
I ONLY MADE SEVEN OF THEM...
HEH!
THAT'S NOT ENOUGH FOR A PRODUCT LINE.
SO I EXPANDED PRODUCTION.

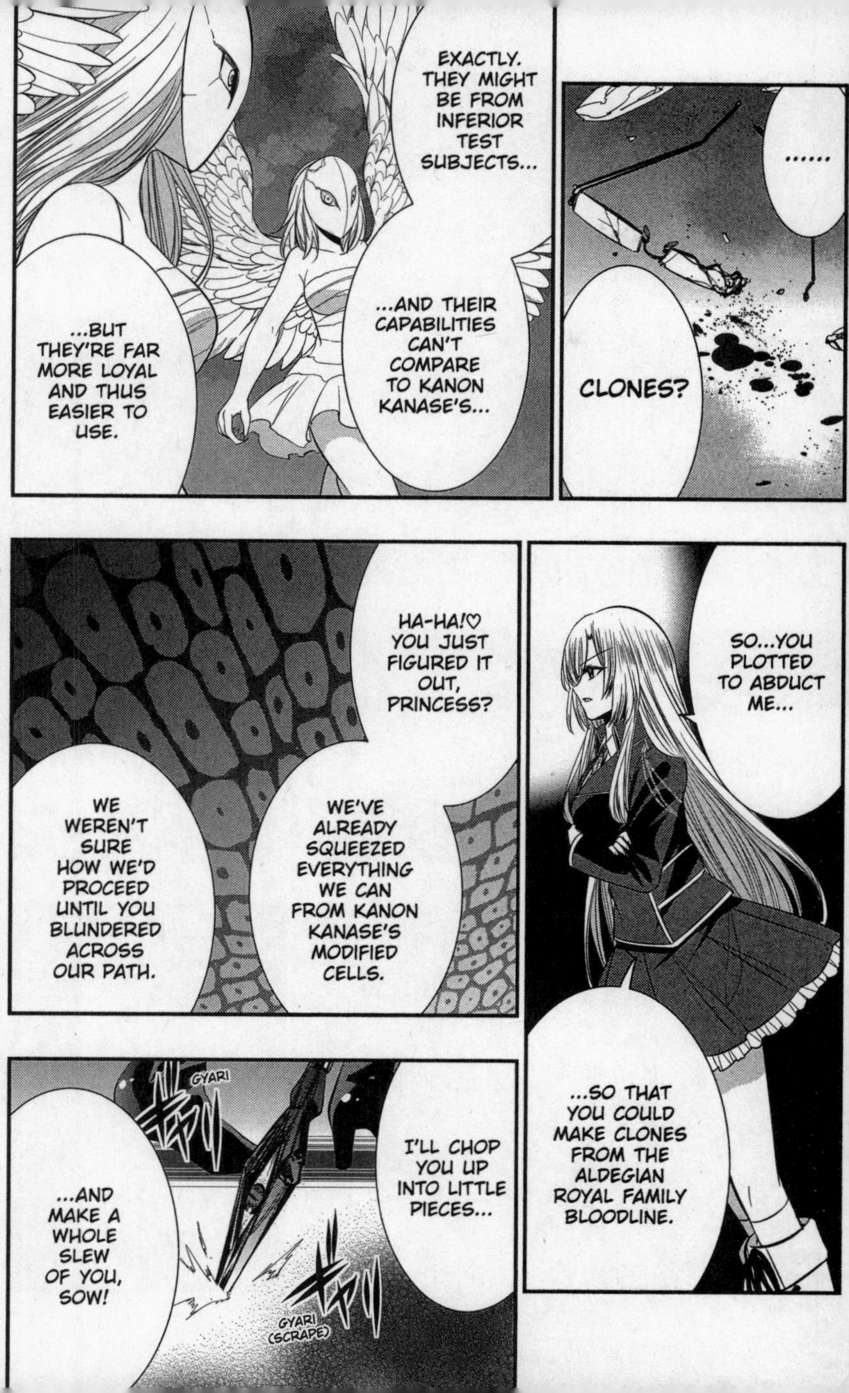
......
CLONES?
EXACTLY. THEY MIGHT BE FROM INFERIOR TEST SUBJECTS...
...AND THEIR CAPABILITIES CAN'T COMPARE TO KANON KANASE'S...
...BUT THEY'RE FAR MORE LOYAL AND THUS EASIER TO USE.
SO...YOU PLOTTED TO ABDUCT ME...
...SO THAT YOU COULD MAKE CLONES FROM THE ALDEGIAN ROYAL FAMILY BLOODLINE.
HA-HA!♡ YOU JUST FIGURED IT OUT, PRINCESS?
WE'VE ALREADY SQUEEZED EVERYTHING WE CAN FROM KANON KANASE'S MODIFIED CELLS.
WE WEREN'T SURE HOW WE'D PROCEED UNTIL YOU BLUNDERED ACROSS OUR PATH.
GYARI
I'LL CHOP YOU UP INTO LITTLE PIECES...
...AND MAKE A WHOLE SLEW OF YOU, SOW!
GYARI (SCRAPE)

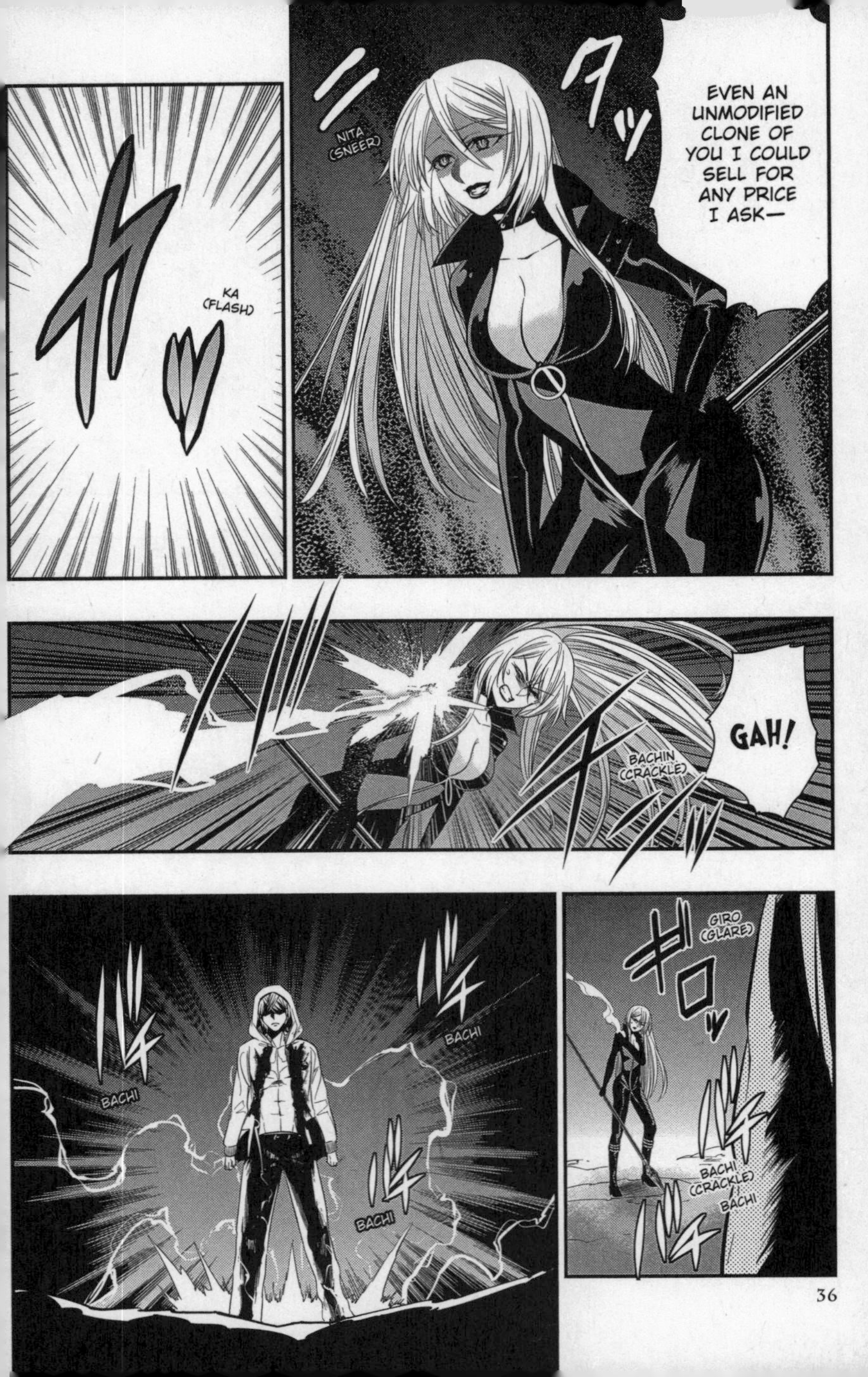
NITA (SNEER)
EVEN AN UNMODIFIED CLONE OF YOU I COULD SELL FOR ANY PRICE I ASK—
KA (FLASH)
GAH!
BACHIN (CRACKLE)
GIRO (GLARE)
BACHI (CRACKLE)
BACHI
BACHI
BACHI
BACHI

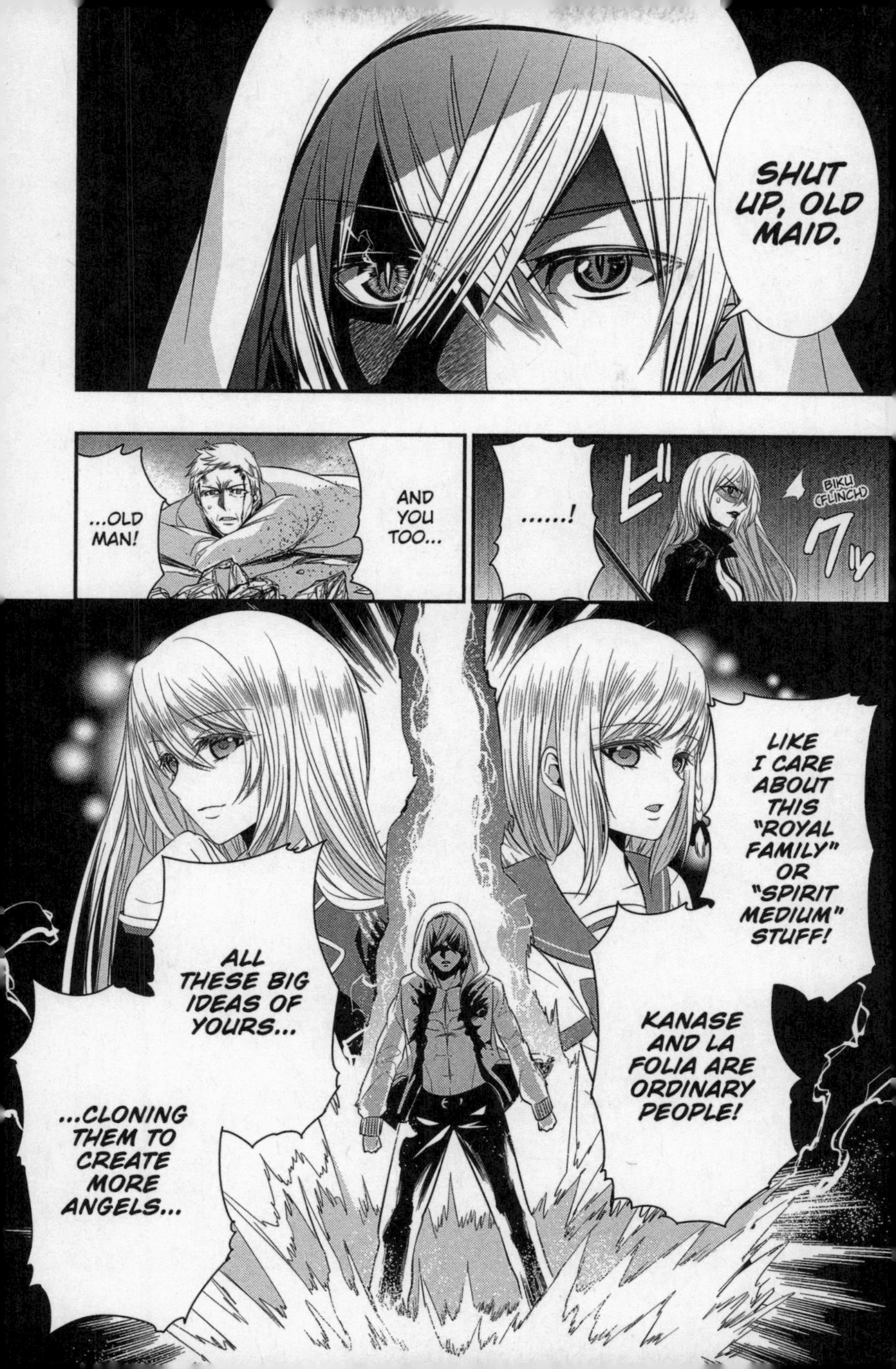
SHUT UP, OLD MAID.
......!
ビクッ
BIKU (FLINCH)
AND YOU TOO...
...OLD MAN!
LIKE I CARE ABOUT THIS "ROYAL FAMILY" OR "SPIRIT MEDIUM" STUFF!
KANASE AND LA FOLIA ARE ORDINARY PEOPLE!
ALL THESE BIG IDEAS OF YOURS...
...CLONING THEM TO CREATE MORE ANGELS...

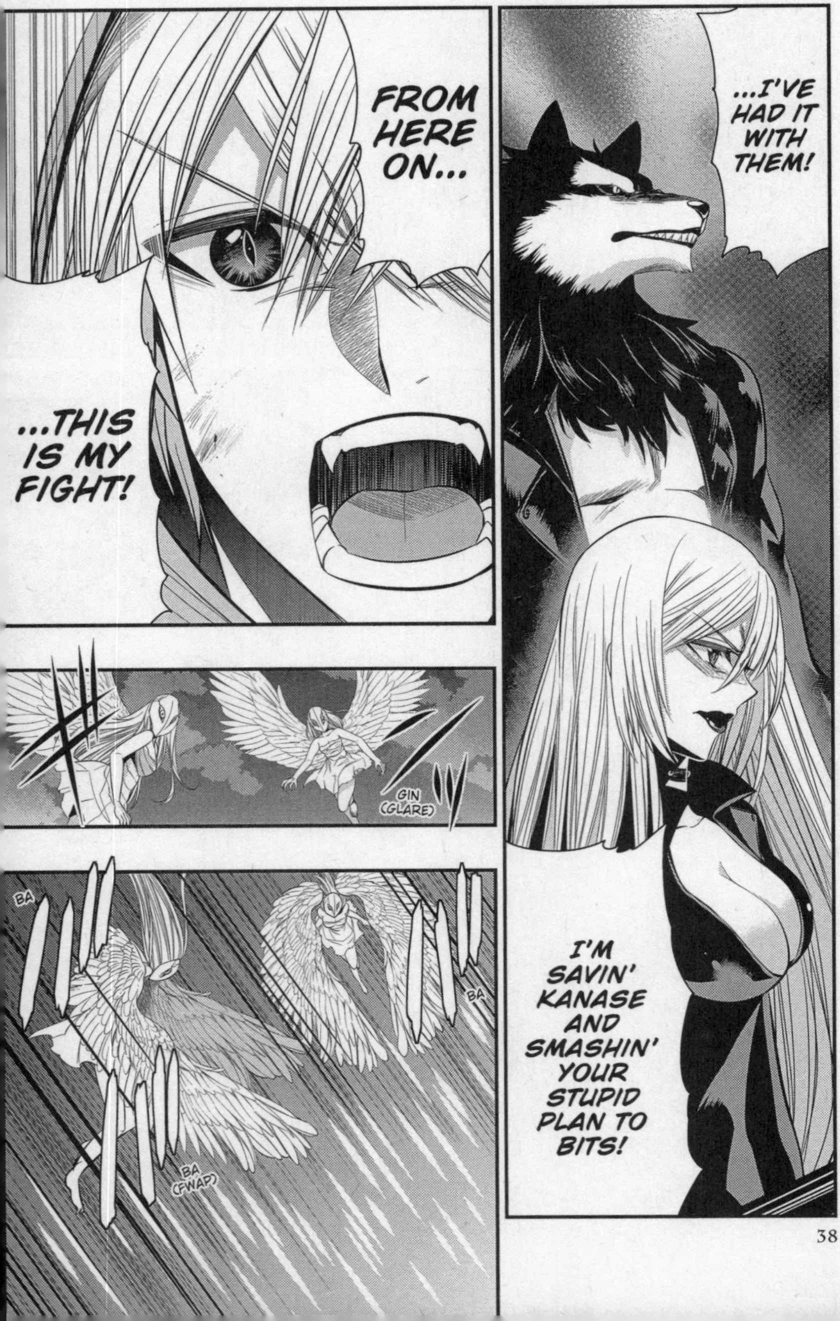
...I'VE HAD IT WITH THEM!
I'M SAVIN' KANASE AND SMASHIN' YOUR STUPID PLAN TO BITS!
FROM HERE ON...
...THIS IS MY FIGHT!
GIN (GLARE)
BA
BA
BA (FWAP)

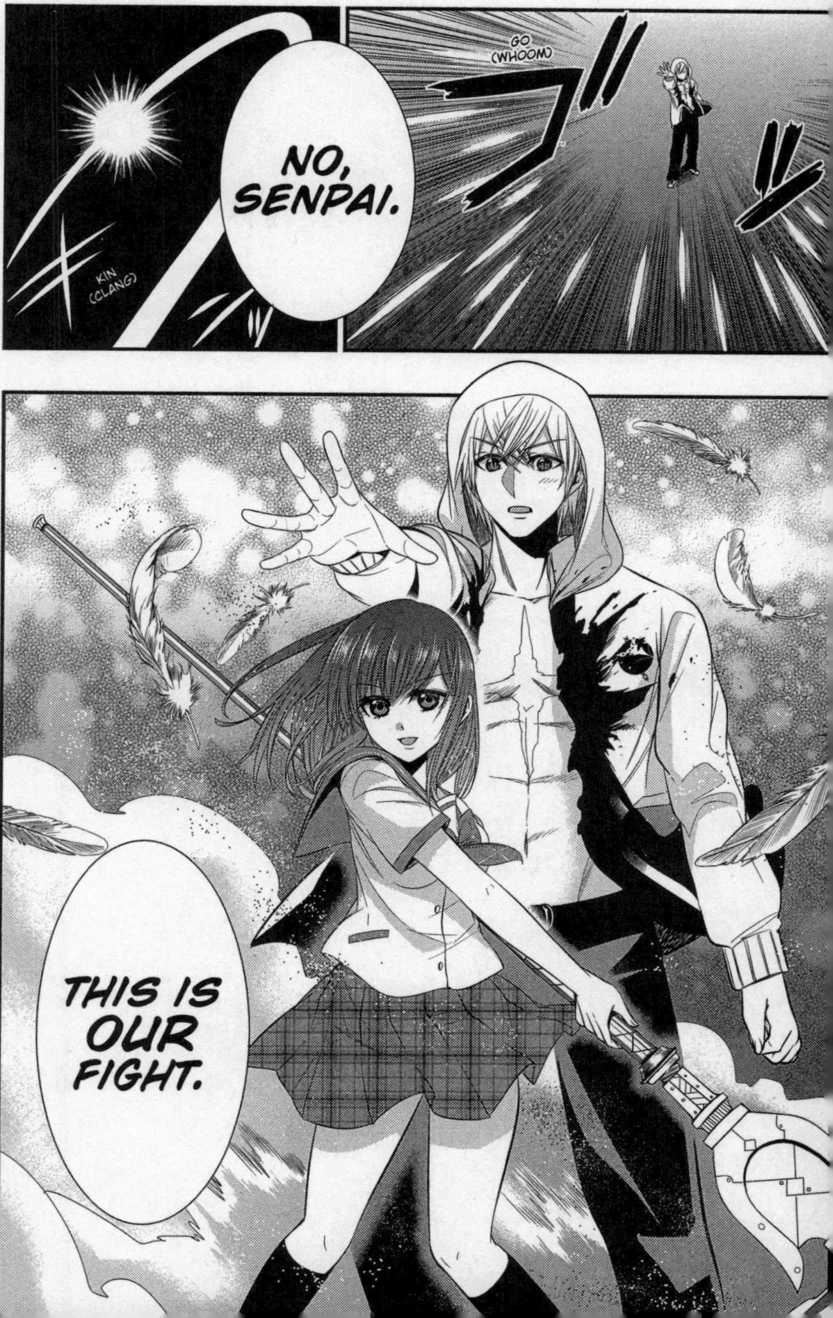
GO
(WHOOM)
NO, SENPAI.
KIN
(CLANG)
THIS IS OUR FIGHT.

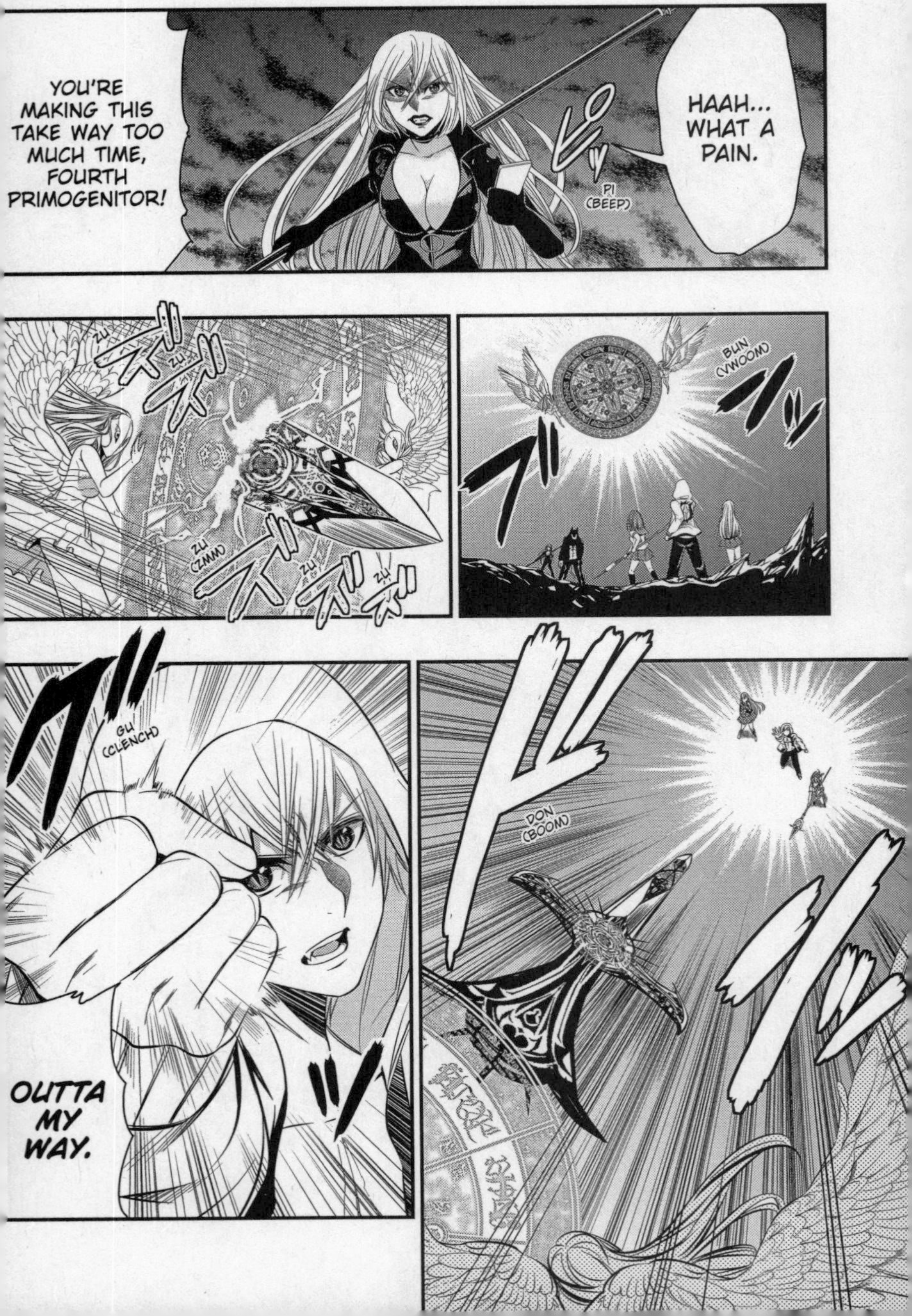
HAAH... WHAT A PAIN.
PI (BEEP)
YOU'RE MAKING THIS TAKE WAY TOO MUCH TIME, FOURTH PRIMOGENITOR!
BUN (VWOOM)
ZU
ZU
ZU (ZMM)
ZU
ZU
DON (BOOM)
GU (CLENCH)
OUTTA MY WAY.

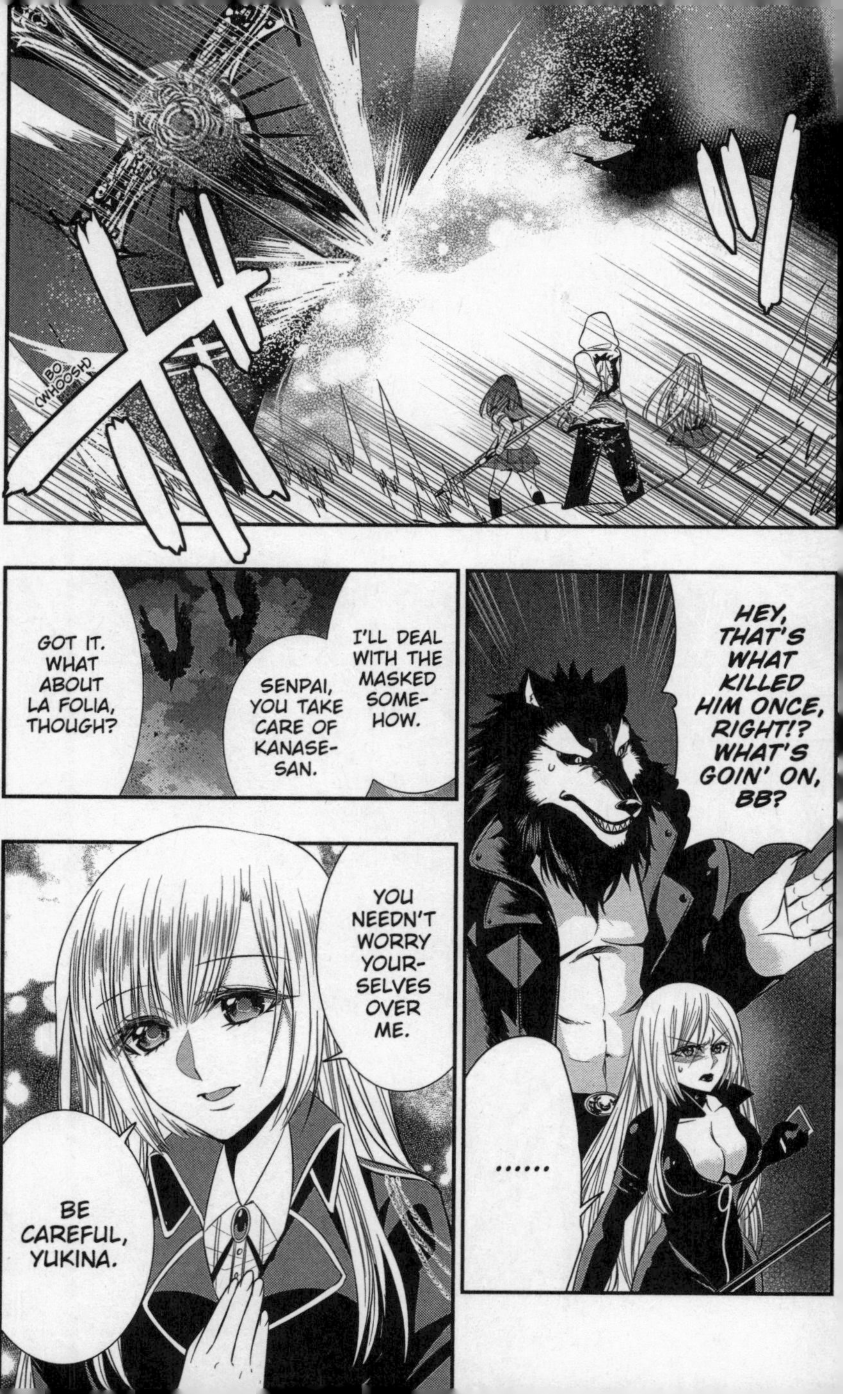
BO (WHOOSH)
HEY, THAT'S WHAT KILLED HIM ONCE, RIGHT!? WHAT'S GOIN' ON, BB?
......
I'LL DEAL WITH THE MASKED SOME-HOW.
SENPAI, YOU TAKE CARE OF KANASE-SAN.
GOT IT. WHAT ABOUT LA FOLIA, THOUGH?
YOU NEEDN'T WORRY YOUR-SELVES OVER ME.
BE CAREFUL, YUKINA.

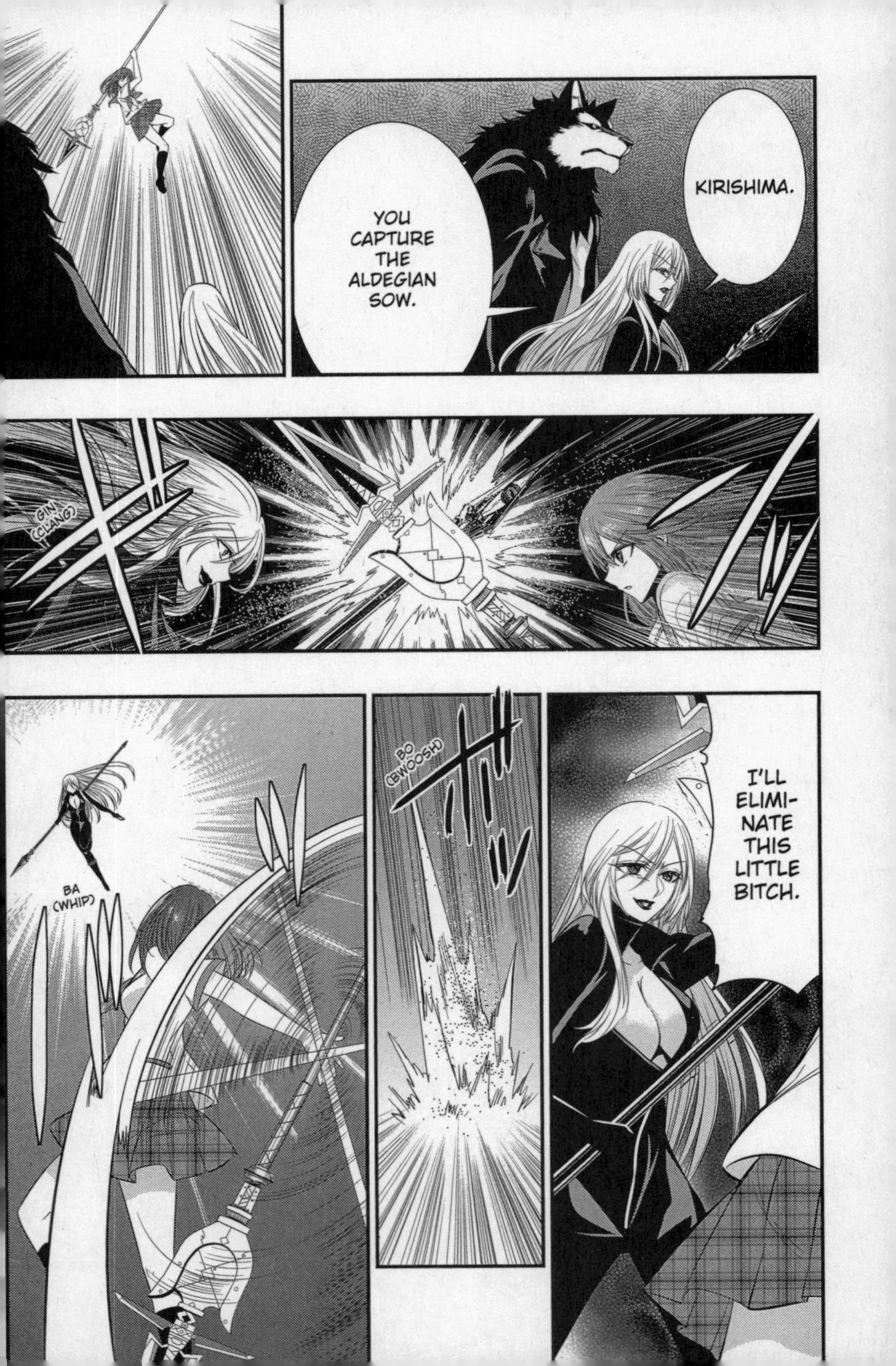
KIRISHIMA.
YOU CAPTURE THE ALDEGIAN SOW.
GIN (CLANG)
I'LL ELIMI- NATE THIS LITTLE BITCH.
BO (BWOOSH)
BA (WHIP)

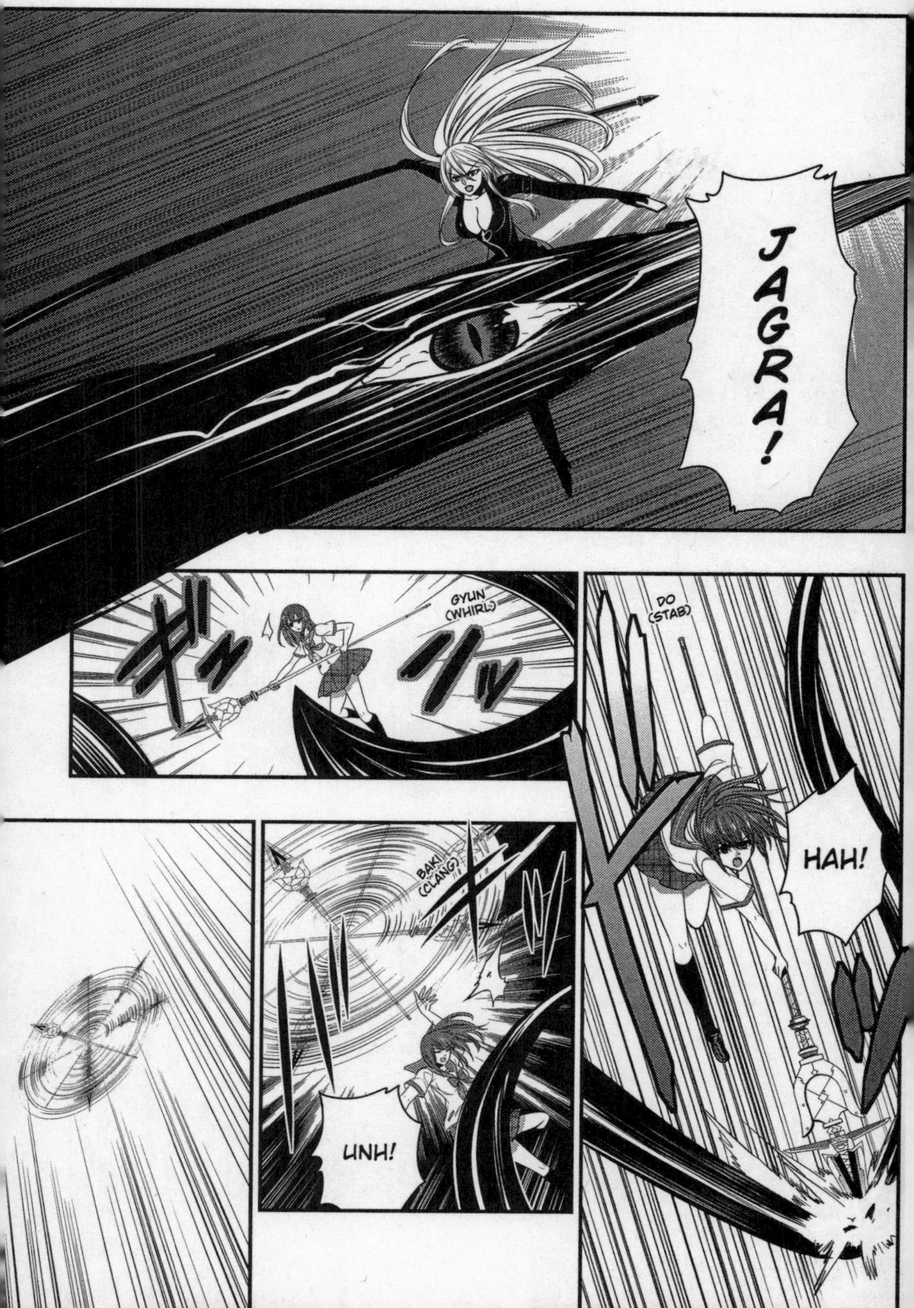
JAGRA!
DO (STAB)
HAH!
GYUN (WHIRL)
BAKI (CLANG)
UNH!

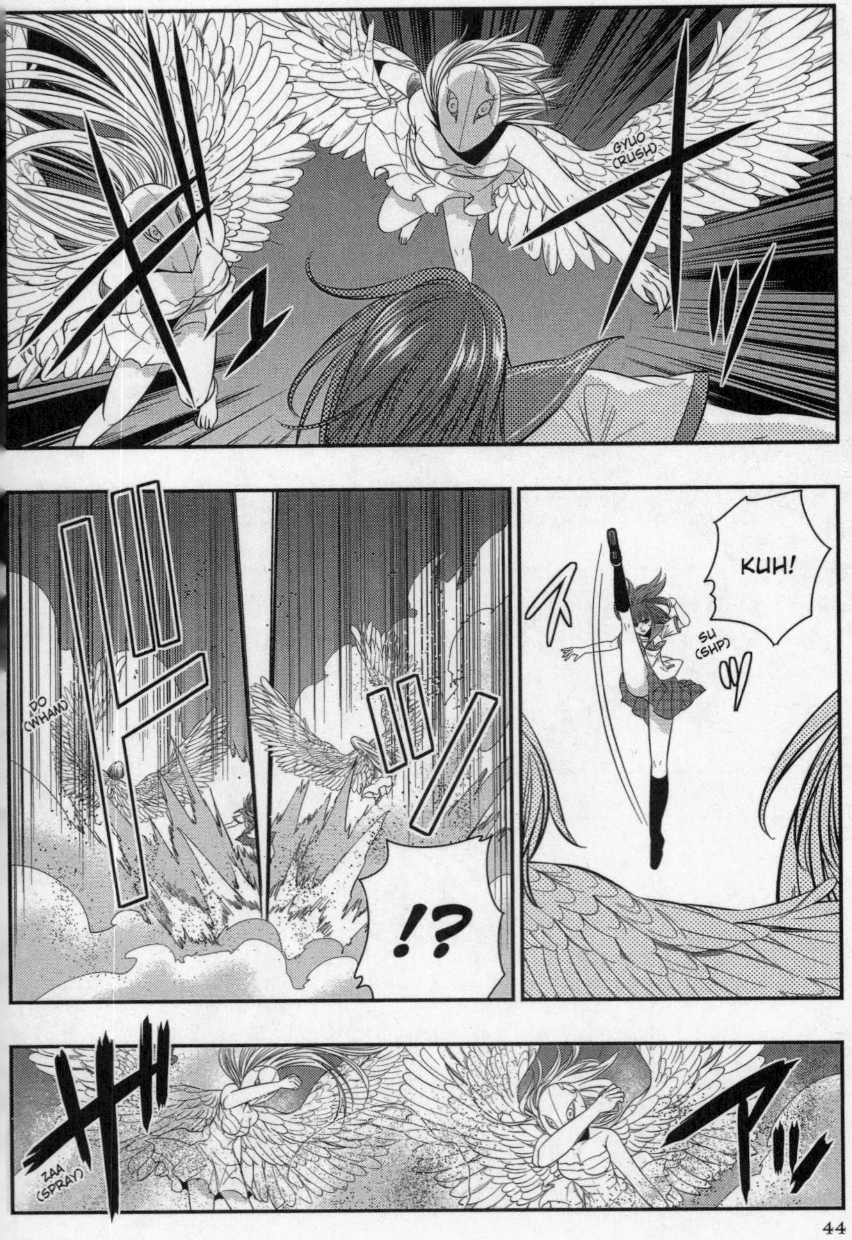
GYUO (RUSH)
KUH!
SU (SHP)
DO (WHAM)
!?
ZAA (SPRAY)

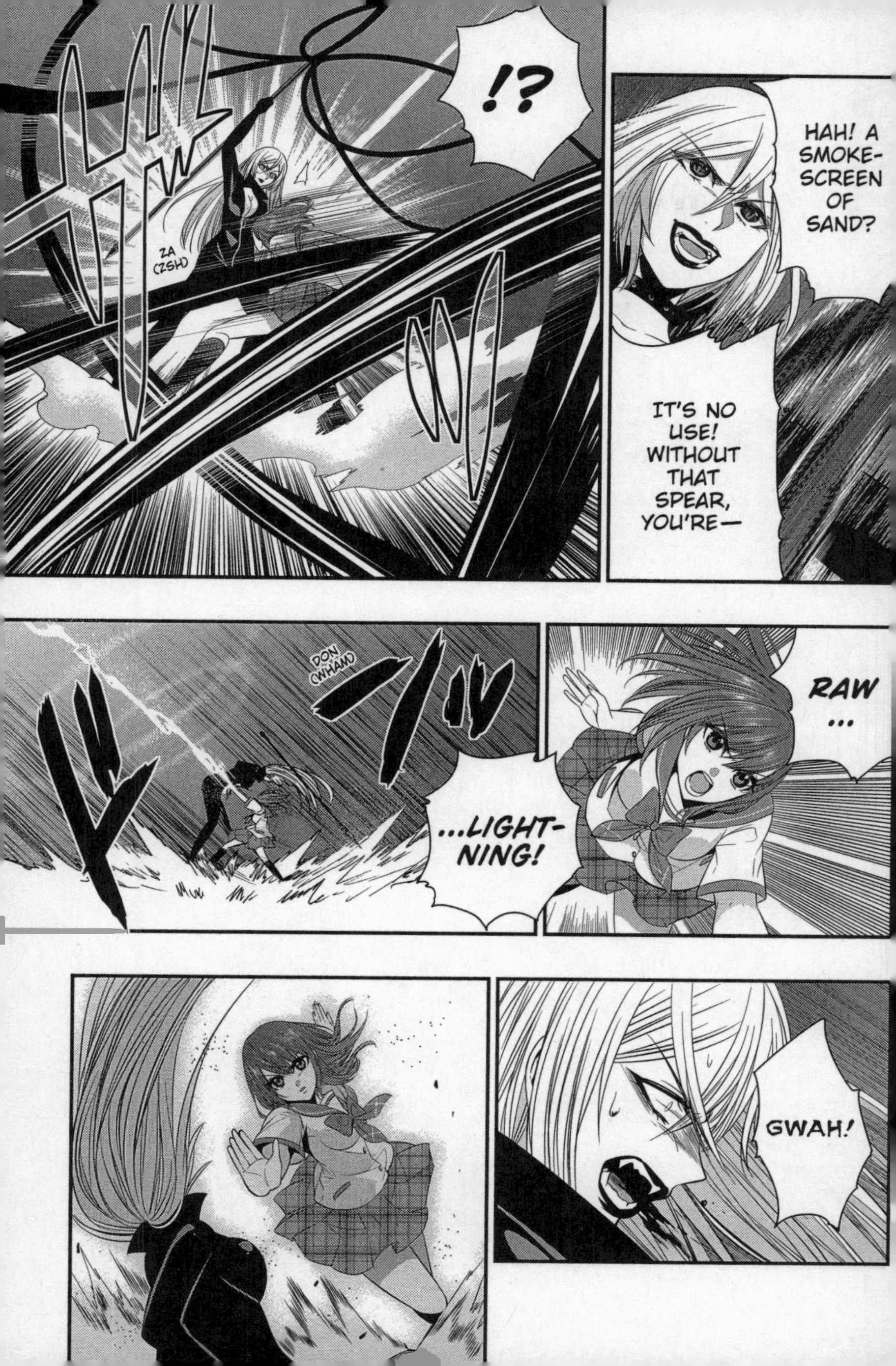
HAH! A SMOKE-SCREEN OF SAND?
IT'S NO USE! WITHOUT THAT SPEAR, YOU'RE—
!?
ZA (ZSH)
RAW...
...LIGHT-NING!
DON (WHAM)
GWAH!

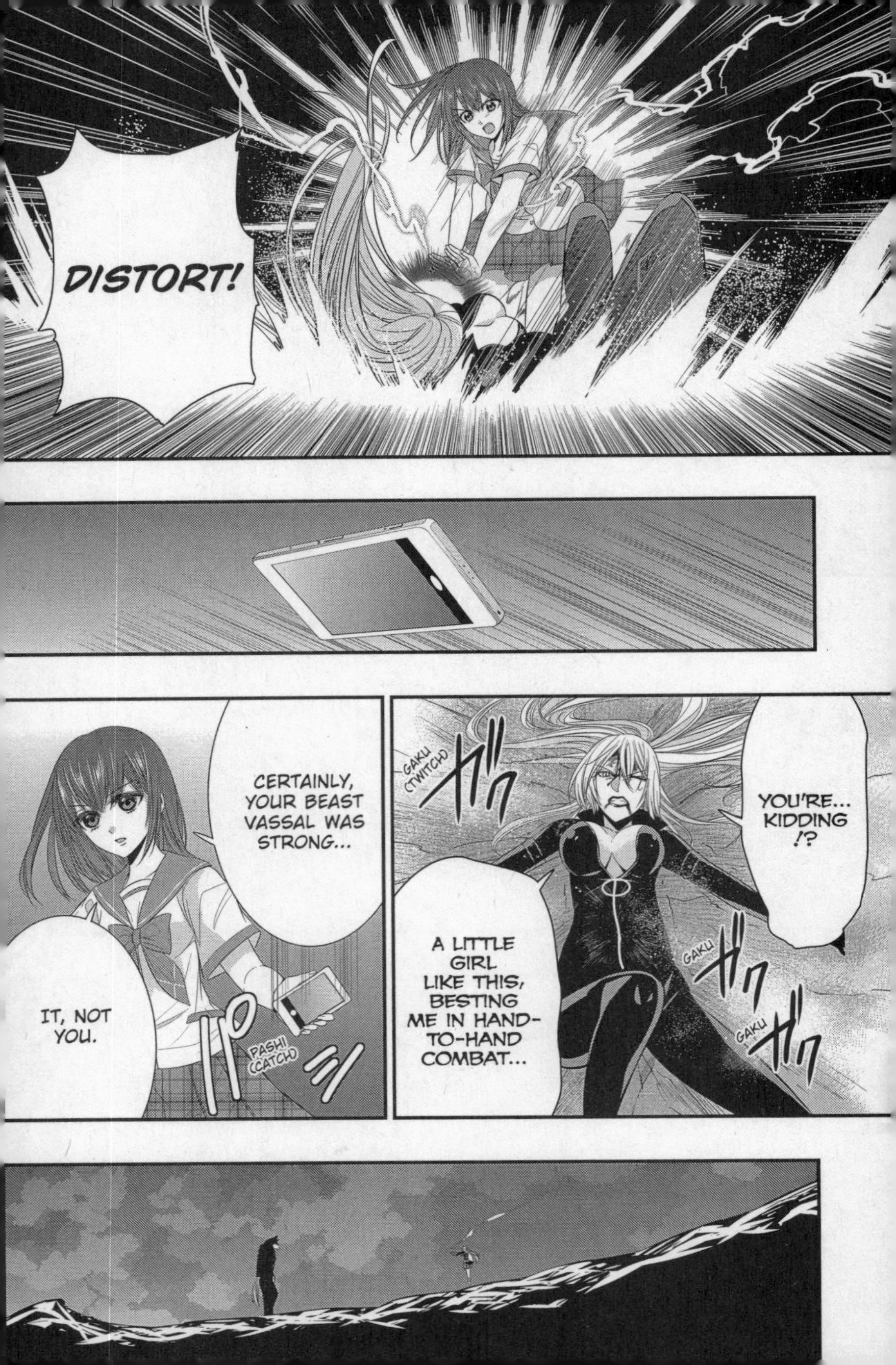
DISTORT!
GAKU (TWITCH)
YOU'RE... KIDDING!?
A LITTLE GIRL LIKE THIS, BESTING ME IN HAND-TO-HAND COMBAT...
GAKU
GAKU
CERTAINLY, YOUR BEAST VASSAL WAS STRONG...
IT, NOT YOU.
PASHI (CATCH)

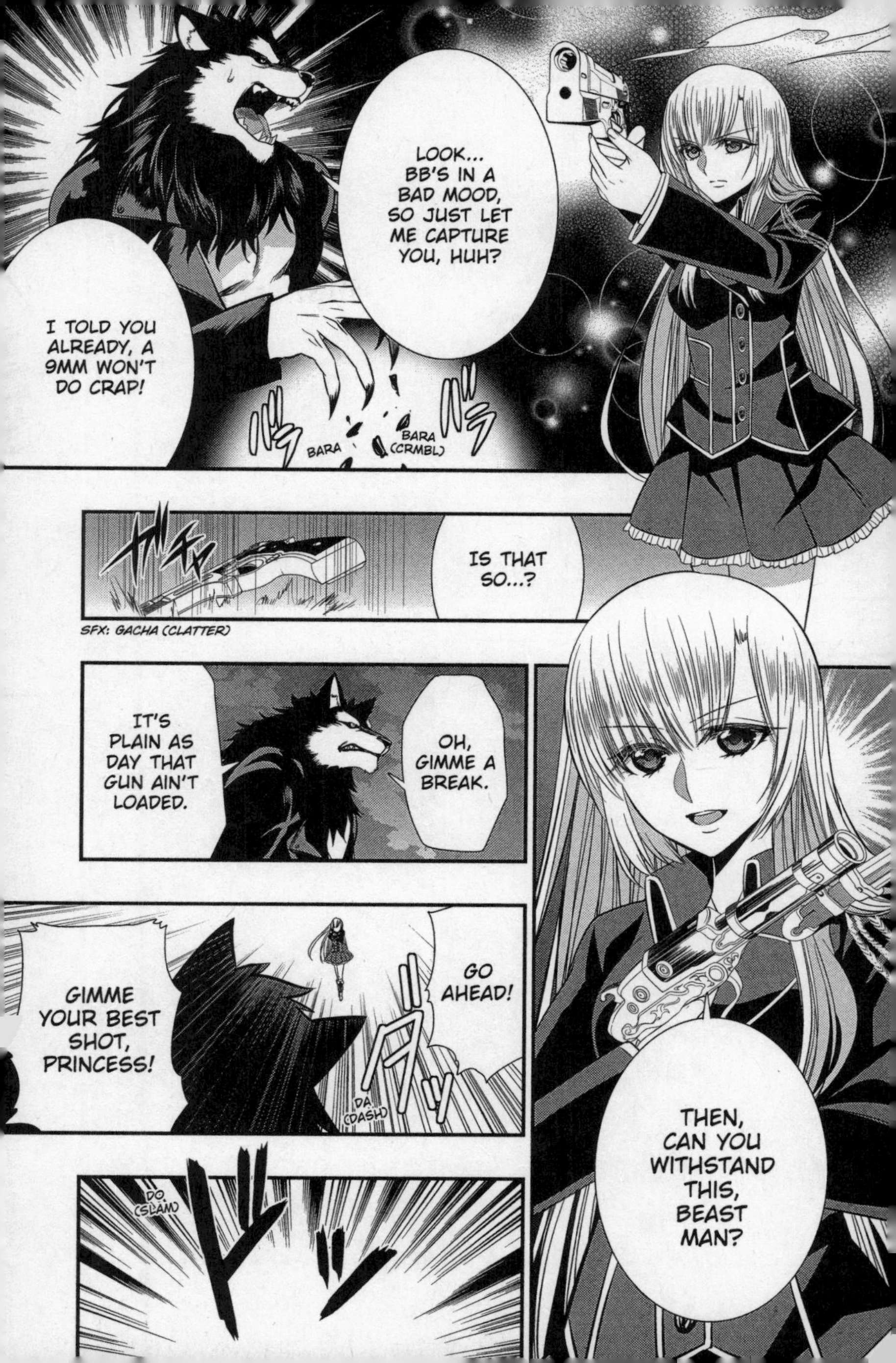
LOOK... BB'S IN A BAD MOOD, SO JUST LET ME CAPTURE YOU, HUH?
I TOLD YOU ALREADY, A 9MM WON'T DO CRAP!
BARA BARA (CRMBL)
IS THAT SO...?
SFX: GACHA (CLATTER)
OH, GIMME A BREAK.
IT'S PLAIN AS DAY THAT GUN AIN'T LOADED.
THEN, CAN YOU WITHSTAND THIS, BEAST MAN?
GO AHEAD!
GIMME YOUR BEST SHOT, PRINCESS!
DA (DASH)
DO (SLAM)

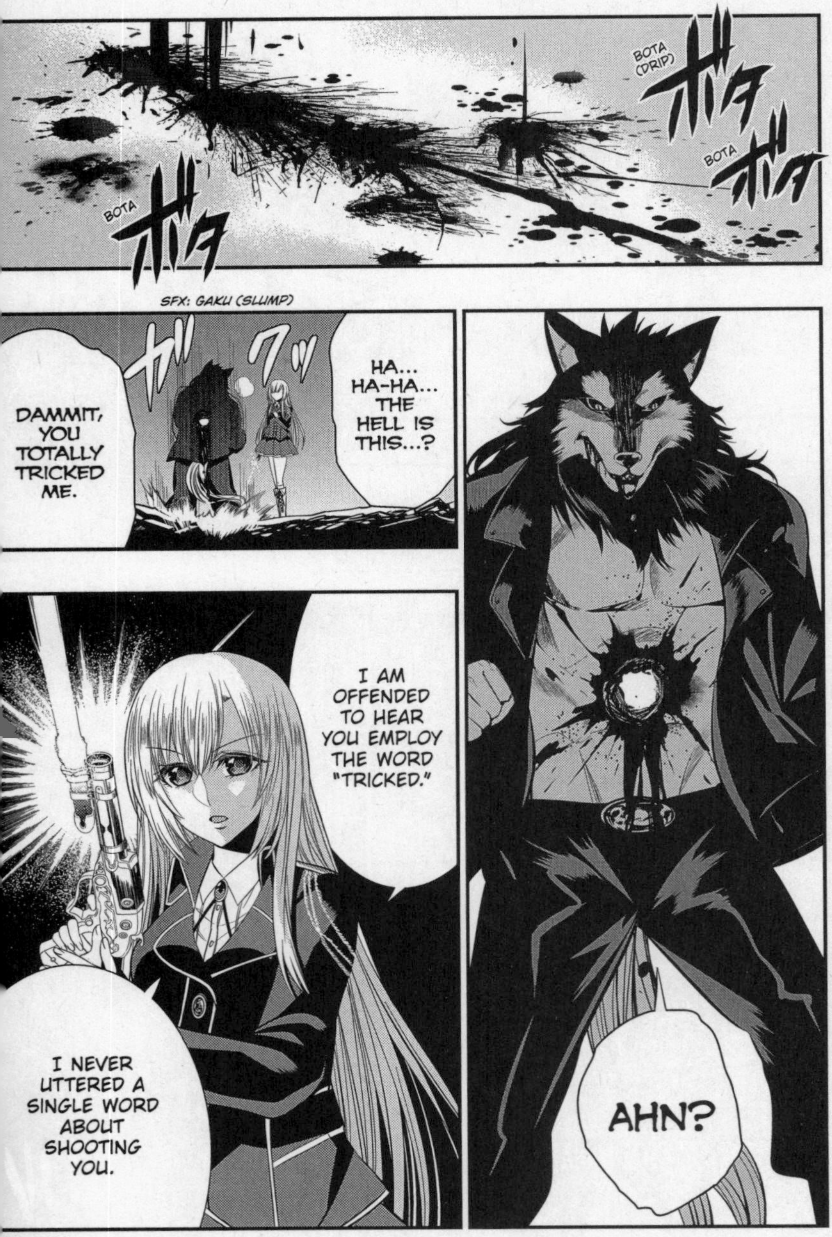

BOTA (DRIP)
ボタ
BOTA
ボタ
BOTA
ボタ
SFX: GAKU (SLUMP)
AHN?
ガクッ
HA... HA-HA... THE HELL IS THIS...?
DAMMIT, YOU TOTALLY TRICKED ME.
I AM OFFENDED TO HEAR YOU EMPLOY THE WORD "TRICKED."
I NEVER UTTERED A SINGLE WORD ABOUT SHOOTING YOU.

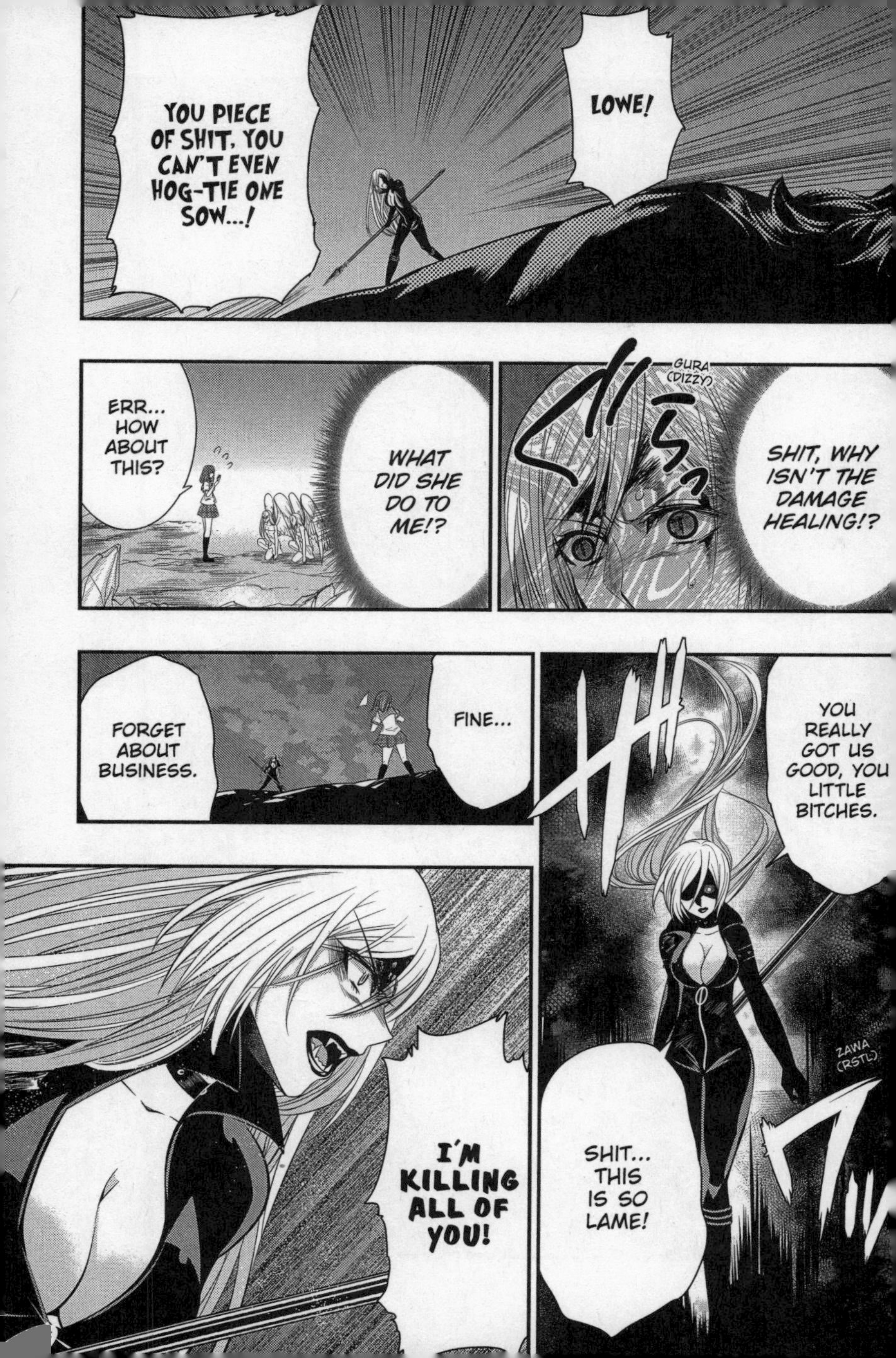
LOWE!
YOU PIECE OF SHIT, YOU CAN'T EVEN HOG-TIE ONE SOW...!
GURA (DIZZY)
SHIT, WHY ISN'T THE DAMAGE HEALING!?
WHAT DID SHE DO TO ME!?
ERR... HOW ABOUT THIS?
YOU REALLY GOT US GOOD, YOU LITTLE BITCHES.
ZAWA (RSTL)
SHIT... THIS IS SO LAME!
FINE...
FORGET ABOUT BUSINESS.
I'M KILLING ALL OF YOU!

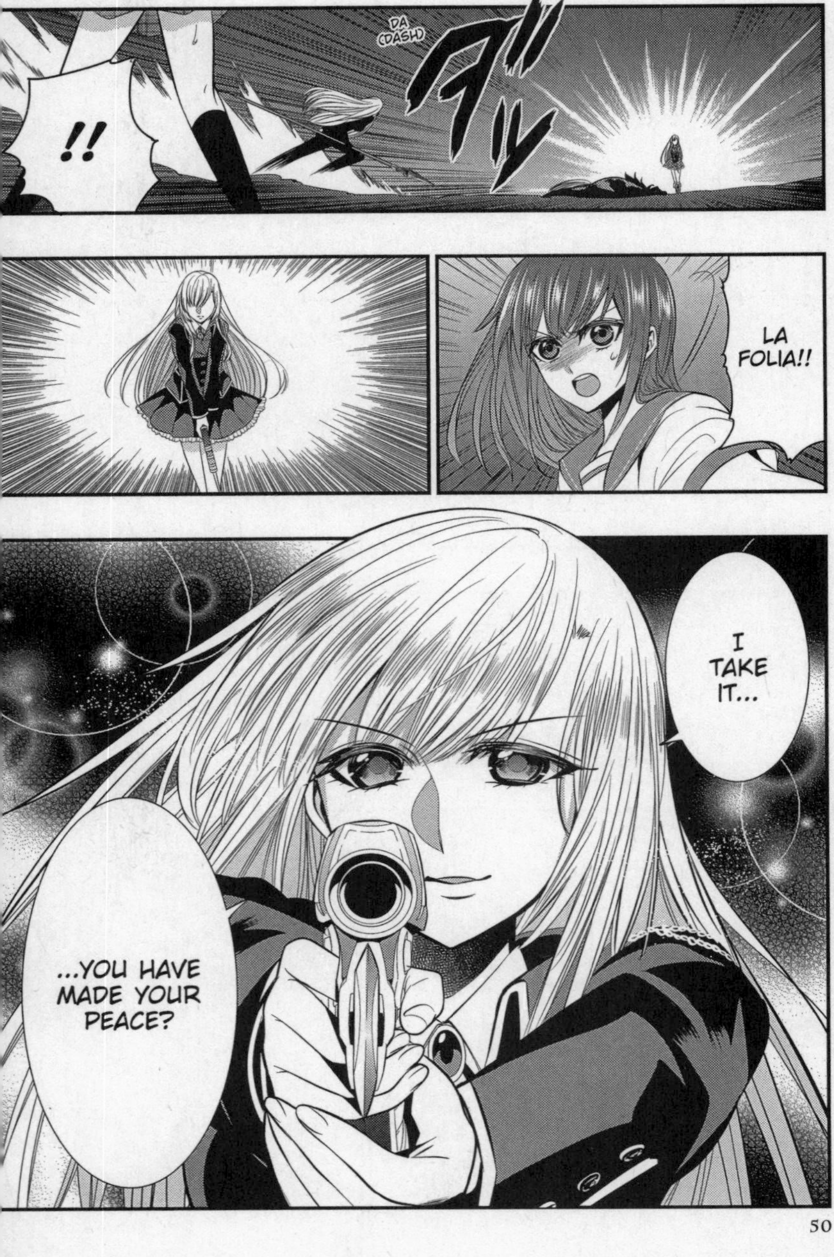

DA (DASH)
!!
LA FOLIA!!
I TAKE IT...
...YOU HAVE MADE YOUR PEACE?

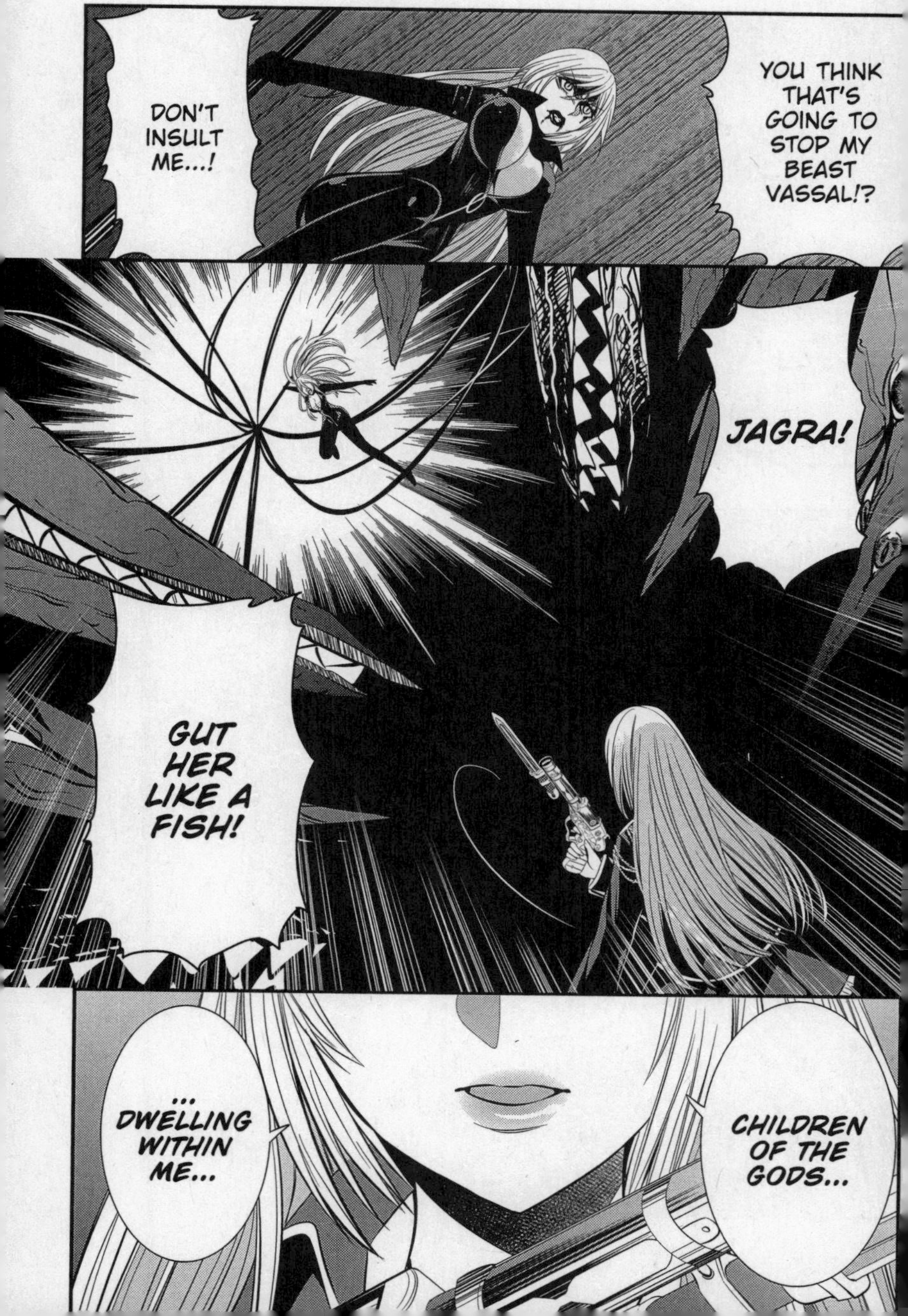
YOU THINK THAT'S GOING TO STOP MY BEAST VASSAL!?
DON'T INSULT ME...!
JAGRA!
GUT HER LIKE A FISH!
CHILDREN OF THE GODS...
... DWELLING WITHIN ME...

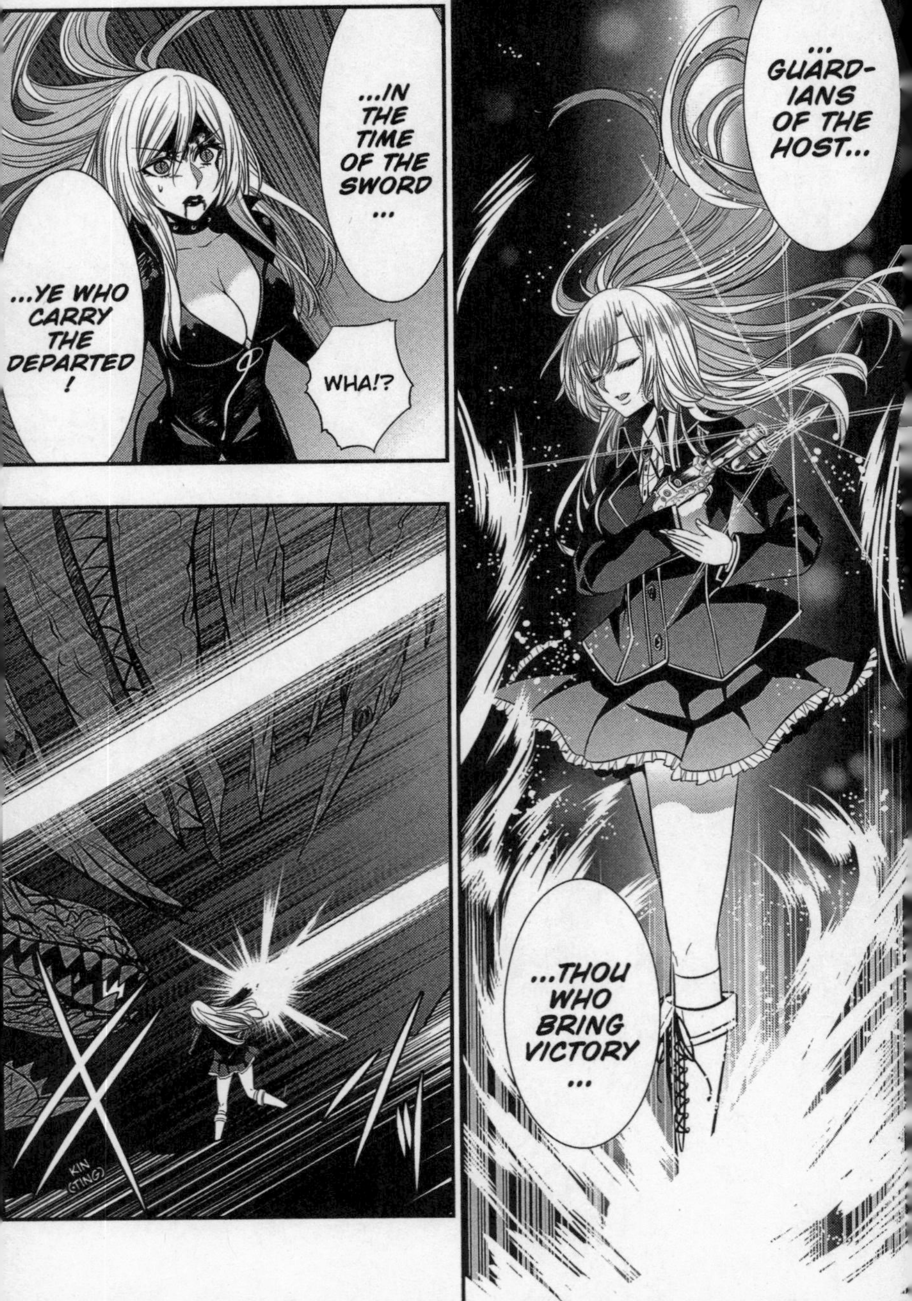
...GUARDIANS OF THE HOST...
...THOU WHO BRING VICTORY...
...IN THE TIME OF THE SWORD...
WHA!?
...YE WHO CARRY THE DEPARTED!
KIN (TING)

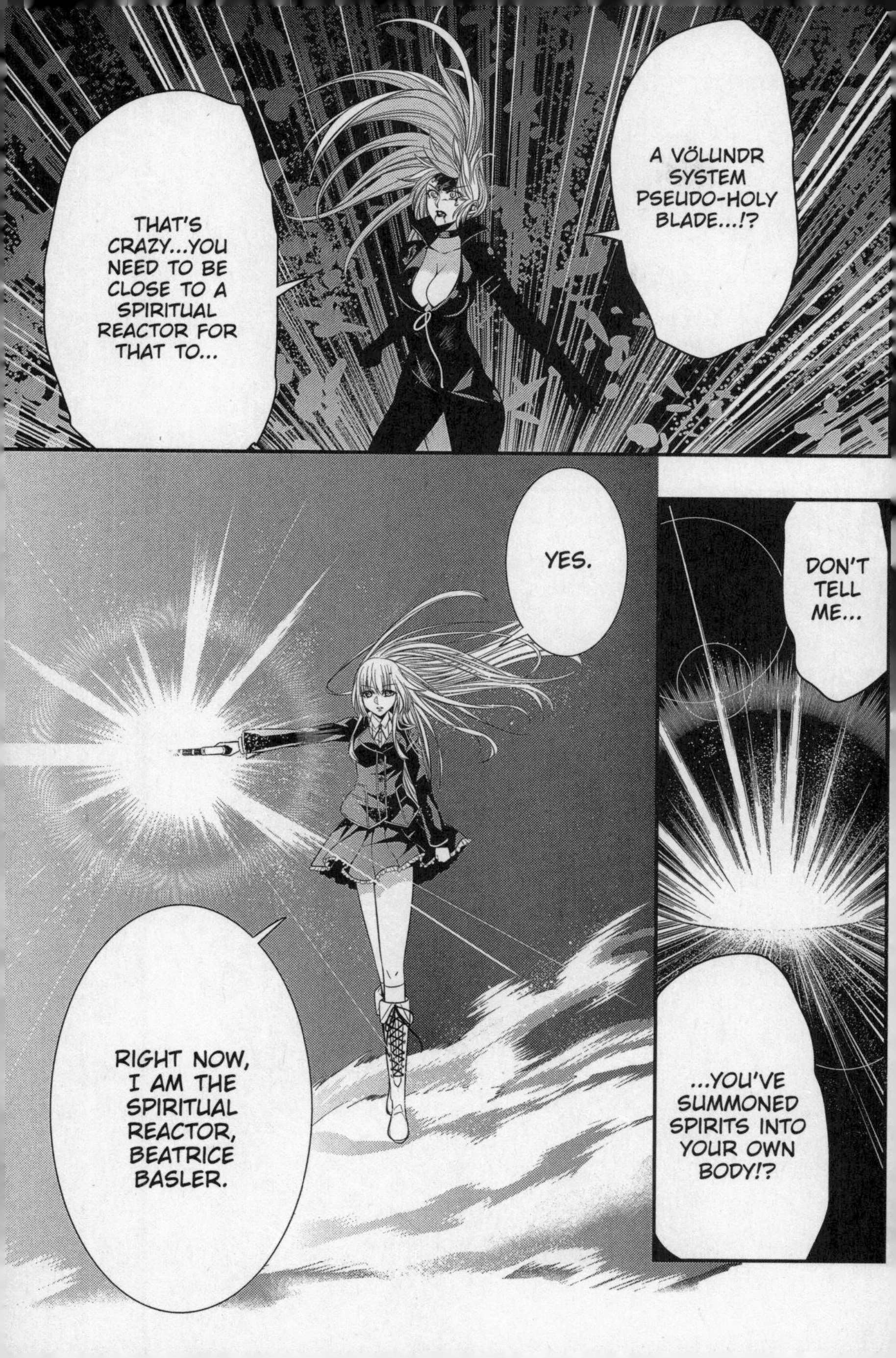
A VÖLUNDR SYSTEM PSEUDO-HOLY BLADE...!?
THAT'S CRAZY...YOU NEED TO BE CLOSE TO A SPIRITUAL REACTOR FOR THAT TO...
DON'T TELL ME...
...YOU'VE SUMMONED SPIRITS INTO YOUR OWN BODY!?
YES.
RIGHT NOW, I AM THE SPIRITUAL REACTOR, BEATRICE BASLER.

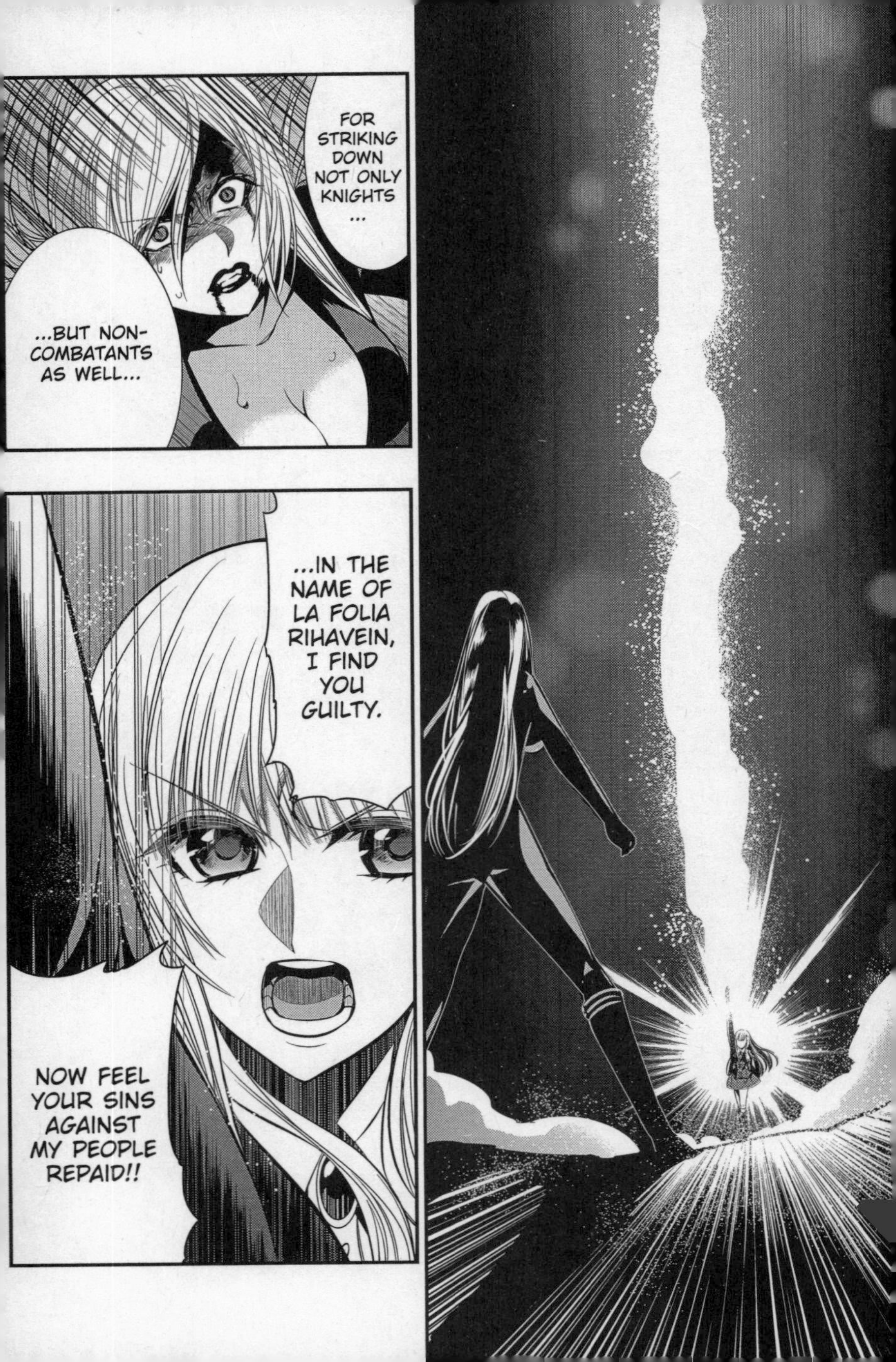
FOR STRIKING DOWN NOT ONLY KNIGHTS...
...BUT NON-COMBATANTS AS WELL...
...IN THE NAME OF LA FOLIA RIHAVEIN, I FIND YOU GUILTY.
NOW FEEL YOUR SINS AGAINST MY PEOPLE REPAID!!

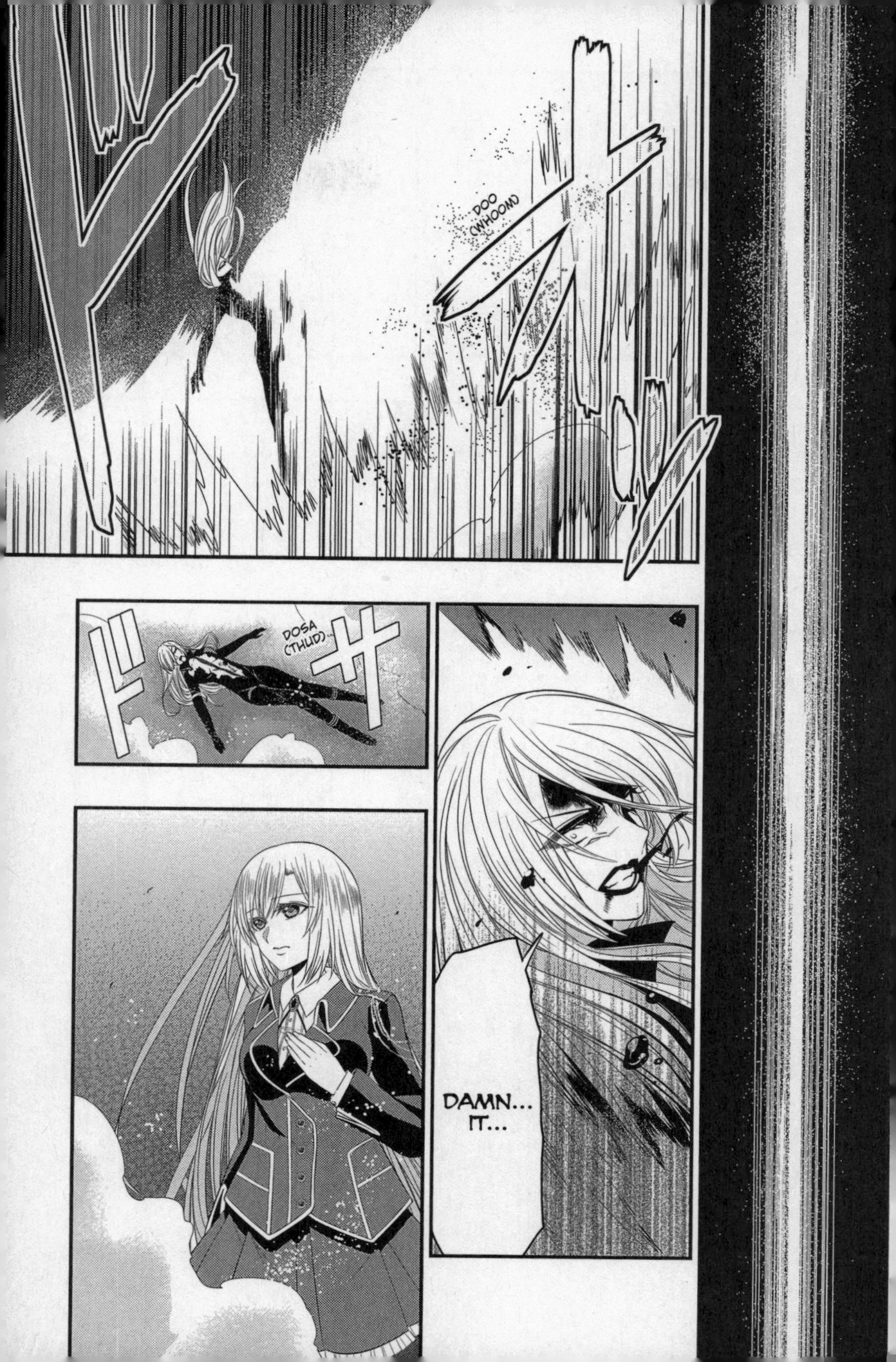
DOO (WHOOM)
DAMN... IT...
DOSA (THUD)

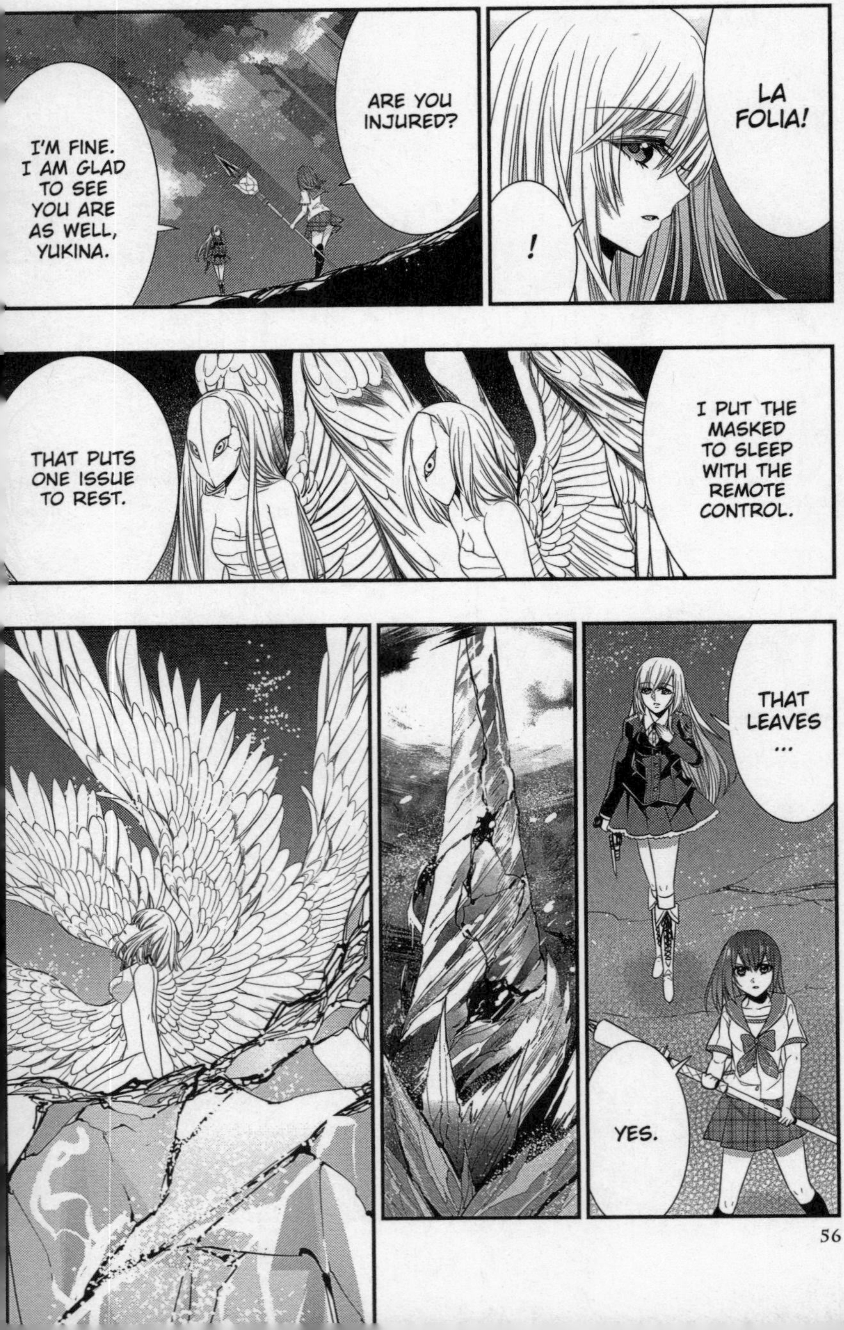
LA FOLIA!
!
ARE YOU INJURED?
I'M FINE. I AM GLAD TO SEE YOU ARE AS WELL, YUKINA.
I PUT THE MASKED TO SLEEP WITH THE REMOTE CONTROL.
THAT PUTS ONE ISSUE TO REST.
THAT LEAVES ...
YES.

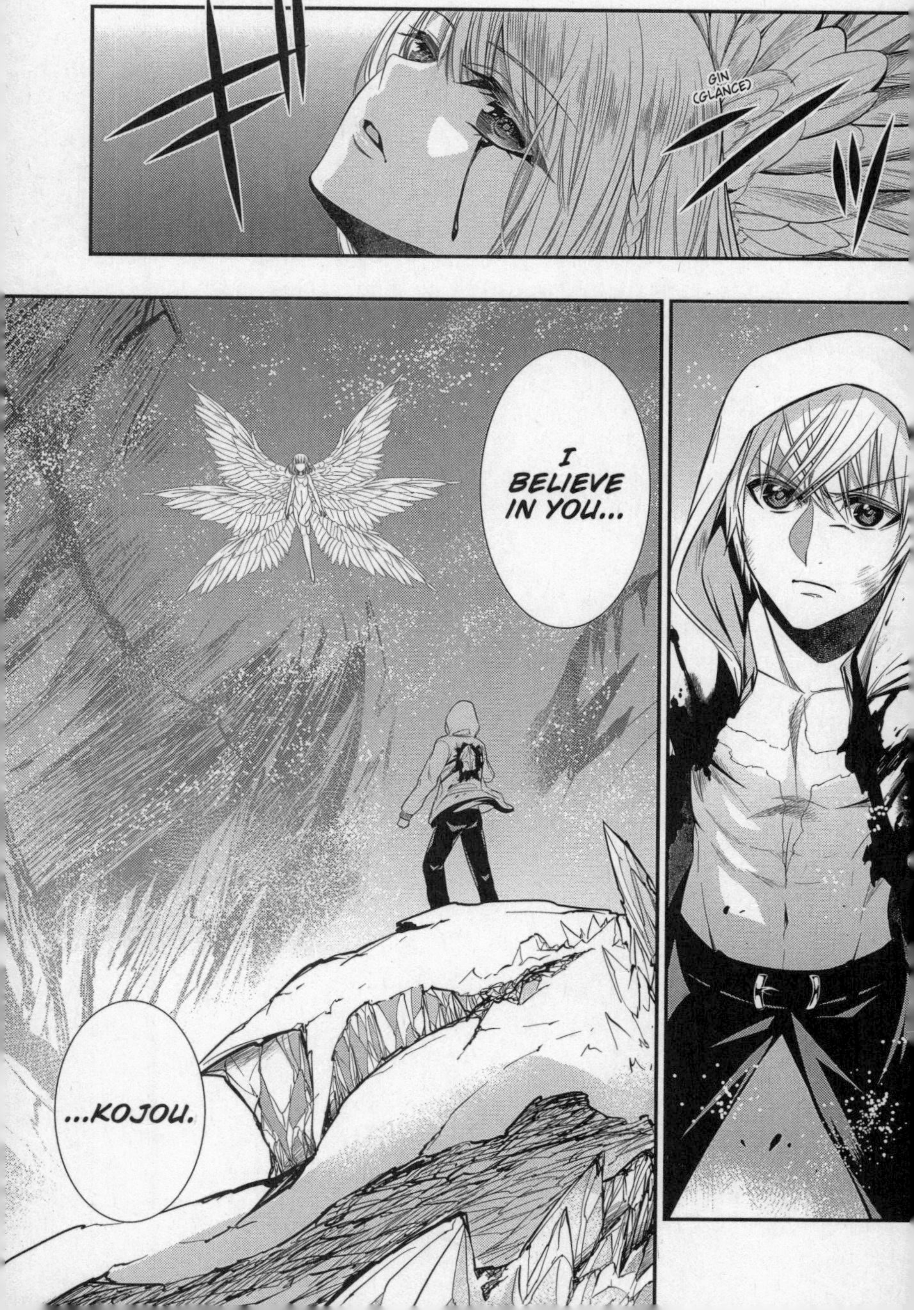
GIN (GLANCE)
I BELIEVE IN YOU...
...KOJOU.

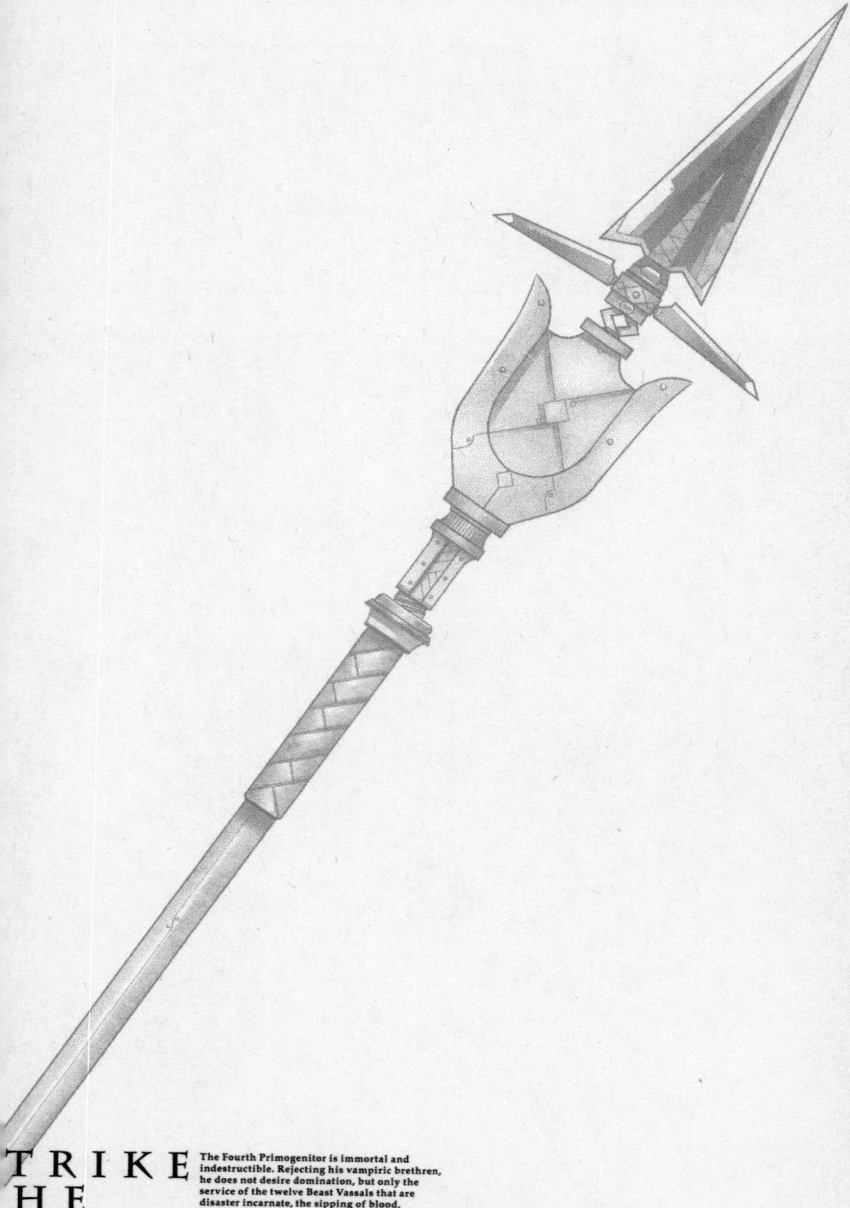

TRIKE
HE
LOOD

The Fourth Primogenitor is immortal and indestructible. Rejecting his vampiric brethren, he does not desire domination, but only the service of the twelve Beast Vassals that are disaster incarnate, the sipping of blood, carnage, and destruction. The vampire is said to be ruthless and heartless, completely beyond the doctrines of the world, a monster who has laid waste to innumerable cities in the past.

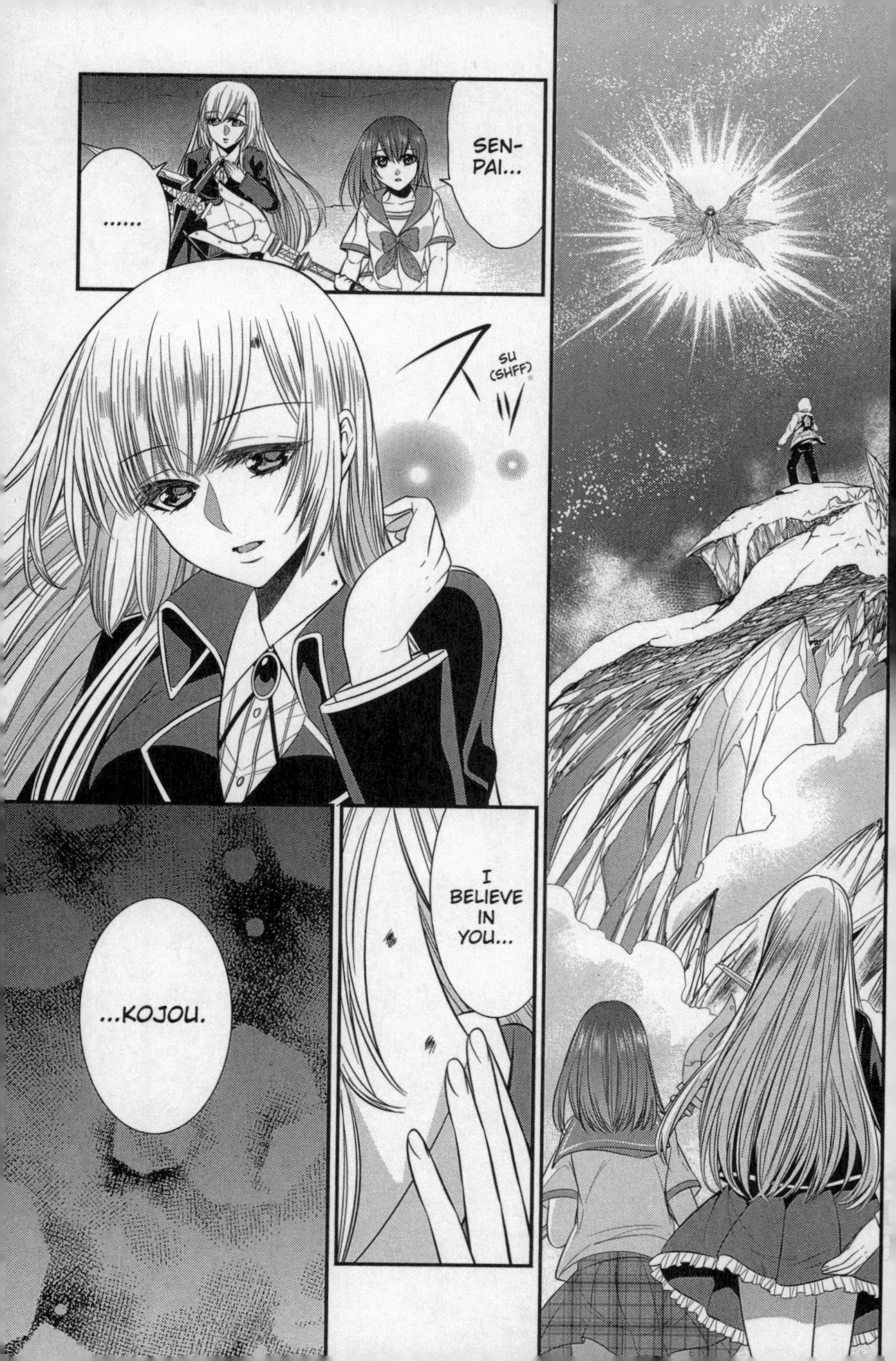
SEN-PAI...
......
SU (SHFF)
I BELIEVE IN YOU...
...KOJOU.

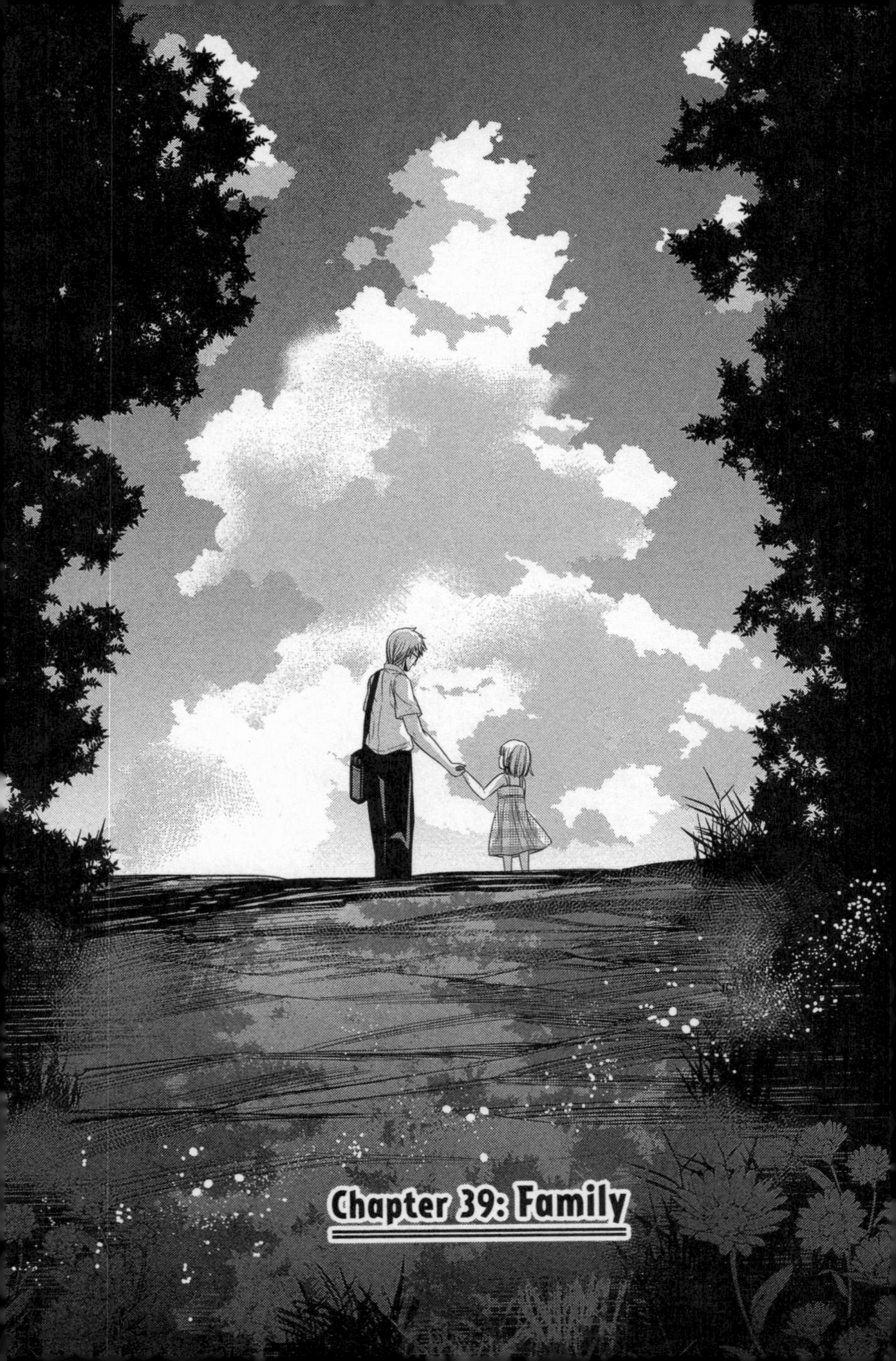
Chapter 39: Family

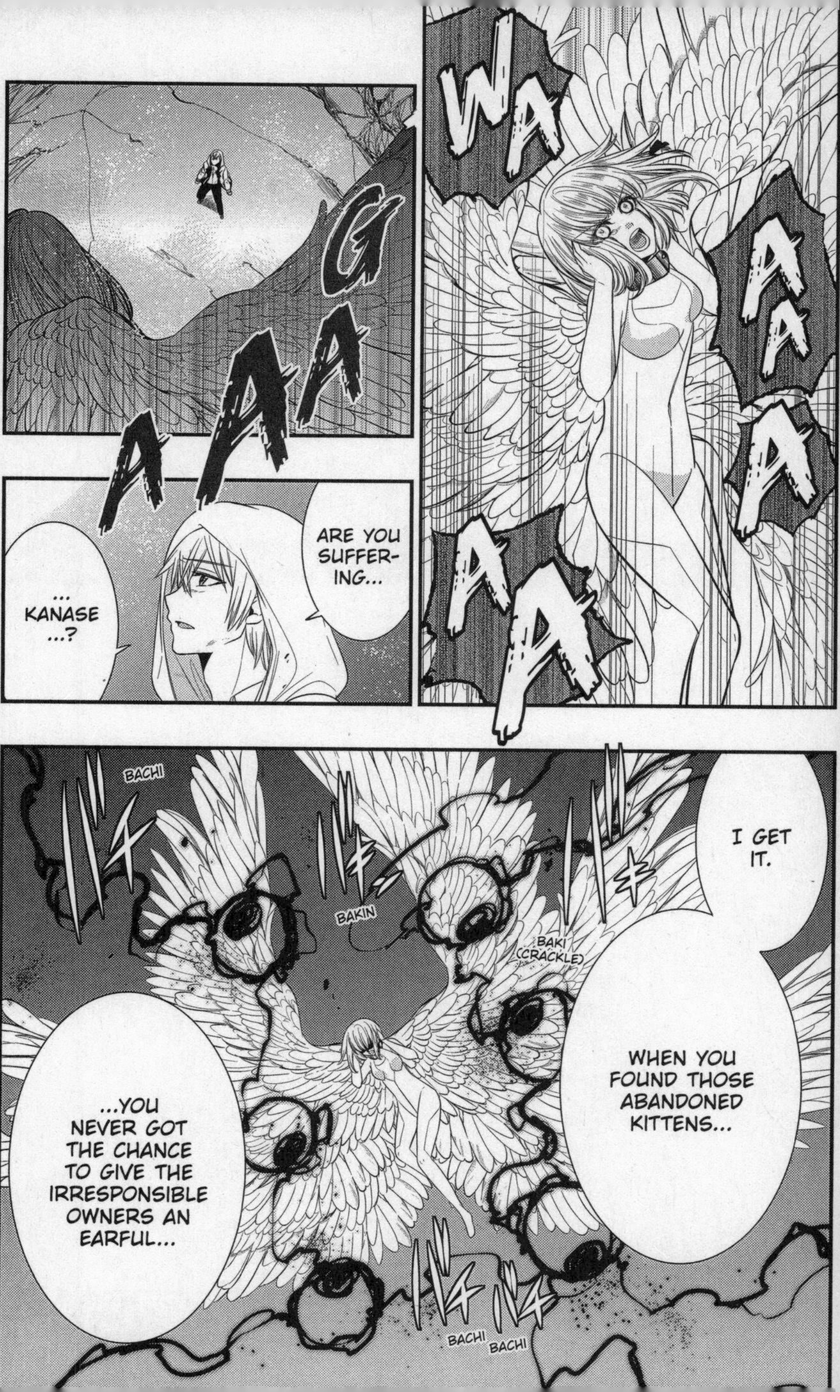

WAAAAAA
GAAAA
ARE YOU SUFFERING...
...KANASE...?
I GET IT.
WHEN YOU FOUND THOSE ABANDONED KITTENS...
BAKI (CRACKLE)
BAKIN
BACHI
...YOU NEVER GOT THE CHANCE TO GIVE THE IRRESPONSIBLE OWNERS AN EARFUL...
BACHI BACHI

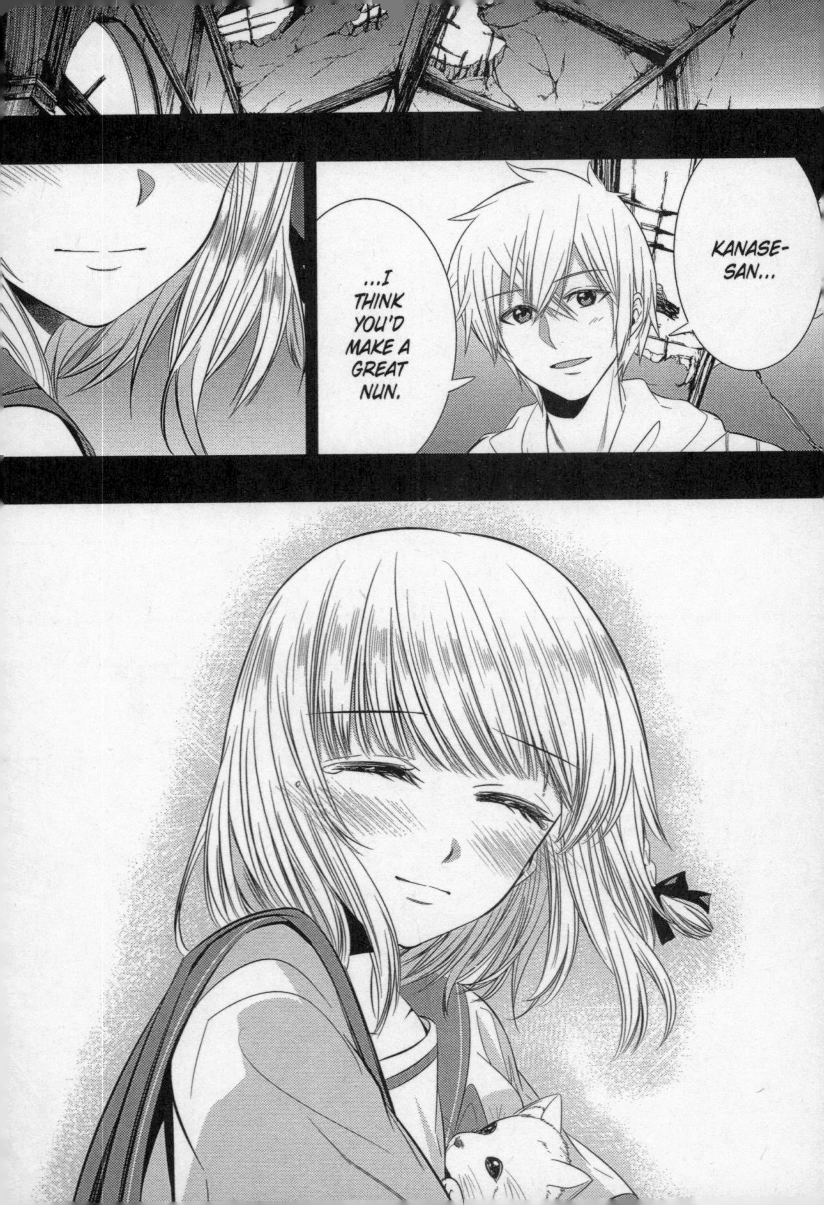
KANASE-SAN...
...I THINK YOU'D MAKE A GREAT NUN.

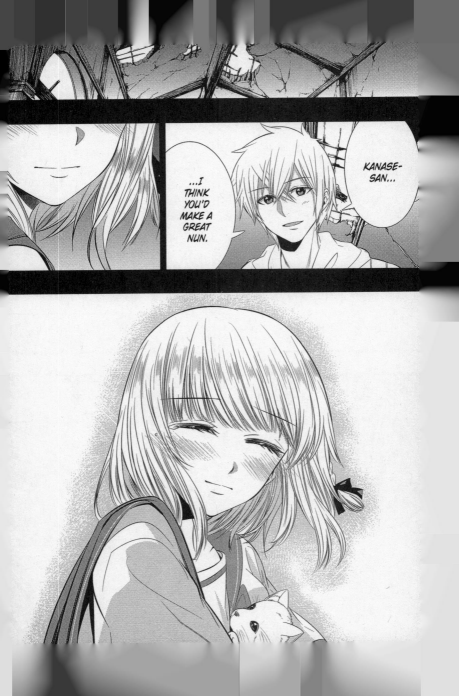

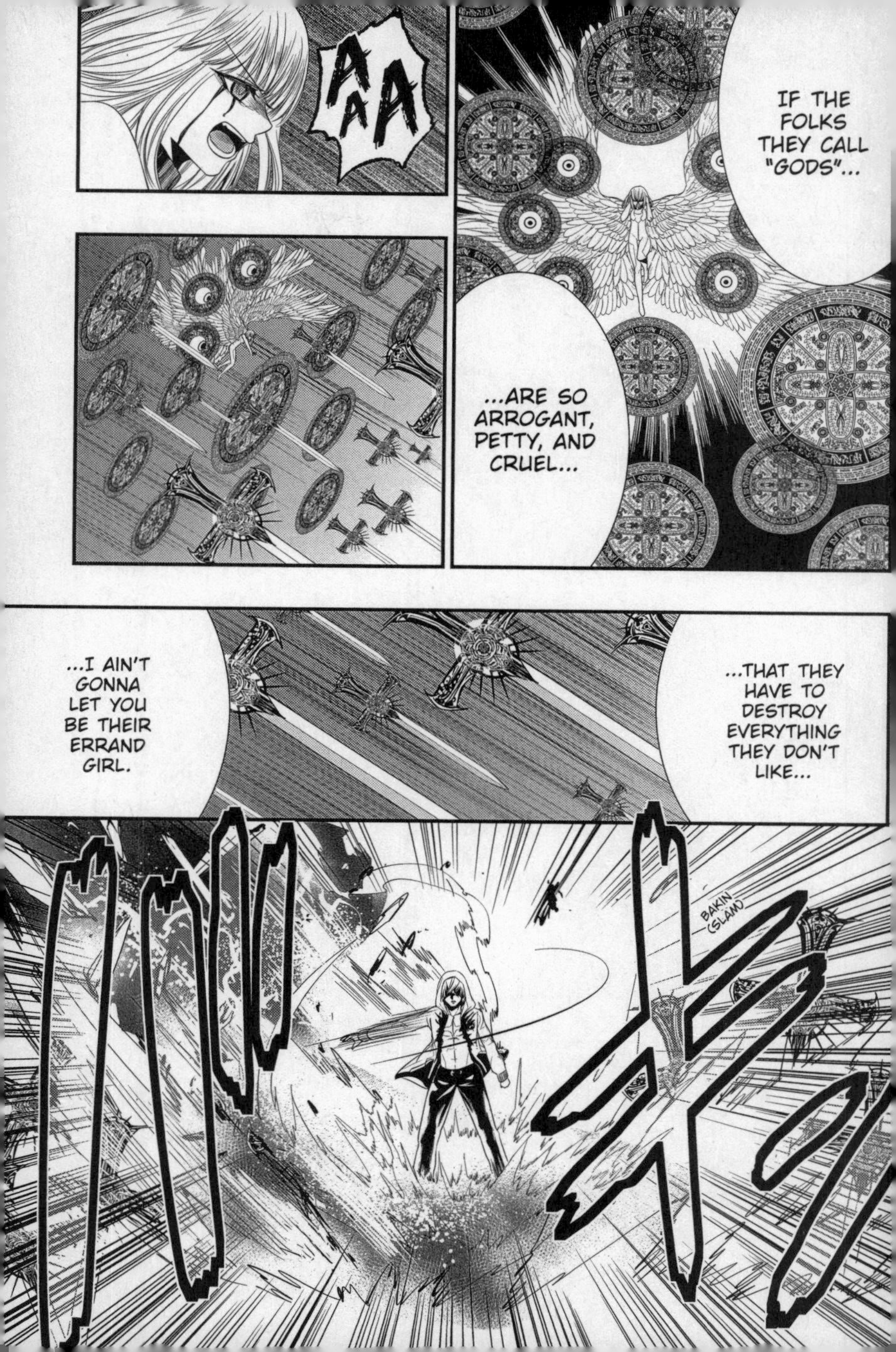
IF THE FOLKS THEY CALL "GODS"...
...ARE SO ARROGANT, PETTY, AND CRUEL...
AAA
...THAT THEY HAVE TO DESTROY EVERYTHING THEY DON'T LIKE...
...I AIN'T GONNA LET YOU BE THEIR ERRAND GIRL.
BAKIN (SLAM)

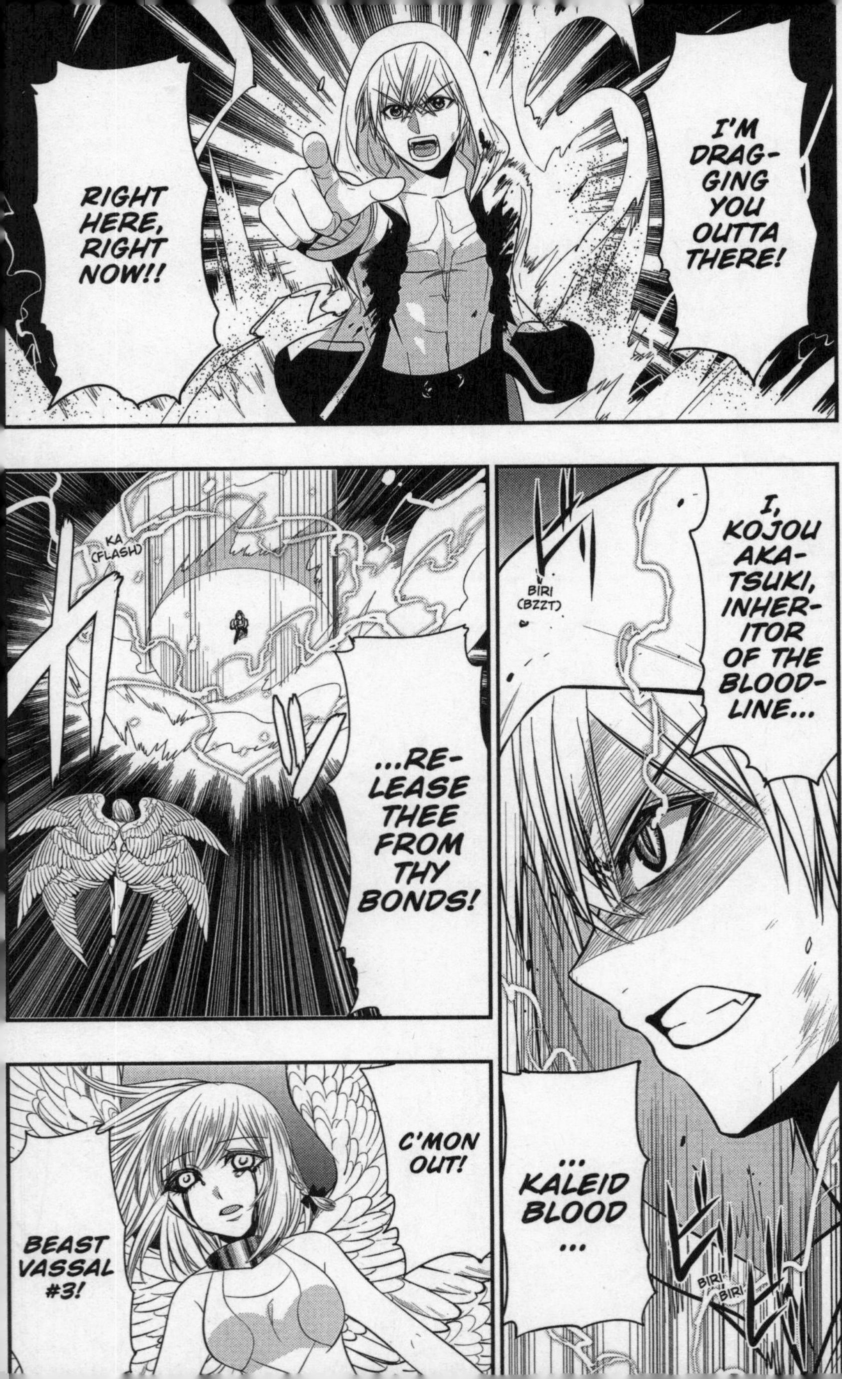
I'M DRAG- GING YOU OUTTA THERE!
RIGHT HERE, RIGHT NOW!!
BIRI (BZZT)
I, KOJOU AKA- TSUKI, INHER- ITOR OF THE BLOOD- LINE...
... KALEID BLOOD ...
BIRI BIRI
KA (FLASH)
...RE- LEASE THEE FROM THY BONDS!
C'MON OUT!
BEAST VASSAL #3!

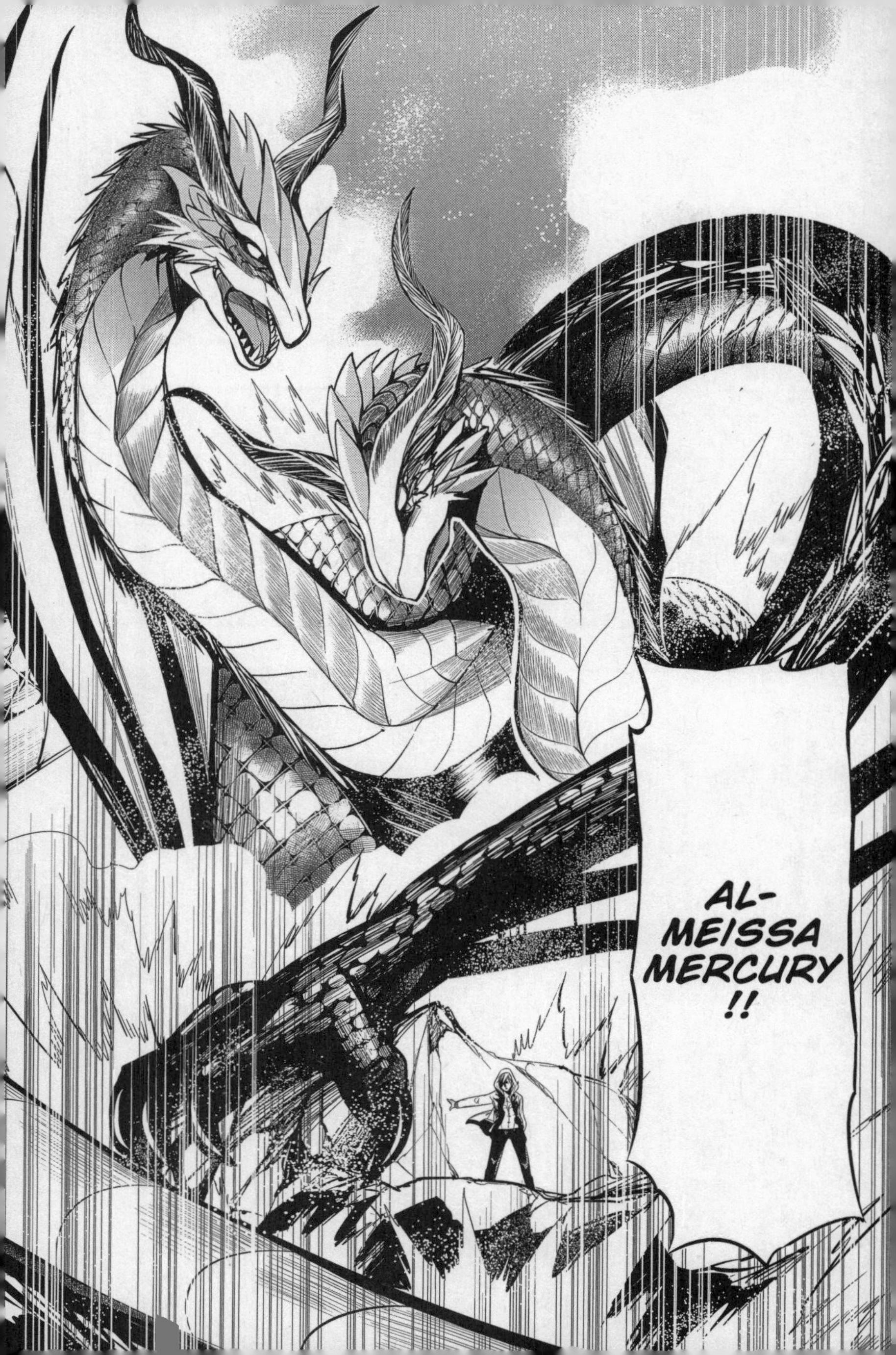
AL-MEISSA MERCURY !!

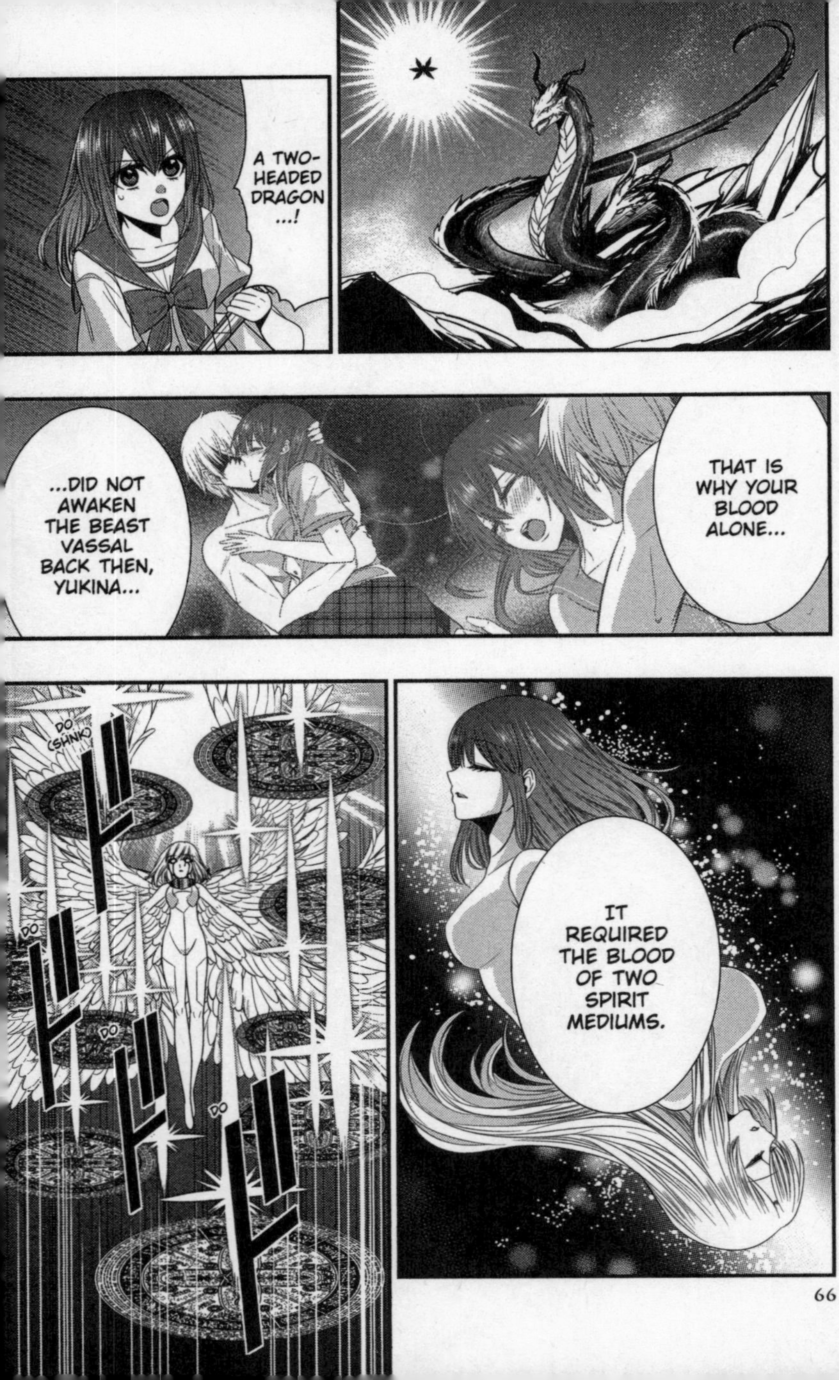
A TWO-HEADED DRAGON...!
THAT IS WHY YOUR BLOOD ALONE...
...DID NOT AWAKEN THE BEAST VASSAL BACK THEN, YUKINA...
IT REQUIRED THE BLOOD OF TWO SPIRIT MEDIUMS.
DO (SHNK)
DO
DO
DO

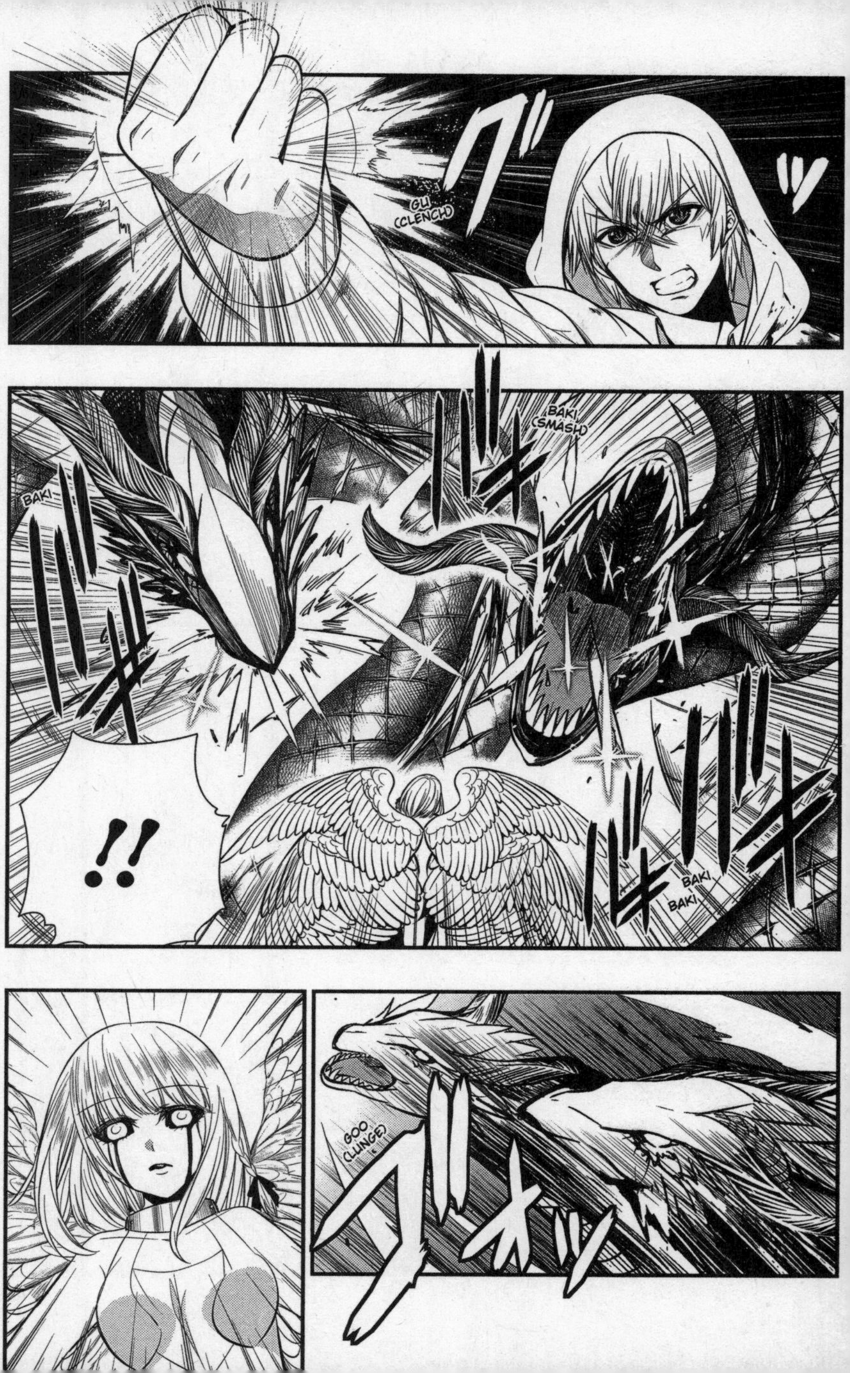
GU (CLENCH)
BAKI (SMASH)
BAKI BAKI
BAKI
!!
GOO (LUNGE)

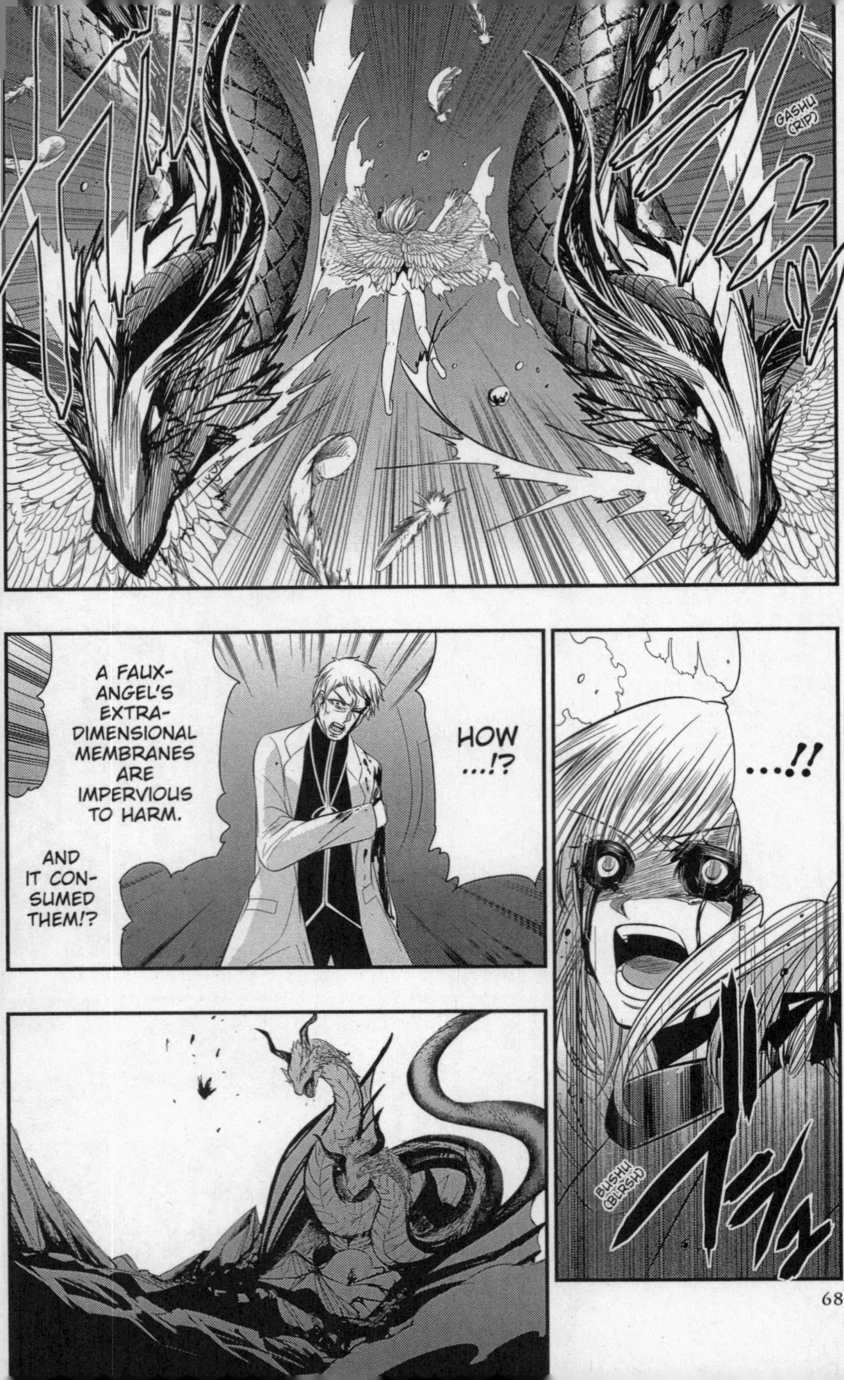
GASHU (RIP)
...!!
BUSHU (BLRSH)
HOW ...!?
A FAUX-ANGEL'S EXTRA-DIMENSIONAL MEMBRANES ARE IMPERVIOUS TO HARM.
AND IT CONSUMED THEM!?

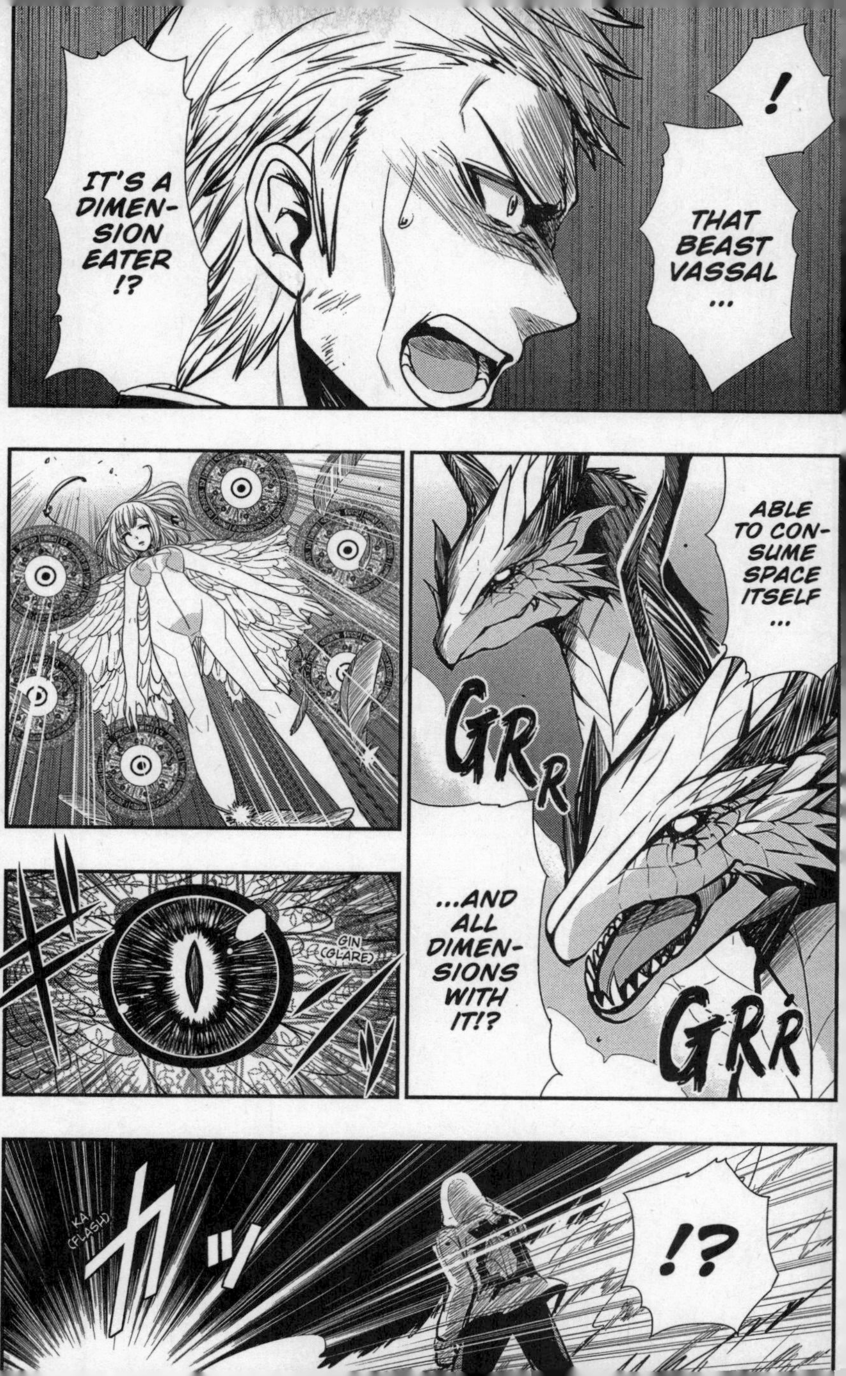
!
THAT BEAST VASSAL ...
IT'S A DIMENSION EATER !?
ABLE TO CONSUME SPACE ITSELF ...
GRR
...AND ALL DIMENSIONS WITH IT!?
GRR
GIN (GLARE)
!?
KA (FLASH)

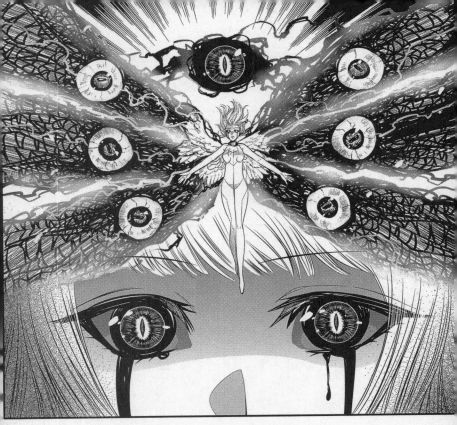

THAT'S RIGHT! SHE'S ONLY FALLEN INTO THE SAME DIMENSION...

...SHE HAS NOT LOST HER FLOW OF HIGHER-PLANAR DIVINE ENERGY.

JU
(SIZZLE)

GN... WAH!?

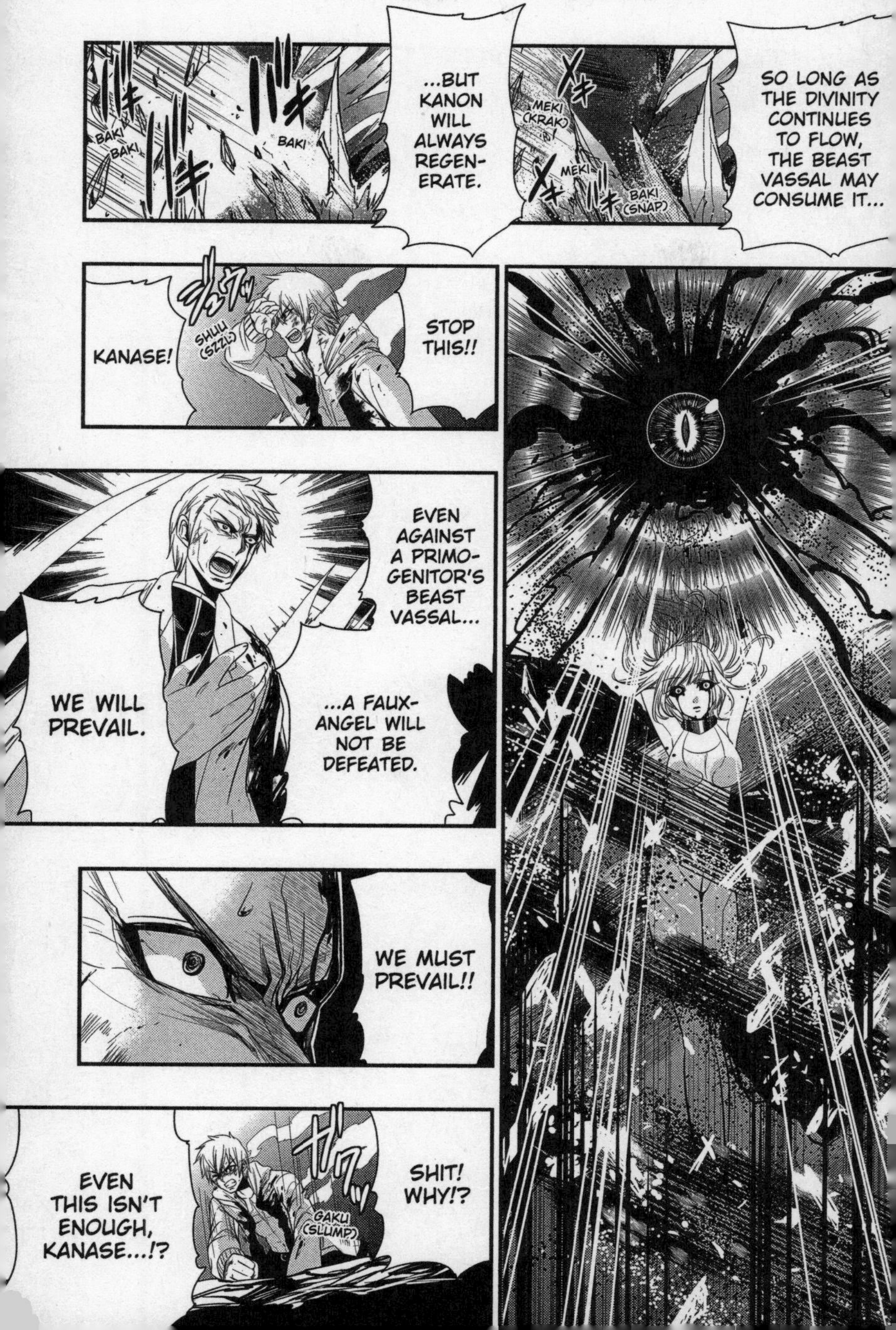
SO LONG AS THE DIVINITY CONTINUES TO FLOW, THE BEAST VASSAL MAY CONSUME IT...
MEKI (KRAK)
MEKI
BAKI (SNAP)
...BUT KANON WILL ALWAYS REGENERATE.
BAKI
BAKI
BAKI
STOP THIS!!
SHUU (SZZL)
KANASE!
EVEN AGAINST A PRIMOGENITOR'S BEAST VASSAL...
...A FAUX-ANGEL WILL NOT BE DEFEATED.
WE WILL PREVAIL.
WE MUST PREVAIL!!
SHIT! WHY!?
GAKU (SLUMP)
EVEN THIS ISN'T ENOUGH, KANASE...!?

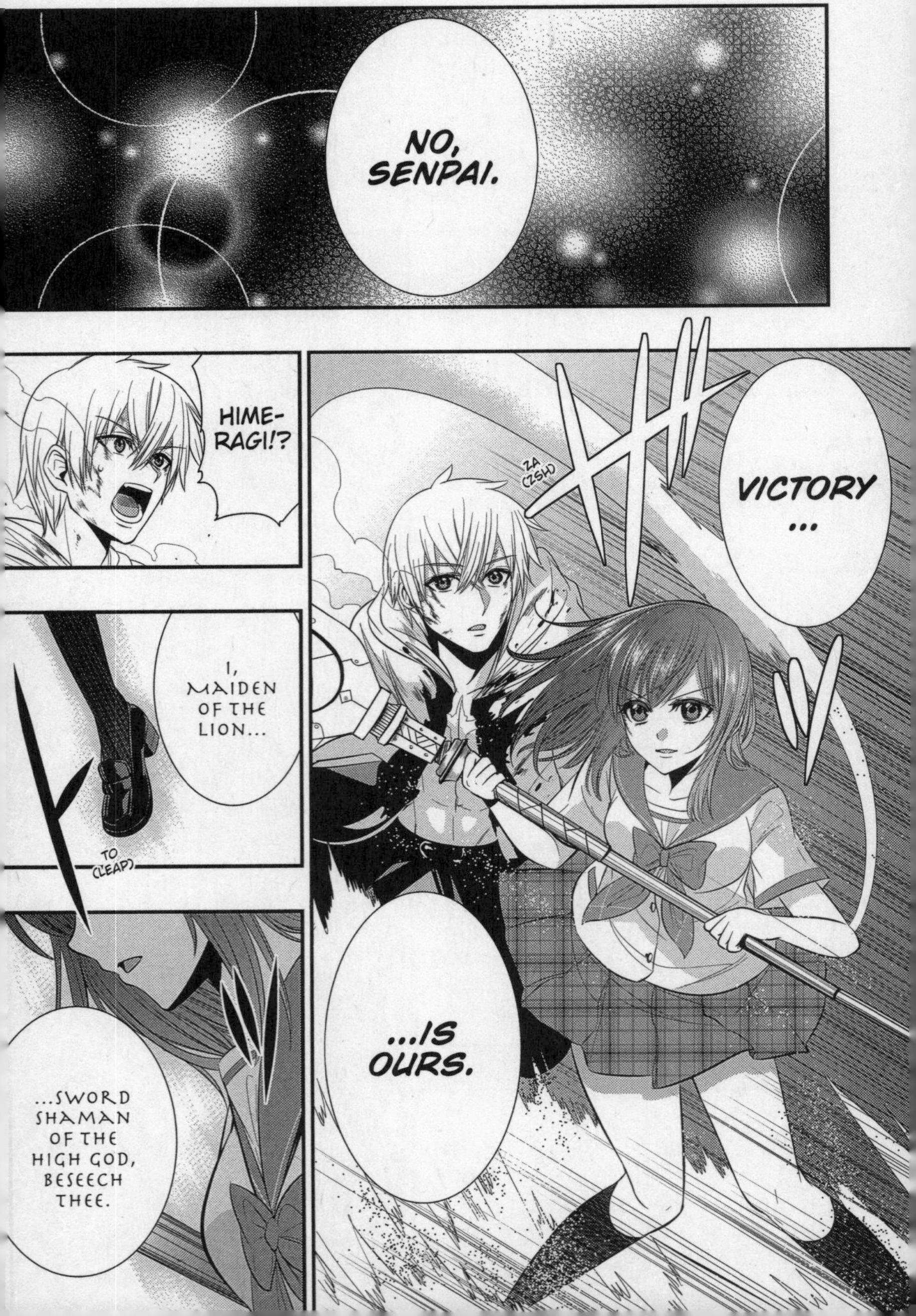
NO, SENPAI.
VICTORY ...
ZA (ZSH)
...IS OURS.
HIME-RAGI!?
I, MAIDEN OF THE LION...
TO (LEAP)
...SWORD SHAMAN OF THE HIGH GOD, BESEECH THEE.

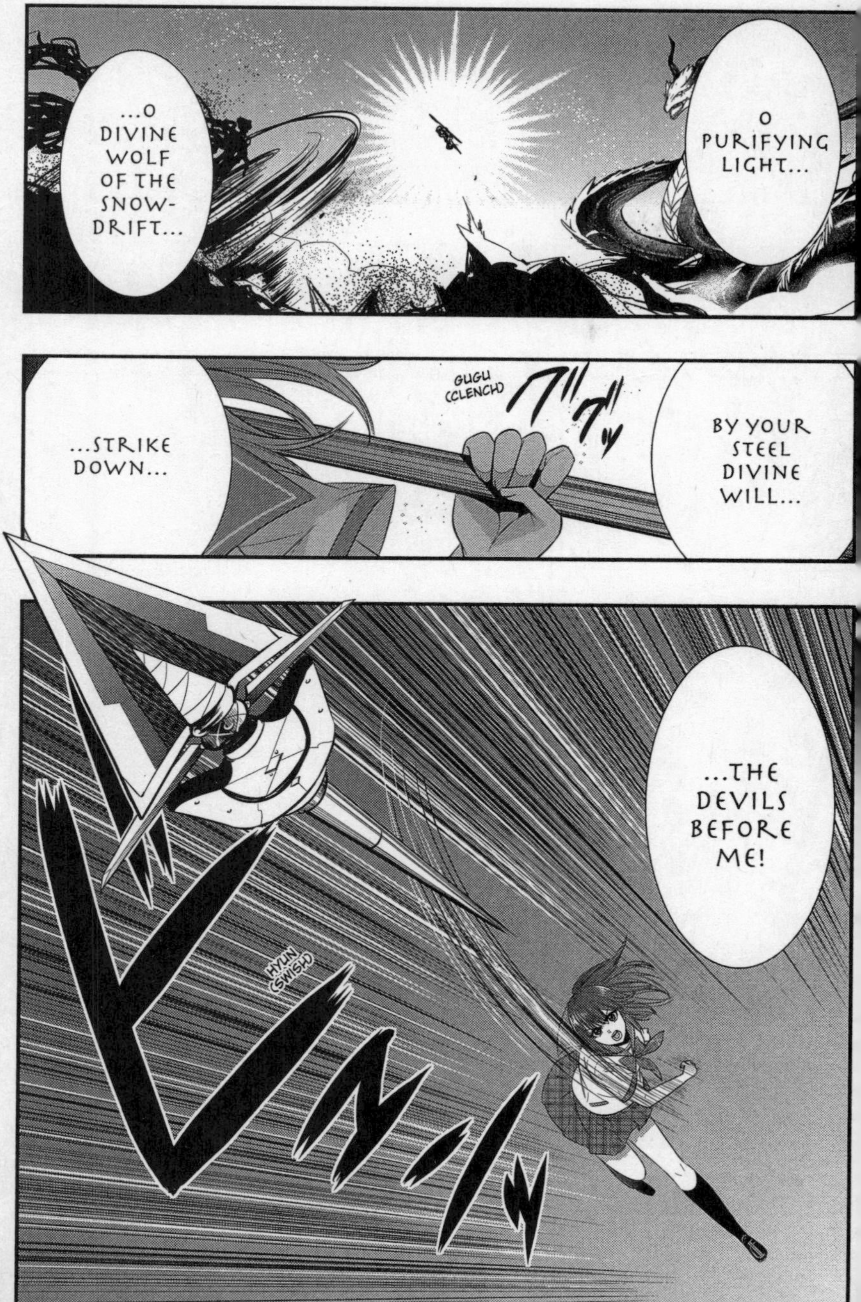
O PURIFYING LIGHT...
...O DIVINE WOLF OF THE SNOW-DRIFT...
BY YOUR STEEL DIVINE WILL...
GUGU (CLENCH)
...STRIKE DOWN...
...THE DEVILS BEFORE ME!
HYUN (SWISH)

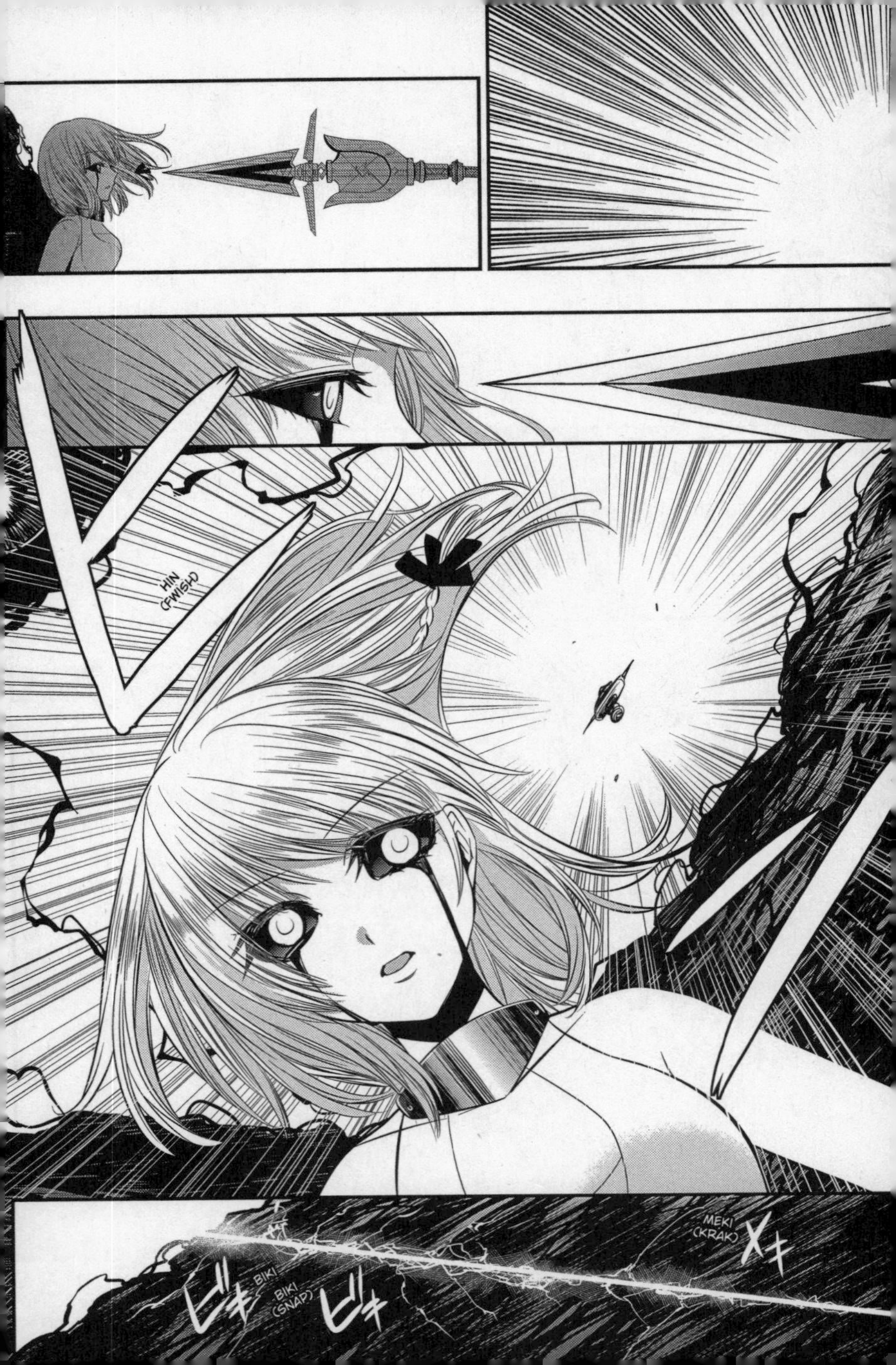
HIN
(FWISH)
メキ
MEKI
(KRAK)
ビキ
BIKI
BIKI
(SNAP)
ビキ

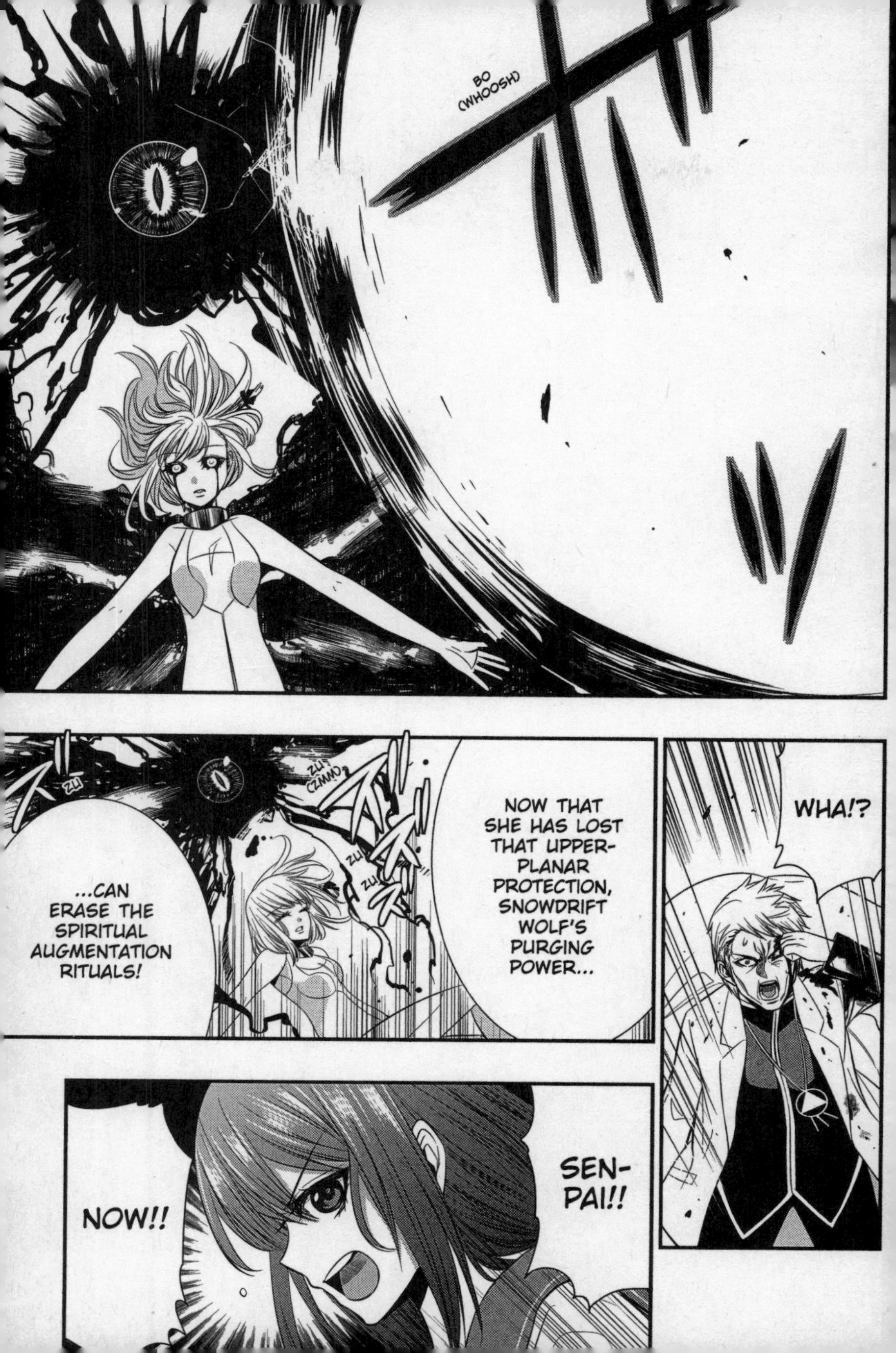

BO (WHOOSH)
WHA!?
ZU ZU (ZMMM)
NOW THAT SHE HAS LOST THAT UPPER-PLANAR PROTECTION, SNOWDRIFT WOLF'S PURGING POWER...
...CAN ERASE THE SPIRITUAL AUGMENTATION RITUALS!
SEN-PAI!!
NOW!!

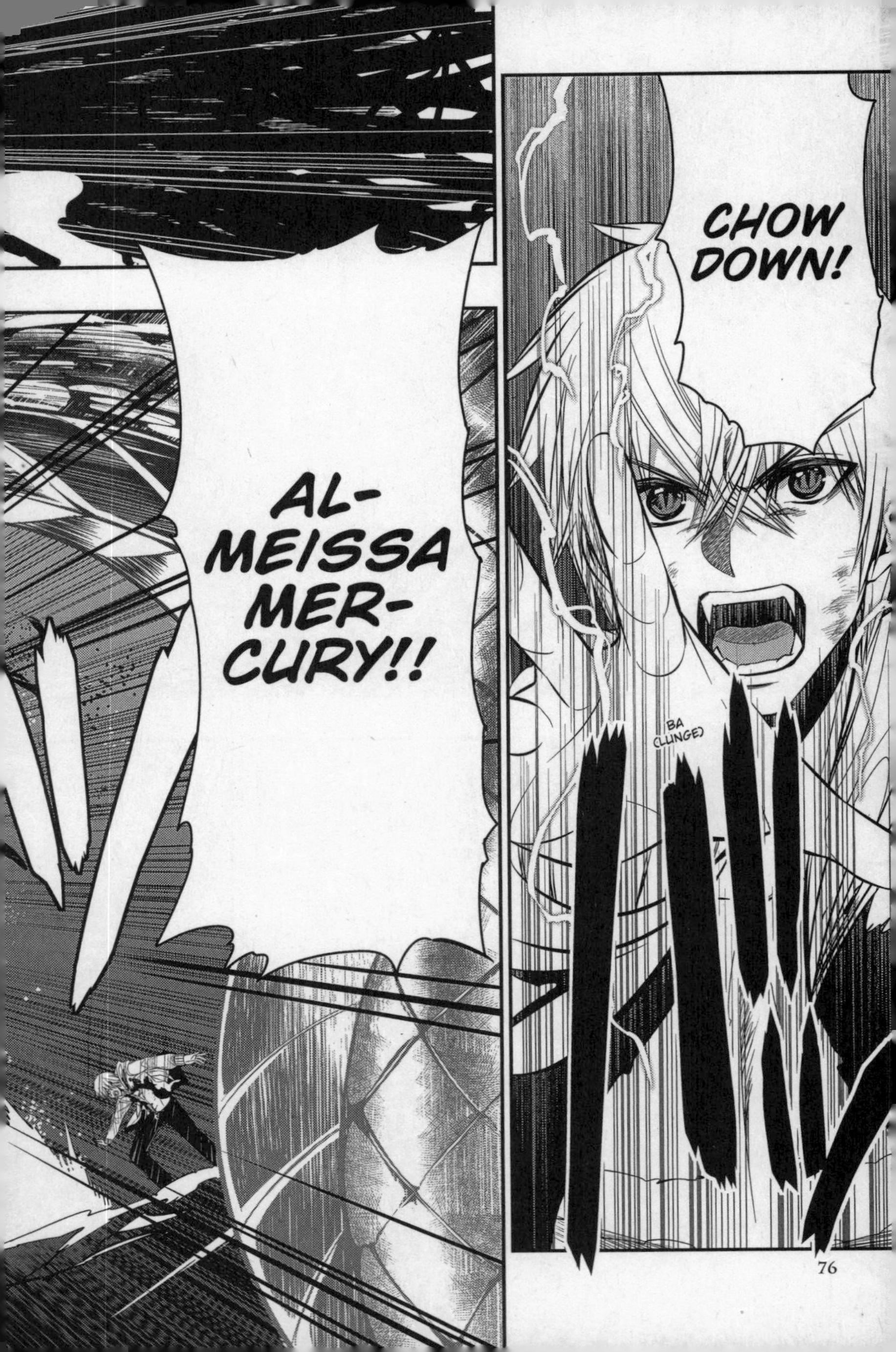
CHOW DOWN!
BA (LUNGE)
AL-MEISSA MER-CURY!!

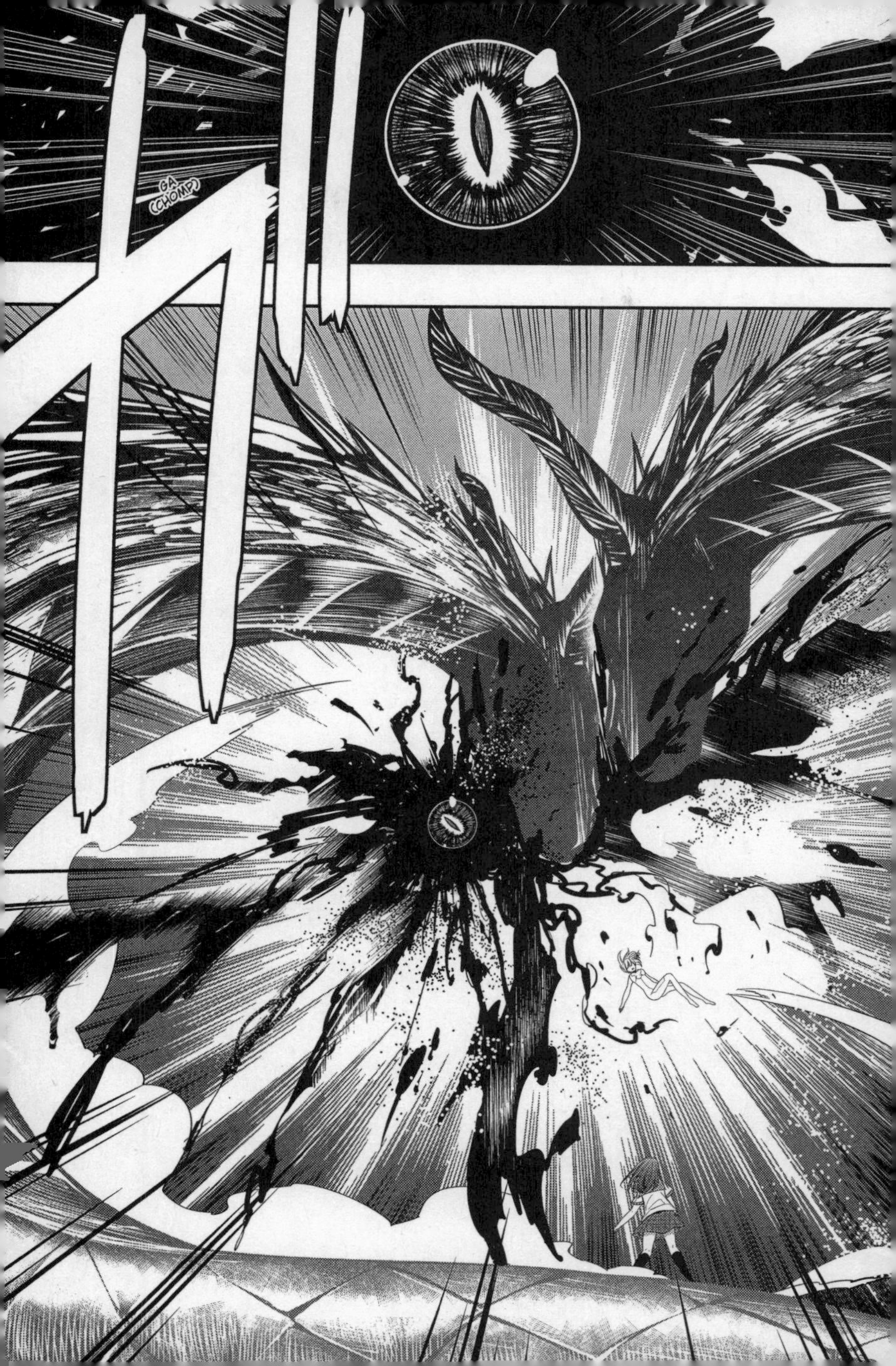
GA
(CHOMP)

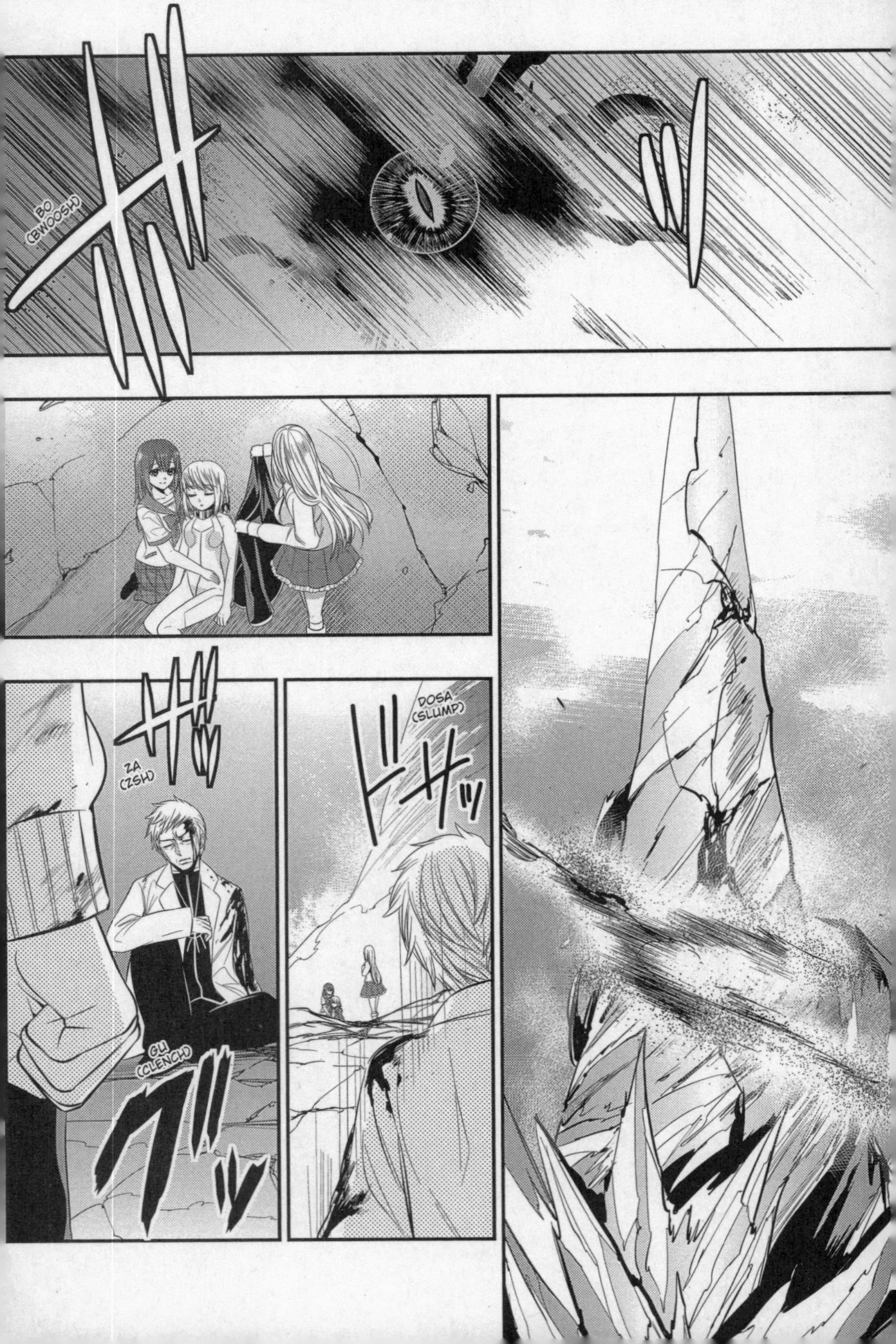
BO (BWOOSH)
DOSA (SLUMP)
ドサッ
ZA (ZSH)
GU (CLENCH)
グッ

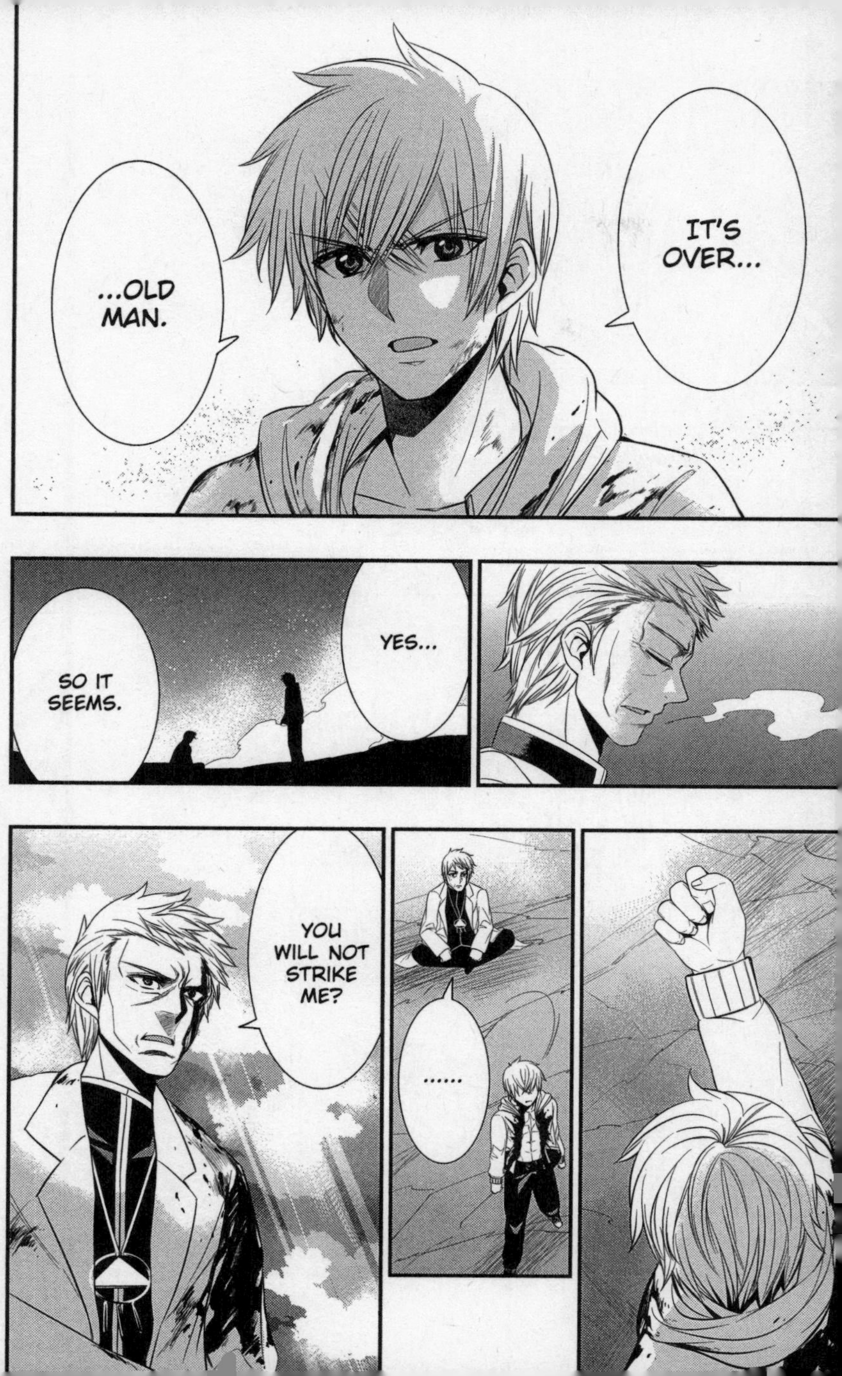
IT'S OVER...
...OLD MAN.
YES...
SO IT SEEMS.
......
YOU WILL NOT STRIKE ME?

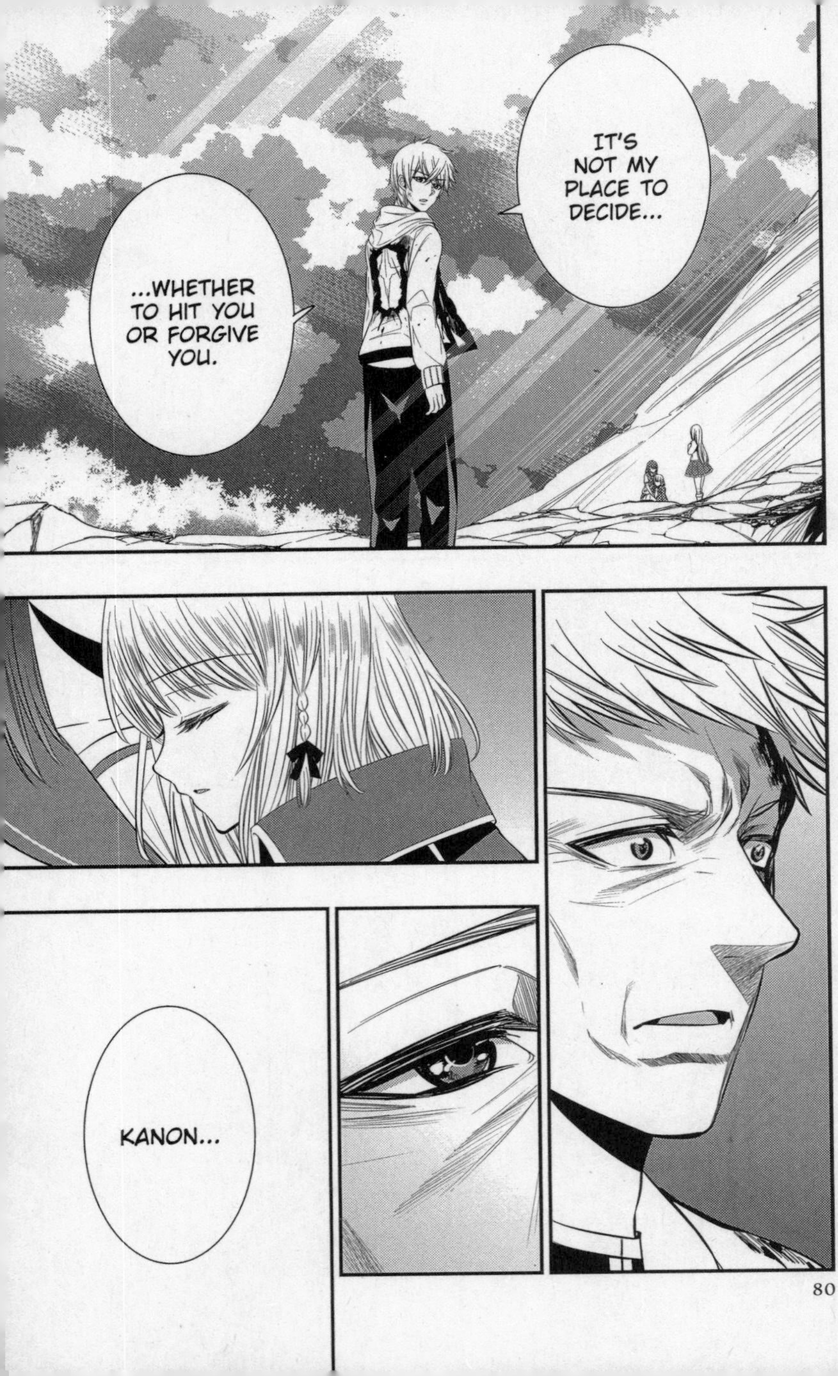
IT'S NOT MY PLACE TO DECIDE...
...WHETHER TO HIT YOU OR FORGIVE YOU.
KANON...

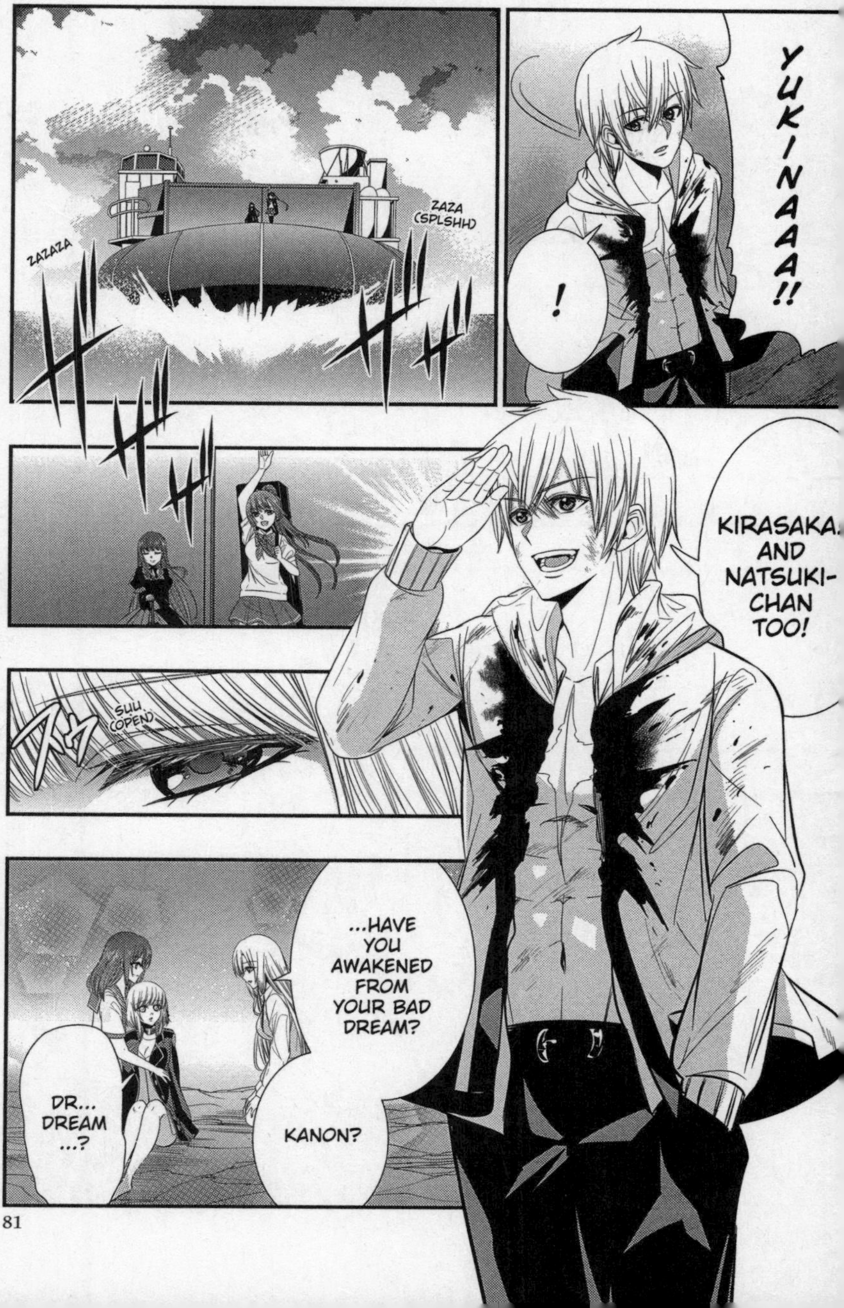
YUKINAAAA!!
!
ZAZA (SPLSHH)
ZAZAZA
KIRASAKA... AND NATSUKI-CHAN TOO!
SUU (OPEN)
...HAVE YOU AWAKENED FROM YOUR BAD DREAM?
KANON?
DR... DREAM ...?

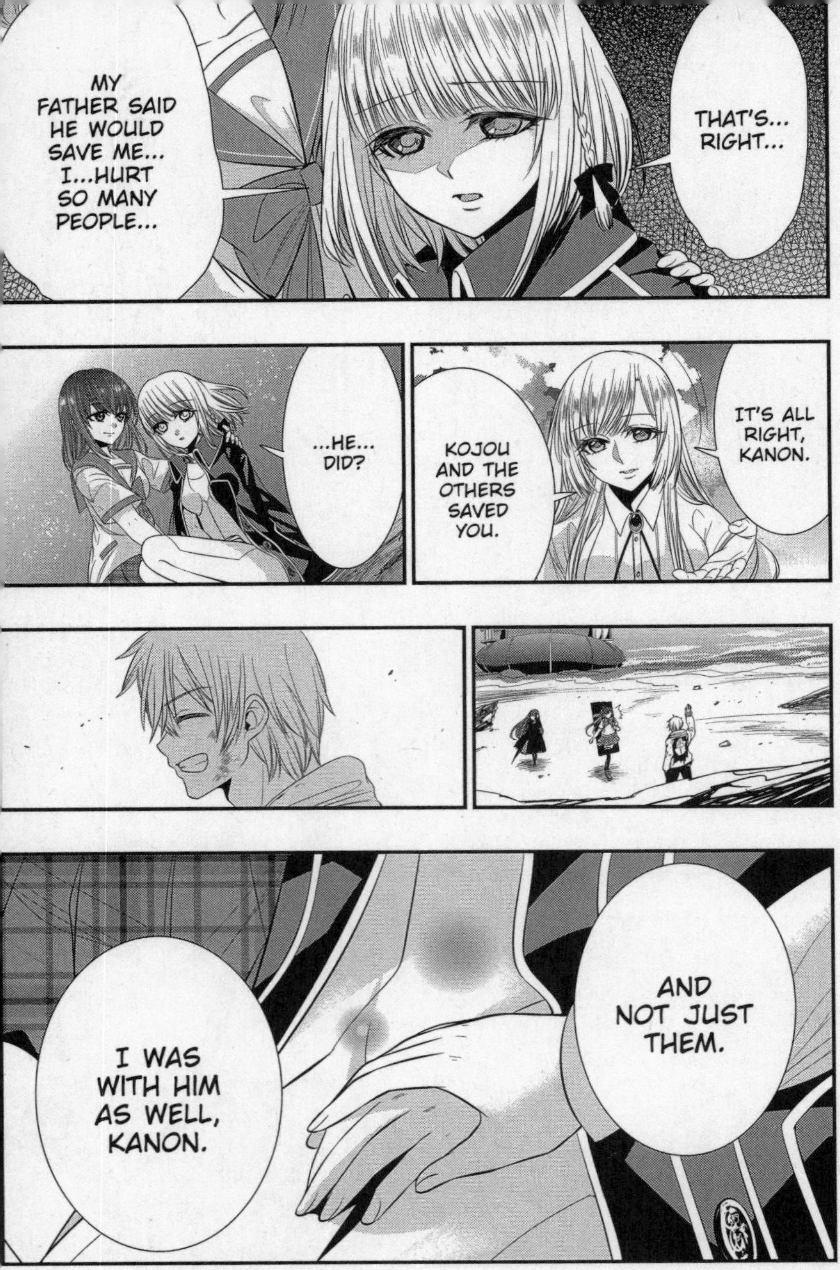
THAT'S... RIGHT...
MY FATHER SAID HE WOULD SAVE ME... I...HURT SO MANY PEOPLE...
IT'S ALL RIGHT, KANON.
KOJOU AND THE OTHERS SAVED YOU.
...HE... DID?
AND NOT JUST THEM.
I WAS WITH HIM AS WELL, KANON.

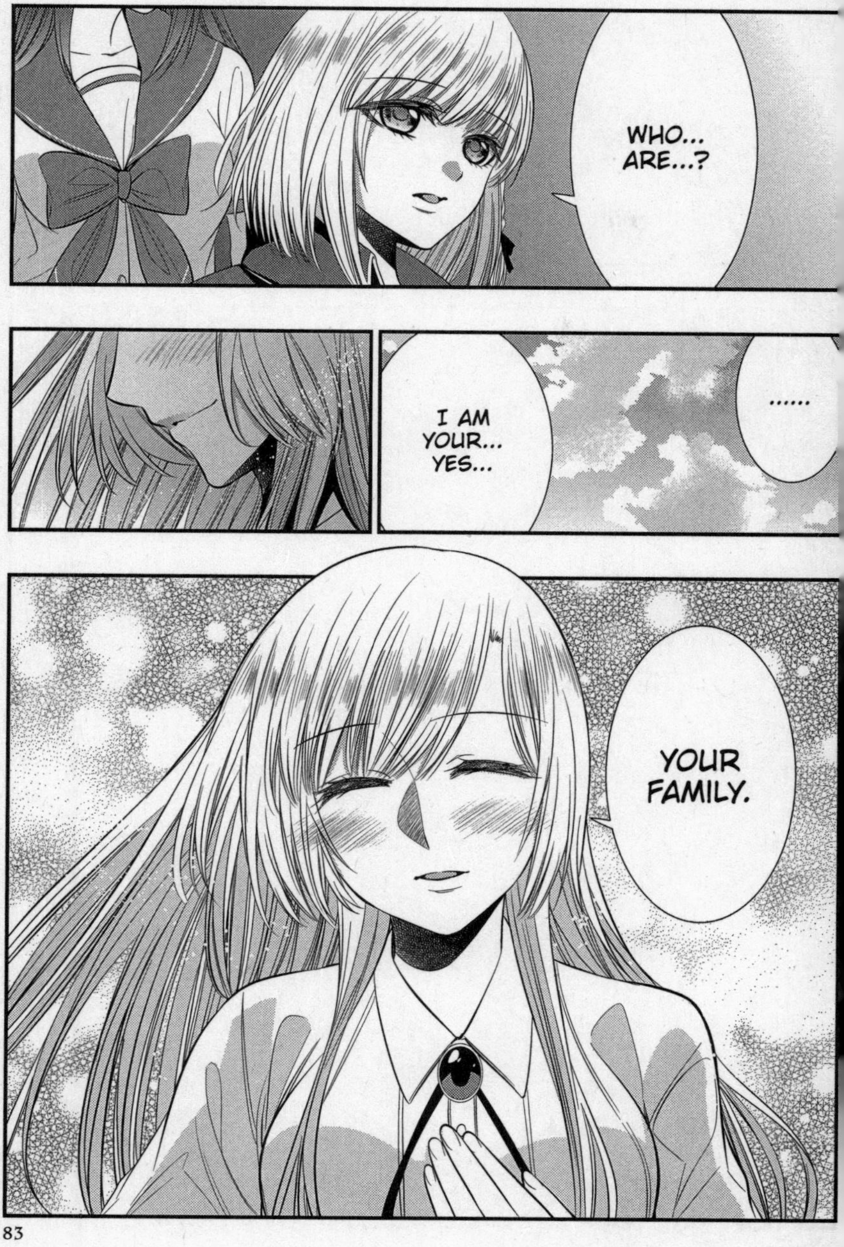
WHO... ARE...?
......
I AM YOUR... YES...
YOUR FAMILY.

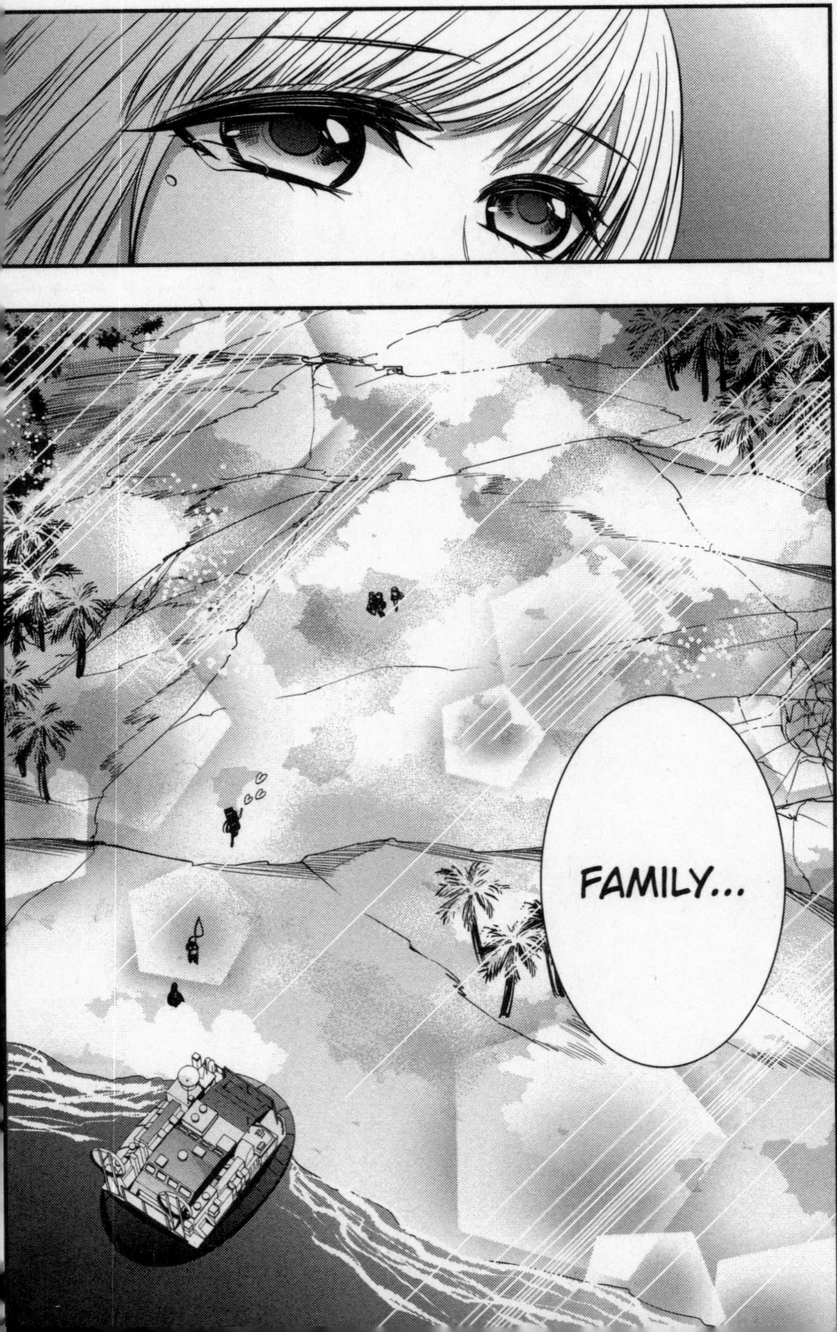
FAMILY...

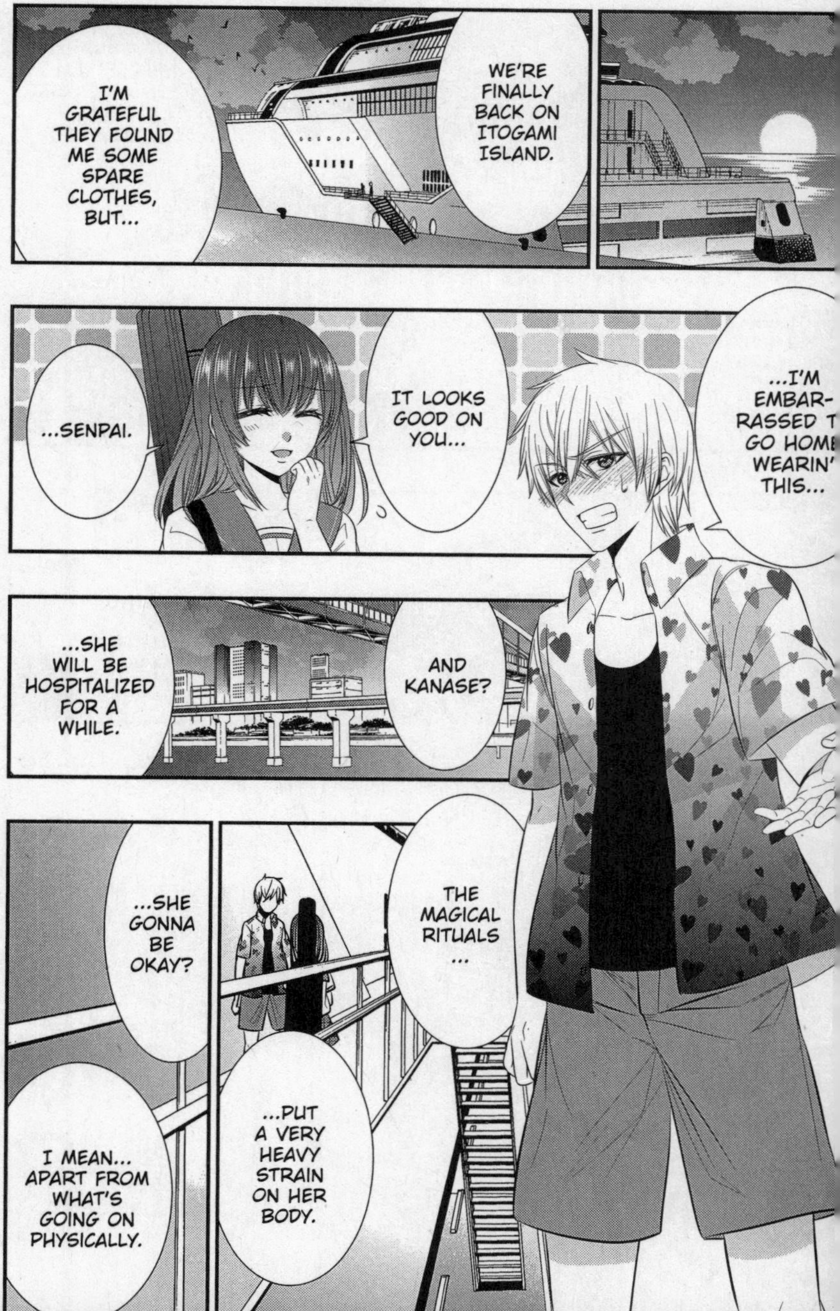
WE'RE FINALLY BACK ON ITOGAMI ISLAND.
I'M GRATEFUL THEY FOUND ME SOME SPARE CLOTHES, BUT...
...I'M EMBAR-RASSED T GO HOME WEARIN' THIS...
IT LOOKS GOOD ON YOU...
...SENPAI.
AND KANASE?
...SHE WILL BE HOSPITALIZED FOR A WHILE.
THE MAGICAL RITUALS ...
...PUT A VERY HEAVY STRAIN ON HER BODY.
...SHE GONNA BE OKAY?
I MEAN... APART FROM WHAT'S GOING ON PHYSICALLY.

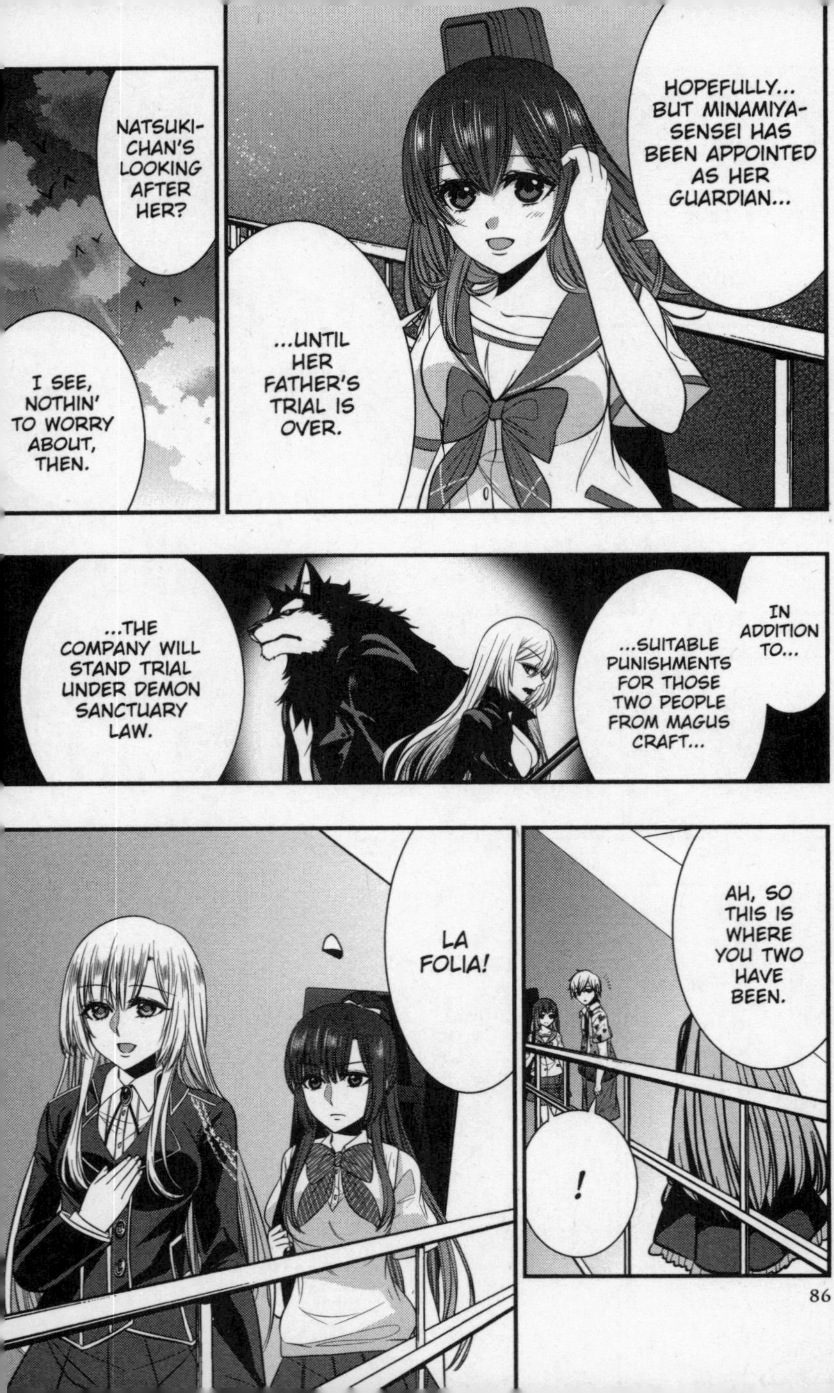
HOPEFULLY... BUT MINAMIYA-SENSEI HAS BEEN APPOINTED AS HER GUARDIAN...
...UNTIL HER FATHER'S TRIAL IS OVER.
NATSUKI-CHAN'S LOOKING AFTER HER?
I SEE, NOTHIN' TO WORRY ABOUT, THEN.
IN ADDITION TO...
...SUITABLE PUNISHMENTS FOR THOSE TWO PEOPLE FROM MAGUS CRAFT...
...THE COMPANY WILL STAND TRIAL UNDER DEMON SANCTUARY LAW.
AH, SO THIS IS WHERE YOU TWO HAVE BEEN.
!
LA FOLIA!

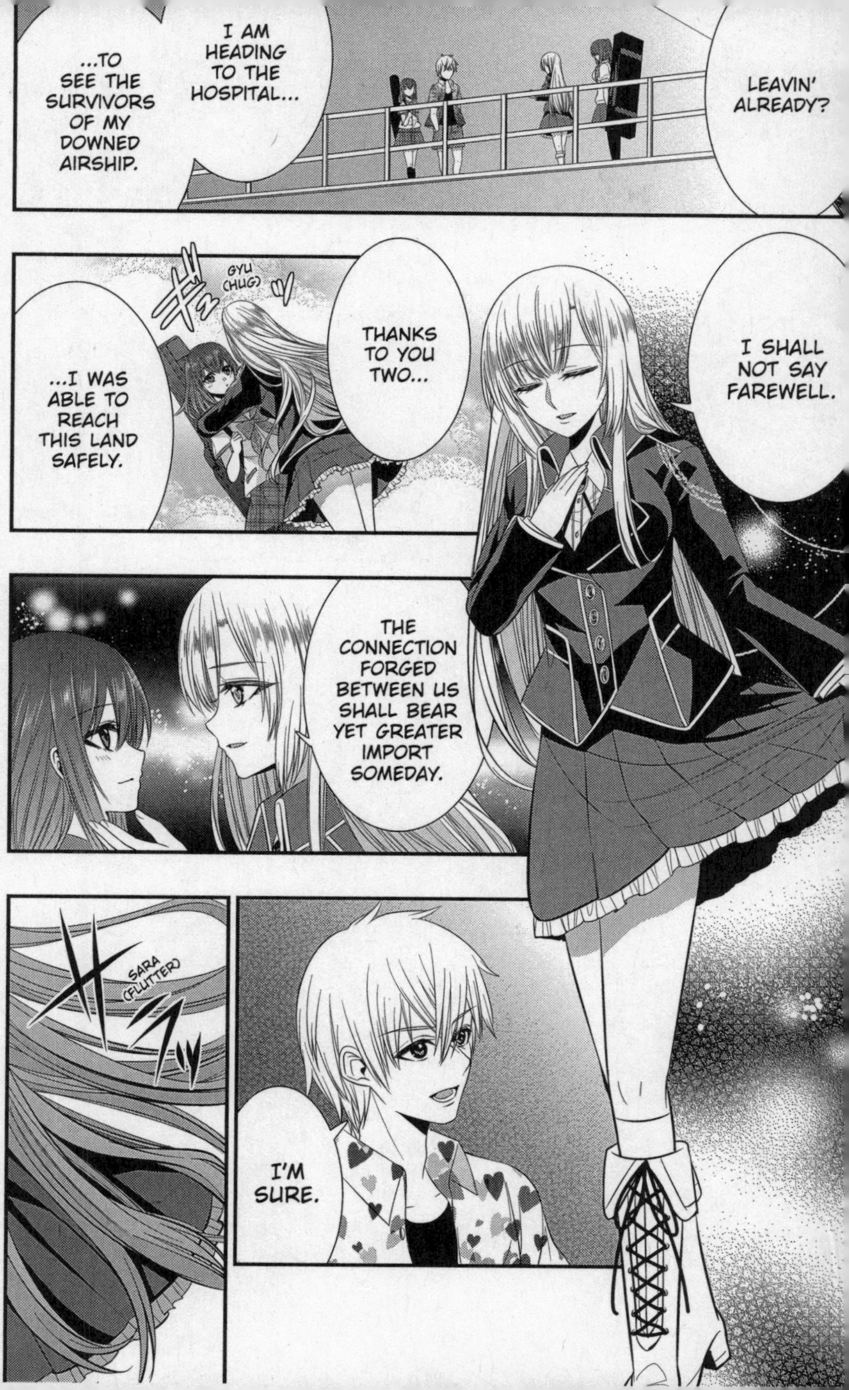
LEAVIN' ALREADY?
I AM HEADING TO THE HOSPITAL...
...TO SEE THE SURVIVORS OF MY DOWNED AIRSHIP.
I SHALL NOT SAY FAREWELL.
THANKS TO YOU TWO...
GYU (HUG)
...I WAS ABLE TO REACH THIS LAND SAFELY.
THE CONNECTION FORGED BETWEEN US SHALL BEAR YET GREATER IMPORT SOMEDAY.
I'M SURE.
SARA (FLUTTER)

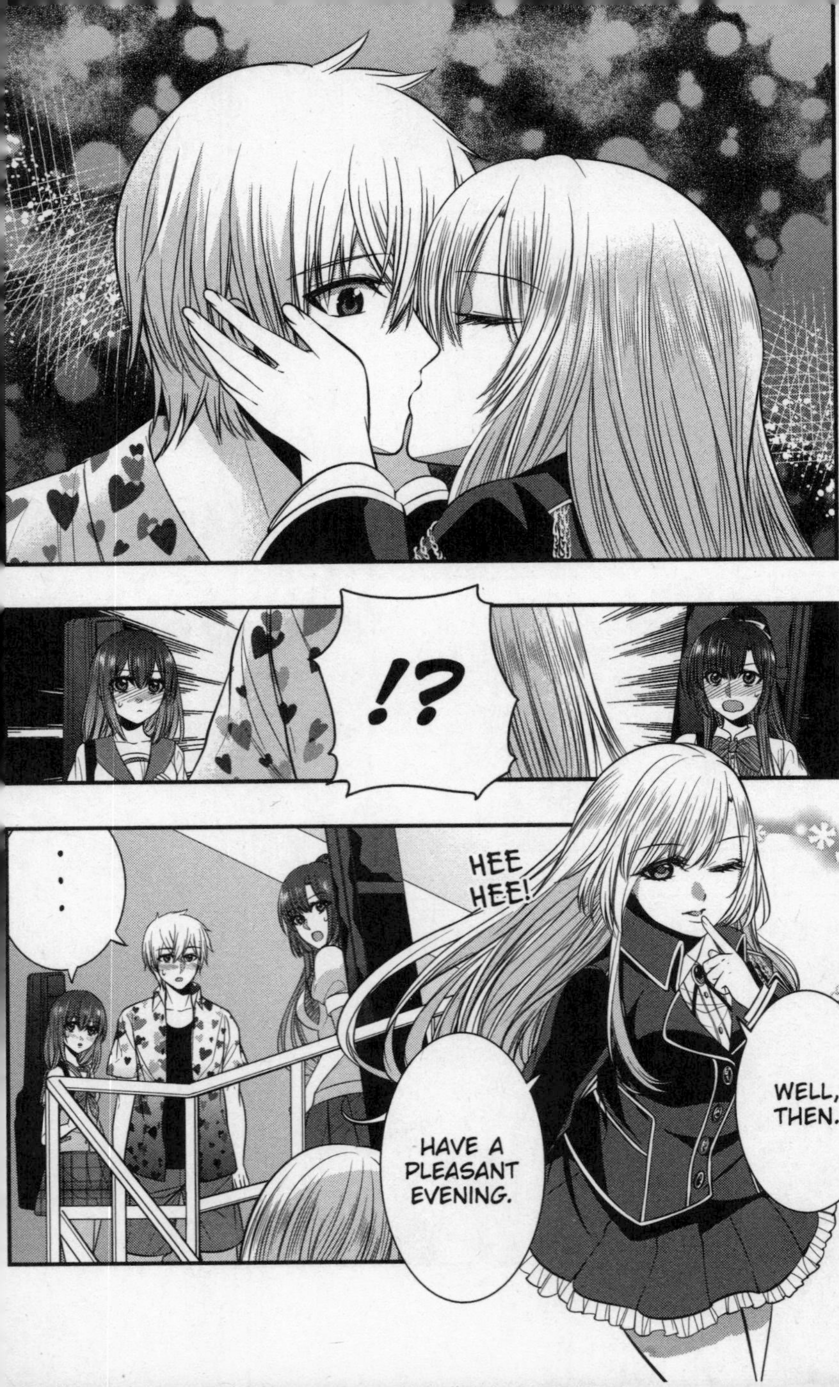
!?
HEE HEE!
WELL, THEN.
HAVE A PLEASANT EVENING.
...

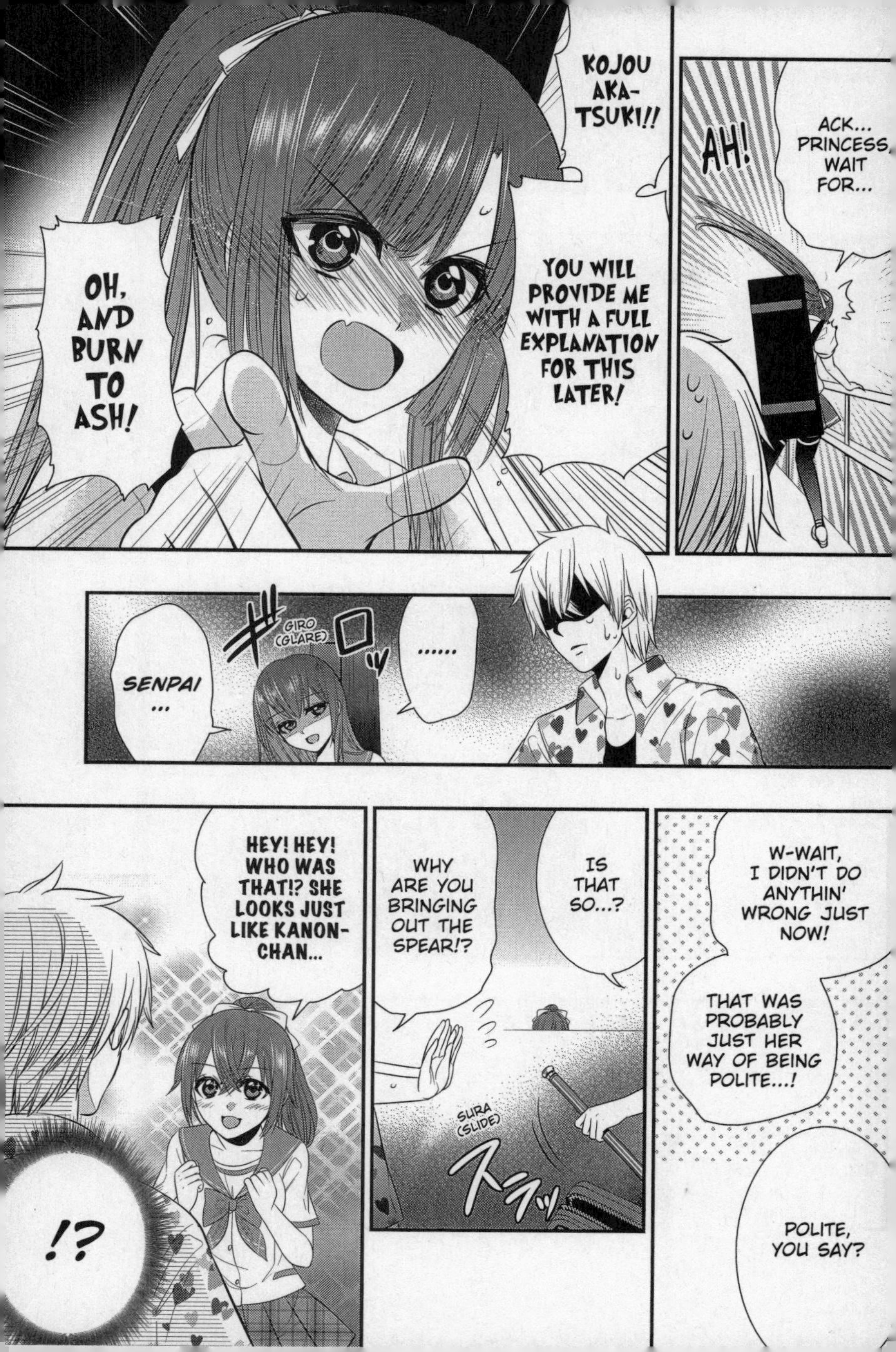
AH!
ACK... PRINCESS, WAIT FOR...
KOJOU AKA-TSUKI!!
YOU WILL PROVIDE ME WITH A FULL EXPLANATION FOR THIS LATER!
OH, AND BURN TO ASH!
......
GIRO (GLARE)
SENPAI ...
W-WAIT, I DIDN'T DO ANYTHIN' WRONG JUST NOW!
THAT WAS PROBABLY JUST HER WAY OF BEING POLITE...!
POLITE, YOU SAY?
IS THAT SO...?
WHY ARE YOU BRINGING OUT THE SPEAR!?
SURA (SLIDE)
HEY! HEY! WHO WAS THAT!? SHE LOOKS JUST LIKE KANON-CHAN...
!?

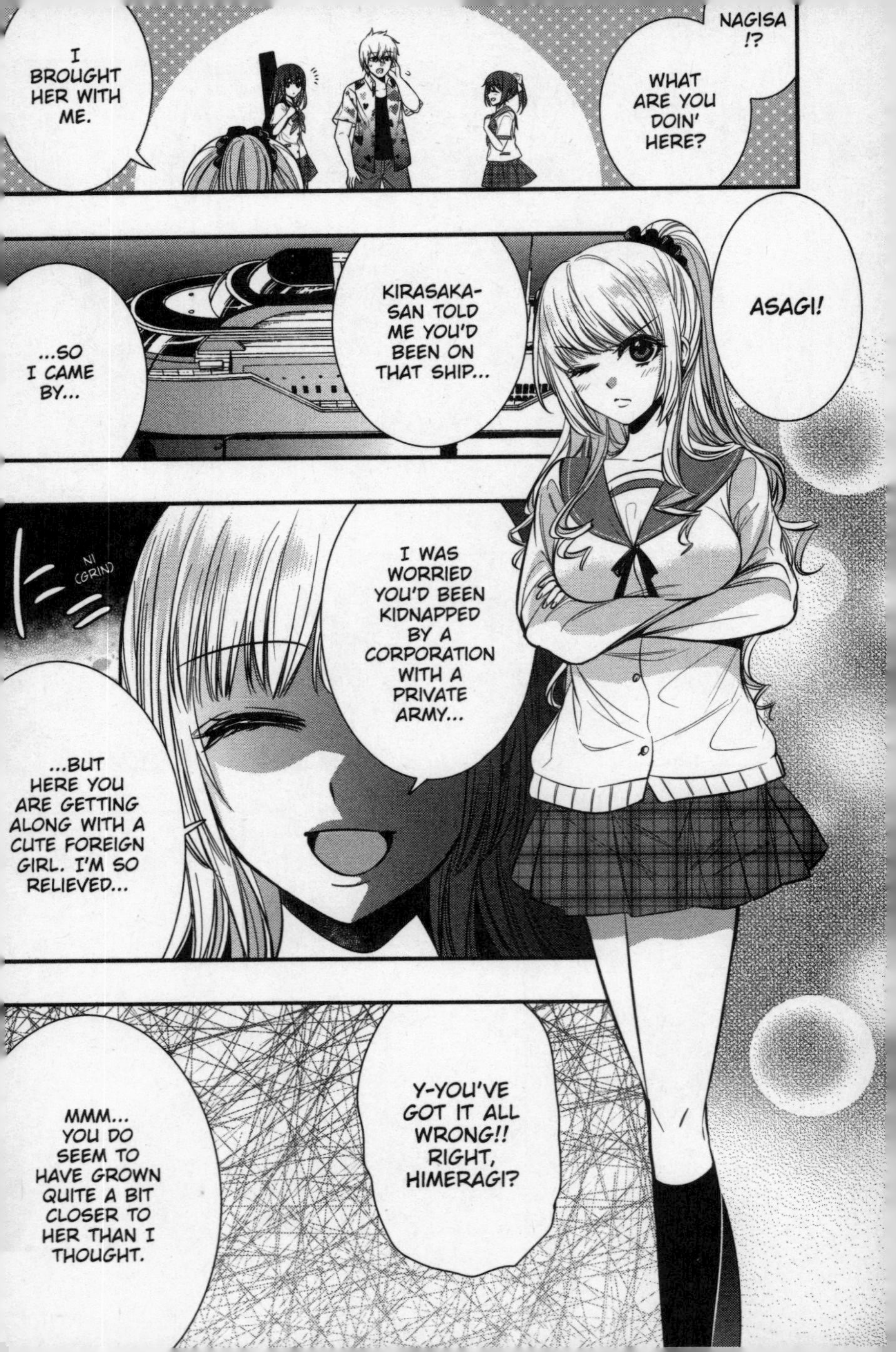
NAGISA!?
WHAT ARE YOU DOIN' HERE?
I BROUGHT HER WITH ME.
ASAGI!
KIRASAKA-SAN TOLD ME YOU'D BEEN ON THAT SHIP...
...SO I CAME BY...
NI (GRIN)
I WAS WORRIED YOU'D BEEN KIDNAPPED BY A CORPORATION WITH A PRIVATE ARMY...
...BUT HERE YOU ARE GETTING ALONG WITH A CUTE FOREIGN GIRL. I'M SO RELIEVED...
Y-YOU'VE GOT IT ALL WRONG!! RIGHT, HIMERAGI?
MMM... YOU DO SEEM TO HAVE GROWN QUITE A BIT CLOSER TO HER THAN I THOUGHT.

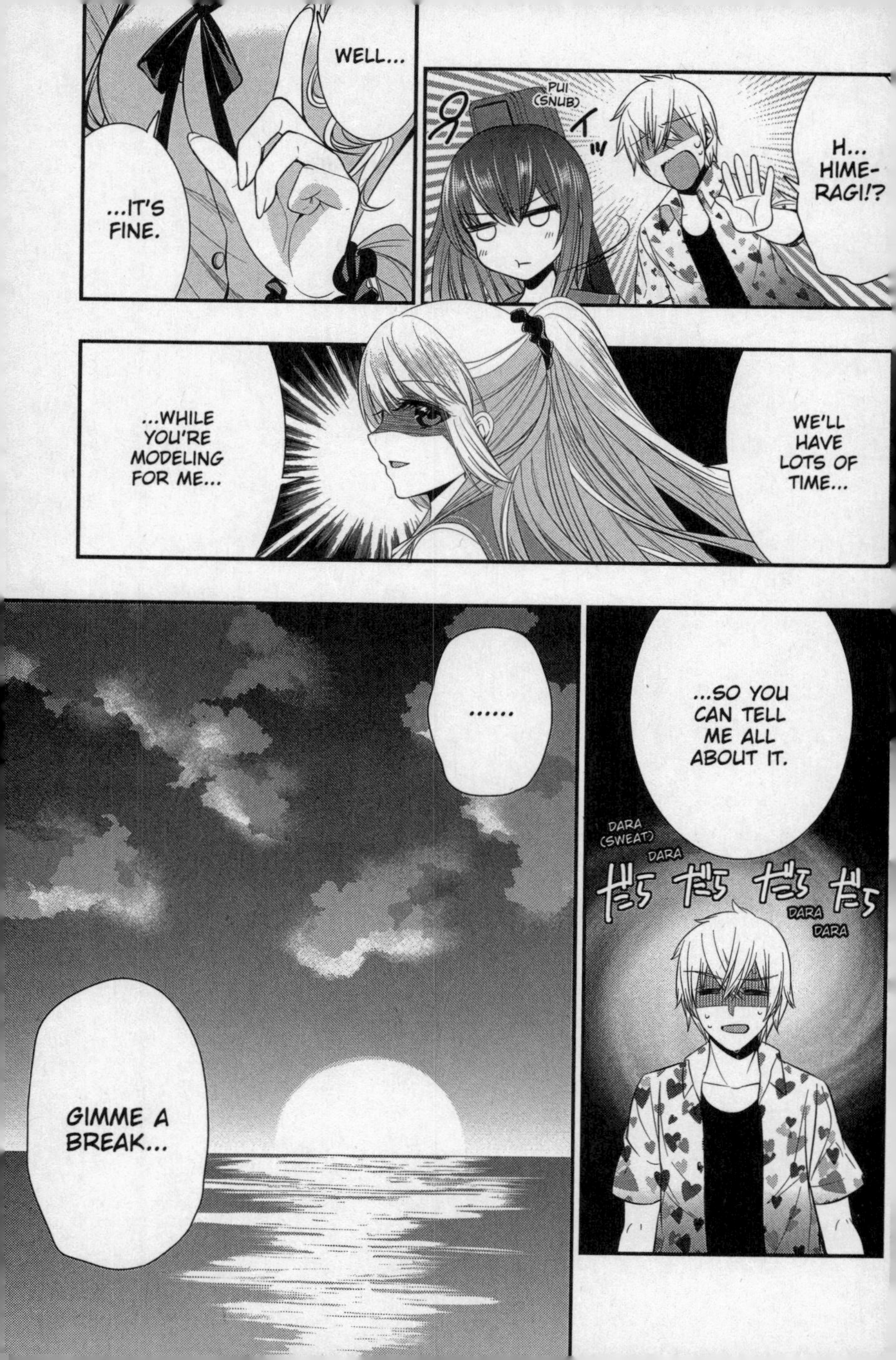
H... HIME-RAGI!?
PUI (SNUB)
WELL...
...IT'S FINE.
WE'LL HAVE LOTS OF TIME...
...WHILE YOU'RE MODELING FOR ME...
...SO YOU CAN TELL ME ALL ABOUT IT.
DARA (SWEAT) DARA DARA DARA
だら だら だら だら
......
GIMME A BREAK...

STRIKE THE BLOOD

DEFINITION

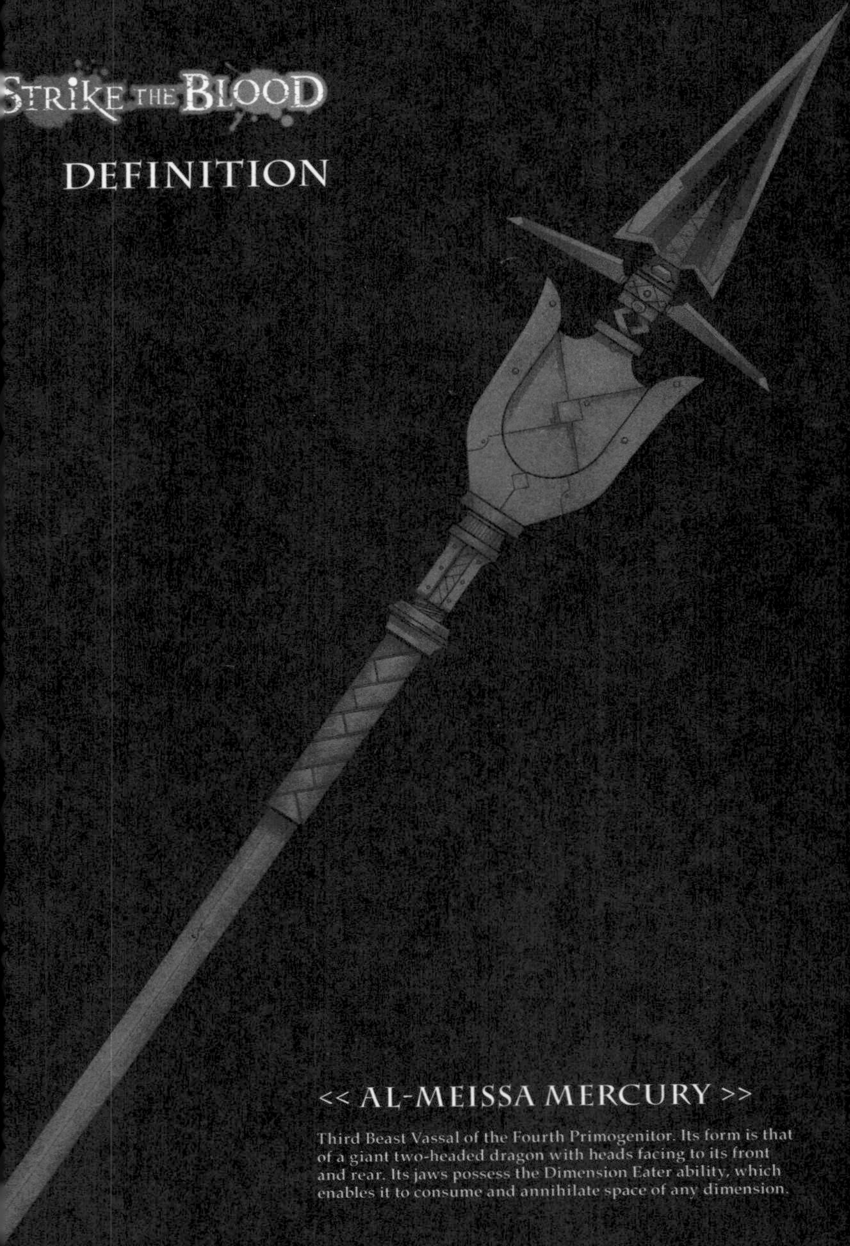

<< AL-MEISSA MERCURY >>

Third Beast Vassal of the Fourth Primogenitor. Its form is that of a giant two-headed dragon with heads facing to its front and rear. Its jaws possess the Dimension Eater ability, which enables it to consume and annihilate space of any dimension.

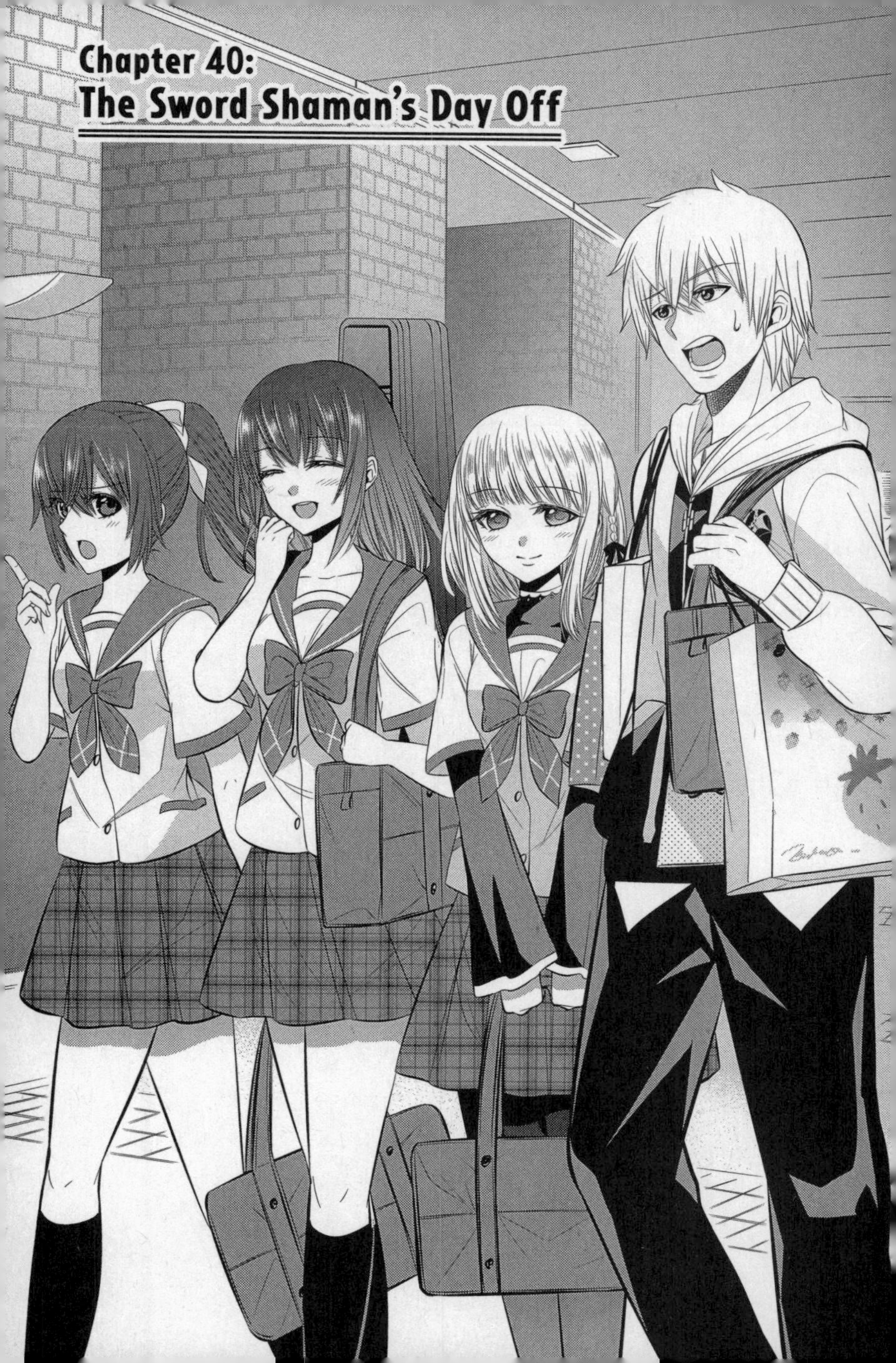
Chapter 40:
The Sword Shaman's Day Off

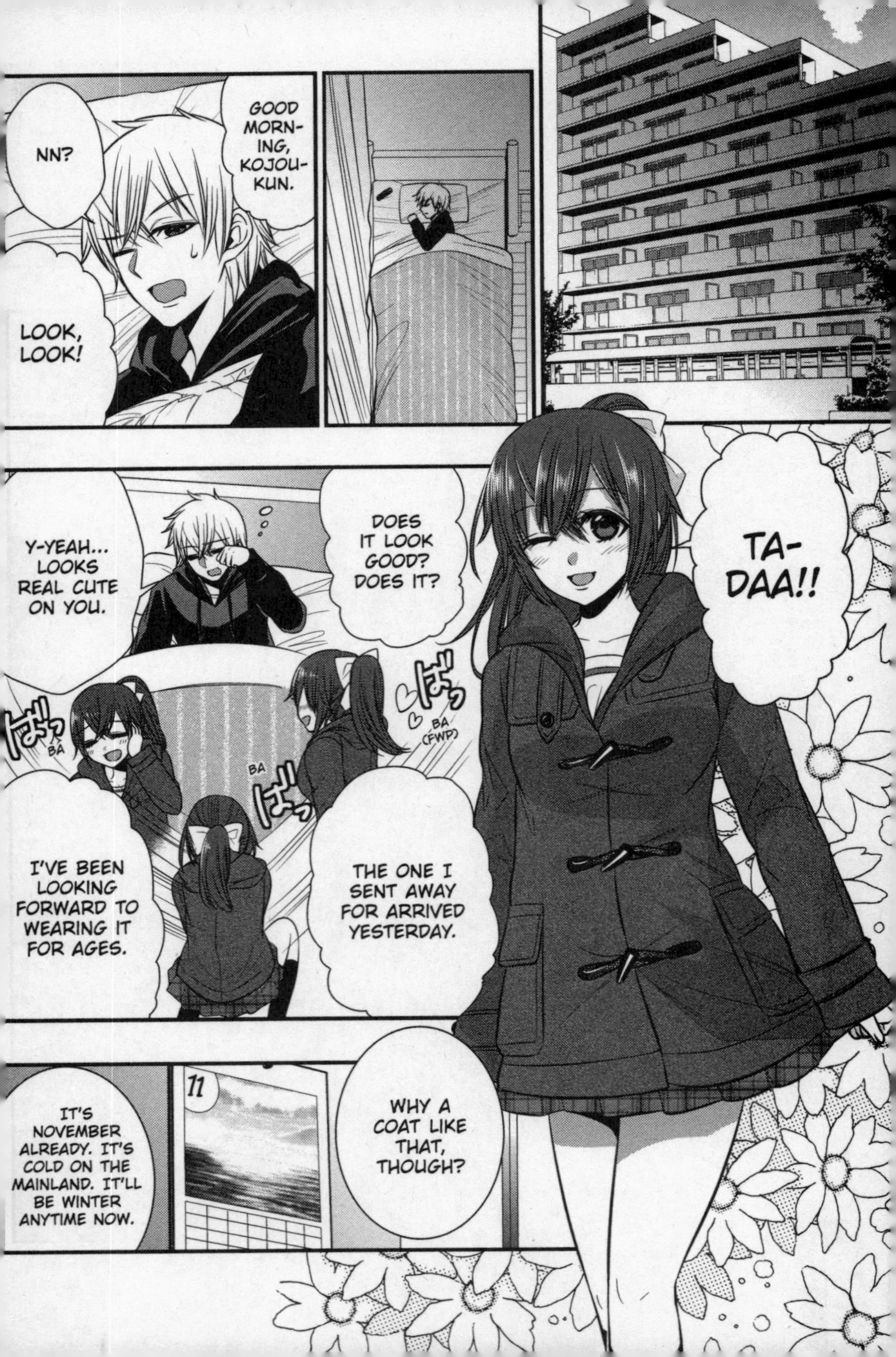
GOOD MORNING, KOJOU-KUN.
NN?
LOOK, LOOK!
TA-DAA!!
DOES IT LOOK GOOD? DOES IT?
Y-YEAH... LOOKS REAL CUTE ON YOU.
ばっ BA (FWP)
ばっ BA
ばっ BA
THE ONE I SENT AWAY FOR ARRIVED YESTERDAY.
I'VE BEEN LOOKING FORWARD TO WEARING IT FOR AGES.
WHY A COAT LIKE THAT, THOUGH?
11
IT'S NOVEMBER ALREADY. IT'S COLD ON THE MAINLAND. IT'LL BE WINTER ANYTIME NOW.

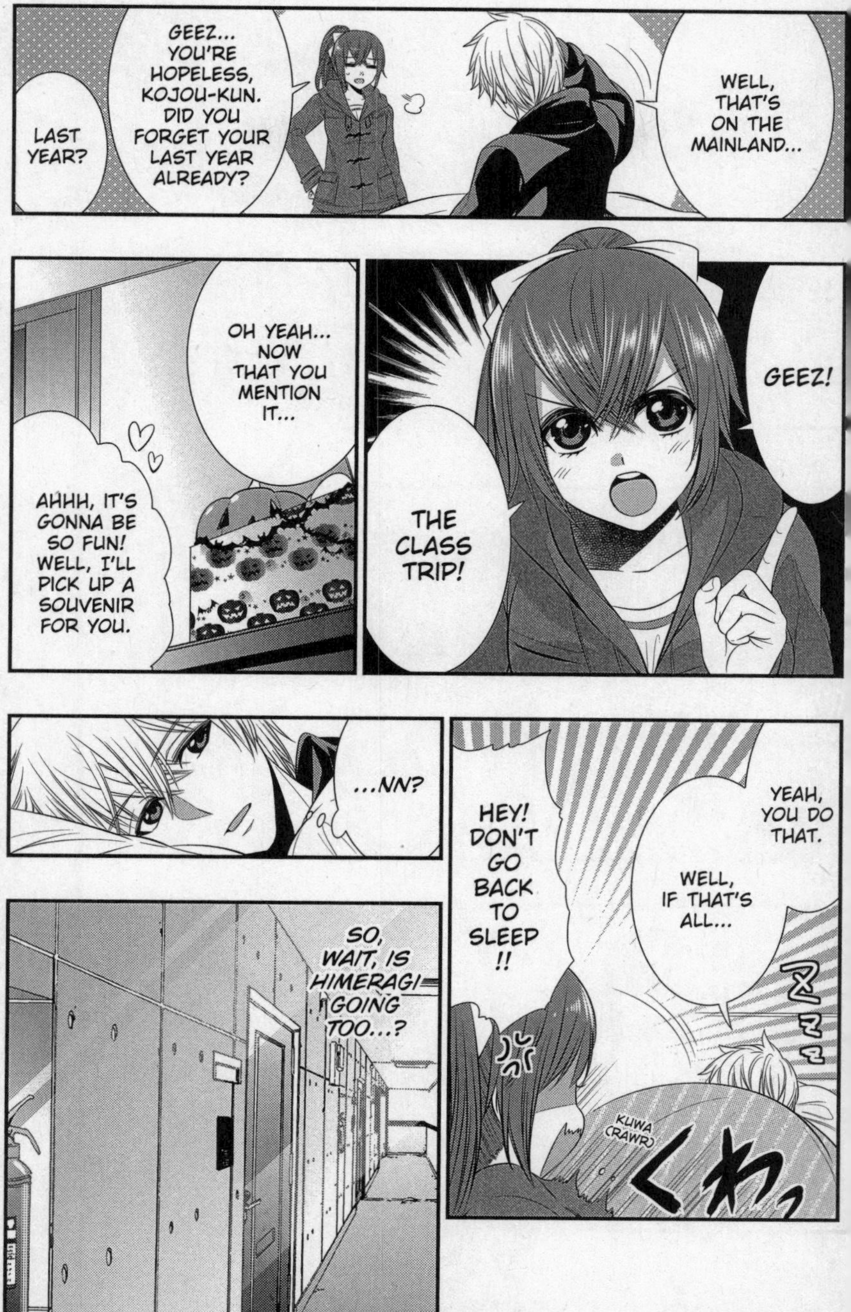
WELL, THAT'S ON THE MAINLAND...
GEEZ... YOU'RE HOPELESS, KOJOU-KUN. DID YOU FORGET YOUR LAST YEAR ALREADY?
LAST YEAR?
GEEZ!
THE CLASS TRIP!
OH YEAH... NOW THAT YOU MENTION IT...
AHHH, IT'S GONNA BE SO FUN! WELL, I'LL PICK UP A SOUVENIR FOR YOU.
YEAH, YOU DO THAT.
WELL, IF THAT'S ALL...
HEY! DON'T GO BACK TO SLEEP!!
KUWA (RAWR)
くわっ
...NN?
SO, WAIT, IS HIMERAGI GOING TOO...?

SIGN: HIMERAGI

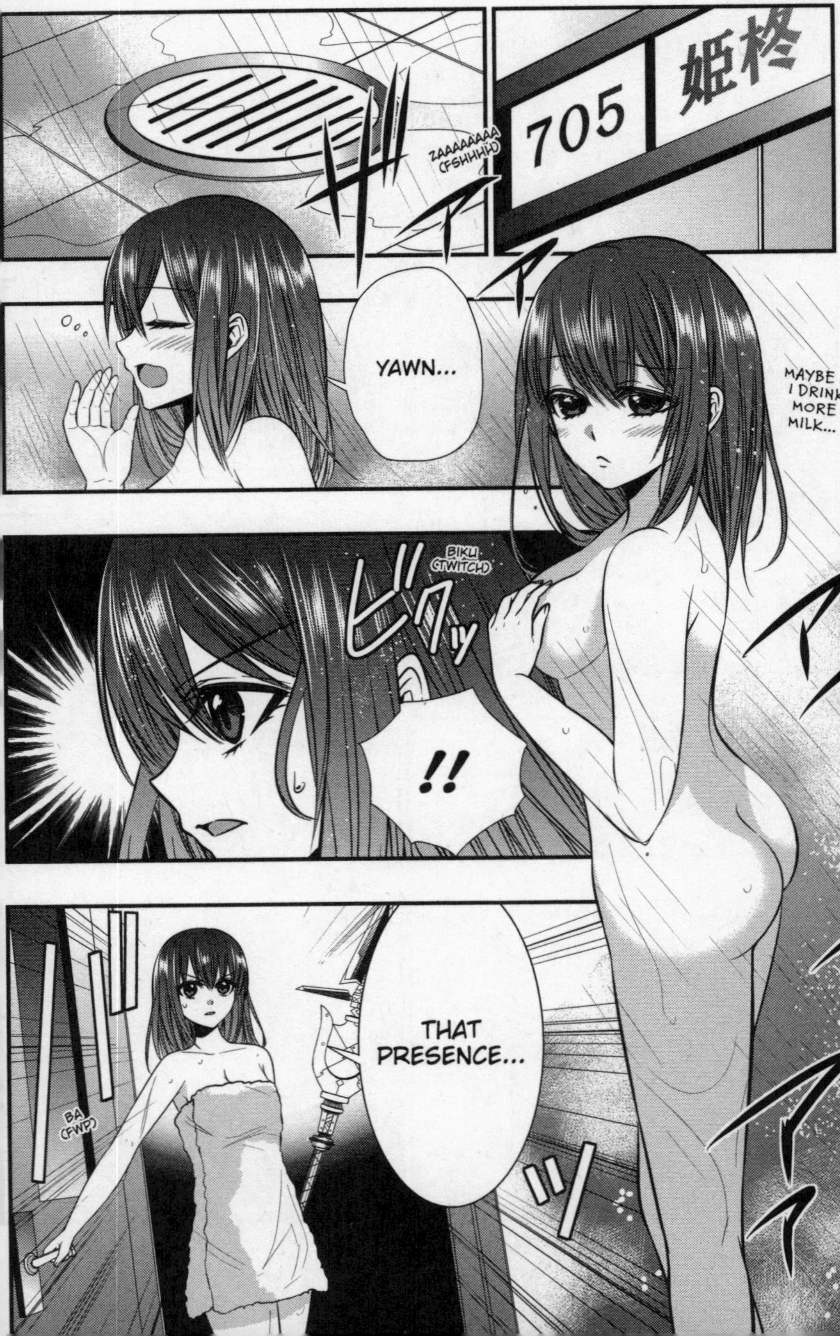
705
姫柊
ZAAAAAAAA (FSHHHH)
MAYBE IF I DRINK MORE MILK...
OOO
YAWN...
BIKU (TWITCH)
!!
THAT PRESENCE...
BA (FWP)

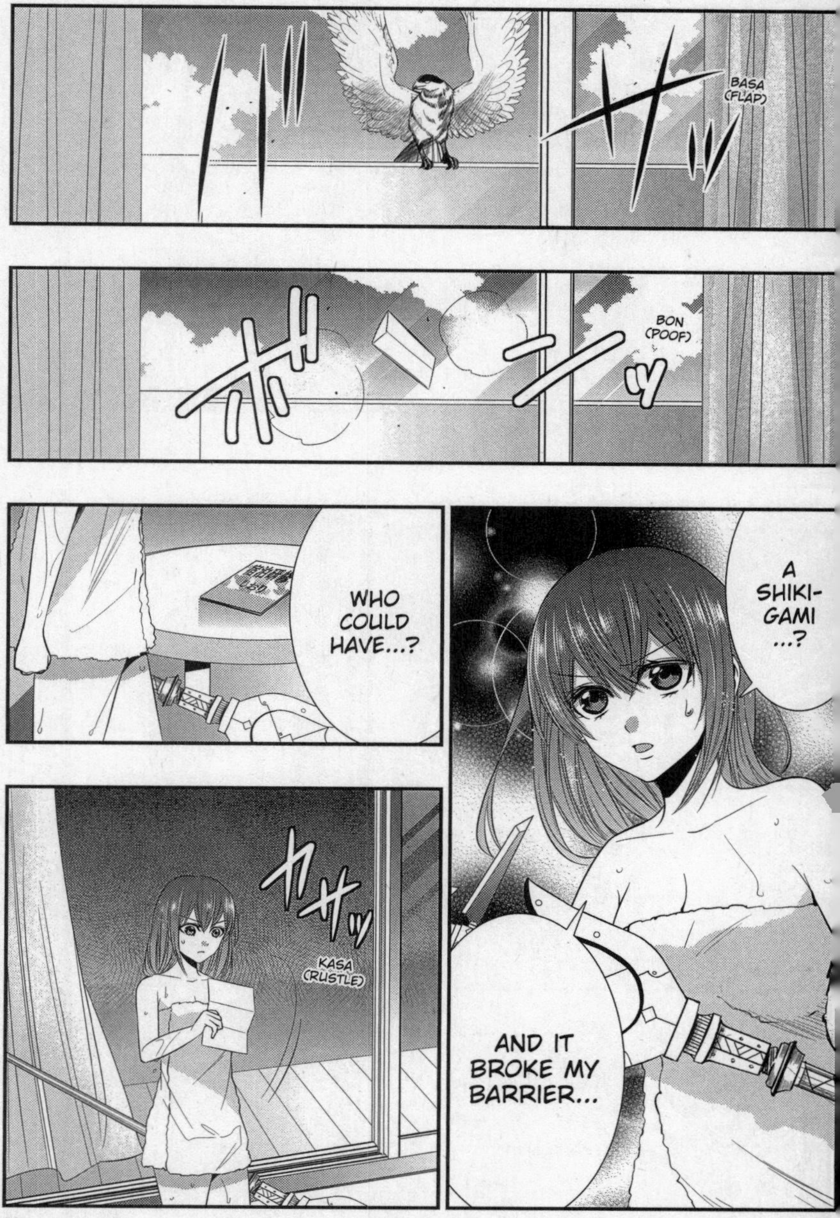
BASA (FLAP)
BON (POOF)
A SHIKI-GAMI ...?
AND IT BROKE MY BARRIER...
WHO COULD HAVE...?
KASA (RUSTLE)

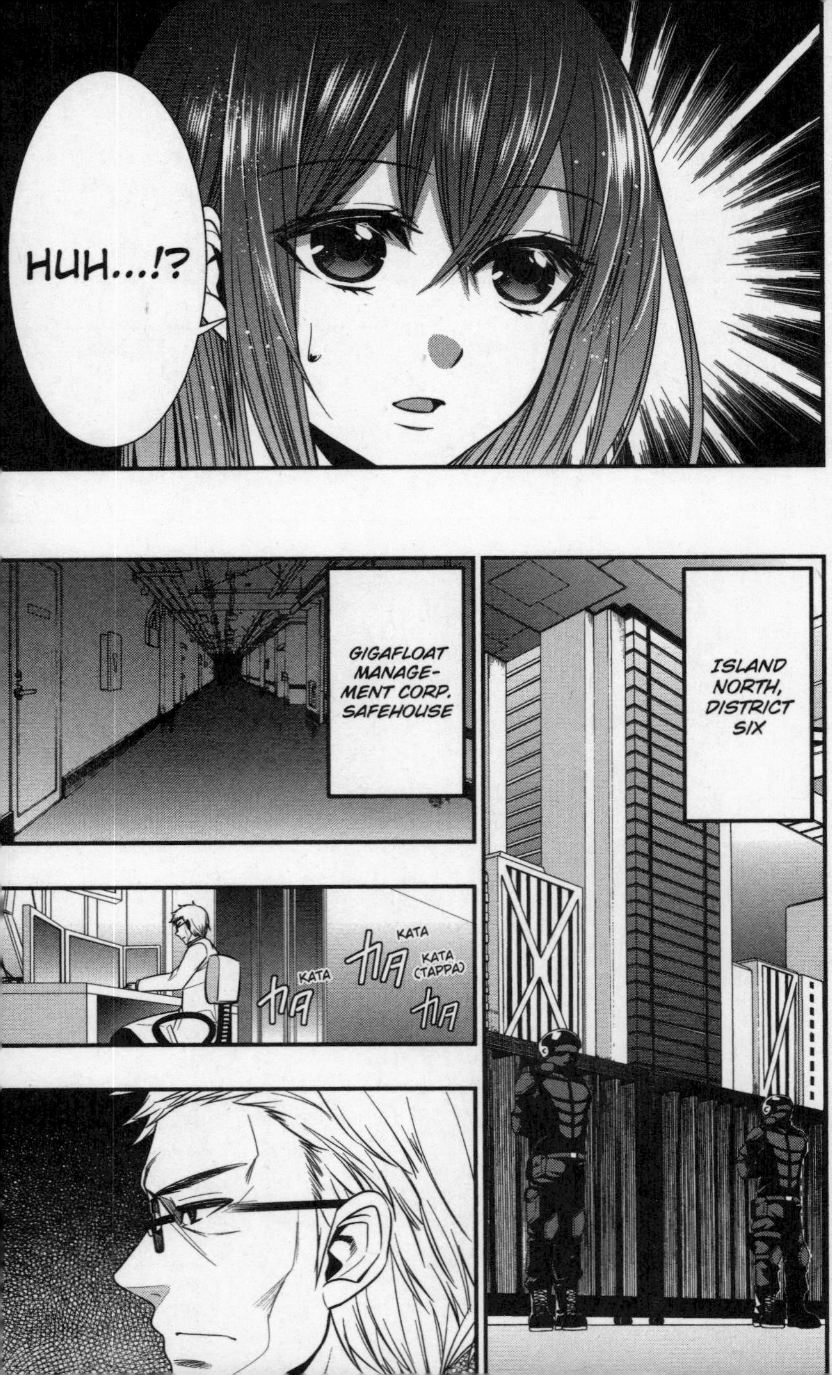
HUH...!?
ISLAND NORTH, DISTRICT SIX
GIGAFLOAT MANAGEMENT CORP. SAFEHOUSE
KATA
KATA (TAPPA)
KATA

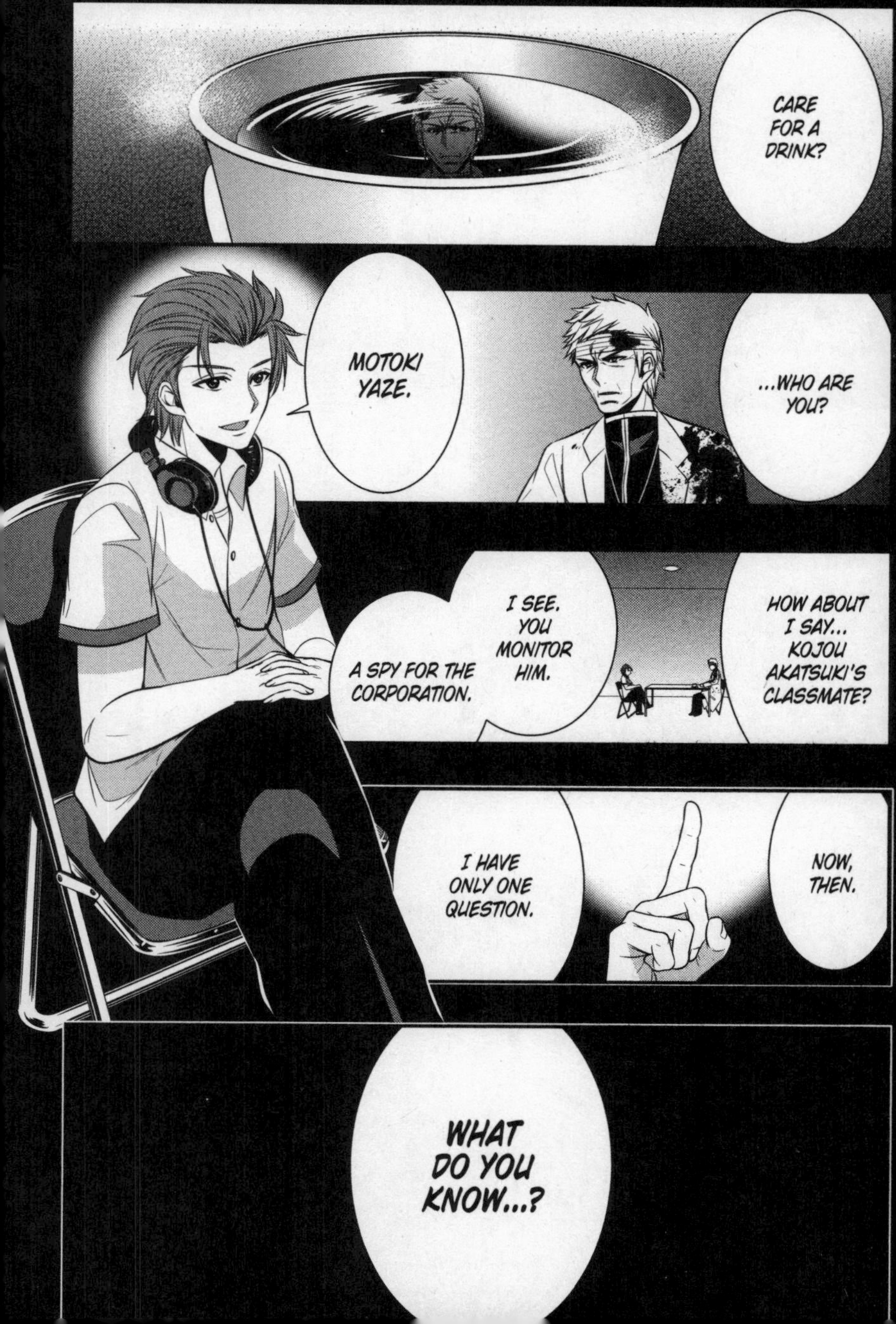
CARE FOR A DRINK?
...WHO ARE YOU?
MOTOKI YAZE.
HOW ABOUT I SAY... KOJOU AKATSUKI'S CLASSMATE?
I SEE. YOU MONITOR HIM.
A SPY FOR THE CORPORATION.
NOW, THEN.
I HAVE ONLY ONE QUESTION.
WHAT DO YOU KNOW...?

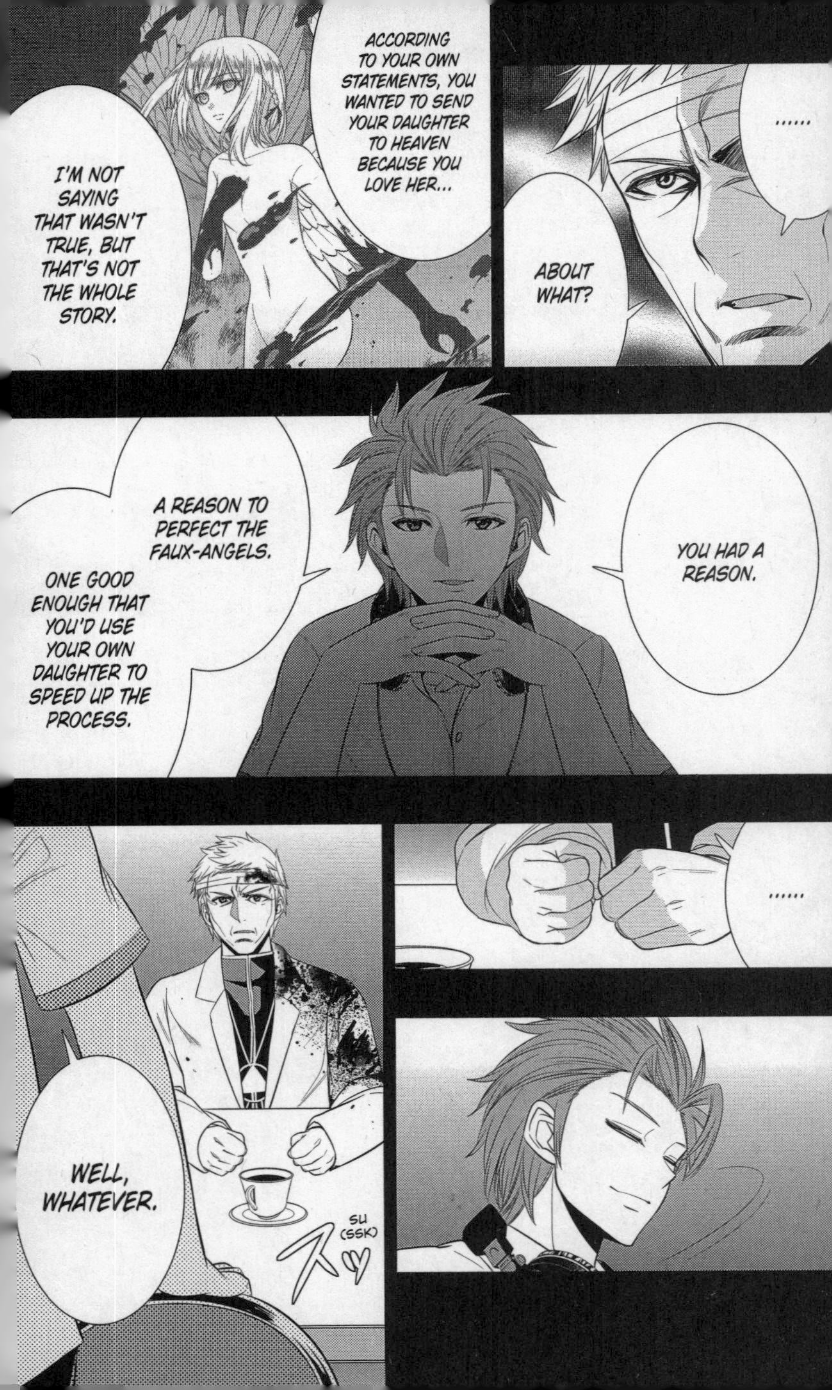
......
ABOUT WHAT?
ACCORDING TO YOUR OWN STATEMENTS, YOU WANTED TO SEND YOUR DAUGHTER TO HEAVEN BECAUSE YOU LOVE HER...
I'M NOT SAYING THAT WASN'T TRUE, BUT THAT'S NOT THE WHOLE STORY.
YOU HAD A REASON.
A REASON TO PERFECT THE FAUX-ANGELS.
ONE GOOD ENOUGH THAT YOU'D USE YOUR OWN DAUGHTER TO SPEED UP THE PROCESS.
......
WELL, WHATEVER.
スッ
SU (SSK)

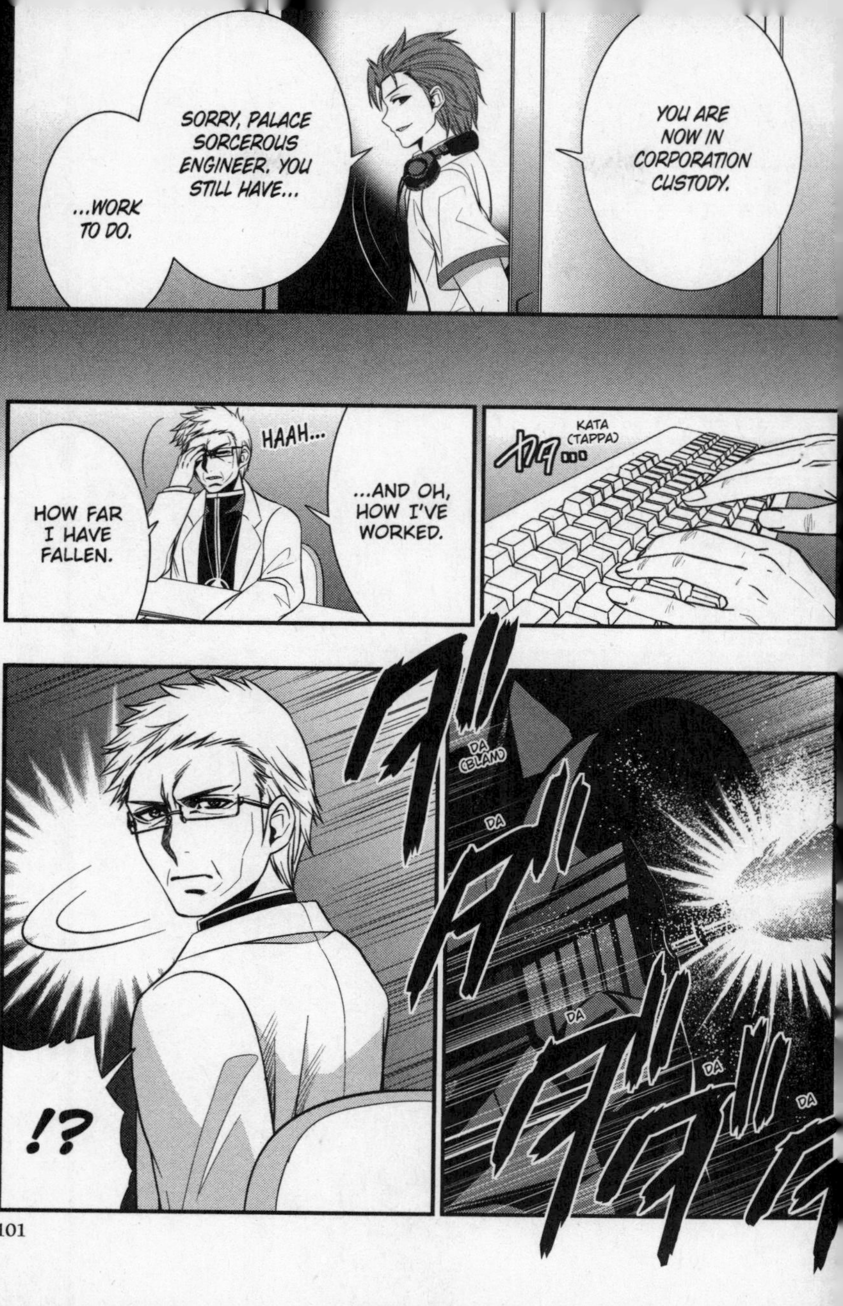
YOU ARE NOW IN CORPORATION CUSTODY.
SORRY, PALACE SORCEROUS ENGINEER. YOU STILL HAVE...
...WORK TO DO.
KATA (TAPPA)
...AND OH, HOW I'VE WORKED.
HAAH...
HOW FAR I HAVE FALLEN.
DA (BLAM)
DA
DA
DA
DA
!?

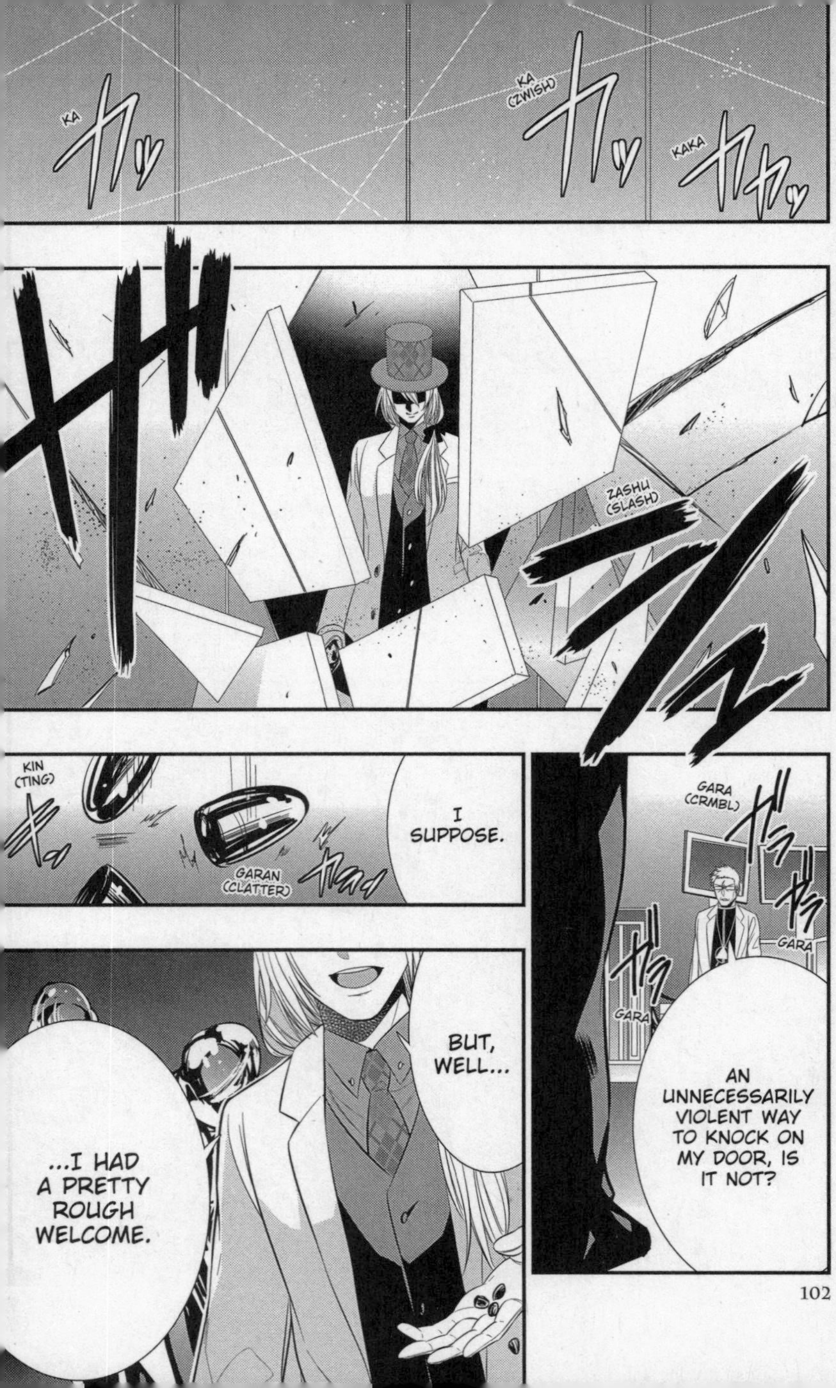
KAKA
KA (ZWISH)
KA
ZASHU (SLASH)
GARA (CRMBL)
GARA
GARA
AN UNNECESSARILY VIOLENT WAY TO KNOCK ON MY DOOR, IS IT NOT?
I SUPPOSE.
GARAN (CLATTER)
KIN (TING)
BUT, WELL...
...I HAD A PRETTY ROUGH WELCOME.

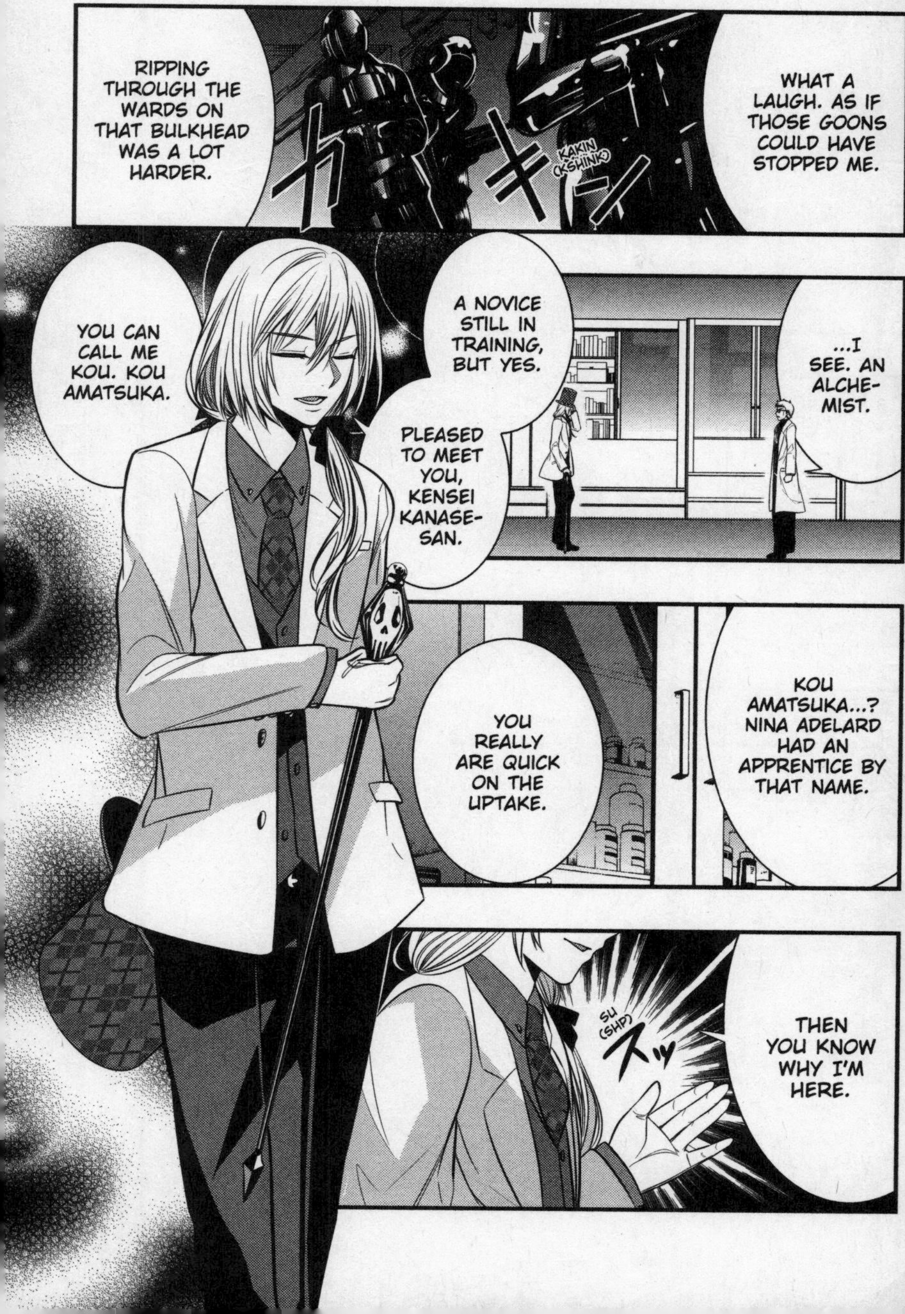
WHAT A LAUGH. AS IF THOSE GOONS COULD HAVE STOPPED ME.
KAKIN (KSHINK)
RIPPING THROUGH THE WARDS ON THAT BULKHEAD WAS A LOT HARDER.
...I SEE. AN ALCHE-MIST.
A NOVICE STILL IN TRAINING, BUT YES.
PLEASED TO MEET YOU, KENSEI KANASE-SAN.
YOU CAN CALL ME KOU. KOU AMATSUKA.
KOU AMATSUKA...? NINA ADELARD HAD AN APPRENTICE BY THAT NAME.
YOU REALLY ARE QUICK ON THE UPTAKE.
THEN YOU KNOW WHY I'M HERE.
SU (SHP)

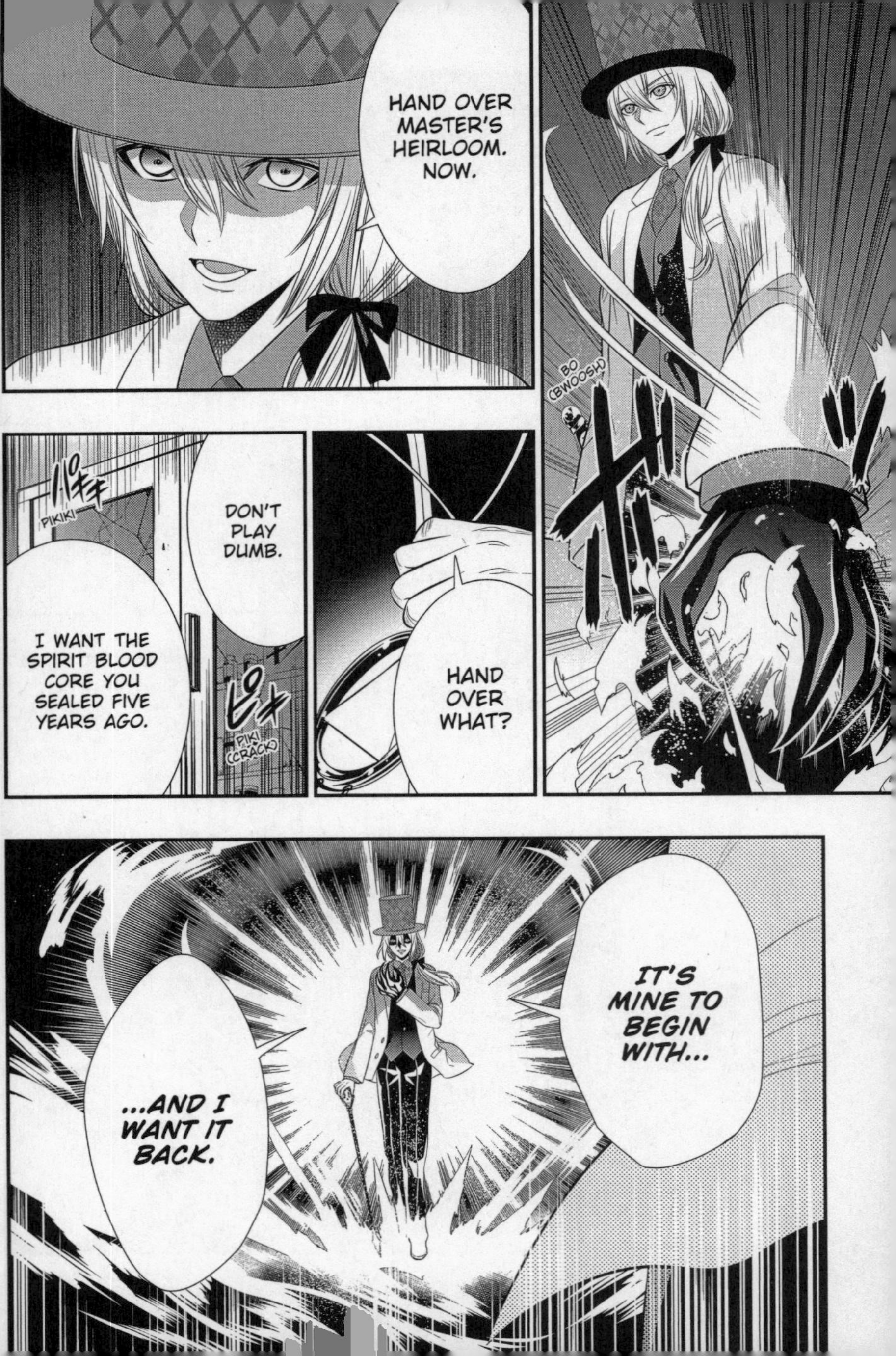
BO (BWOOSH)
HAND OVER MASTER'S HEIRLOOM. NOW.
HAND OVER WHAT?
PIKI (CRACK)
DON'T PLAY DUMB.
PIKIKI
I WANT THE SPIRIT BLOOD CORE YOU SEALED FIVE YEARS AGO.
IT'S MINE TO BEGIN WITH...
...AND I WANT IT BACK.

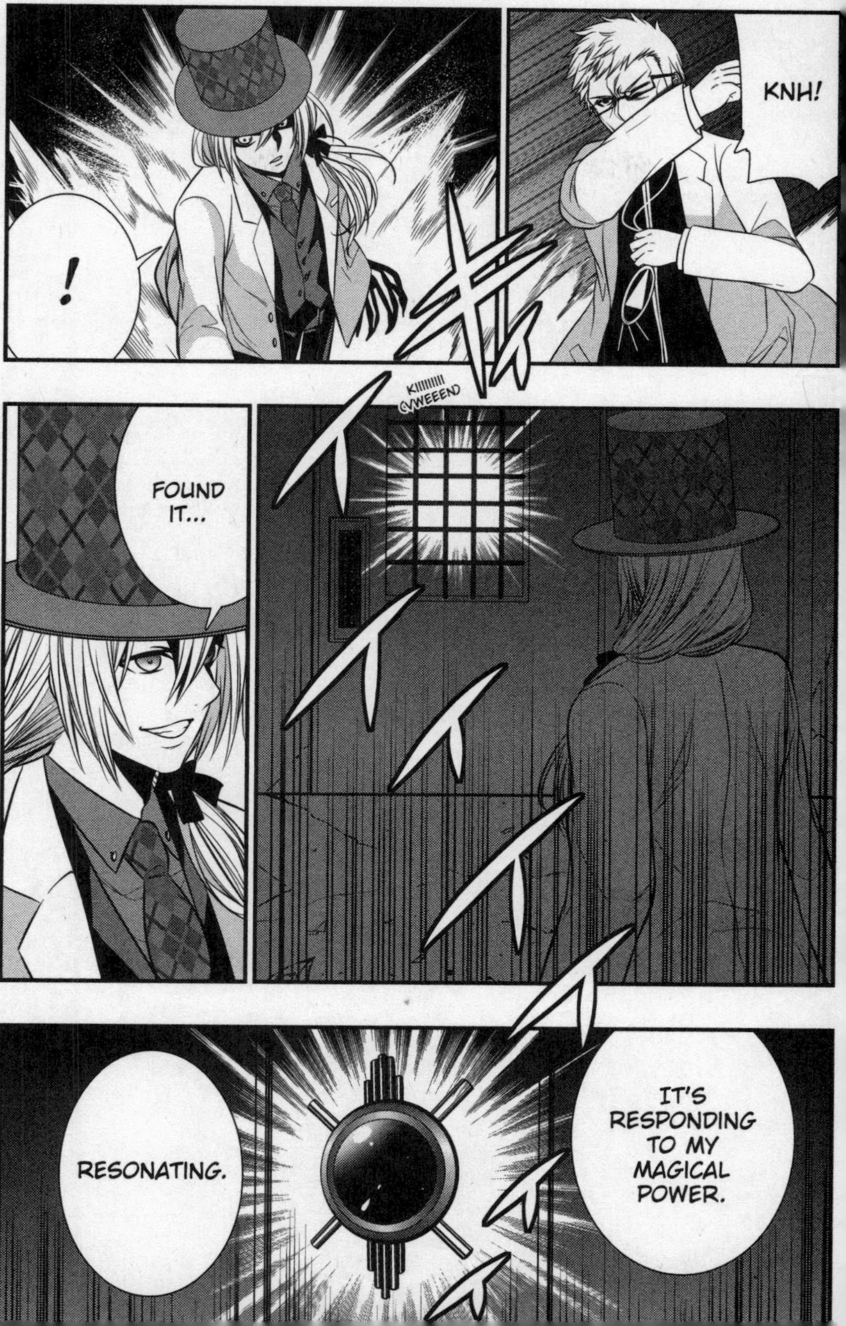
KNH!
!
KIIIIIIIIII
VVWEEEND
FOUND IT...
IT'S RESPONDING TO MY MAGICAL POWER.
RESONATING.

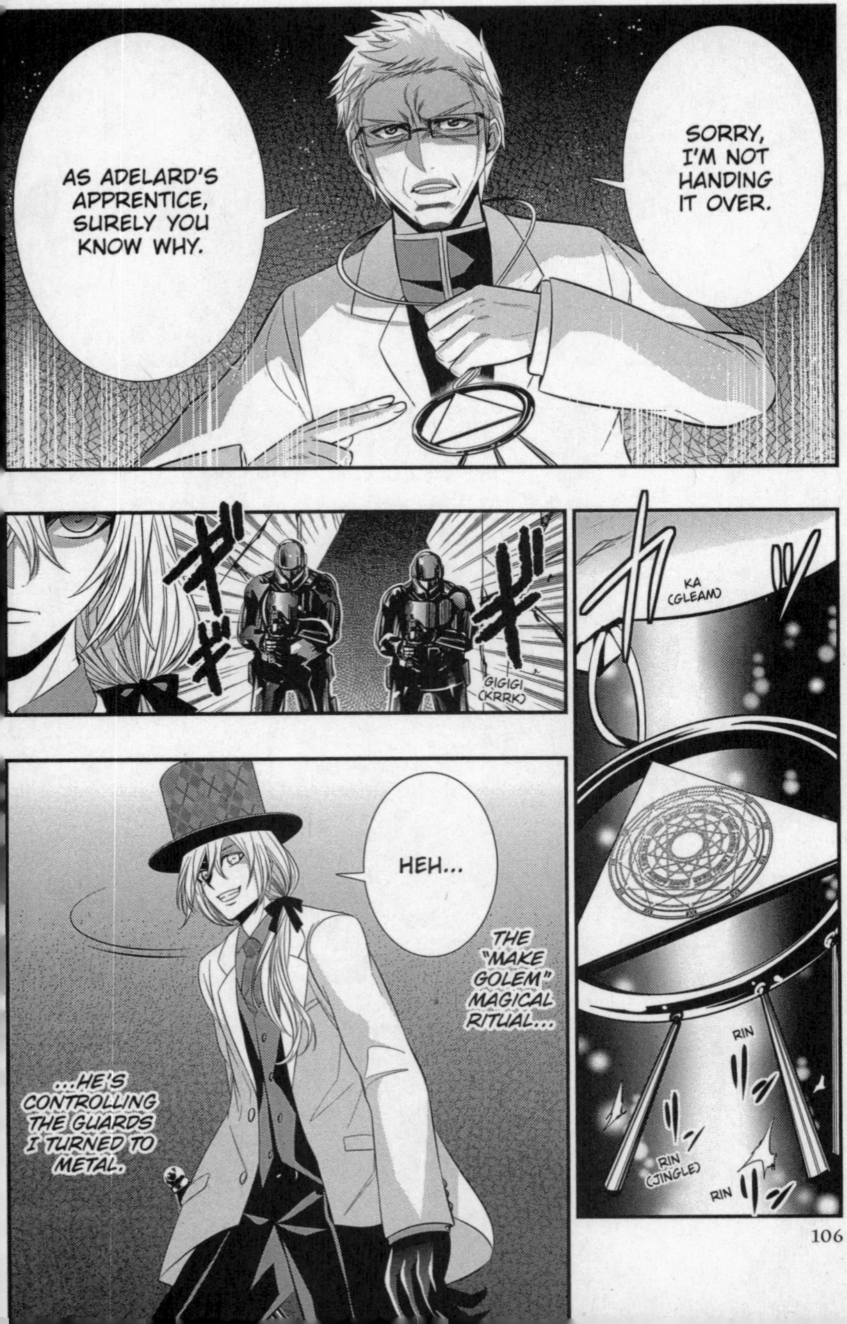
SORRY, I'M NOT HANDING IT OVER.
AS ADELARD'S APPRENTICE, SURELY YOU KNOW WHY.
KA (GLEAM)
RIN
RIN (JINGLE)
RIN
GIGIGI (KRRK)
HEH...
THE "MAKE GOLEM" MAGICAL RITUAL...
...HE'S CONTROLLING THE GUARDS I TURNED TO METAL.

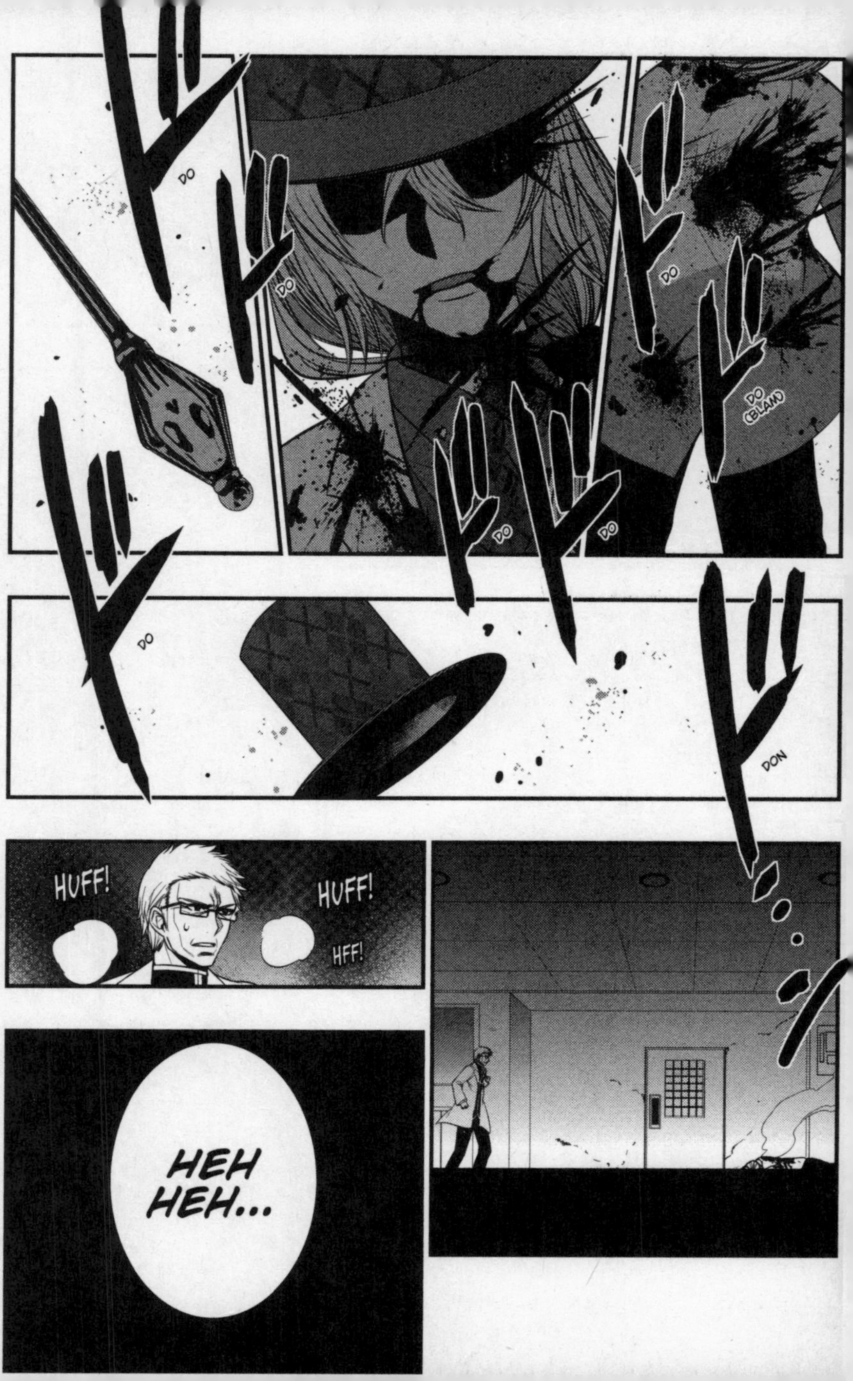

DO
DO
(BLAM)
DO
DO
DO
DO
DON
DO
HUFF!
HUFF!
HFF!
HEH HEH...

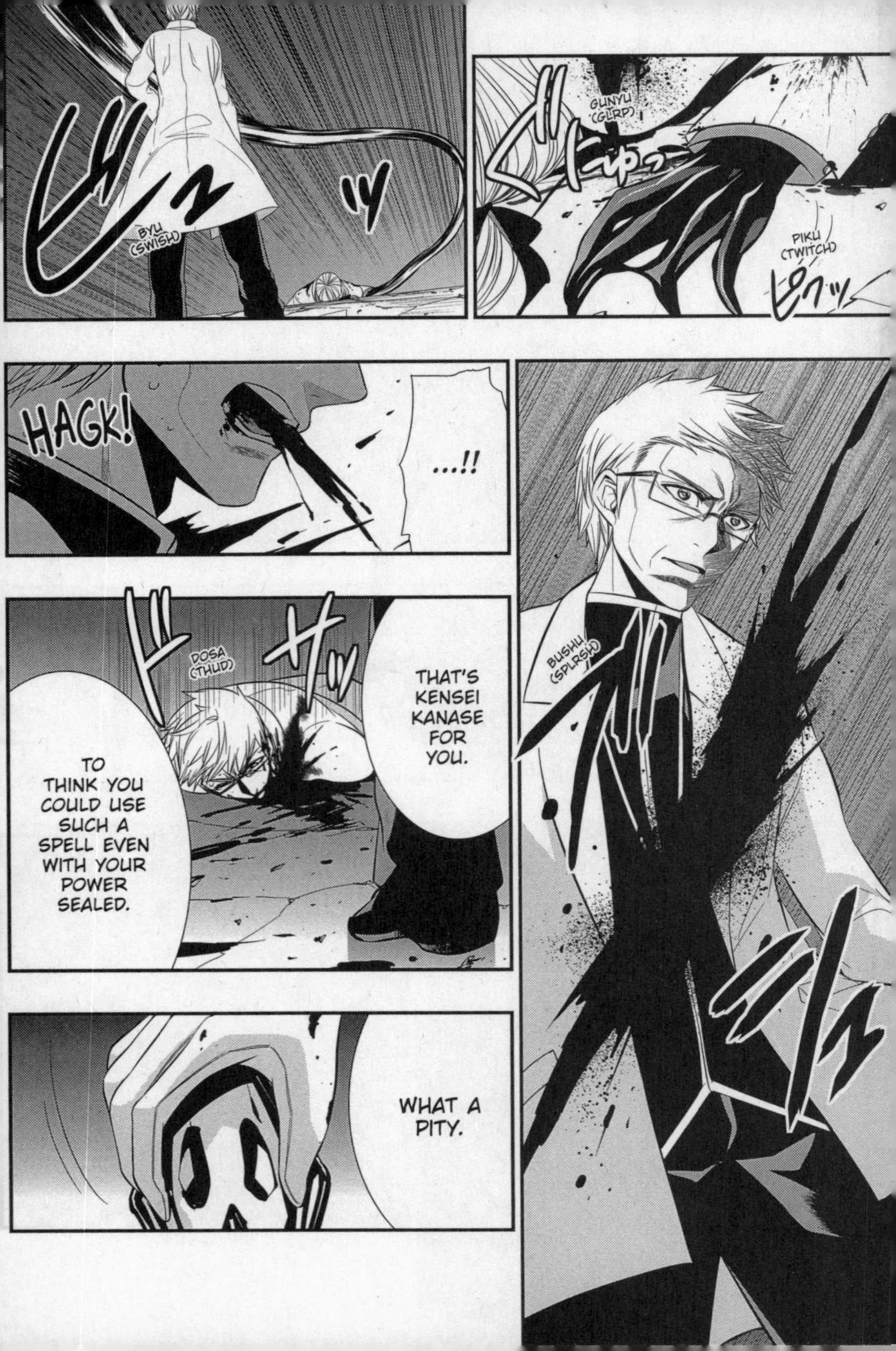

GUNYU (GLRP)
PIKU (TWITCH)
BYU (SWISH)
BUSHU (SPLRSH)
...!!
HAGK!
THAT'S KENSEI KANASE FOR YOU.
DOSA (THUD)
TO THINK YOU COULD USE SUCH A SPELL EVEN WITH YOUR POWER SEALED.
WHAT A PITY.

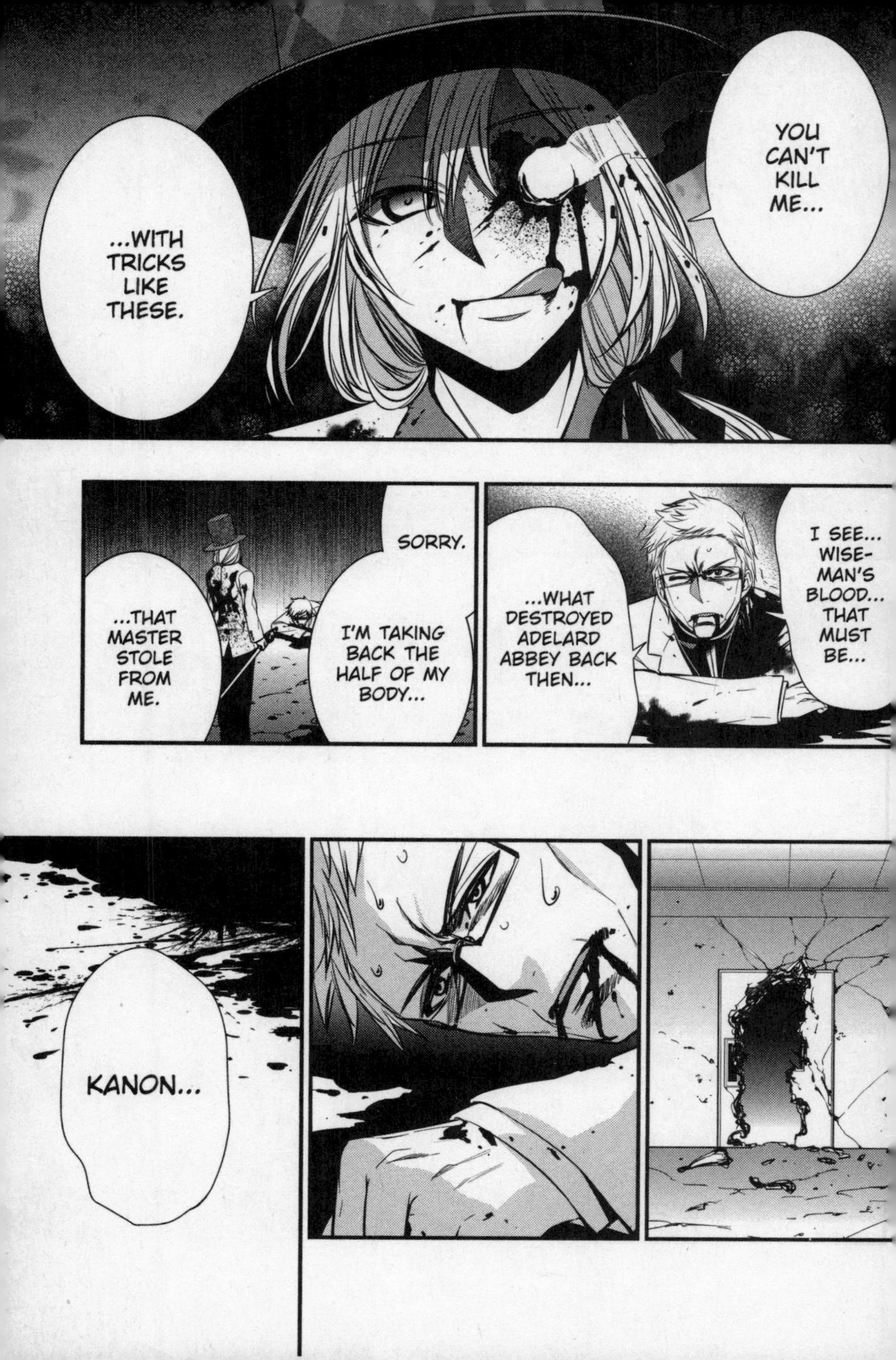
YOU CAN'T KILL ME...
...WITH TRICKS LIKE THESE.
I SEE... WISE-MAN'S BLOOD... THAT MUST BE...
...WHAT DESTROYED ADELARD ABBEY BACK THEN...
SORRY.
I'M TAKING BACK THE HALF OF MY BODY...
...THAT MASTER STOLE FROM ME.
KANON...

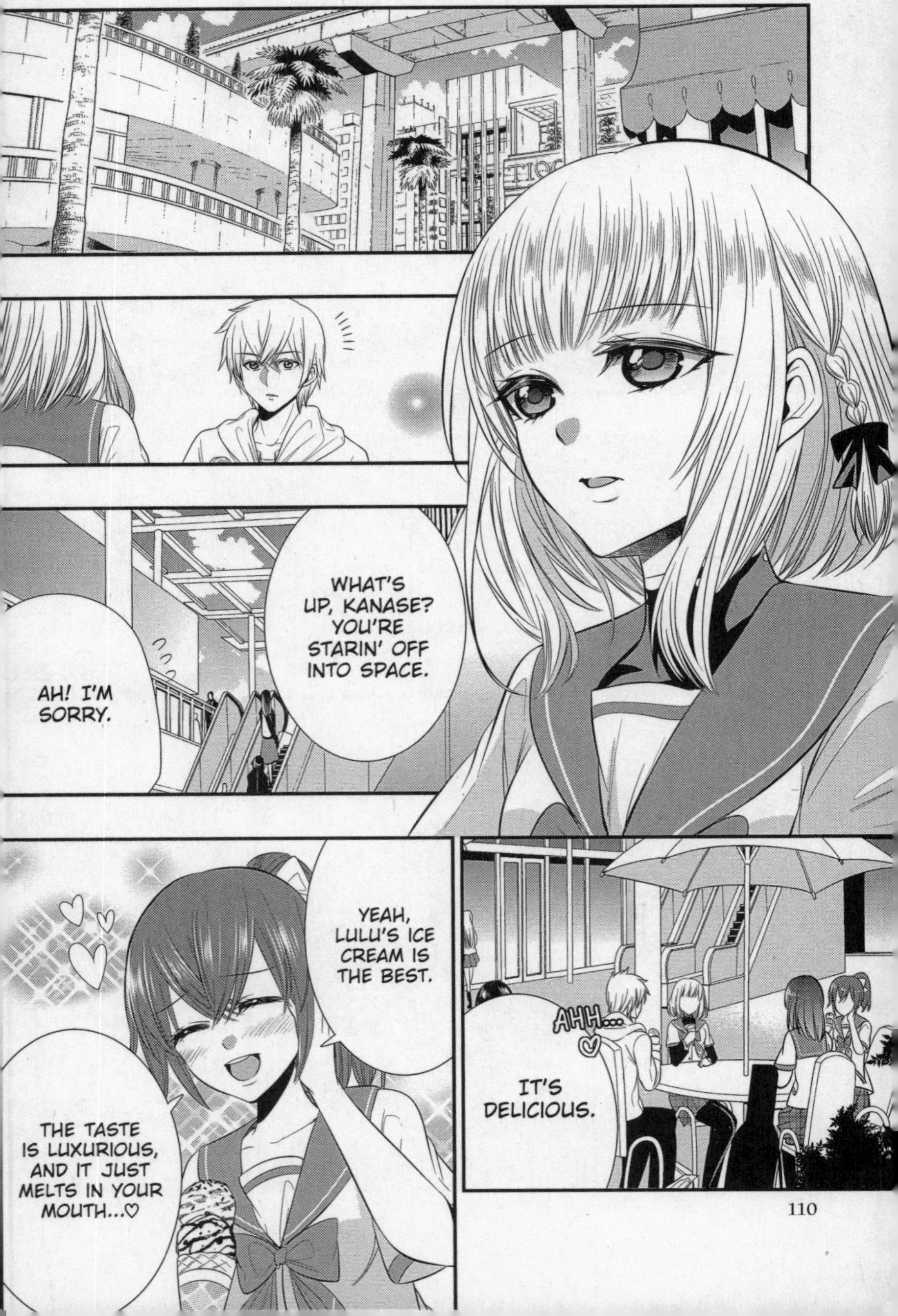
WHAT'S UP, KANASE? YOU'RE STARIN' OFF INTO SPACE.
AH! I'M SORRY.
AHH...♡
IT'S DELICIOUS.
YEAH, LULU'S ICE CREAM IS THE BEST.
THE TASTE IS LUXURIOUS, AND IT JUST MELTS IN YOUR MOUTH...♡

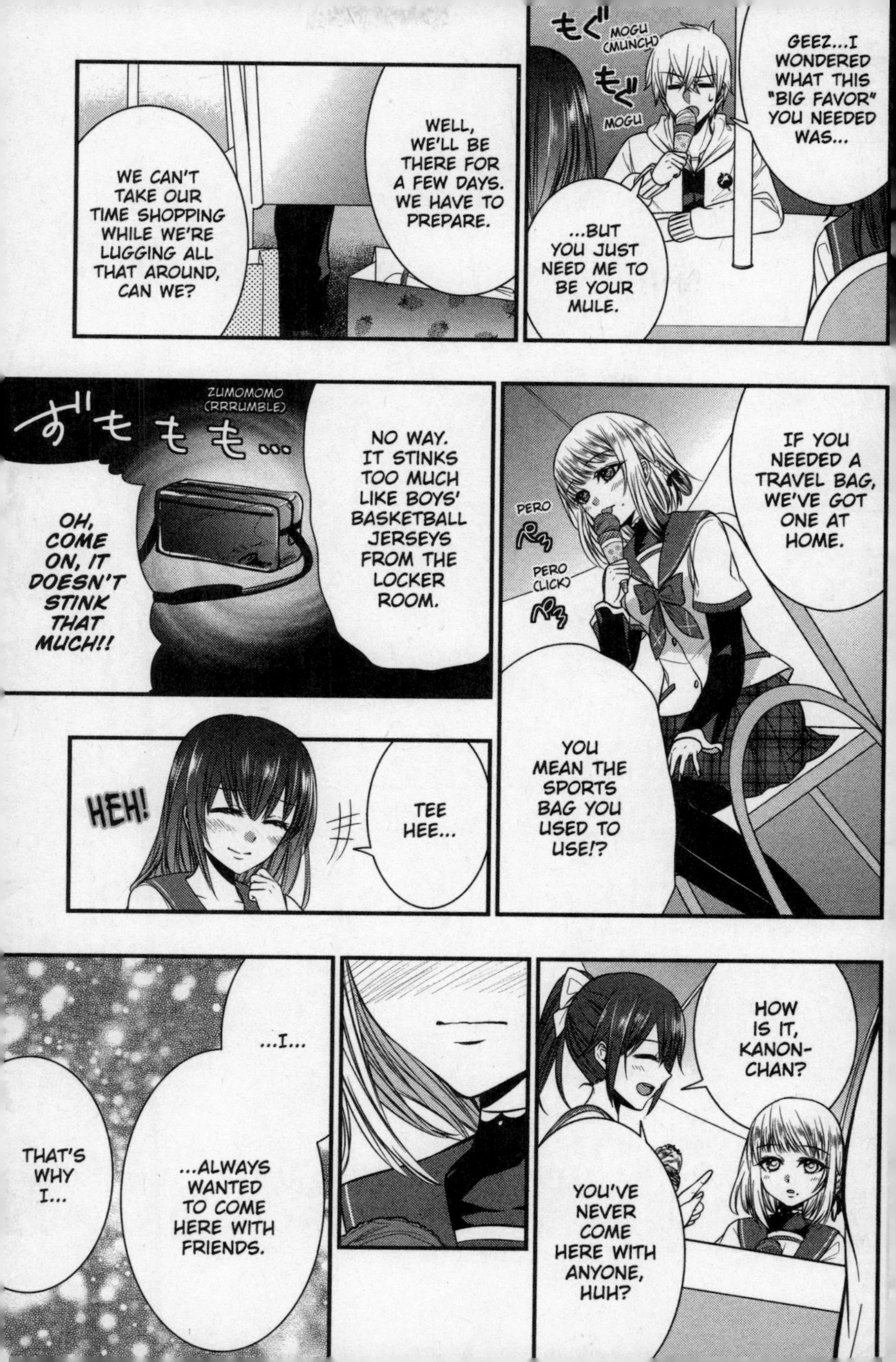
GEEZ...I WONDERED WHAT THIS "BIG FAVOR" YOU NEEDED WAS...
もぐ
MOGU (MUNCH)
もぐ
MOGU
...BUT YOU JUST NEED ME TO BE YOUR MULE.
WELL, WE'LL BE THERE FOR A FEW DAYS. WE HAVE TO PREPARE.
WE CAN'T TAKE OUR TIME SHOPPING WHILE WE'RE LUGGING ALL THAT AROUND, CAN WE?
IF YOU NEEDED A TRAVEL BAG, WE'VE GOT ONE AT HOME.
PERO
ぺろ
PERO (LICK)
ぺろ
YOU MEAN THE SPORTS BAG YOU USED TO USE!?
ずももも...
ZUMOMOMO (RRRUMBLE)
NO WAY. IT STINKS TOO MUCH LIKE BOYS' BASKETBALL JERSEYS FROM THE LOCKER ROOM.
OH, COME ON, IT DOESN'T STINK THAT MUCH!!
TEE HEE...
HEH!
HOW IS IT, KANON-CHAN?
YOU'VE NEVER COME HERE WITH ANYONE, HUH?
...I...
...ALWAYS WANTED TO COME HERE WITH FRIENDS.
THAT'S WHY I...

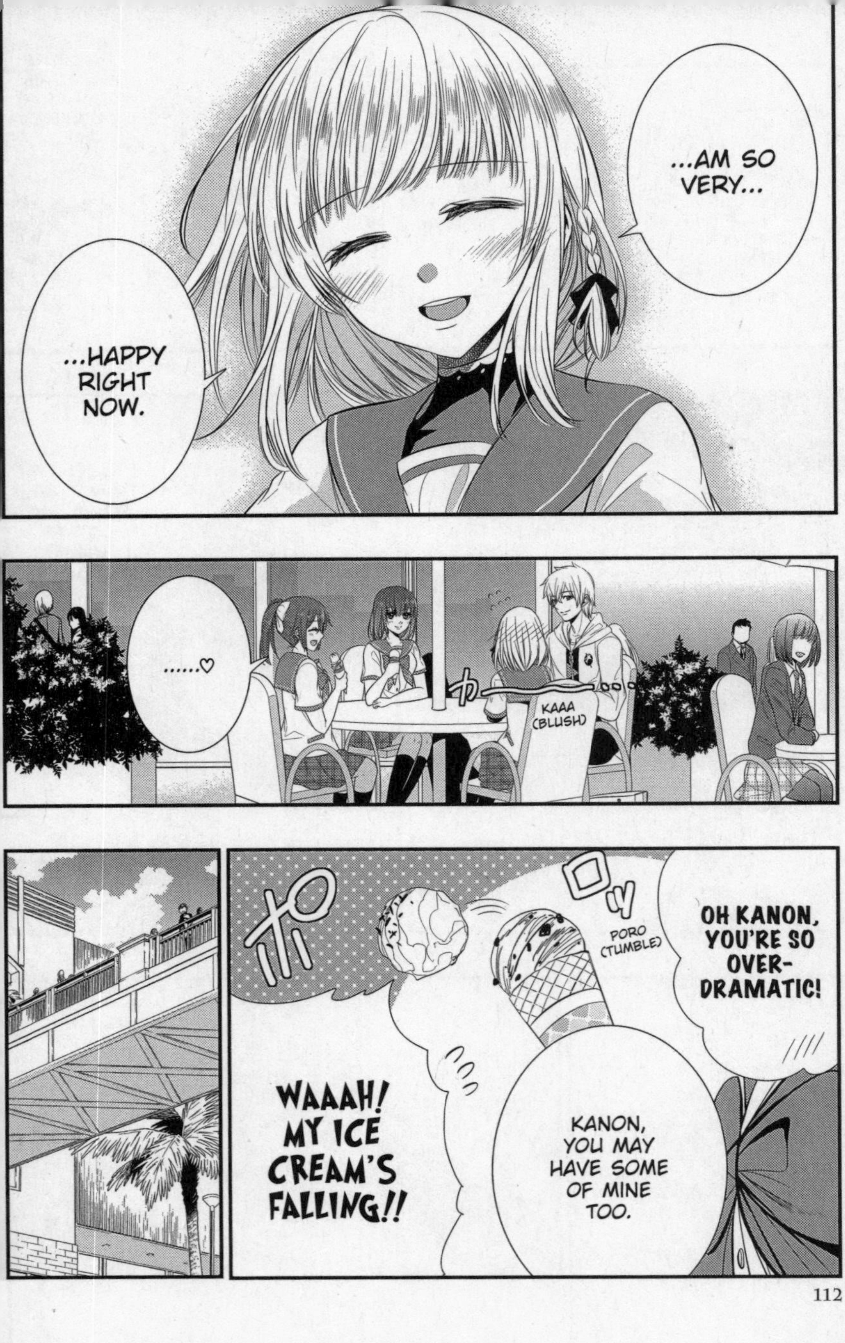
...AM SO VERY...
...HAPPY RIGHT NOW.
KAAA (BLUSH)
......♡
OH KANON, YOU'RE SO OVER-DRAMATIC!
PORO (TUMBLE)
KANON, YOU MAY HAVE SOME OF MINE TOO.
WAAAH! MY ICE CREAM'S FALLING!!

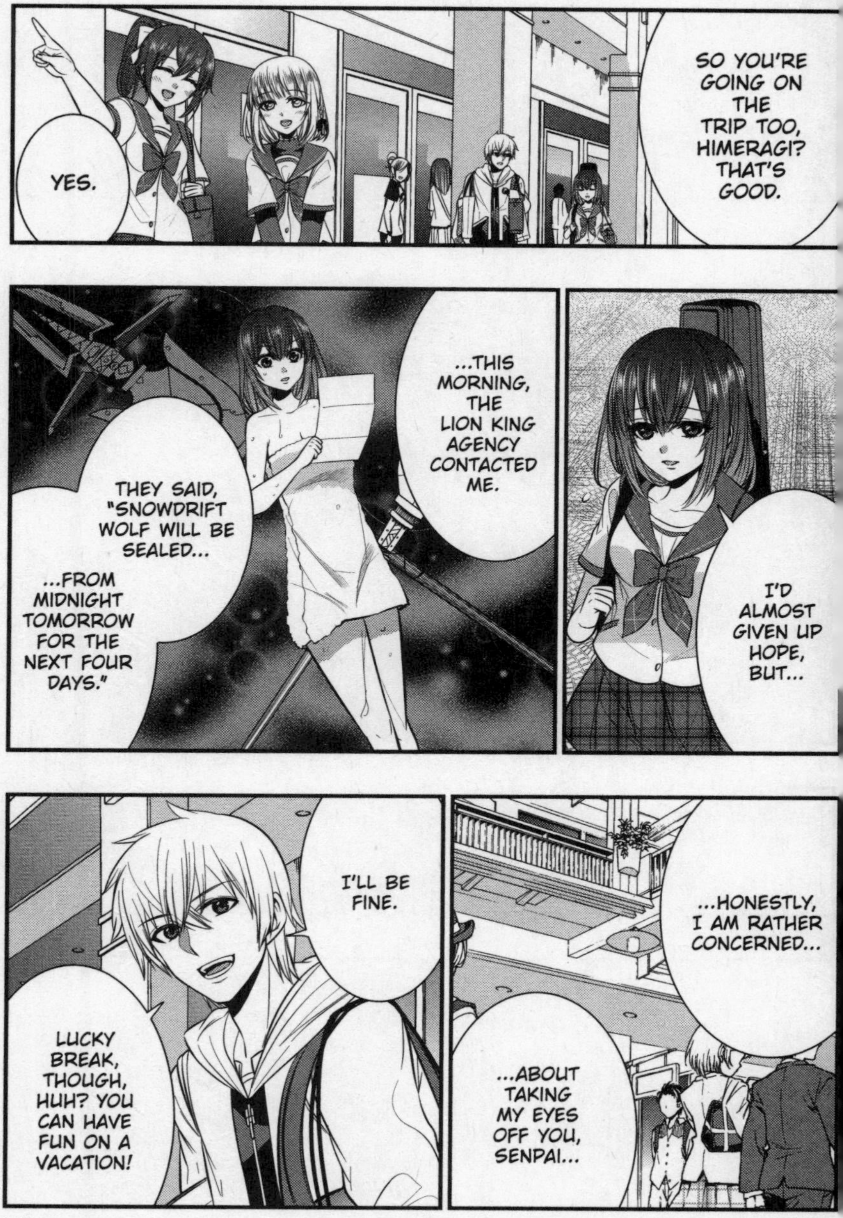
SO YOU'RE GOING ON THE TRIP TOO, HIMERAGI? THAT'S GOOD.
YES.
I'D ALMOST GIVEN UP HOPE, BUT...
...THIS MORNING, THE LION KING AGENCY CONTACTED ME.
THEY SAID, "SNOWDRIFT WOLF WILL BE SEALED...
...FROM MIDNIGHT TOMORROW FOR THE NEXT FOUR DAYS."
...HONESTLY, I AM RATHER CONCERNED...
...ABOUT TAKING MY EYES OFF YOU, SENPAI...
I'LL BE FINE.
LUCKY BREAK, THOUGH, HUH? YOU CAN HAVE FUN ON A VACATION!

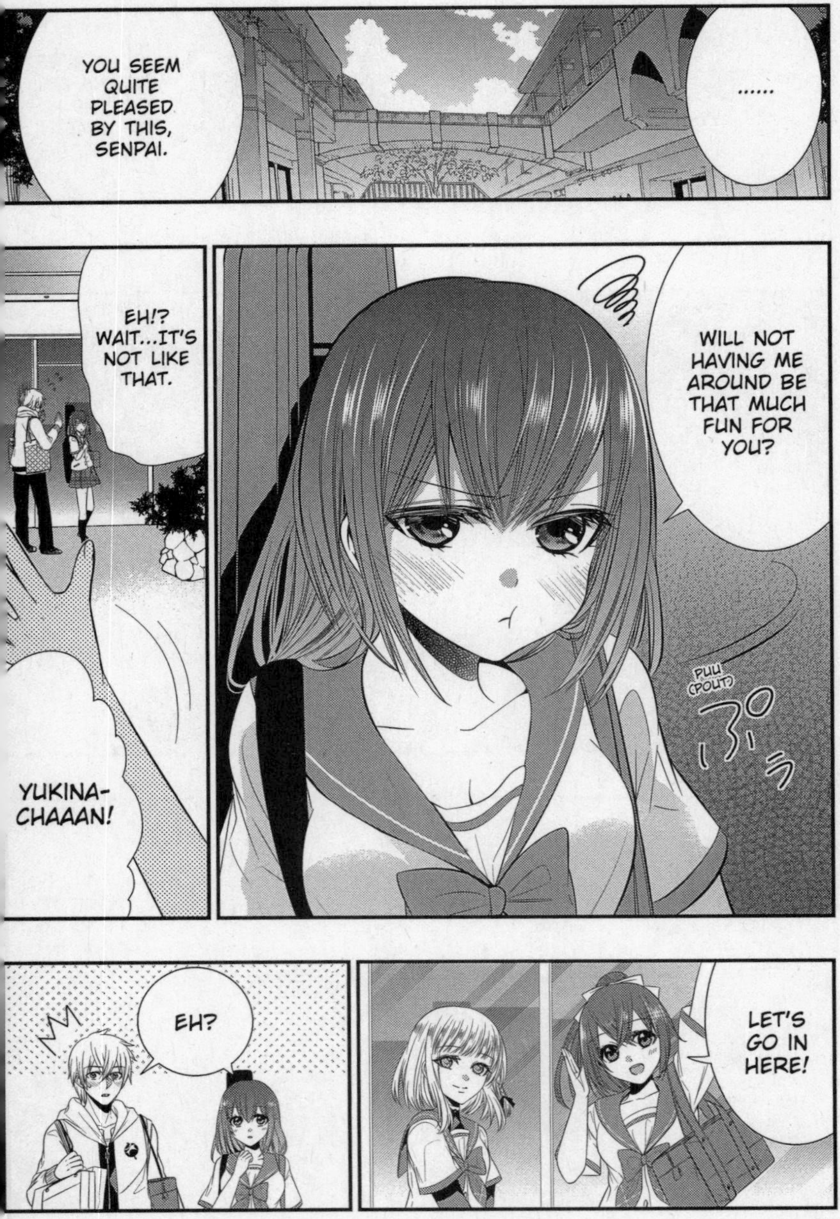
......
YOU SEEM QUITE PLEASED BY THIS, SENPAI.
WILL NOT HAVING ME AROUND BE THAT MUCH FUN FOR YOU?
PUU (POUT)
EH!? WAIT...IT'S NOT LIKE THAT.
YUKINA-CHAAAN!
LET'S GO IN HERE!
EH?

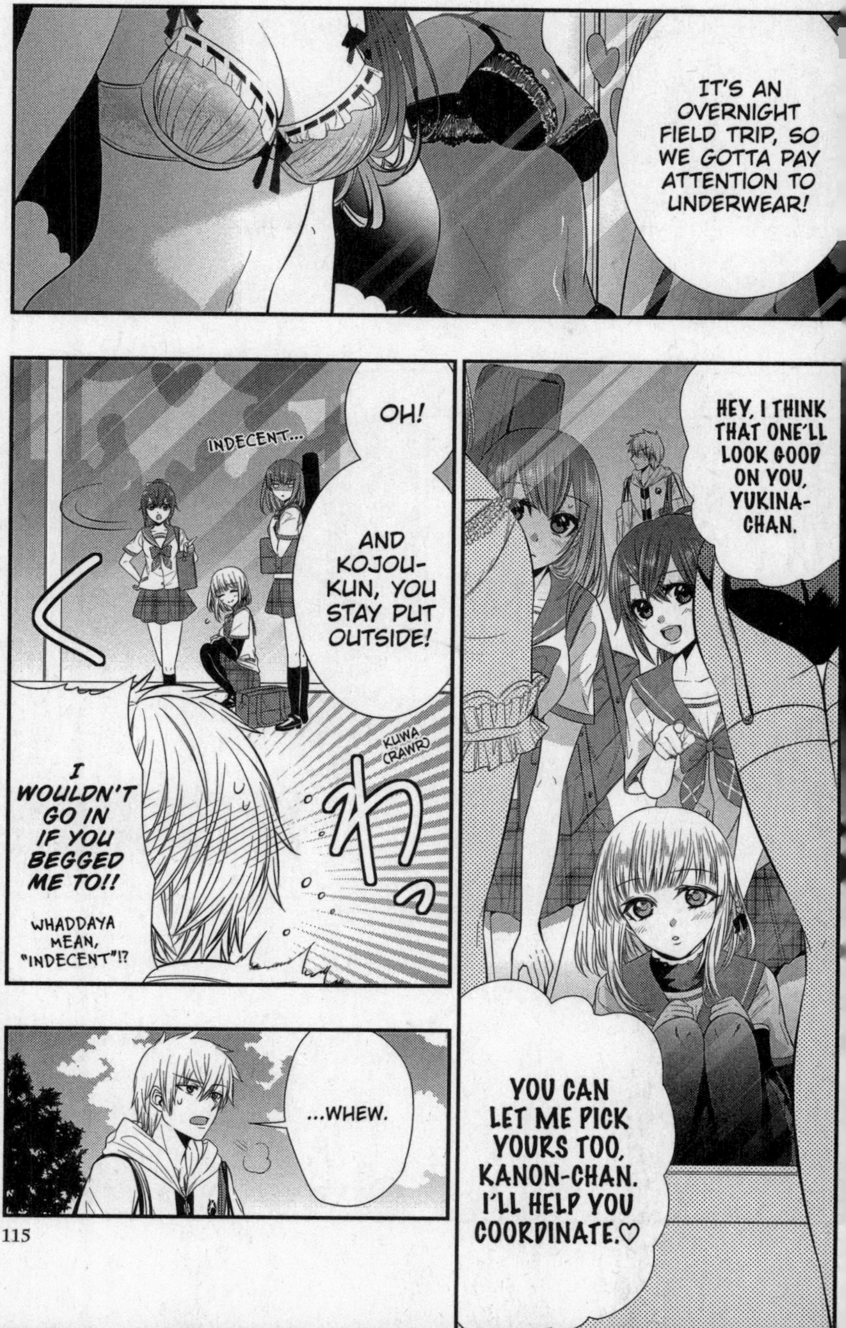
IT'S AN OVERNIGHT FIELD TRIP, SO WE GOTTA PAY ATTENTION TO UNDERWEAR!
HEY, I THINK THAT ONE'LL LOOK GOOD ON YOU, YUKINA-CHAN.
YOU CAN LET ME PICK YOURS TOO, KANON-CHAN. I'LL HELP YOU COORDINATE.♡
OH!
AND KOJOU-KUN, YOU STAY PUT OUTSIDE!
INDECENT...
KUWA (RAWR)
I WOULDN'T GO IN IF YOU BEGGED ME TO!!
WHADDAYA MEAN, "INDECENT"!?
...WHEW.

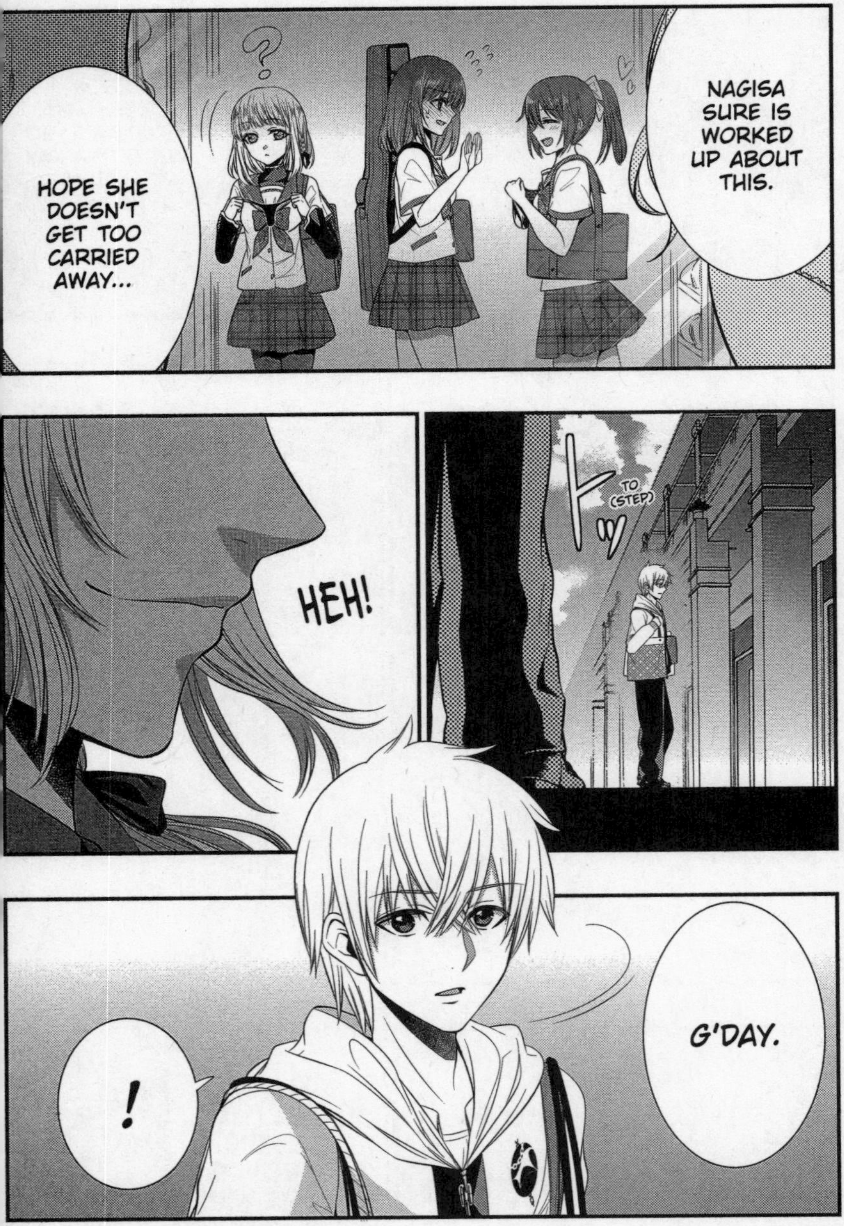
NAGISA SURE IS WORKED UP ABOUT THIS.
HOPE SHE DOESN'T GET TOO CARRIED AWAY...
トッ
TO (STEP)
HEH!
G'DAY.
!

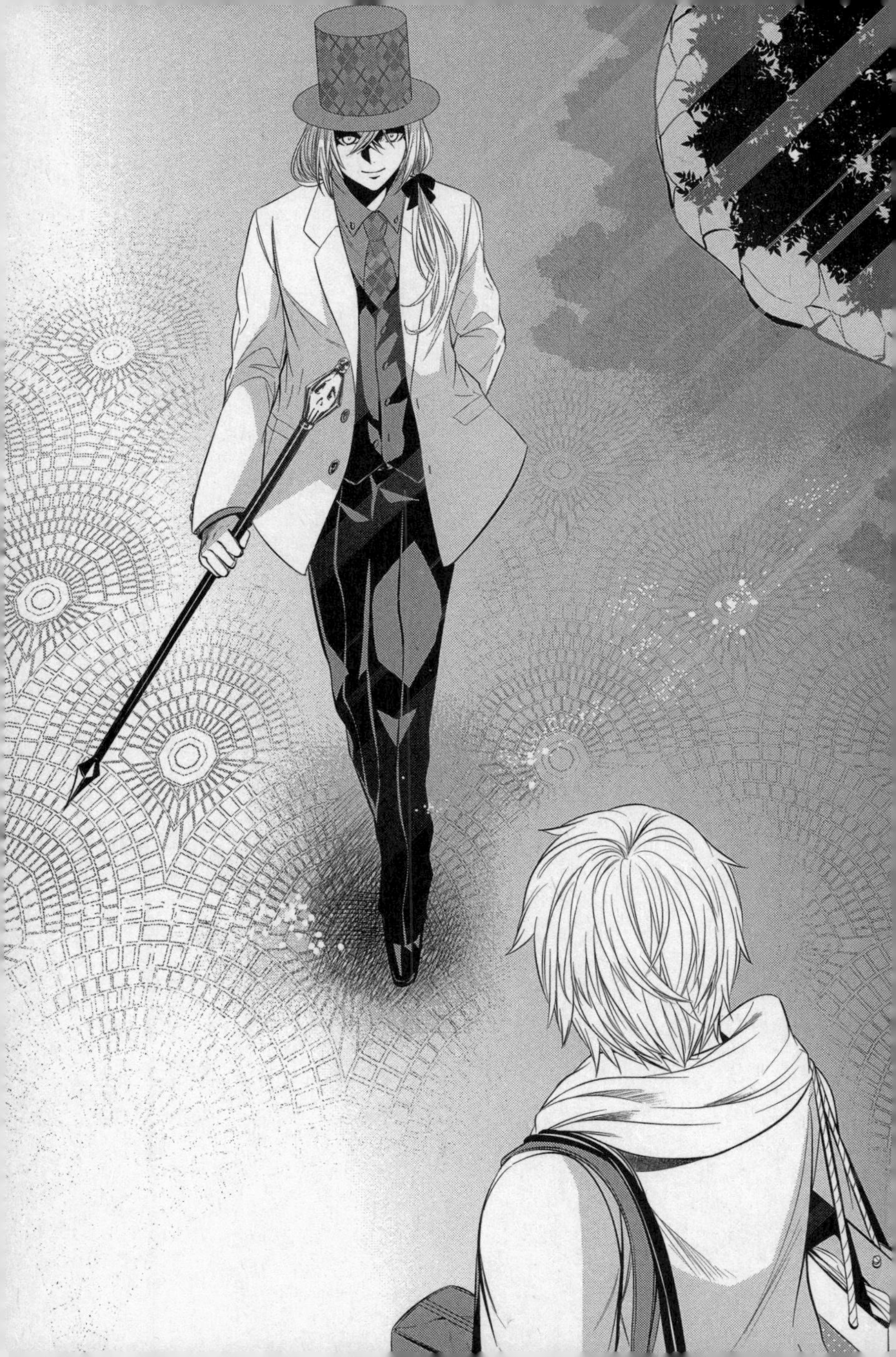

STRIKE THE BLOOD

DEFINITION

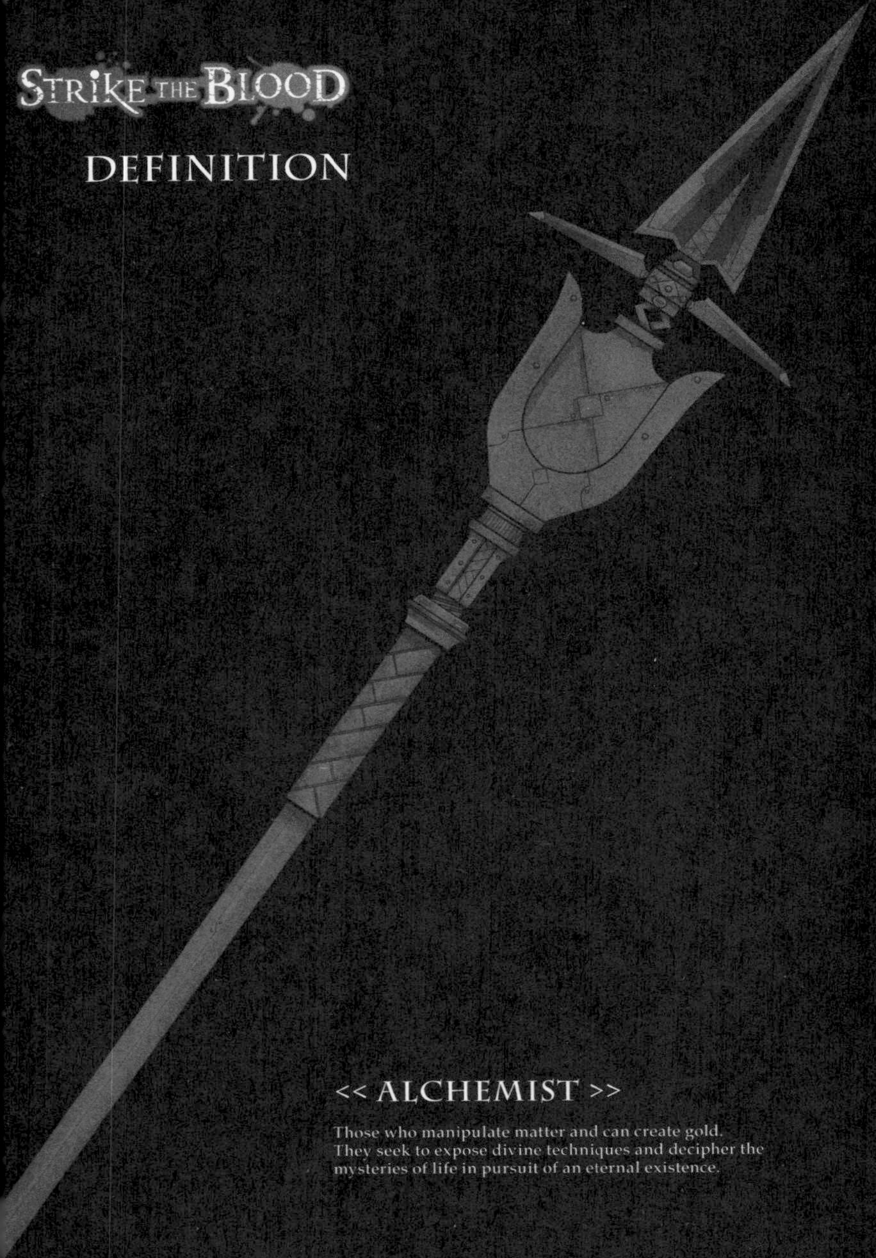

<< ALCHEMIST >>

Those who manipulate matter and can create gold. They seek to expose divine techniques and decipher the mysteries of life in pursuit of an eternal existence.

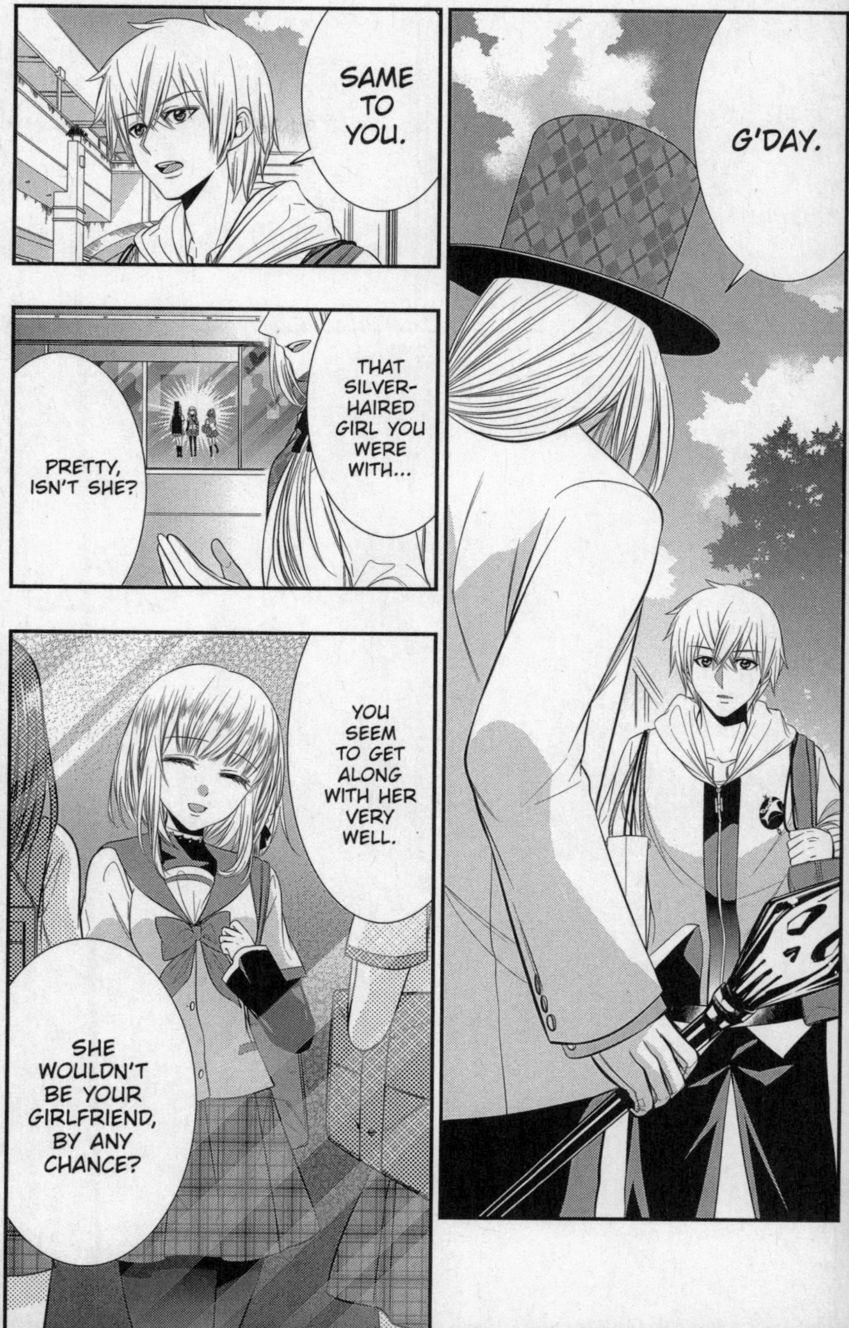
G'DAY.
SAME TO YOU.
THAT SILVER-HAIRED GIRL YOU WERE WITH...
PRETTY, ISN'T SHE?
YOU SEEM TO GET ALONG WITH HER VERY WELL.
SHE WOULDN'T BE YOUR GIRLFRIEND, BY ANY CHANCE?

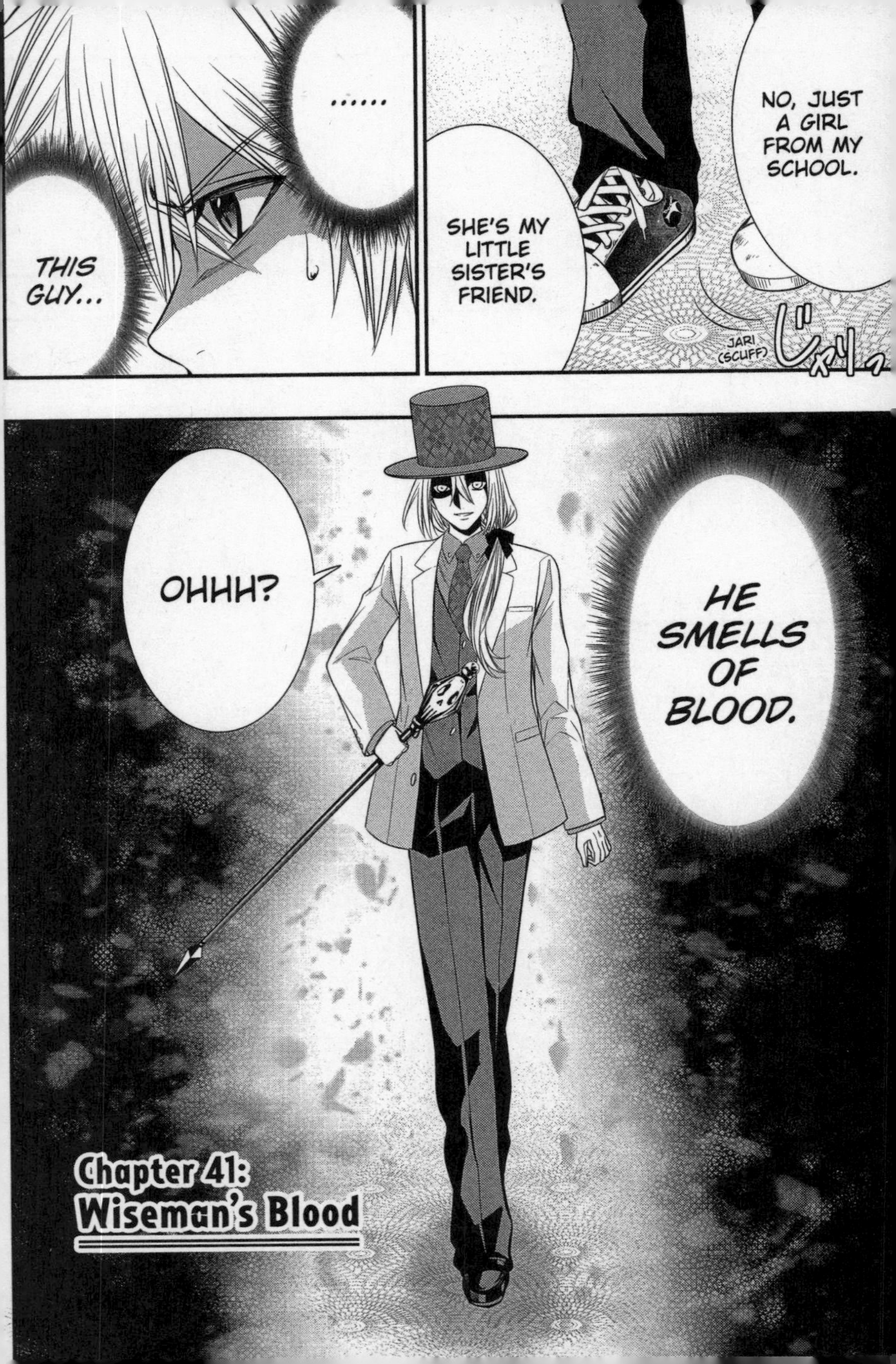
NO, JUST A GIRL FROM MY SCHOOL.
SHE'S MY LITTLE SISTER'S FRIEND.
JARI (SCUFF)
じゃりっ
......
THIS GUY...
HE SMELLS OF BLOOD.
OHHH?
Chapter 41: Wiseman's Blood

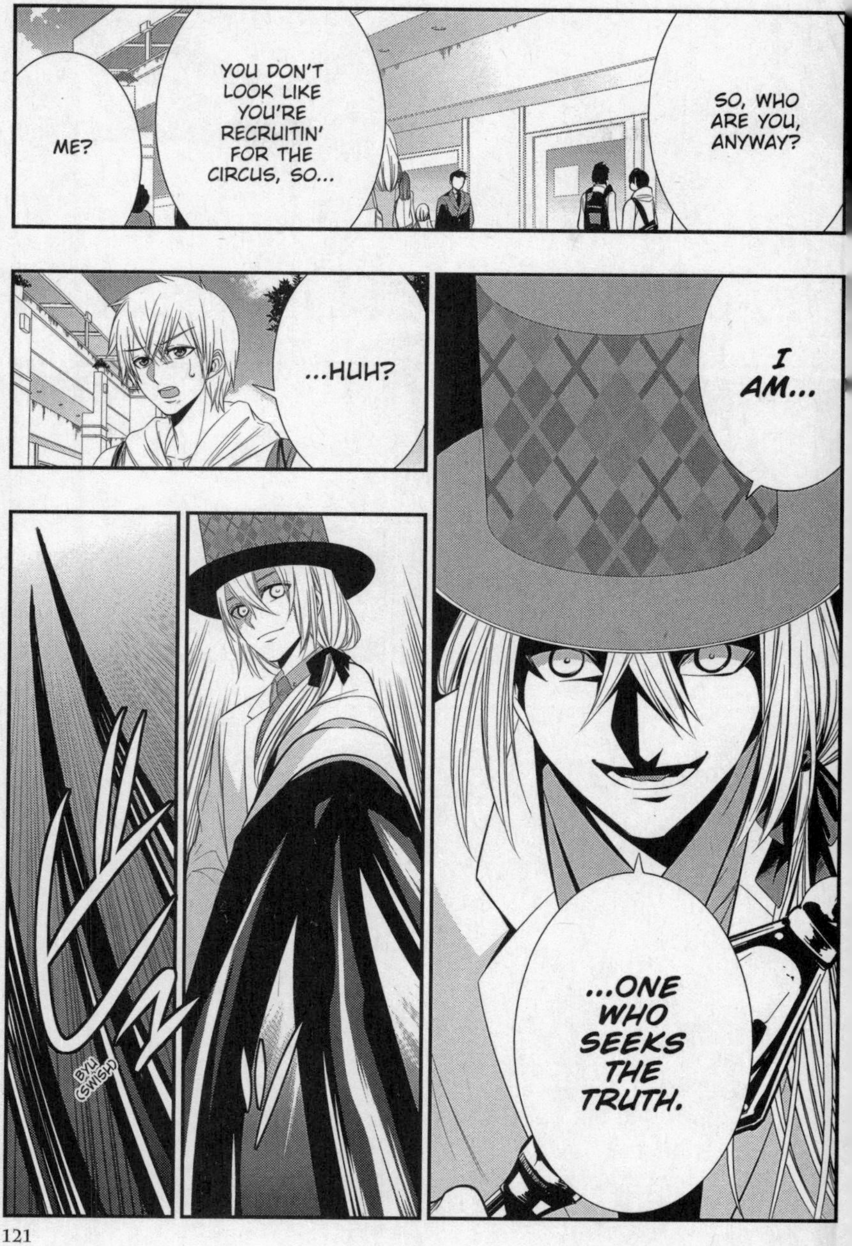
SO, WHO ARE YOU, ANYWAY?
YOU DON'T LOOK LIKE YOU'RE RECRUITIN' FOR THE CIRCUS, SO...
ME?
I AM...
...ONE WHO SEEKS THE TRUTH.
...HUH?
BYU (SWISH)

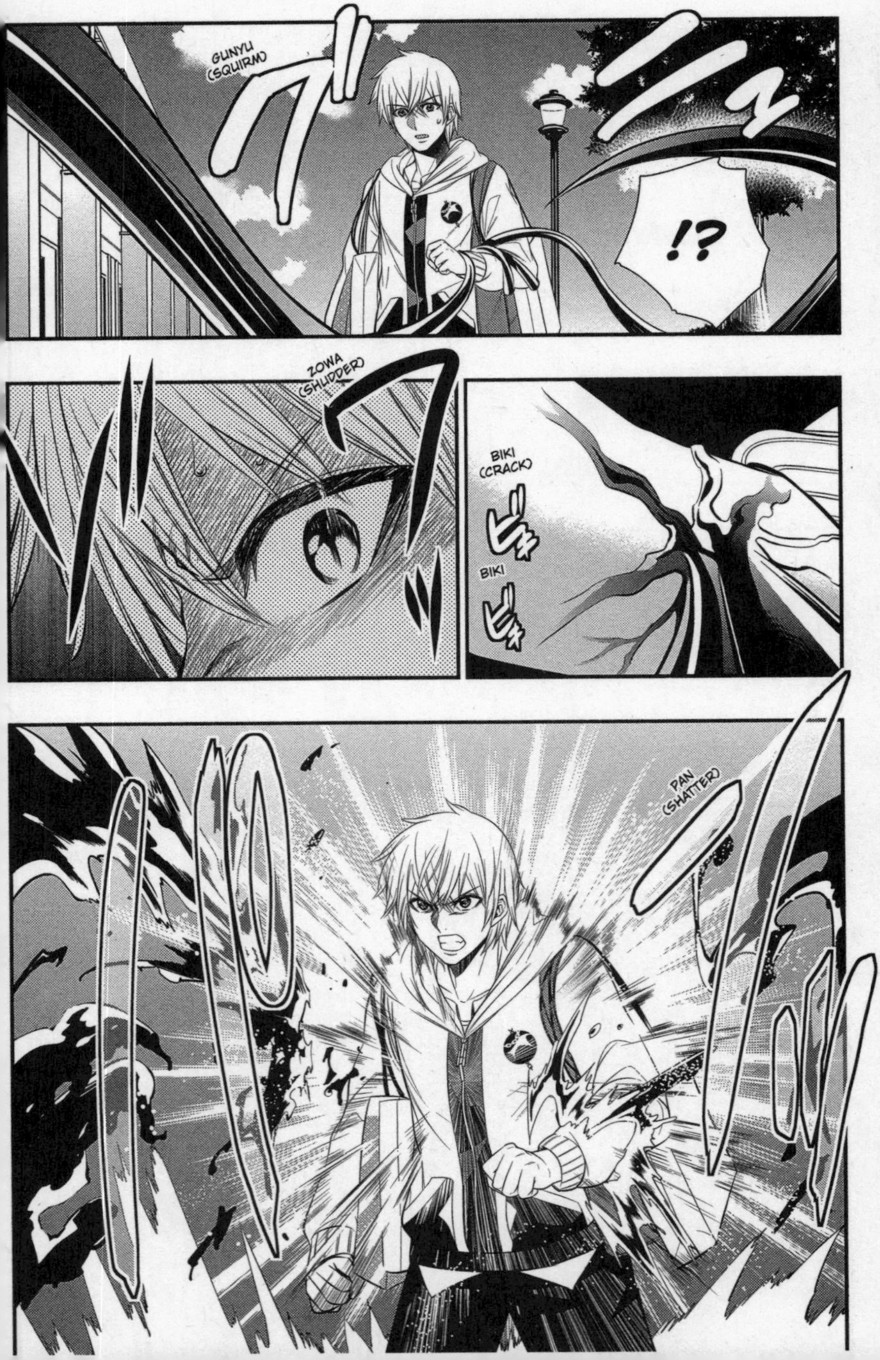
GUNYU (SQUIRM)
!?
ZOWA (SHUDDER)
BIKI (CRACK)
BIKI
PAN (SHATTER)

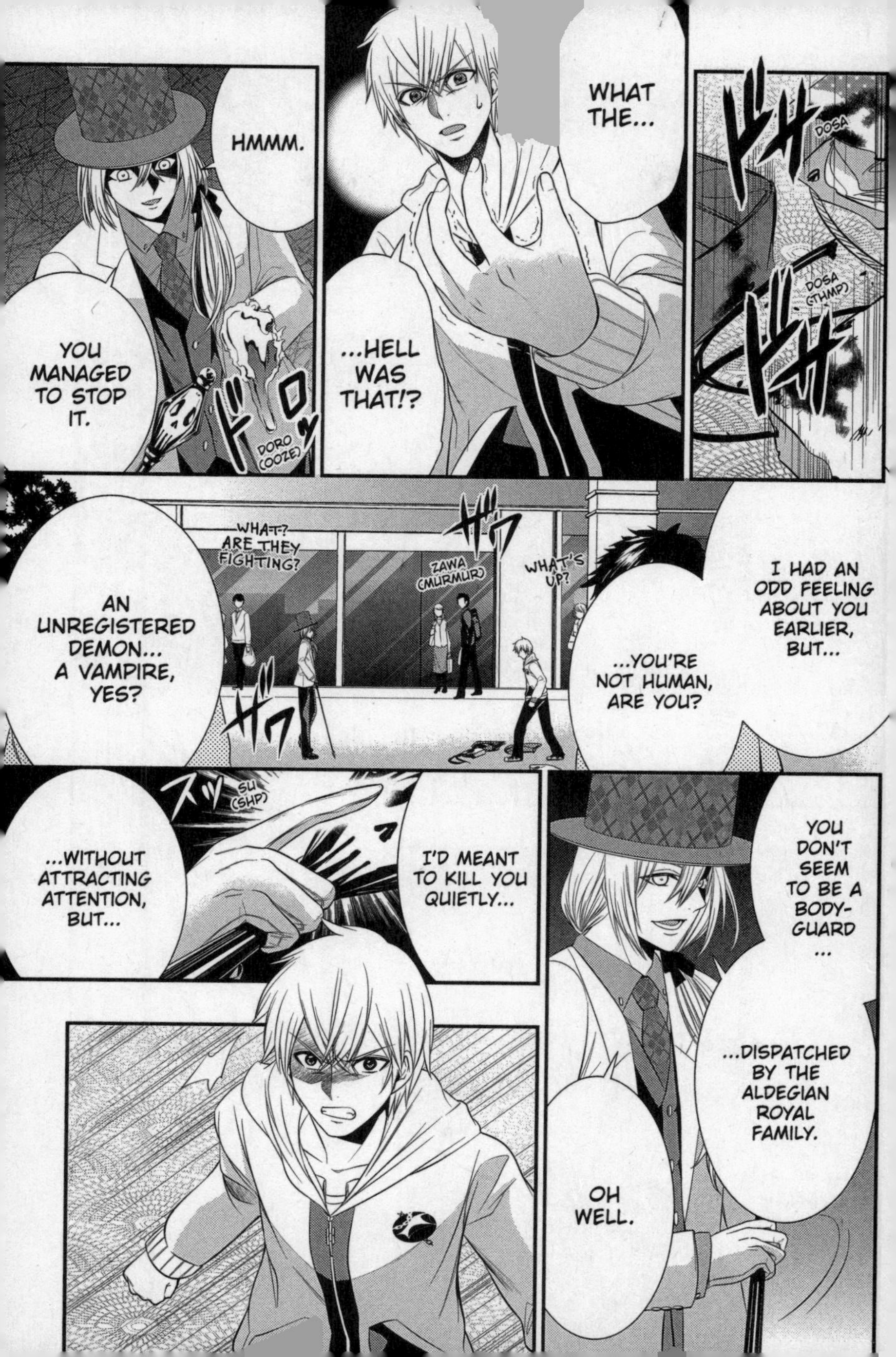
DOSA
DOSA (THMP)
WHAT THE...
...HELL WAS THAT!?
HMMM.
YOU MANAGED TO STOP IT.
DORO (COOZE)
I HAD AN ODD FEELING ABOUT YOU EARLIER, BUT...
...YOU'RE NOT HUMAN, ARE YOU?
WHAT'S UP?
ZAWA (MURMUR)
WHAT? ARE THEY FIGHTING?
AN UNREGISTERED DEMON... A VAMPIRE, YES?
YOU DON'T SEEM TO BE A BODY-GUARD...
...DISPATCHED BY THE ALDEGIAN ROYAL FAMILY.
OH WELL.
I'D MEANT TO KILL YOU QUIETLY...
...WITHOUT ATTRACTING ATTENTION, BUT...
SU (SHP)

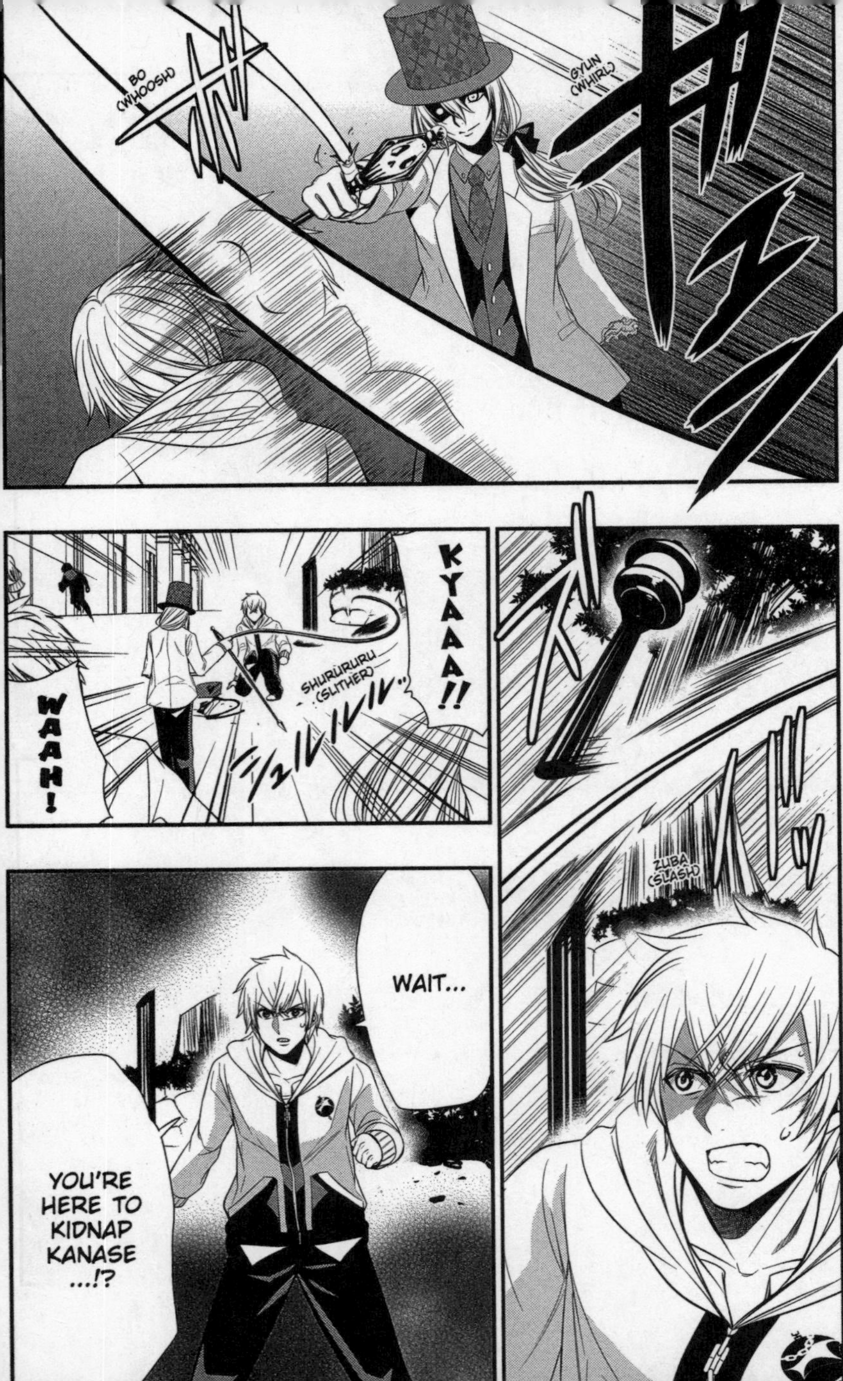
GYUN (WHIRL)
BO (WHOOSH)
ZUBA (SLASH)
KYAAA!!
SHURURURU (SLITHER)
WAAH!
WAIT...
YOU'RE HERE TO KIDNAP KANASE ...!?

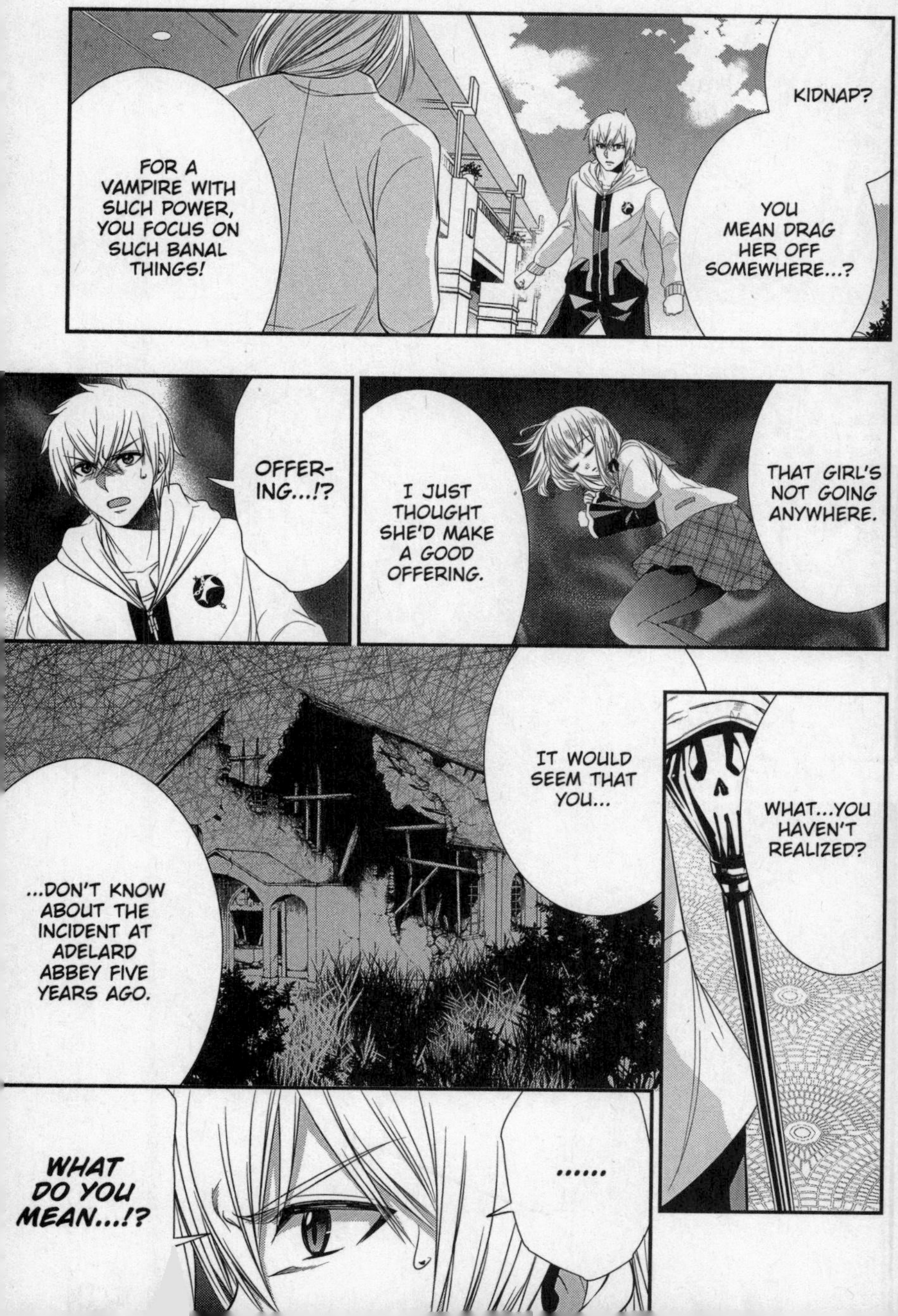
KIDNAP?
YOU MEAN DRAG HER OFF SOMEWHERE...?
FOR A VAMPIRE WITH SUCH POWER, YOU FOCUS ON SUCH BANAL THINGS!
THAT GIRL'S NOT GOING ANYWHERE.
I JUST THOUGHT SHE'D MAKE A GOOD OFFERING.
OFFER-ING...!?
WHAT...YOU HAVEN'T REALIZED?
IT WOULD SEEM THAT YOU...
...DON'T KNOW ABOUT THE INCIDENT AT ADELARD ABBEY FIVE YEARS AGO.
......
WHAT DO YOU MEAN...!?

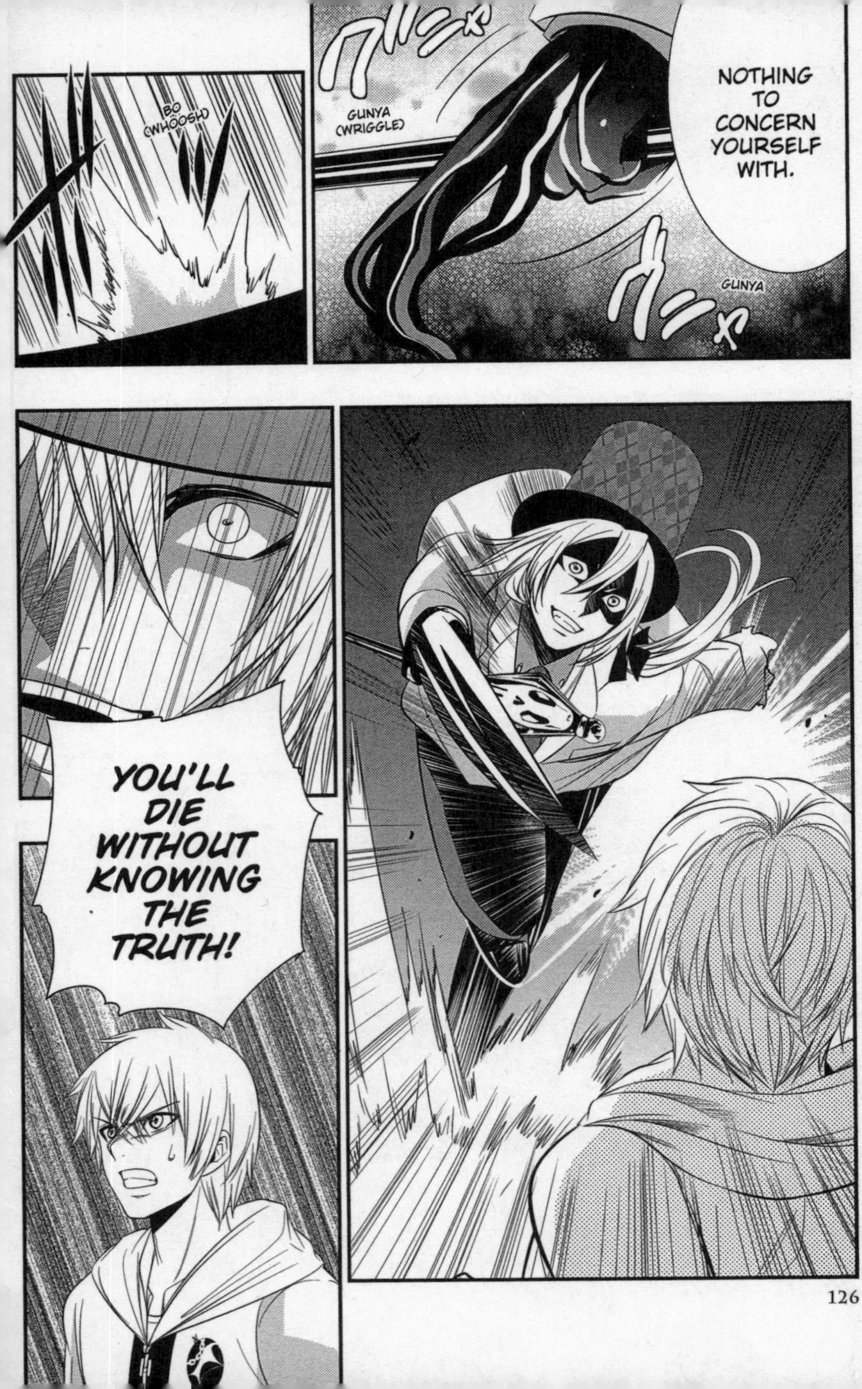
NOTHING TO CONCERN YOURSELF WITH.
GUNYA (WRIGGLE)
GUNYA
BO (WHOOSH)
YOU'LL DIE WITHOUT KNOWING THE TRUTH!

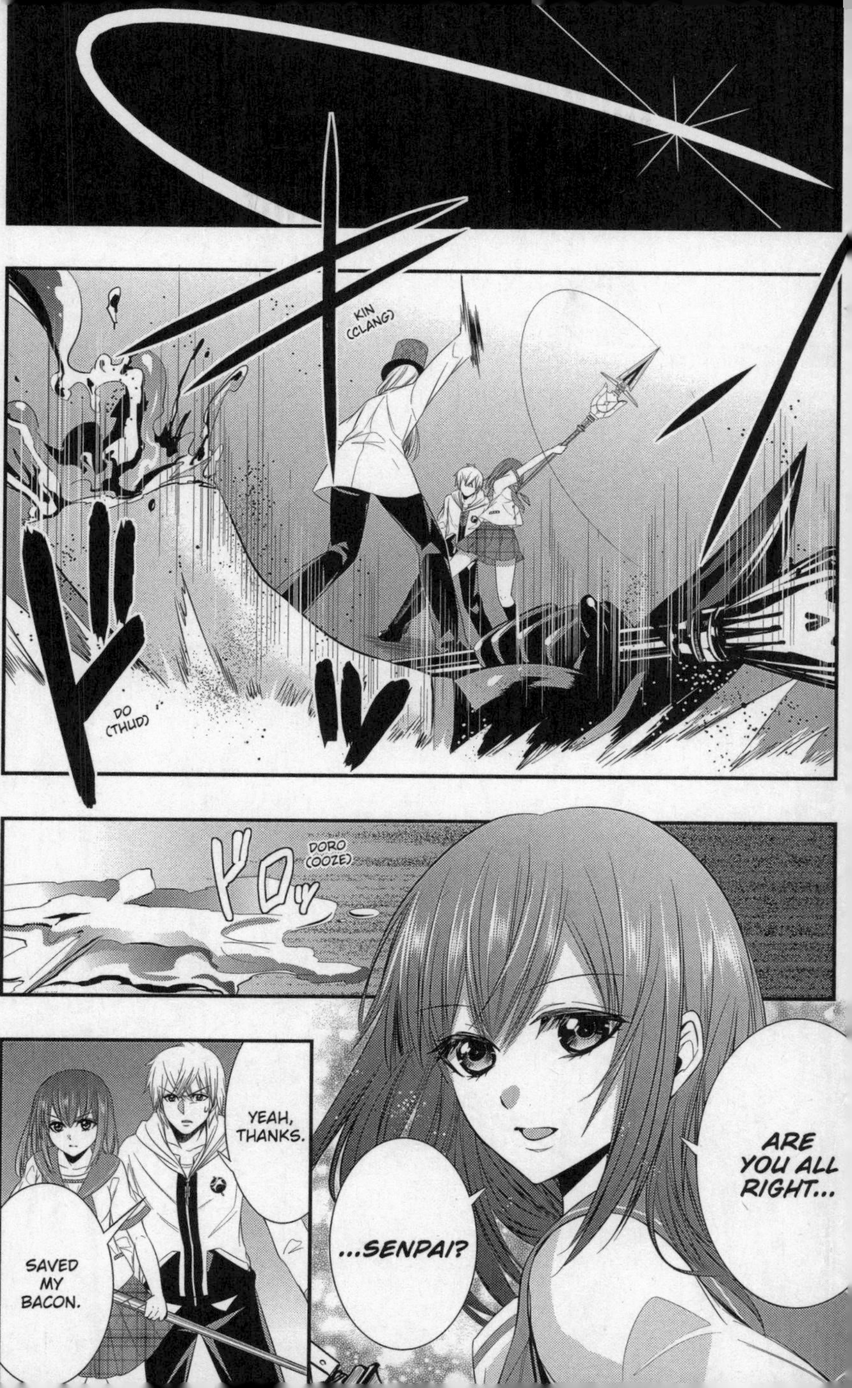
KIN (CLANG)
DO (THUD)
DORO (OOZE)
ARE YOU ALL RIGHT...
...SENPAI?
YEAH, THANKS.
SAVED MY BACON.

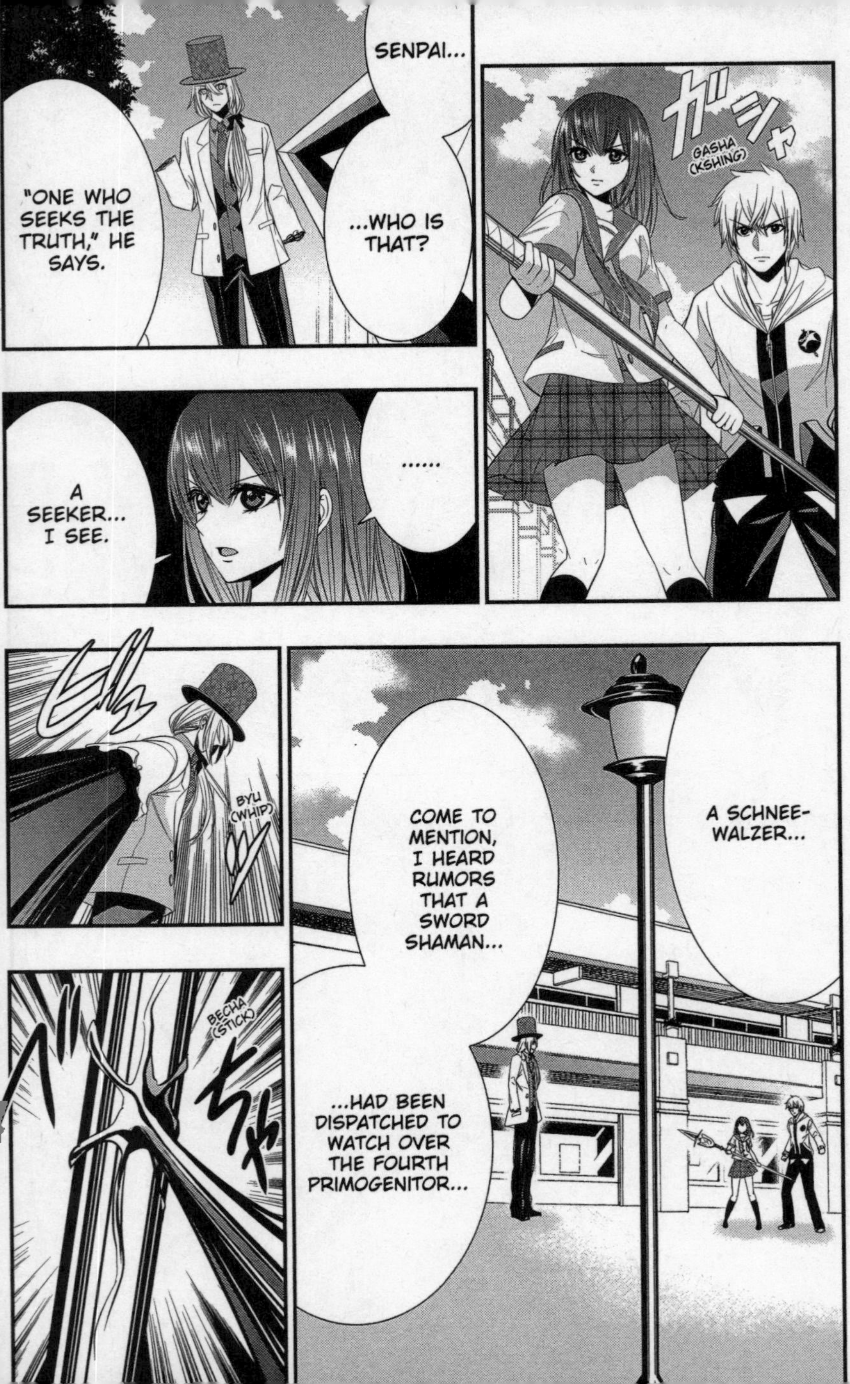
GASHA (KSHING)
SENPAI...
...WHO IS THAT?
"ONE WHO SEEKS THE TRUTH," HE SAYS.
......
A SEEKER... I SEE.
A SCHNEE-WALZER...
COME TO MENTION, I HEARD RUMORS THAT A SWORD SHAMAN...
...HAD BEEN DISPATCHED TO WATCH OVER THE FOURTH PRIMOGENITOR...
BYU (WHIP)
BECHA (STICK)

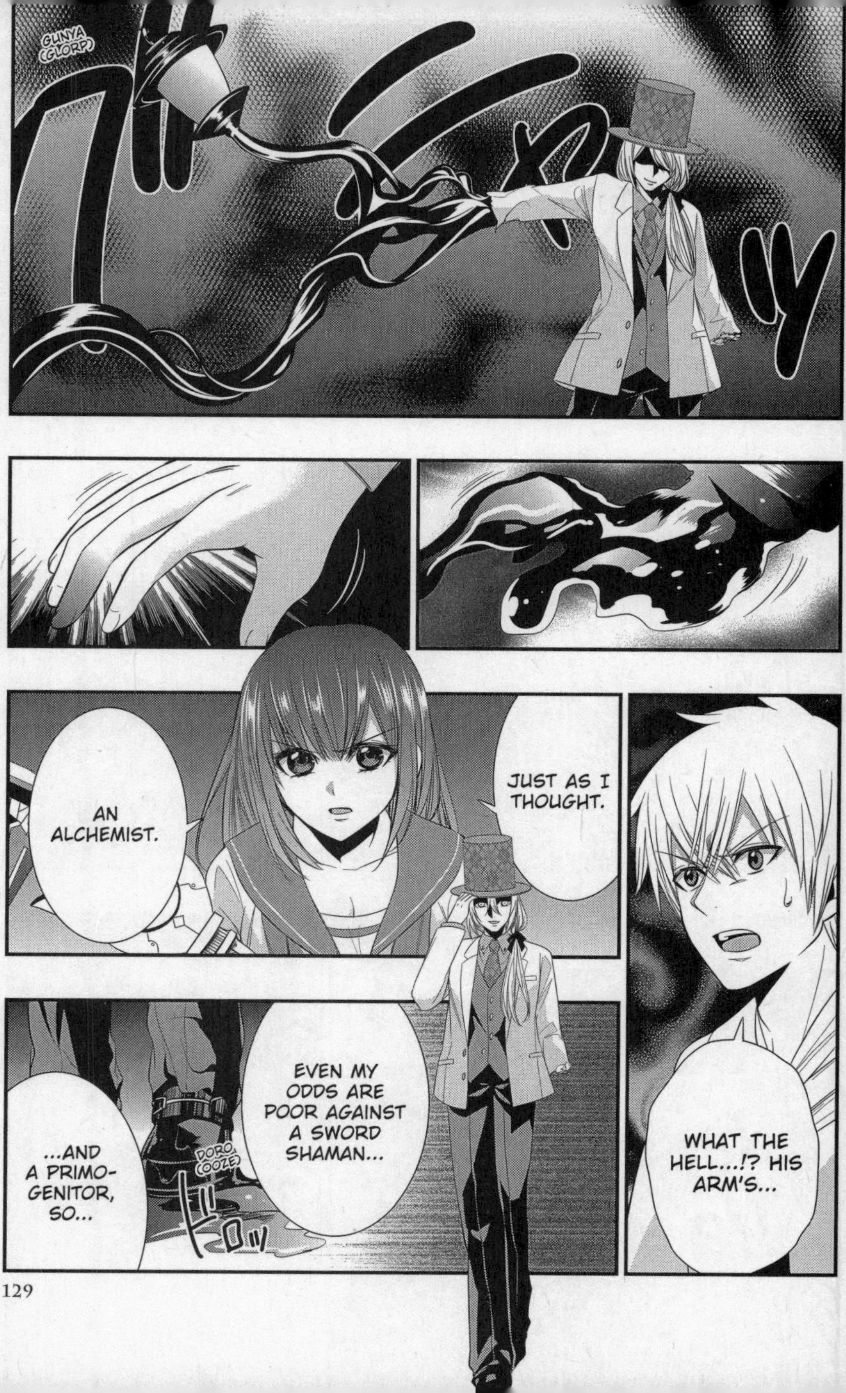
GUNYA (GLORP)
WHAT THE HELL...!? HIS ARM'S...
JUST AS I THOUGHT.
AN ALCHEMIST.
EVEN MY ODDS ARE POOR AGAINST A SWORD SHAMAN...
DORO (OOZE)
...AND A PRIMO-GENITOR, SO...

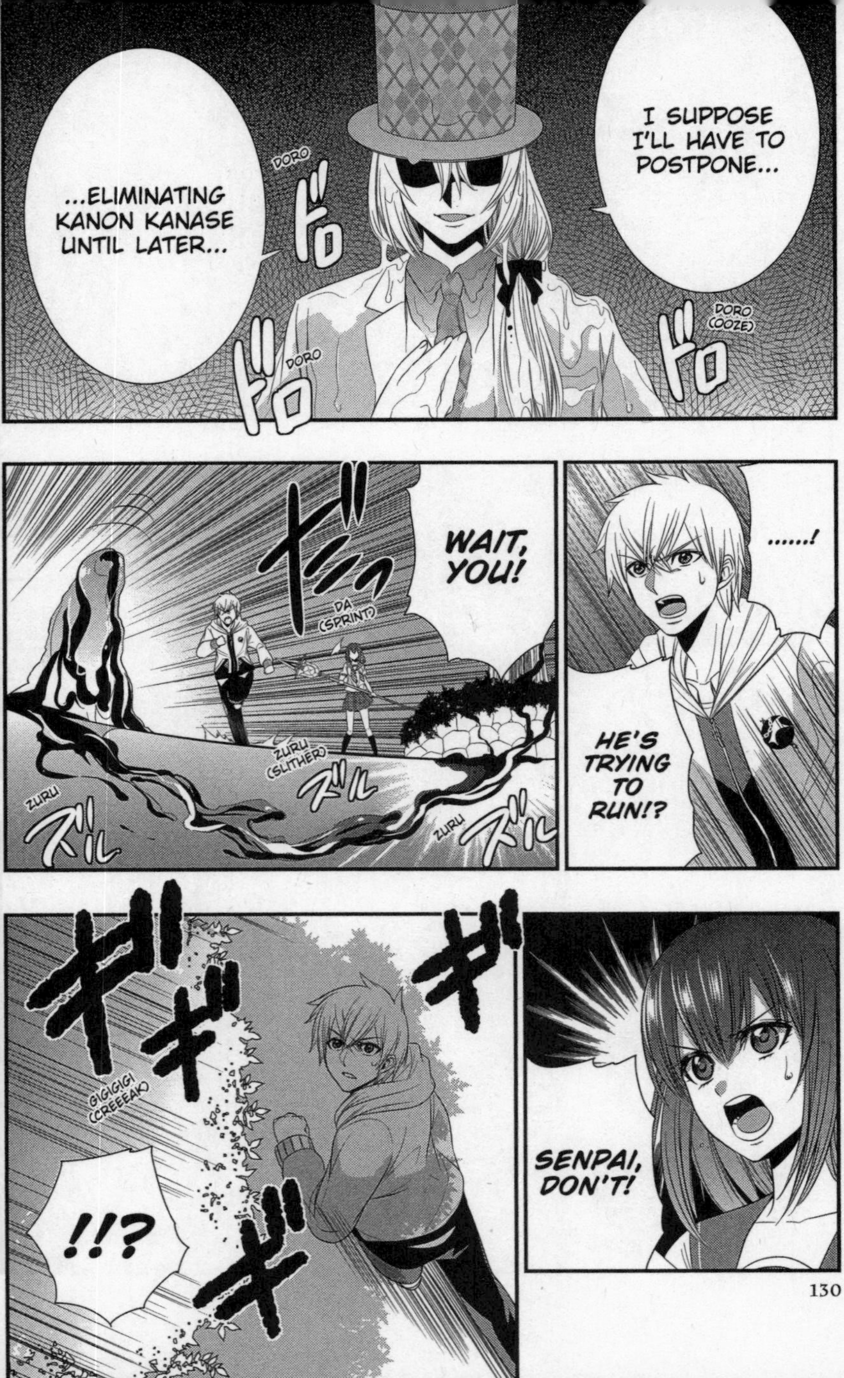
DORO (OOZE)
I SUPPOSE I'LL HAVE TO POSTPONE...
DORO
...ELIMINATING KANON KANASE UNTIL LATER...
DORO
......!
HE'S TRYING TO RUN!?
WAIT, YOU!
DA (SPRINT)
ZURU (SLITHER)
ZURU
ZURU
SENPAI, DON'T!
GIGIGIGI (CREEEAK)
!!?

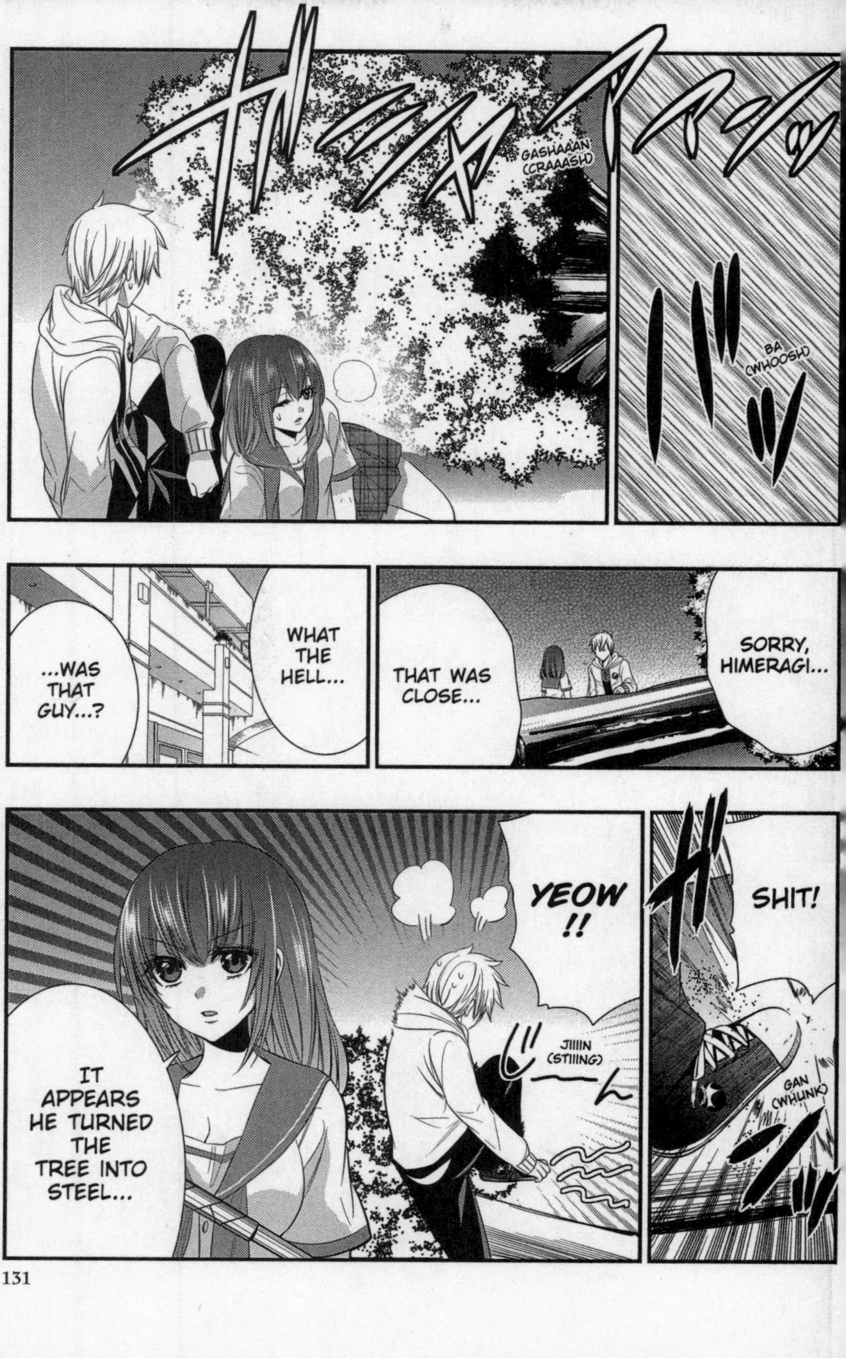
BA (WHOOSH)
GASHAAAN (CRAAASH)
SORRY, HIMERAGI...
THAT WAS CLOSE...
WHAT THE HELL...
...WAS THAT GUY...?
SHIT!
GAN (WHUNK)
YEOW!!
JIIIIN (STIIING)
IT APPEARS HE TURNED THE TREE INTO STEEL...

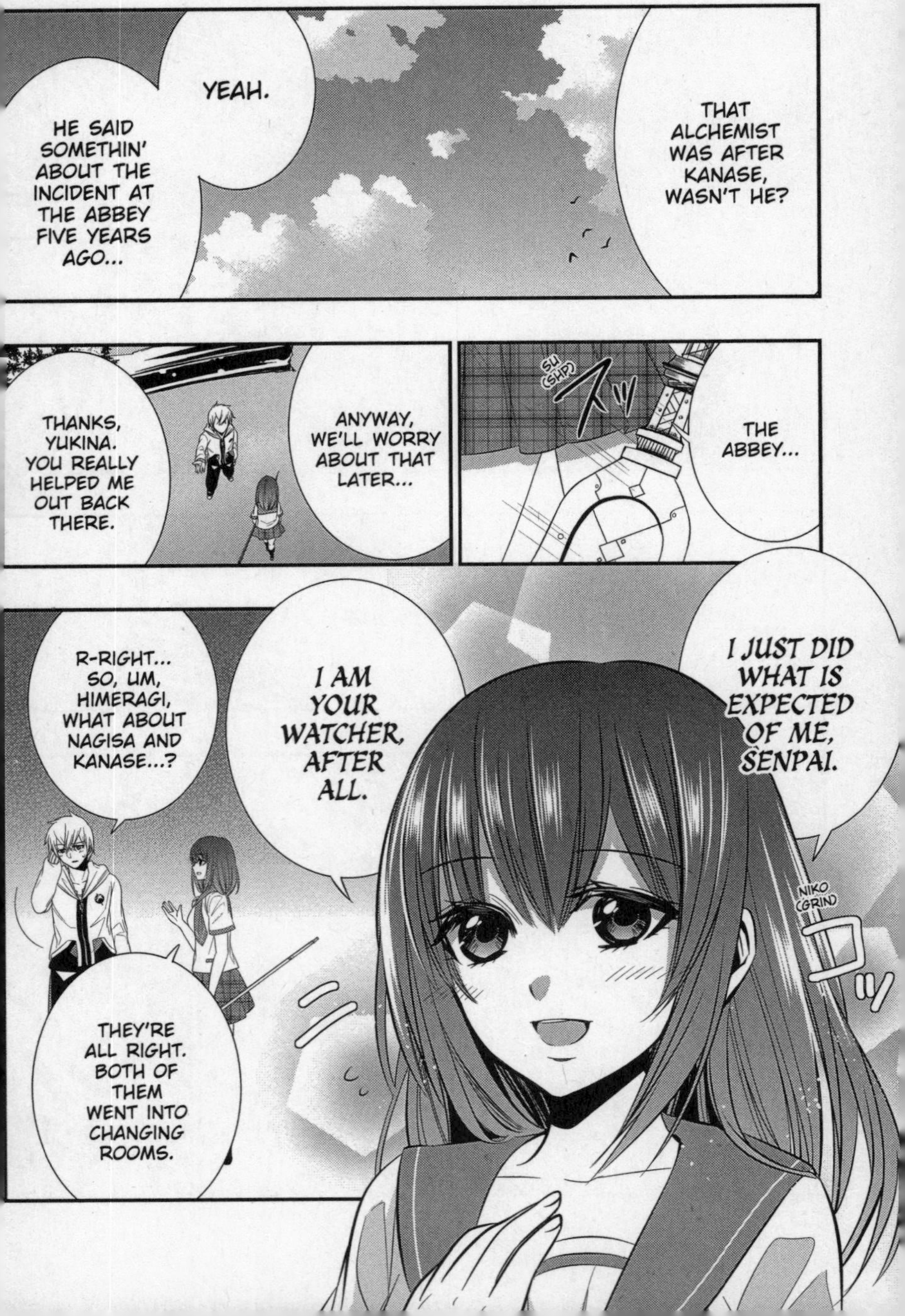
THAT ALCHEMIST WAS AFTER KANASE, WASN'T HE?
YEAH.
HE SAID SOMETHIN' ABOUT THE INCIDENT AT THE ABBEY FIVE YEARS AGO...
SU (SHP)
THE ABBEY...
ANYWAY, WE'LL WORRY ABOUT THAT LATER...
THANKS, YUKINA. YOU REALLY HELPED ME OUT BACK THERE.
I JUST DID WHAT IS EXPECTED OF ME, SENPAI.
I AM YOUR WATCHER, AFTER ALL.
NIKO (GRIN)
R-RIGHT... SO, UM, HIMERAGI, WHAT ABOUT NAGISA AND KANASE...?
THEY'RE ALL RIGHT. BOTH OF THEM WENT INTO CHANGING ROOMS.

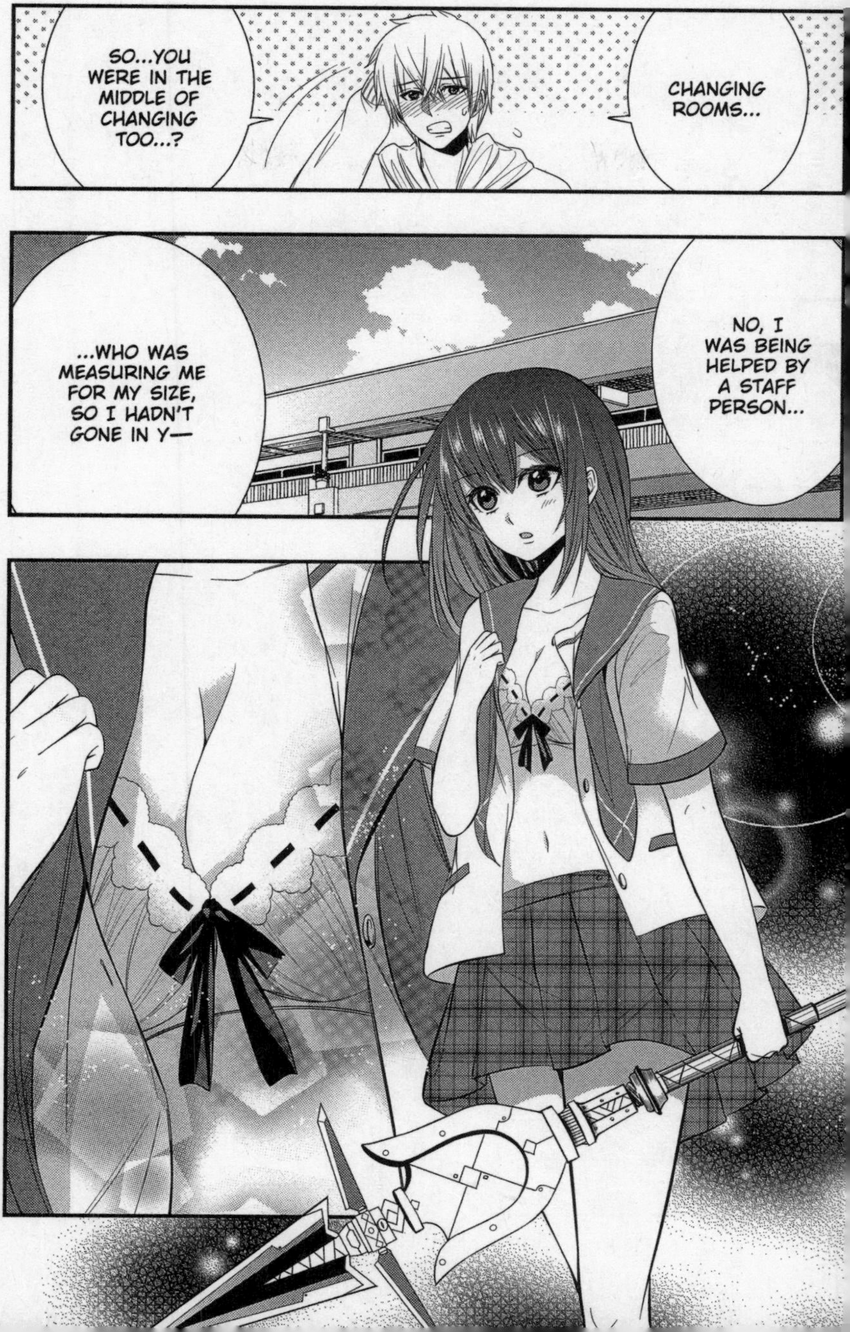
CHANGING ROOMS...
SO...YOU WERE IN THE MIDDLE OF CHANGING TOO...?
NO, I WAS BEING HELPED BY A STAFF PERSON...
...WHO WAS MEASURING ME FOR MY SIZE, SO I HADN'T GONE IN Y—

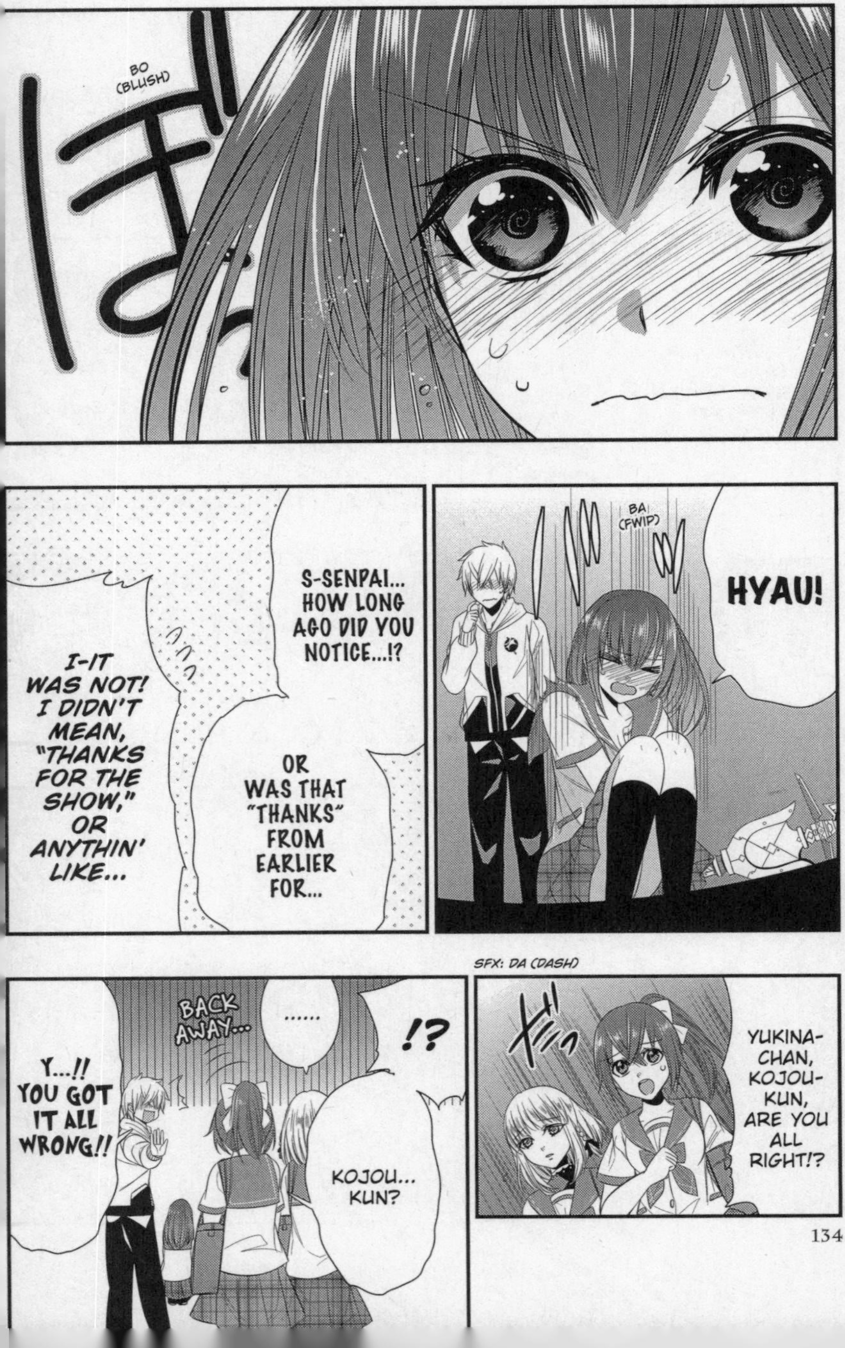
BO (BLUSH)
BA (FWIP)
HYAU!
S-SENPAI... HOW LONG AGO DID YOU NOTICE...!?
OR WAS THAT "THANKS" FROM EARLIER FOR...
I-IT WAS NOT! I DIDN'T MEAN, "THANKS FOR THE SHOW," OR ANYTHIN' LIKE...
SFX: DA (DASH)
YUKINA-CHAN, KOJOU-KUN, ARE YOU ALL RIGHT!?
!?
......
BACK AWAY...
KOJOU... KUN?
Y...!! YOU GOT IT ALL WRONG!!

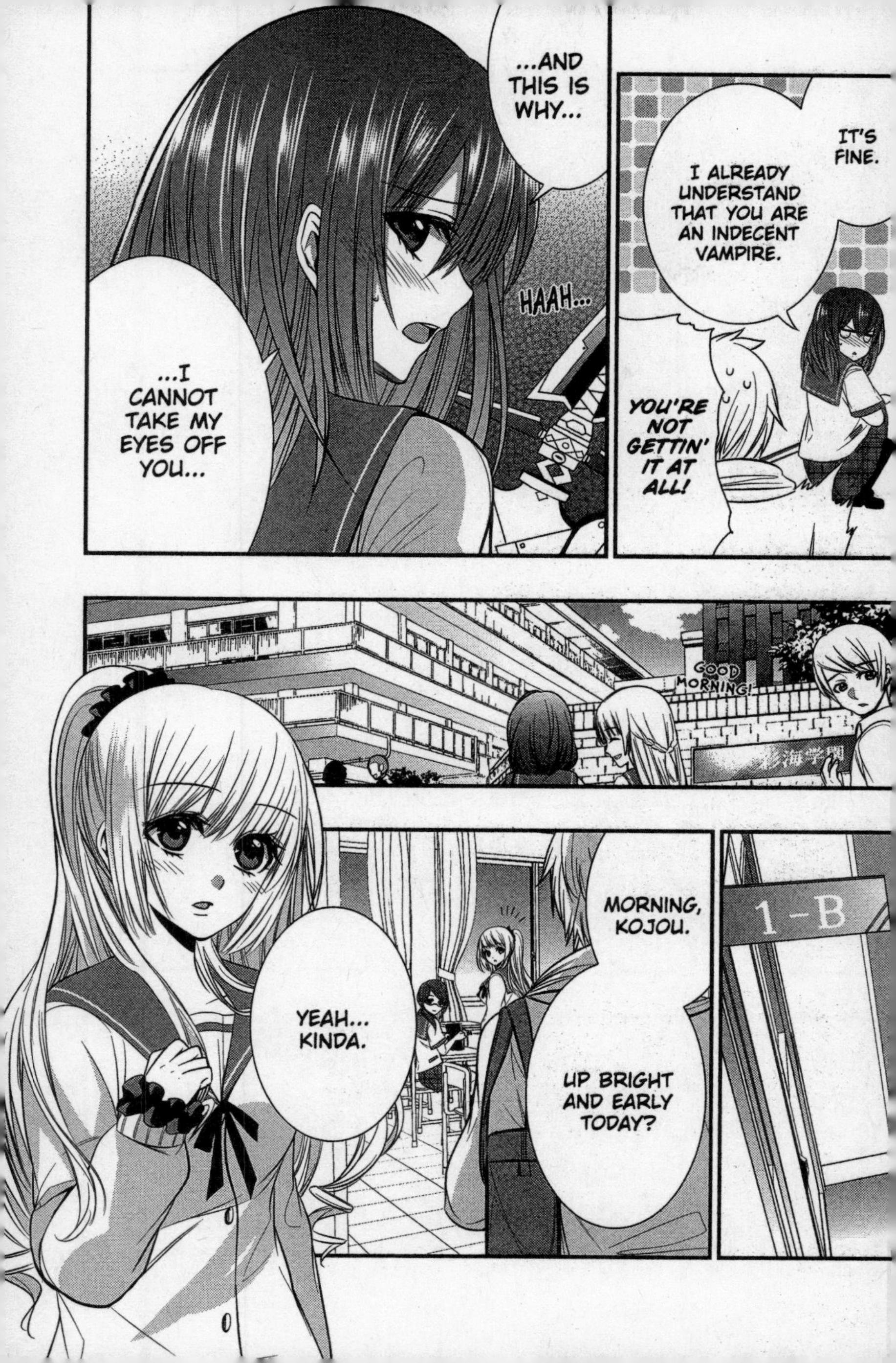
IT'S FINE.
I ALREADY UNDERSTAND THAT YOU ARE AN INDECENT VAMPIRE.
YOU'RE NOT GETTIN' IT AT ALL!
...AND THIS IS WHY...
HAAH...
...I CANNOT TAKE MY EYES OFF YOU...
GOOD MORNING!
彩海学園
1-B
MORNING, KOJOU.
UP BRIGHT AND EARLY TODAY?
YEAH... KINDA.

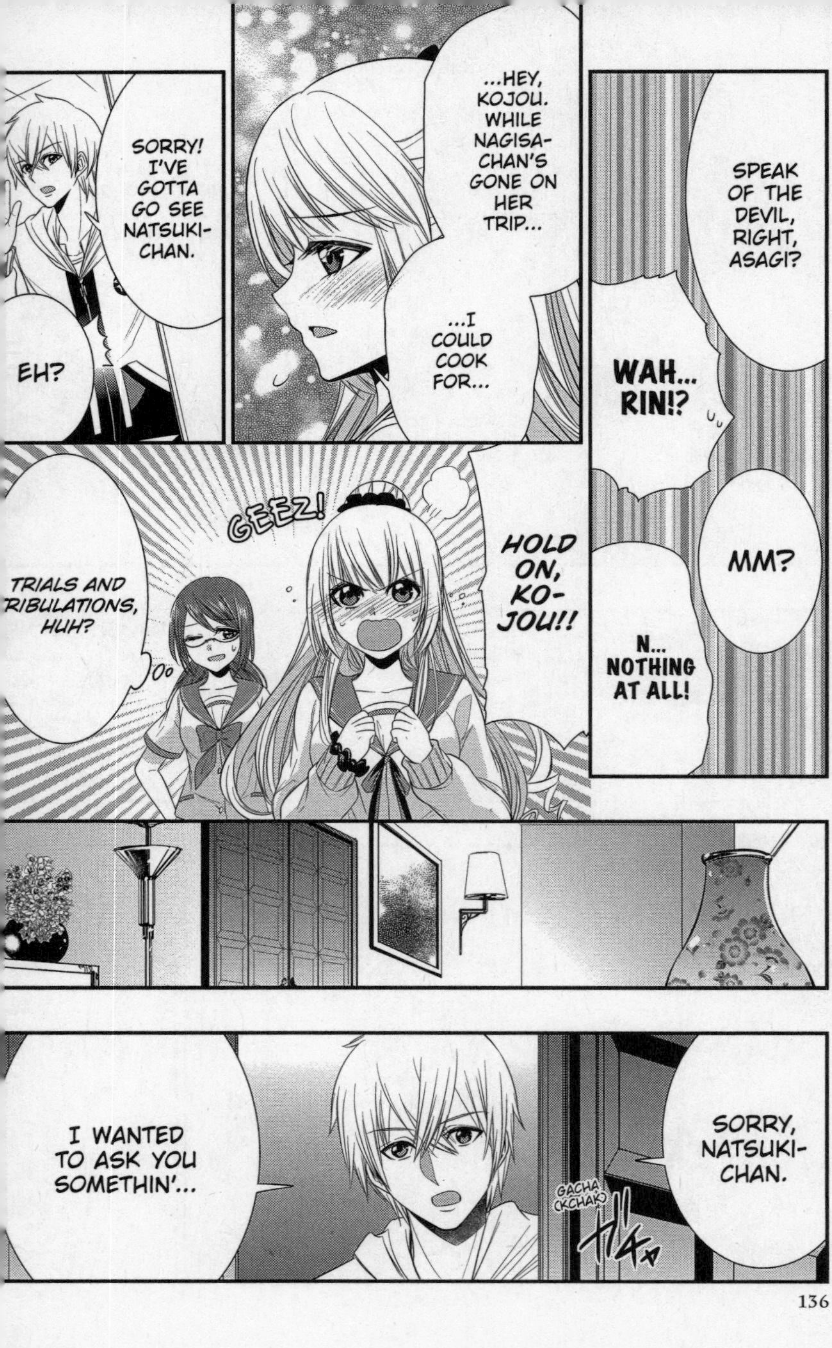
SPEAK OF THE DEVIL, RIGHT, ASAGI?
WAH... RIN!?
...HEY, KOJOU. WHILE NAGISA-CHAN'S GONE ON HER TRIP...
...I COULD COOK FOR...
SORRY! I'VE GOTTA GO SEE NATSUKI-CHAN.
EH?
MM?
N... NOTHING AT ALL!
HOLD ON, KO-JOU!!
GEEZ!
TRIALS AND TRIBULATIONS, HUH?
SORRY, NATSUKI-CHAN.
GACHA (KCHAK)
I WANTED TO ASK YOU SOMETHIN'...

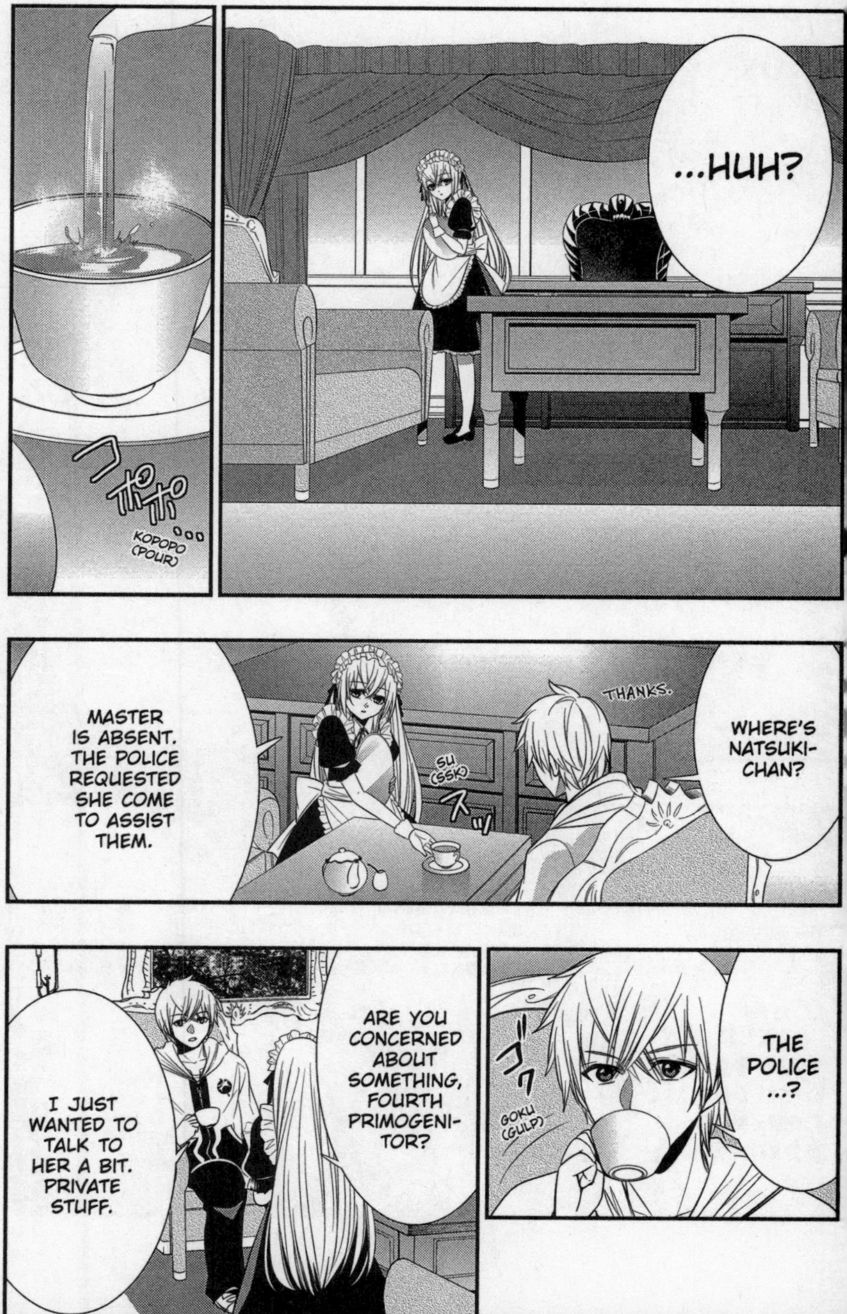
...HUH?
KOPOPO (POUR)
WHERE'S NATSUKI-CHAN?
THANKS.
SU (SSK)
MASTER IS ABSENT. THE POLICE REQUESTED SHE COME TO ASSIST THEM.
THE POLICE ...?
GOKU (GULP)
ARE YOU CONCERNED ABOUT SOMETHING, FOURTH PRIMOGENITOR?
I JUST WANTED TO TALK TO HER A BIT. PRIVATE STUFF.

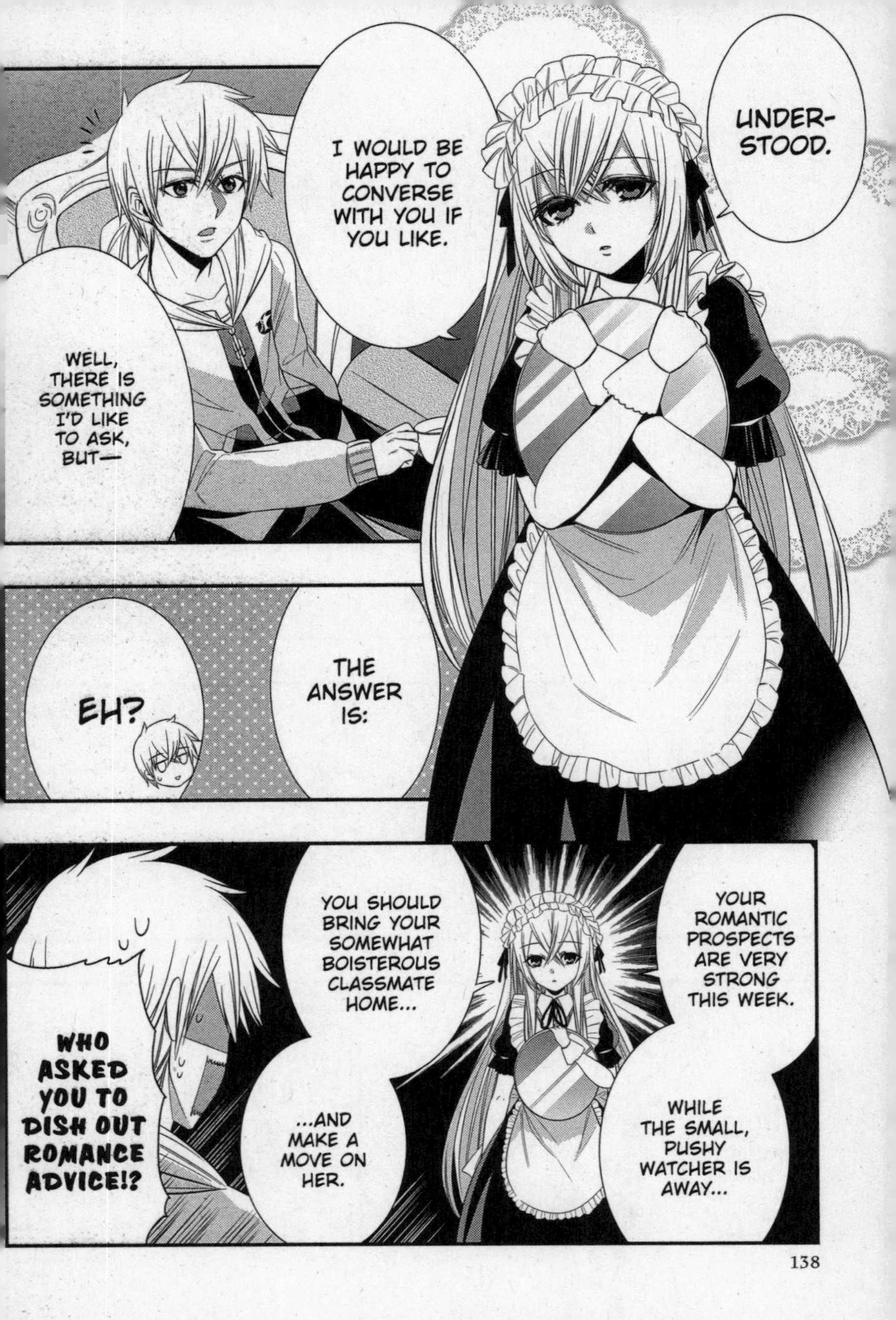
UNDER-STOOD.
I WOULD BE HAPPY TO CONVERSE WITH YOU IF YOU LIKE.
WELL, THERE IS SOMETHING I'D LIKE TO ASK, BUT—
THE ANSWER IS:
EH?
YOUR ROMANTIC PROSPECTS ARE VERY STRONG THIS WEEK.
WHILE THE SMALL, PUSHY WATCHER IS AWAY...
YOU SHOULD BRING YOUR SOMEWHAT BOISTEROUS CLASSMATE HOME...
...AND MAKE A MOVE ON HER.
WHO ASKED YOU TO DISH OUT ROMANCE ADVICE!?

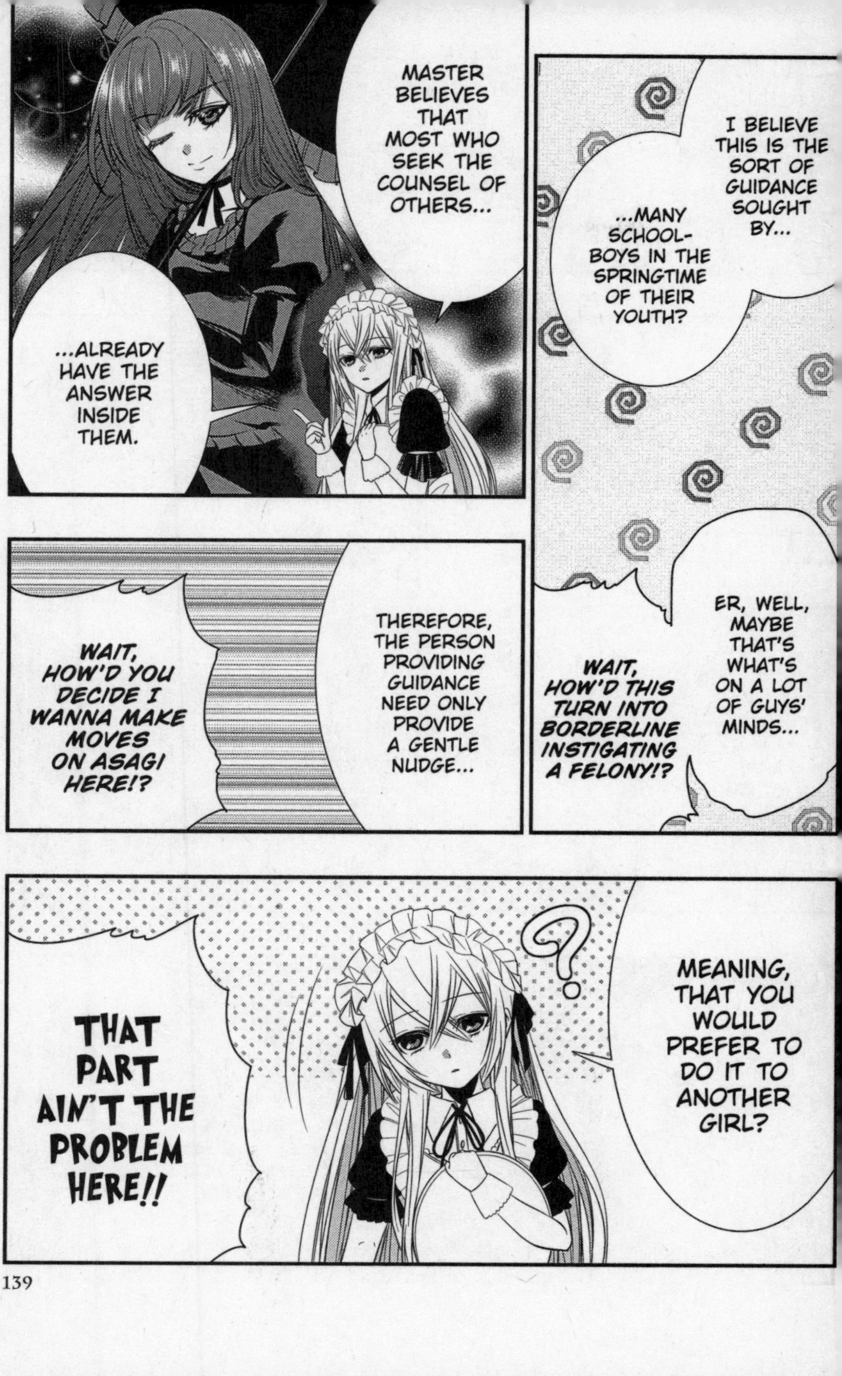
I BELIEVE THIS IS THE SORT OF GUIDANCE SOUGHT BY...
...MANY SCHOOL-BOYS IN THE SPRINGTIME OF THEIR YOUTH?
ER, WELL, MAYBE THAT'S WHAT'S ON A LOT OF GUYS' MINDS...
WAIT, HOW'D THIS TURN INTO BORDERLINE INSTIGATING A FELONY!?
MASTER BELIEVES THAT MOST WHO SEEK THE COUNSEL OF OTHERS...
...ALREADY HAVE THE ANSWER INSIDE THEM.
THEREFORE, THE PERSON PROVIDING GUIDANCE NEED ONLY PROVIDE A GENTLE NUDGE...
WAIT, HOW'D YOU DECIDE I WANNA MAKE MOVES ON ASAGI HERE!?
MEANING, THAT YOU WOULD PREFER TO DO IT TO ANOTHER GIRL?
THAT PART AIN'T THE PROBLEM HERE!!

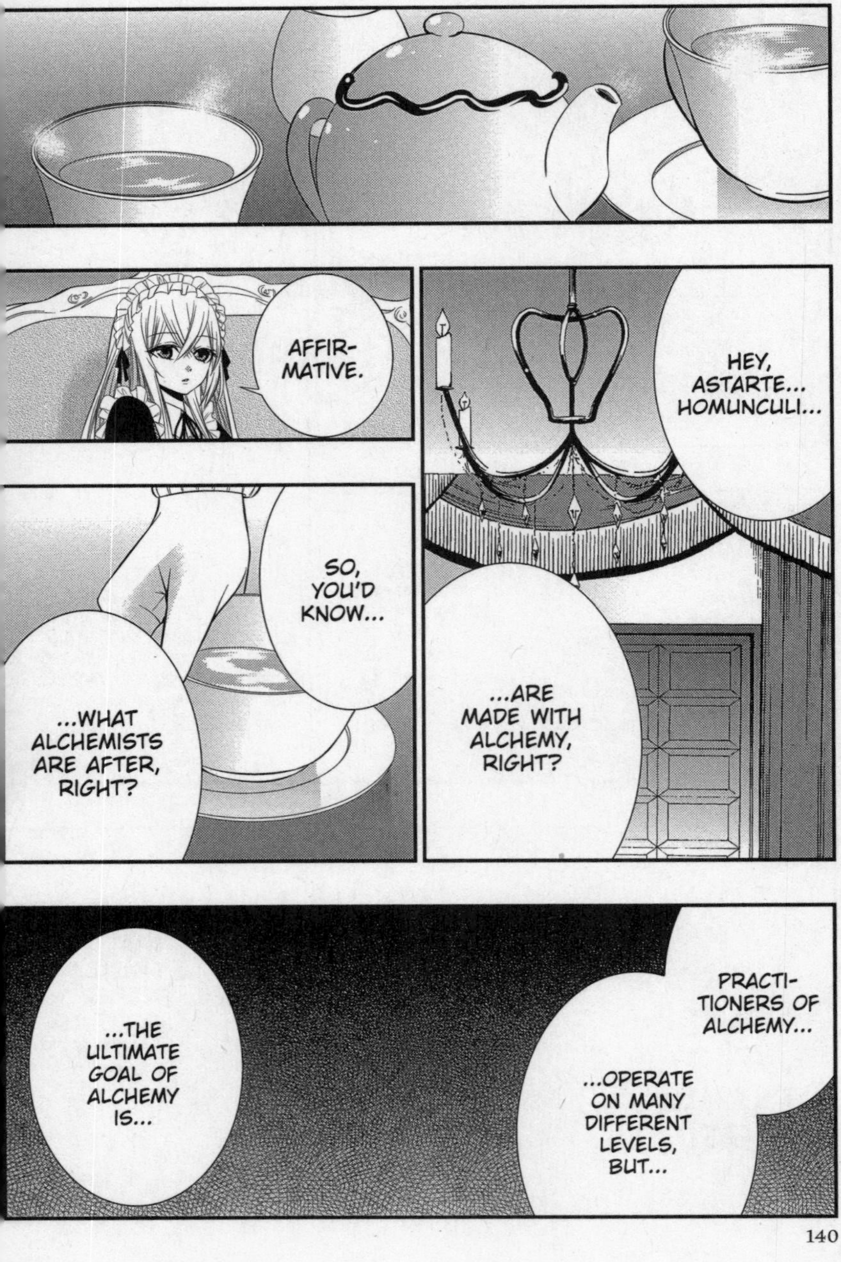
HEY, ASTARTE... HOMUNCULI...
...ARE MADE WITH ALCHEMY, RIGHT?
AFFIR-MATIVE.
SO, YOU'D KNOW...
...WHAT ALCHEMISTS ARE AFTER, RIGHT?
PRACTI-TIONERS OF ALCHEMY...
...OPERATE ON MANY DIFFERENT LEVELS, BUT...
...THE ULTIMATE GOAL OF ALCHEMY IS...

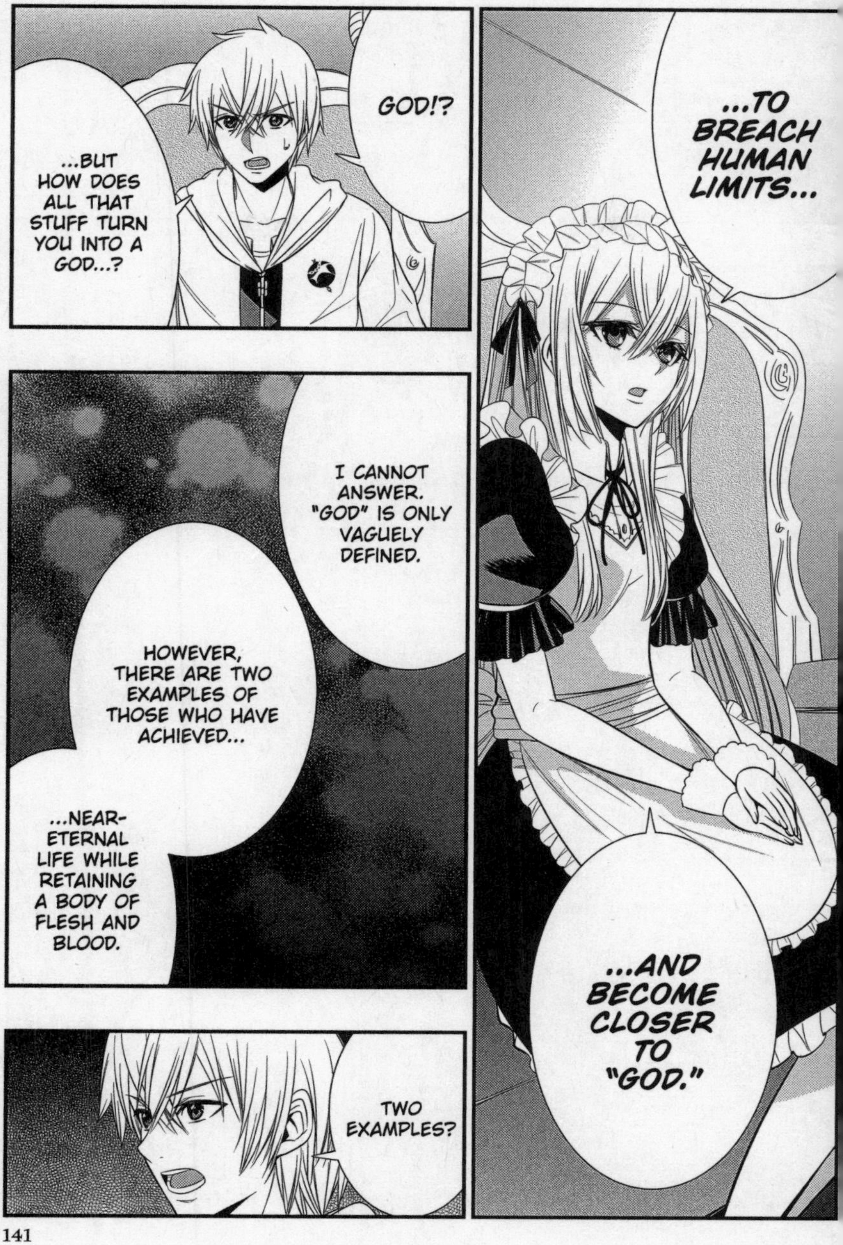
...TO BREACH HUMAN LIMITS...
...AND BECOME CLOSER TO "GOD."
GOD!?
...BUT HOW DOES ALL THAT STUFF TURN YOU INTO A GOD...?
I CANNOT ANSWER. "GOD" IS ONLY VAGUELY DEFINED.
HOWEVER, THERE ARE TWO EXAMPLES OF THOSE WHO HAVE ACHIEVED...
...NEAR-ETERNAL LIFE WHILE RETAINING A BODY OF FLESH AND BLOOD.
TWO EXAMPLES?

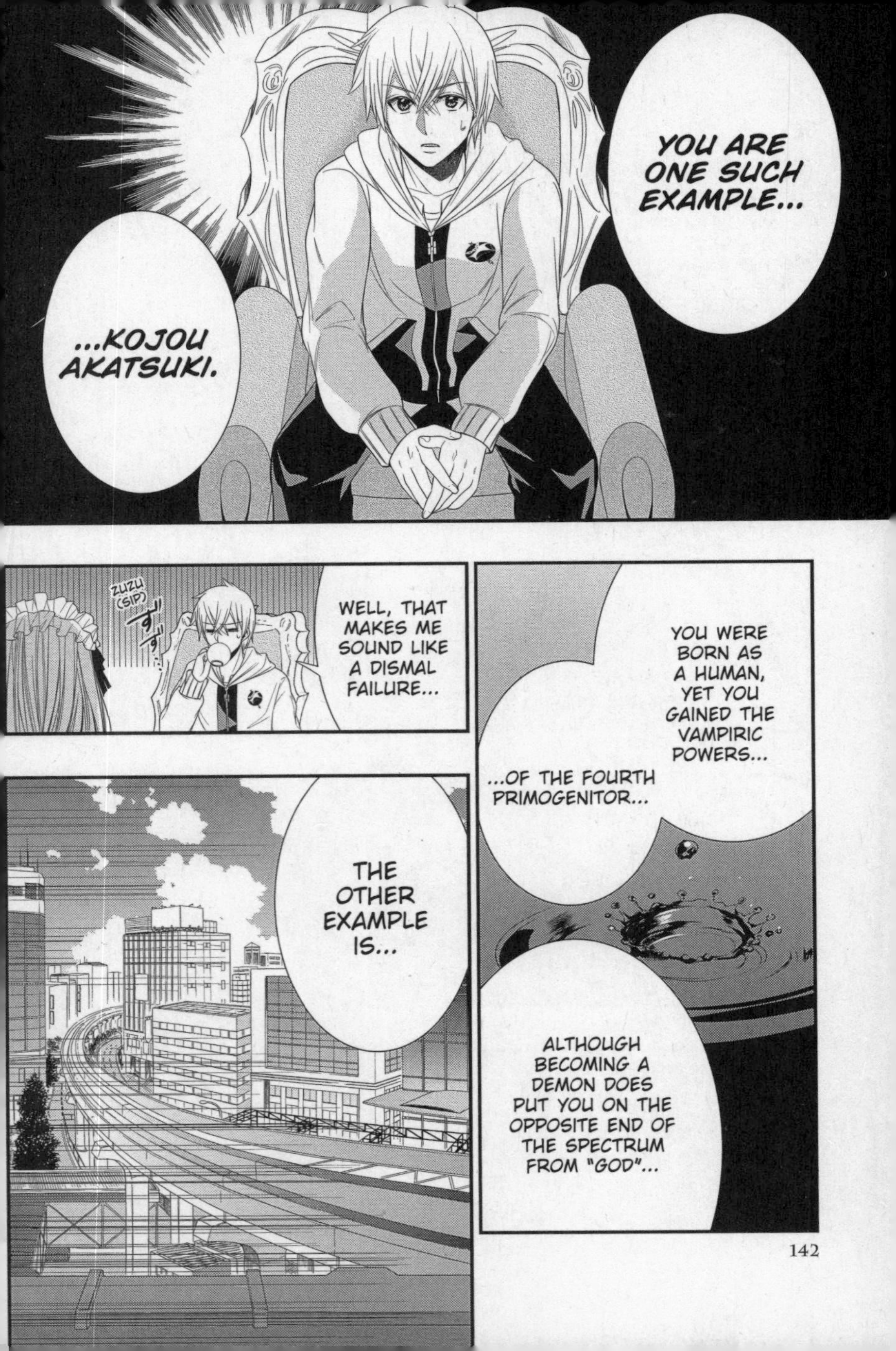
YOU ARE ONE SUCH EXAMPLE...
...KOJOU AKATSUKI.
YOU WERE BORN AS A HUMAN, YET YOU GAINED THE VAMPIRIC POWERS...
...OF THE FOURTH PRIMOGENITOR...
ALTHOUGH BECOMING A DEMON DOES PUT YOU ON THE OPPOSITE END OF THE SPECTRUM FROM "GOD"...
ZUZU (SIP)
WELL, THAT MAKES ME SOUND LIKE A DISMAL FAILURE...
THE OTHER EXAMPLE IS...

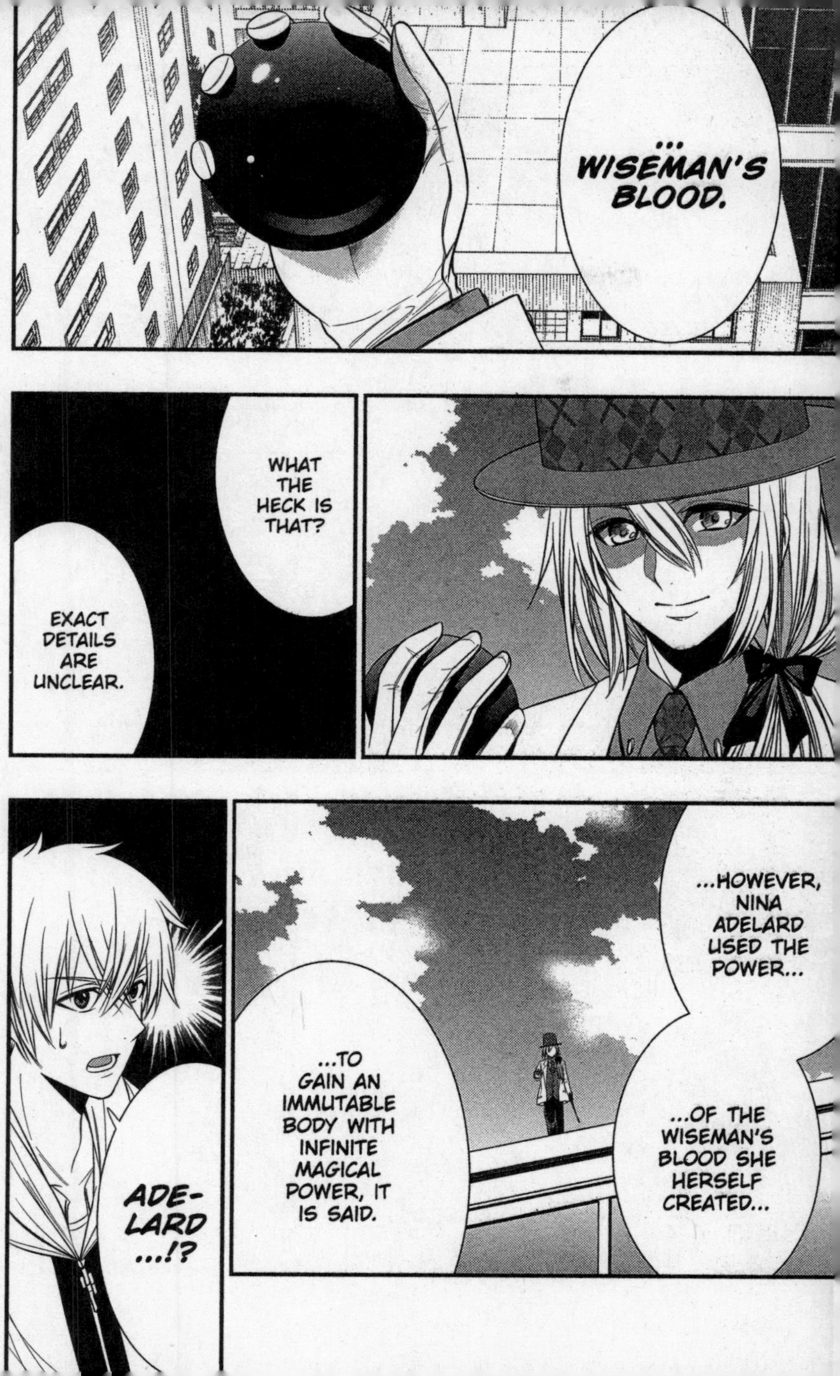
...WISEMAN'S BLOOD.
WHAT THE HECK IS THAT?
EXACT DETAILS ARE UNCLEAR.
...HOWEVER, NINA ADELARD USED THE POWER...
...OF THE WISEMAN'S BLOOD SHE HERSELF CREATED...
...TO GAIN AN IMMUTABLE BODY WITH INFINITE MAGICAL POWER, IT IS SAID.
ADE-LARD...!?

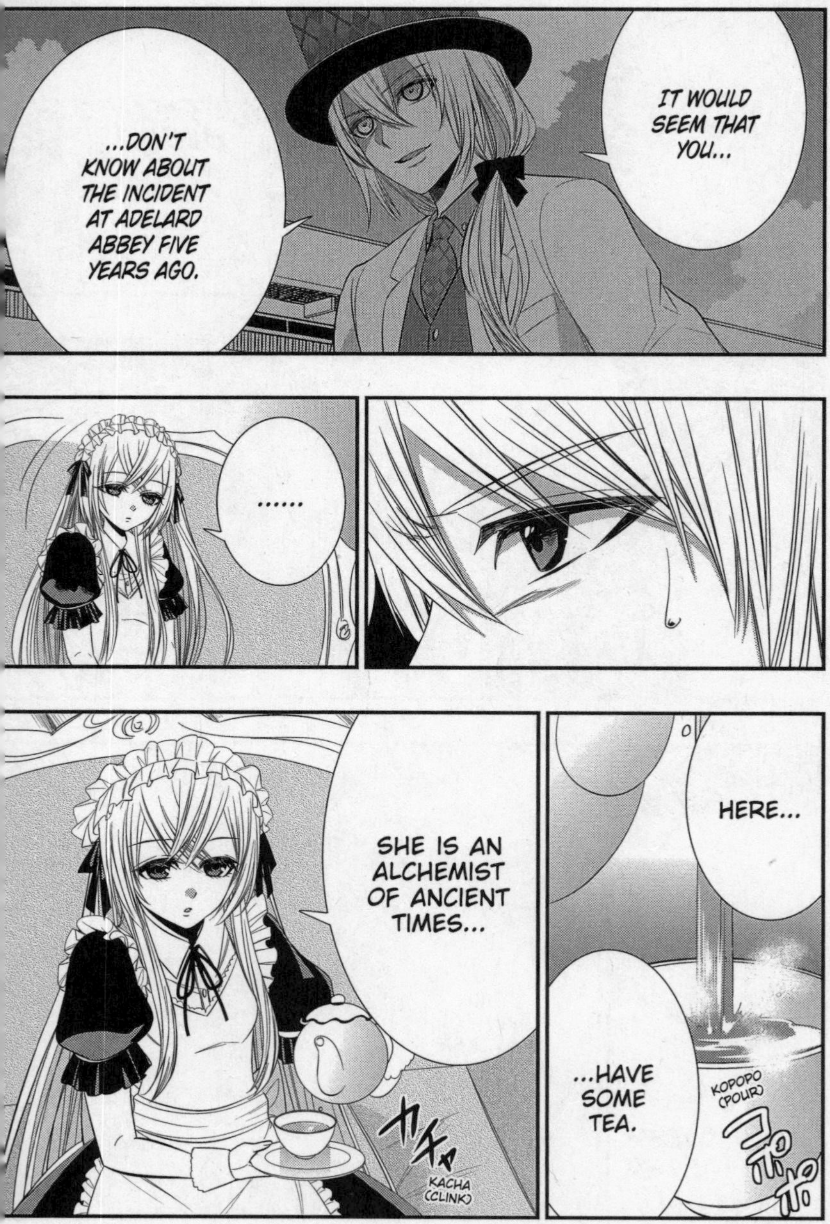
IT WOULD SEEM THAT YOU...
...DON'T KNOW ABOUT THE INCIDENT AT ADELARD ABBEY FIVE YEARS AGO.
......
HERE...
...HAVE SOME TEA.
KOPOPO (POUR)
コポポ
SHE IS AN ALCHEMIST OF ANCIENT TIMES...
カチャ
KACHA (CLINK)

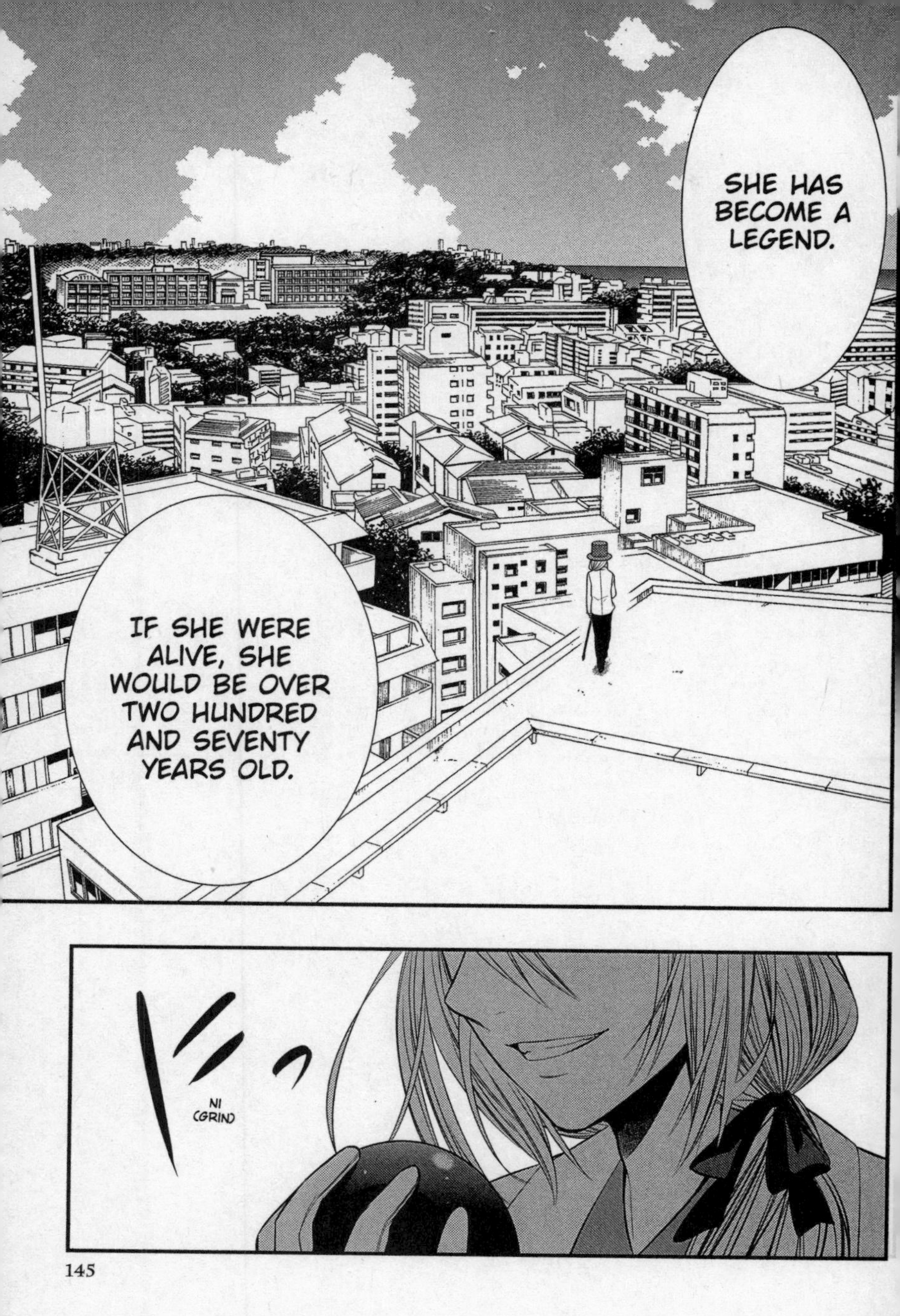
SHE HAS BECOME A LEGEND.
IF SHE WERE ALIVE, SHE WOULD BE OVER TWO HUNDRED AND SEVENTY YEARS OLD.
NI (GRIN)

STRIKE THE BLOOD

DEFINITION

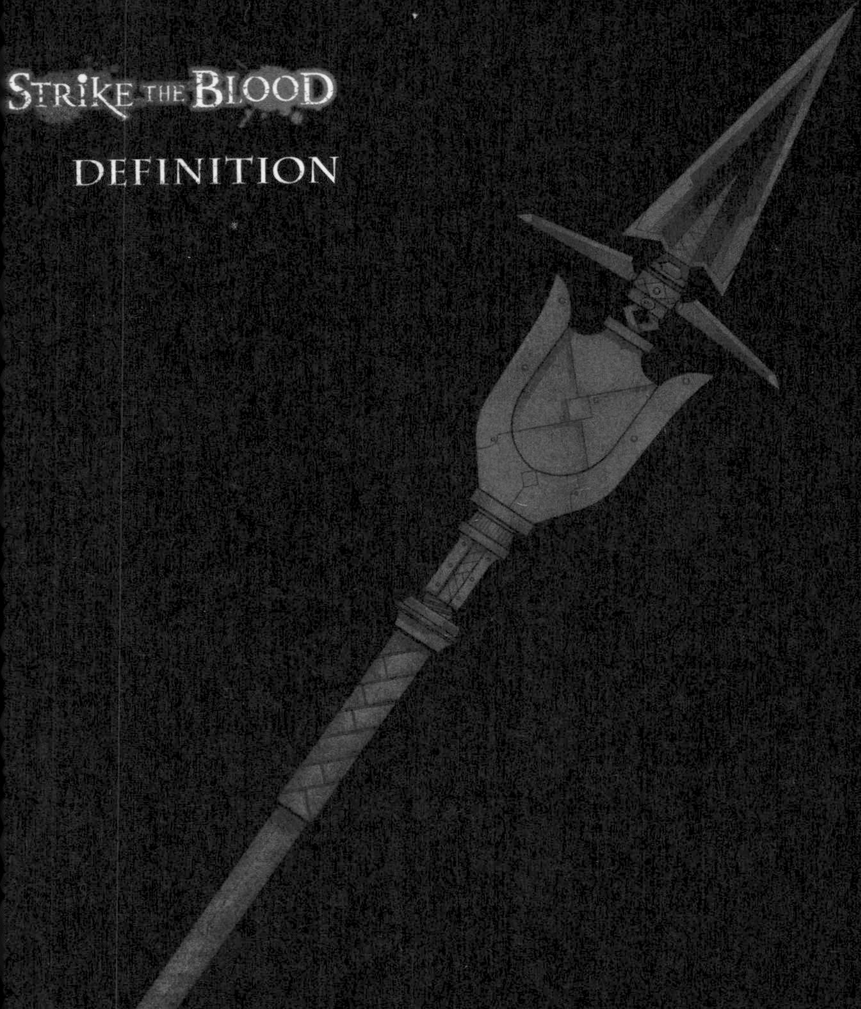

<< NINA ADELARD >>

The Great Alchemist of yore who succeeded in creating the Wiseman's Blood. Possessor of an immutable body and inexhaustible magical power, if still alive she would be over 270 years old. Also, the founder of the abbey where Kanon Kanase was raised.

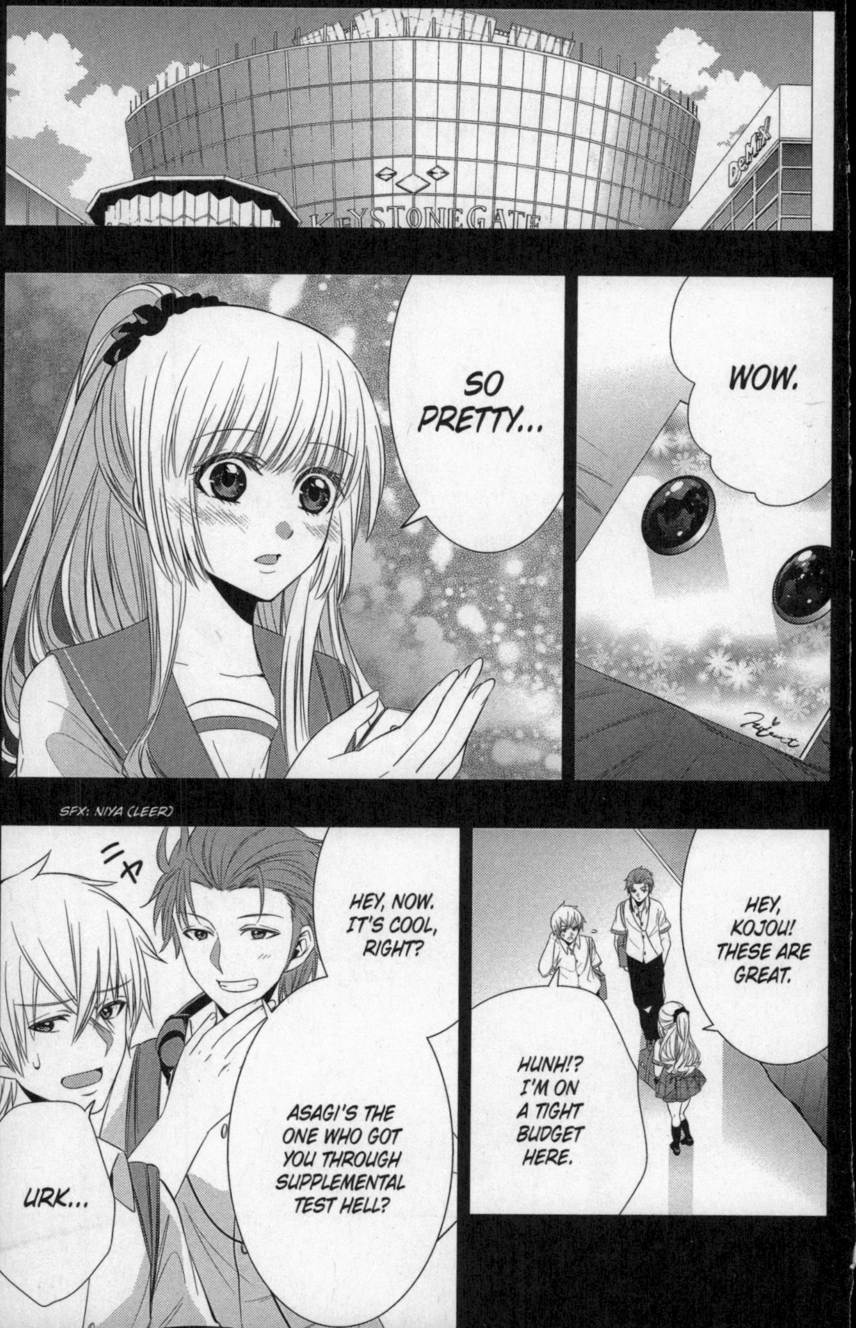
KEYSTONEGATE
DeMiX
WOW.
SO PRETTY...
SFX: NIYA (LEER)
HEY, KOJOU! THESE ARE GREAT.
HUNH!? I'M ON A TIGHT BUDGET HERE.
ニヤ
HEY, NOW. IT'S COOL, RIGHT?
ASAGI'S THE ONE WHO GOT YOU THROUGH SUPPLEMENTAL TEST HELL?
URK...

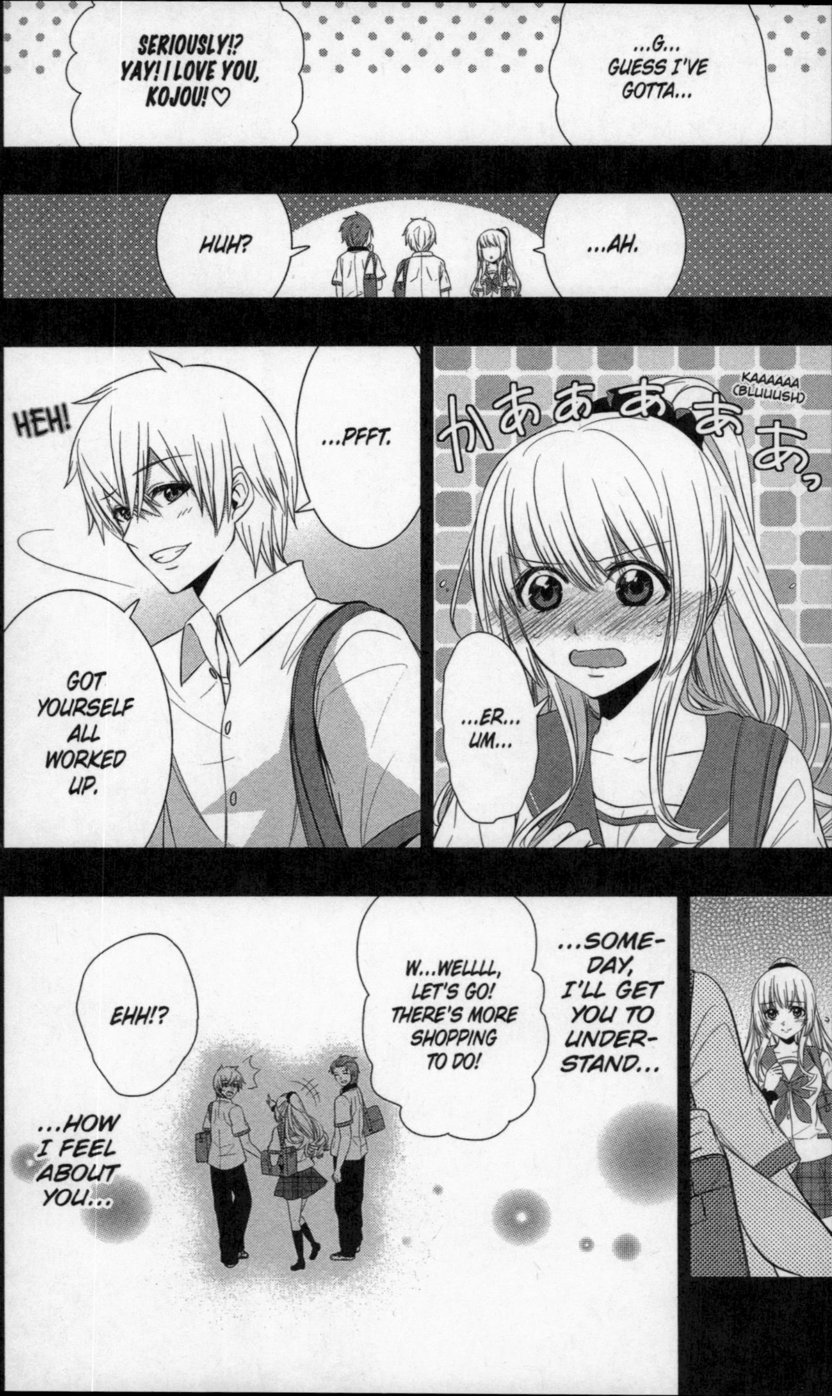
...G... GUESS I'VE GOTTA...
SERIOUSLY!? YAY! I LOVE YOU, KOJOU! ♡
...AH.
HUH?
かあああああっ
KAAAAAA (BLUUUSH)
...ER... UM...
...PFFT.
HEH!
GOT YOURSELF ALL WORKED UP.
...SOME-DAY, I'LL GET YOU TO UNDER-STAND...
W...WELLLL, LET'S GO! THERE'S MORE SHOPPING TO DO!
EHH!?
...HOW I FEEL ABOUT YOU...

Chapter 42: The Lion King Agency

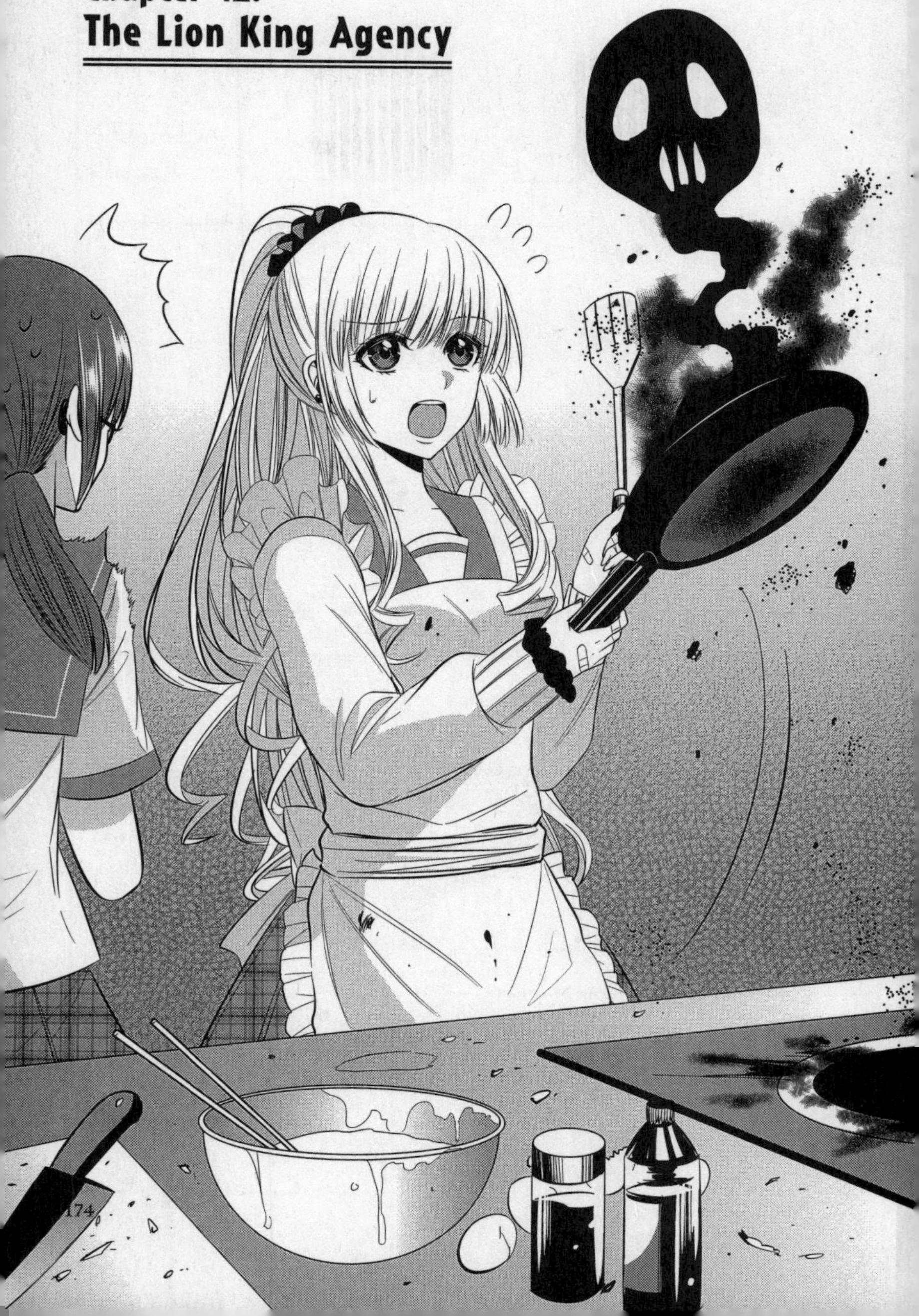

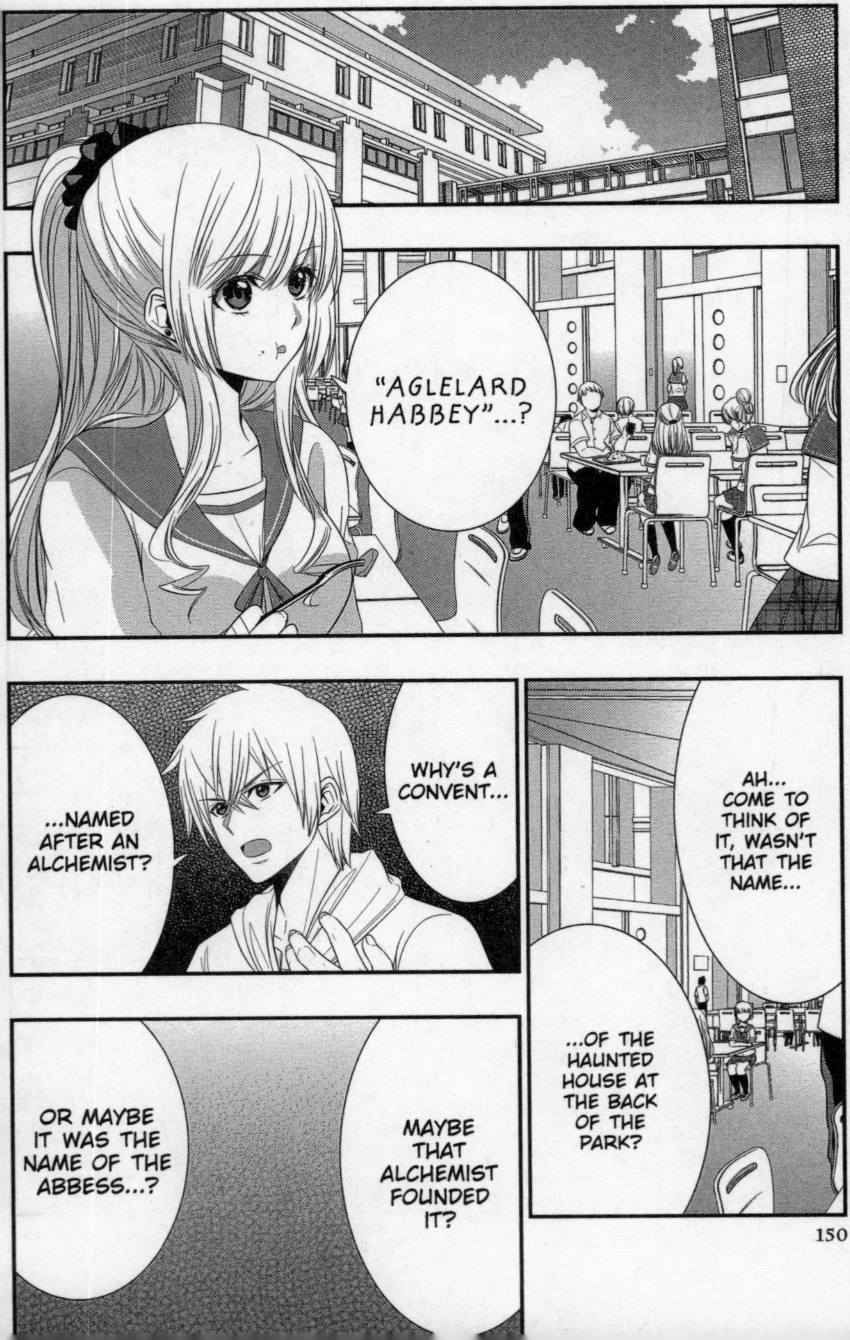
"AGLELARD HABBEY"...?
AH... COME TO THINK OF IT, WASN'T THAT THE NAME...
...OF THE HAUNTED HOUSE AT THE BACK OF THE PARK?
WHY'S A CONVENT...
...NAMED AFTER AN ALCHEMIST?
MAYBE THAT ALCHEMIST FOUNDED IT?
OR MAYBE IT WAS THE NAME OF THE ABBESS...?

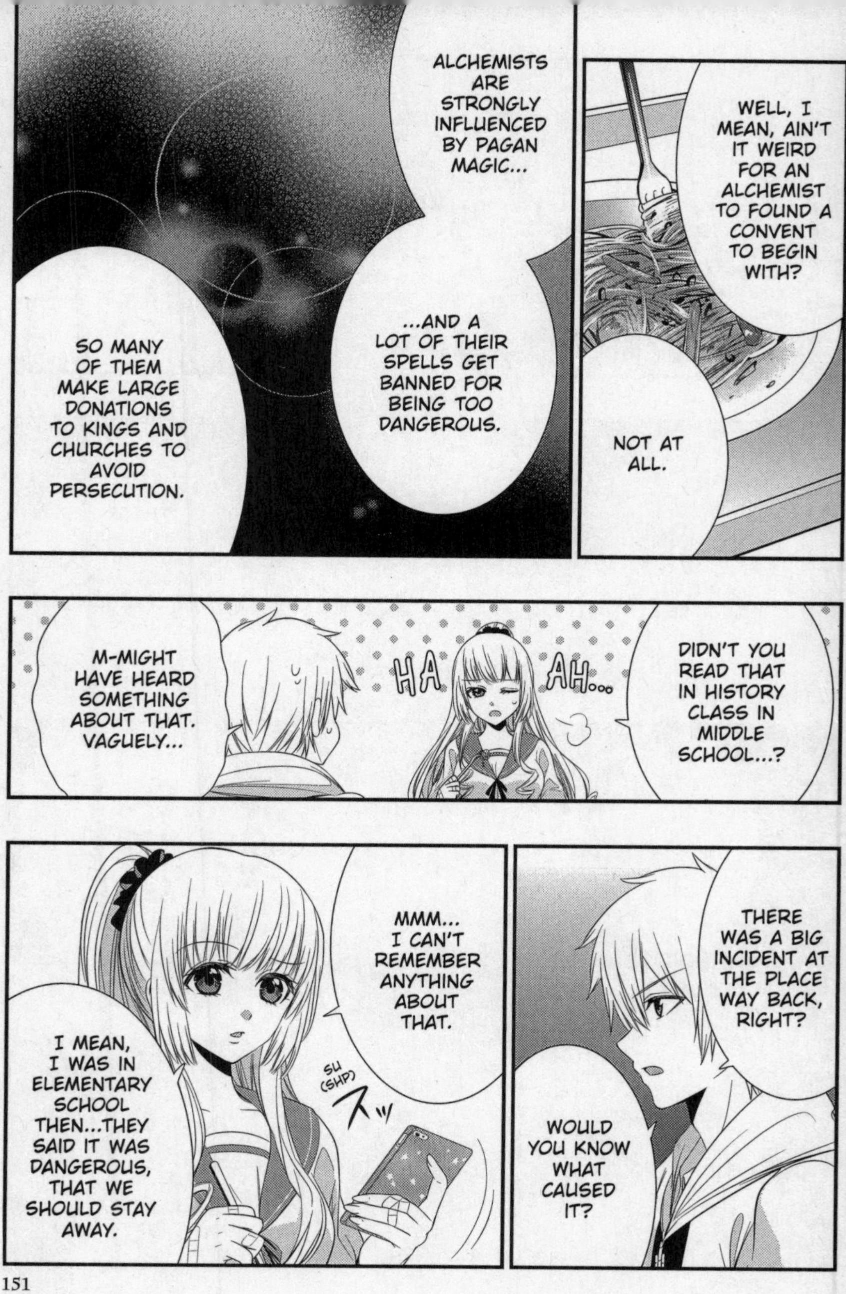
WELL, I MEAN, AIN'T IT WEIRD FOR AN ALCHEMIST TO FOUND A CONVENT TO BEGIN WITH?
NOT AT ALL.
ALCHEMISTS ARE STRONGLY INFLUENCED BY PAGAN MAGIC...
...AND A LOT OF THEIR SPELLS GET BANNED FOR BEING TOO DANGEROUS.
SO MANY OF THEM MAKE LARGE DONATIONS TO KINGS AND CHURCHES TO AVOID PERSECUTION.
DIDN'T YOU READ THAT IN HISTORY CLASS IN MIDDLE SCHOOL...?
HA AH...
M-MIGHT HAVE HEARD SOMETHING ABOUT THAT. VAGUELY...
THERE WAS A BIG INCIDENT AT THE PLACE WAY BACK, RIGHT?
WOULD YOU KNOW WHAT CAUSED IT?
MMM... I CAN'T REMEMBER ANYTHING ABOUT THAT.
SU (SHP)
スッ
I MEAN, I WAS IN ELEMENTARY SCHOOL THEN...THEY SAID IT WAS DANGEROUS, THAT WE SHOULD STAY AWAY.

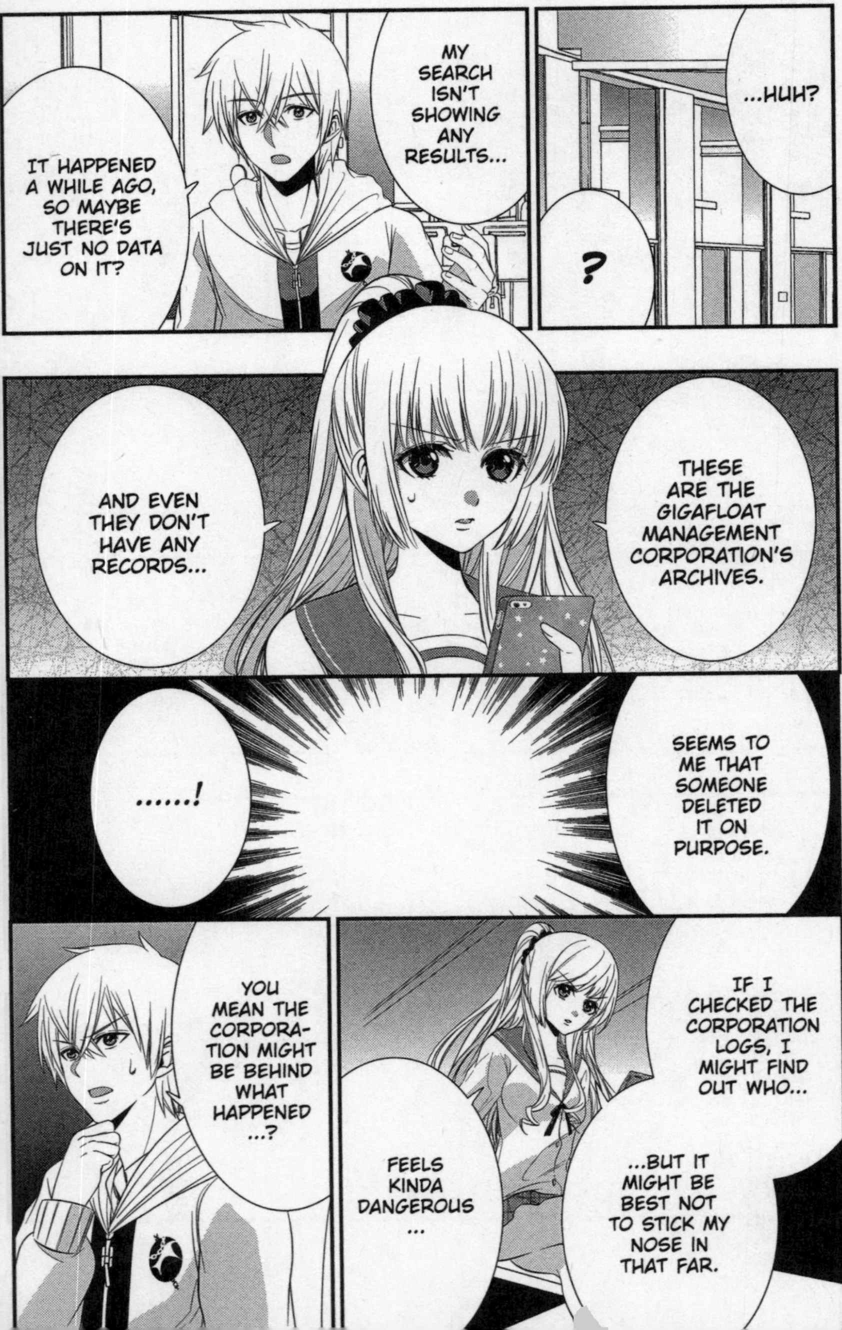
...HUH?
?
MY SEARCH ISN'T SHOWING ANY RESULTS...
IT HAPPENED A WHILE AGO, SO MAYBE THERE'S JUST NO DATA ON IT?
THESE ARE THE GIGAFLOAT MANAGEMENT CORPORATION'S ARCHIVES.
AND EVEN THEY DON'T HAVE ANY RECORDS...
SEEMS TO ME THAT SOMEONE DELETED IT ON PURPOSE.
......!
IF I CHECKED THE CORPORATION LOGS, I MIGHT FIND OUT WHO...
...BUT IT MIGHT BE BEST NOT TO STICK MY NOSE IN THAT FAR.
FEELS KINDA DANGEROUS ...
YOU MEAN THE CORPORA-TION MIGHT BE BEHIND WHAT HAPPENED ...?

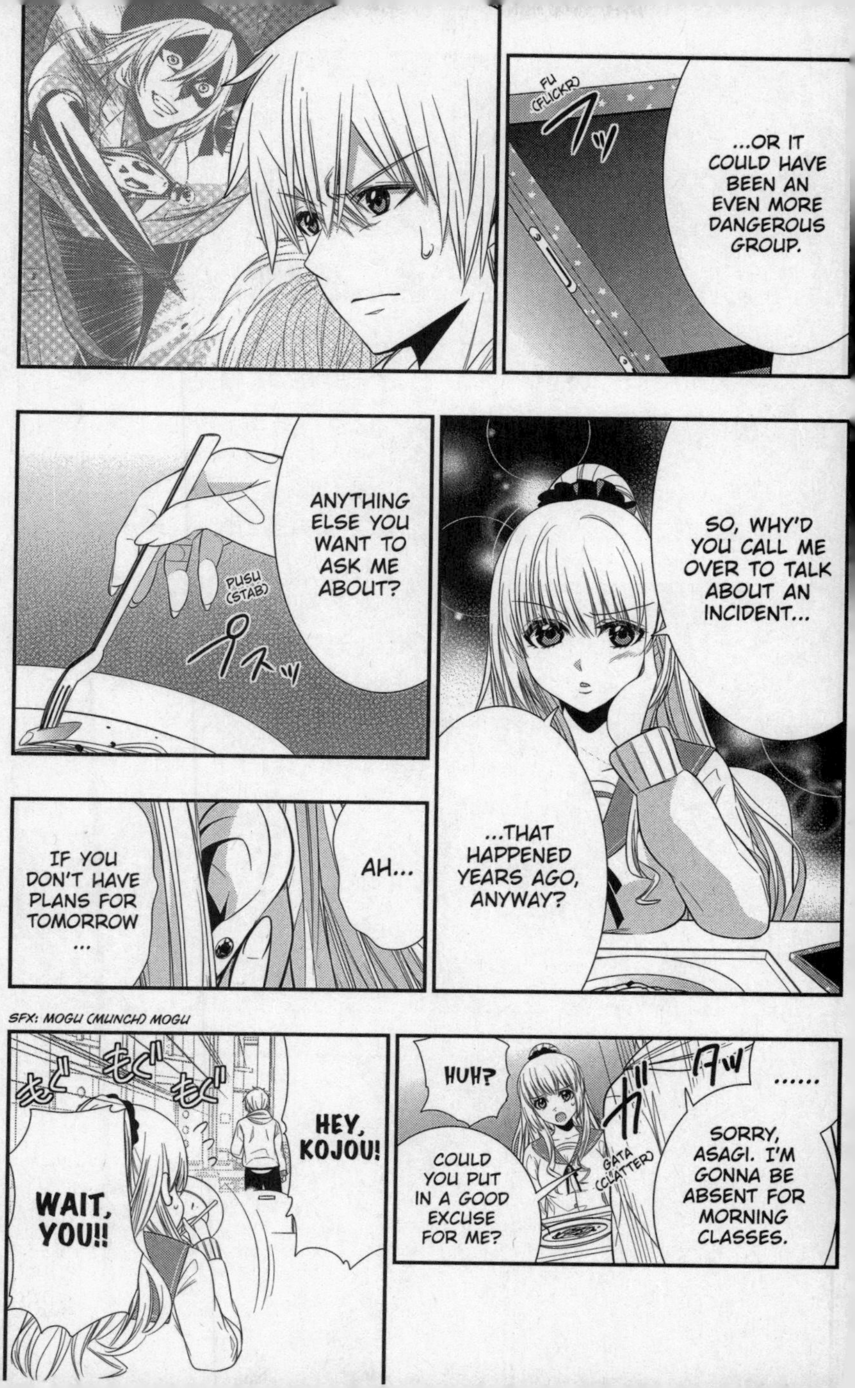
FU (FLICKR)
...OR IT COULD HAVE BEEN AN EVEN MORE DANGEROUS GROUP.
SO, WHY'D YOU CALL ME OVER TO TALK ABOUT AN INCIDENT...
...THAT HAPPENED YEARS AGO, ANYWAY?
ANYTHING ELSE YOU WANT TO ASK ME ABOUT?
PUSU (STAB)
AH...
IF YOU DON'T HAVE PLANS FOR TOMORROW ...
SFX: MOGU (MUNCH) MOGU
......
SORRY, ASAGI. I'M GONNA BE ABSENT FOR MORNING CLASSES.
GATA (CLATTER)
HUH?
COULD YOU PUT IN A GOOD EXCUSE FOR ME?
HEY, KOJOU!
WAIT, YOU!!

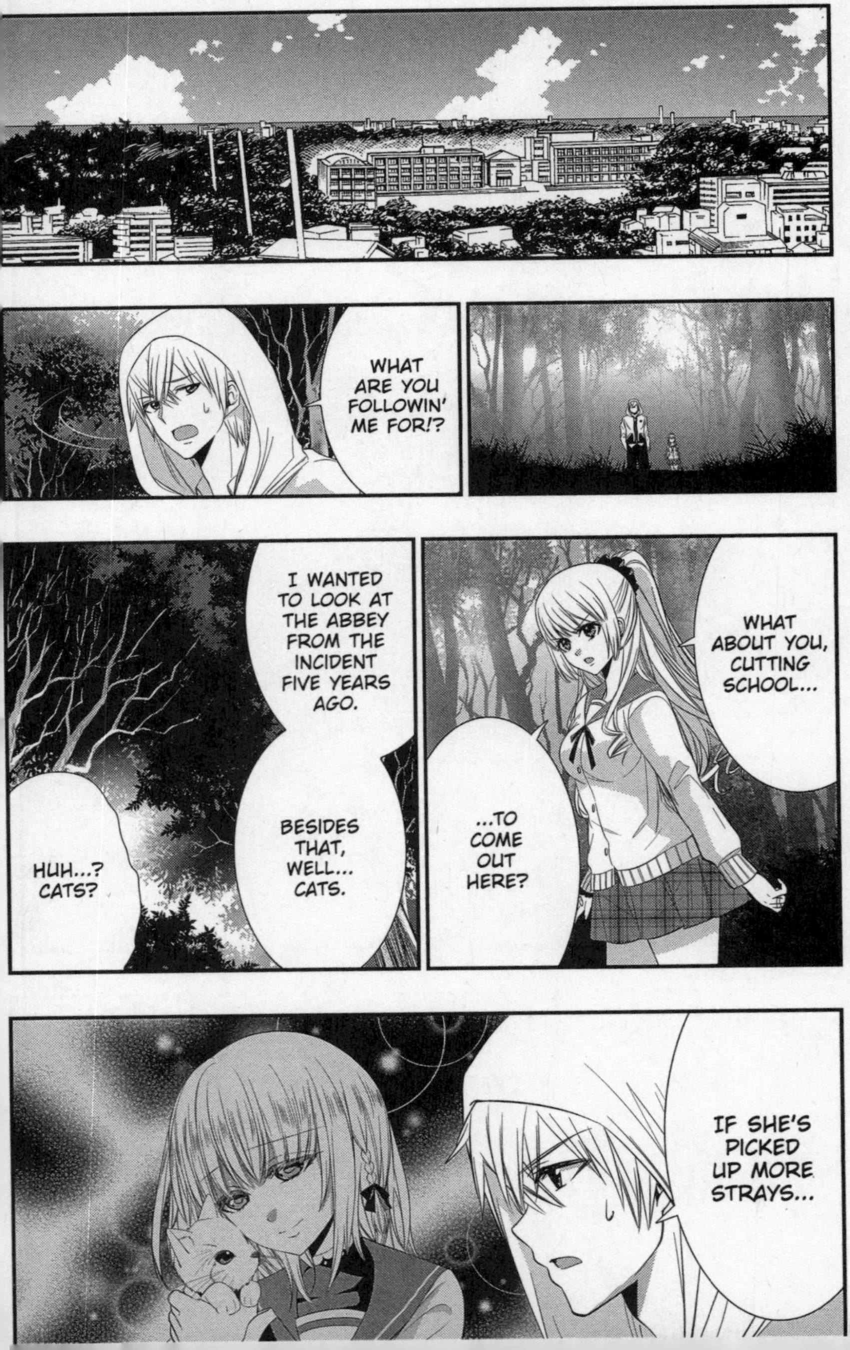
WHAT ARE YOU FOLLOWIN' ME FOR!?
WHAT ABOUT YOU, CUTTING SCHOOL...
...TO COME OUT HERE?
I WANTED TO LOOK AT THE ABBEY FROM THE INCIDENT FIVE YEARS AGO.
BESIDES THAT, WELL... CATS.
HUH...? CATS?
IF SHE'S PICKED UP MORE STRAYS...

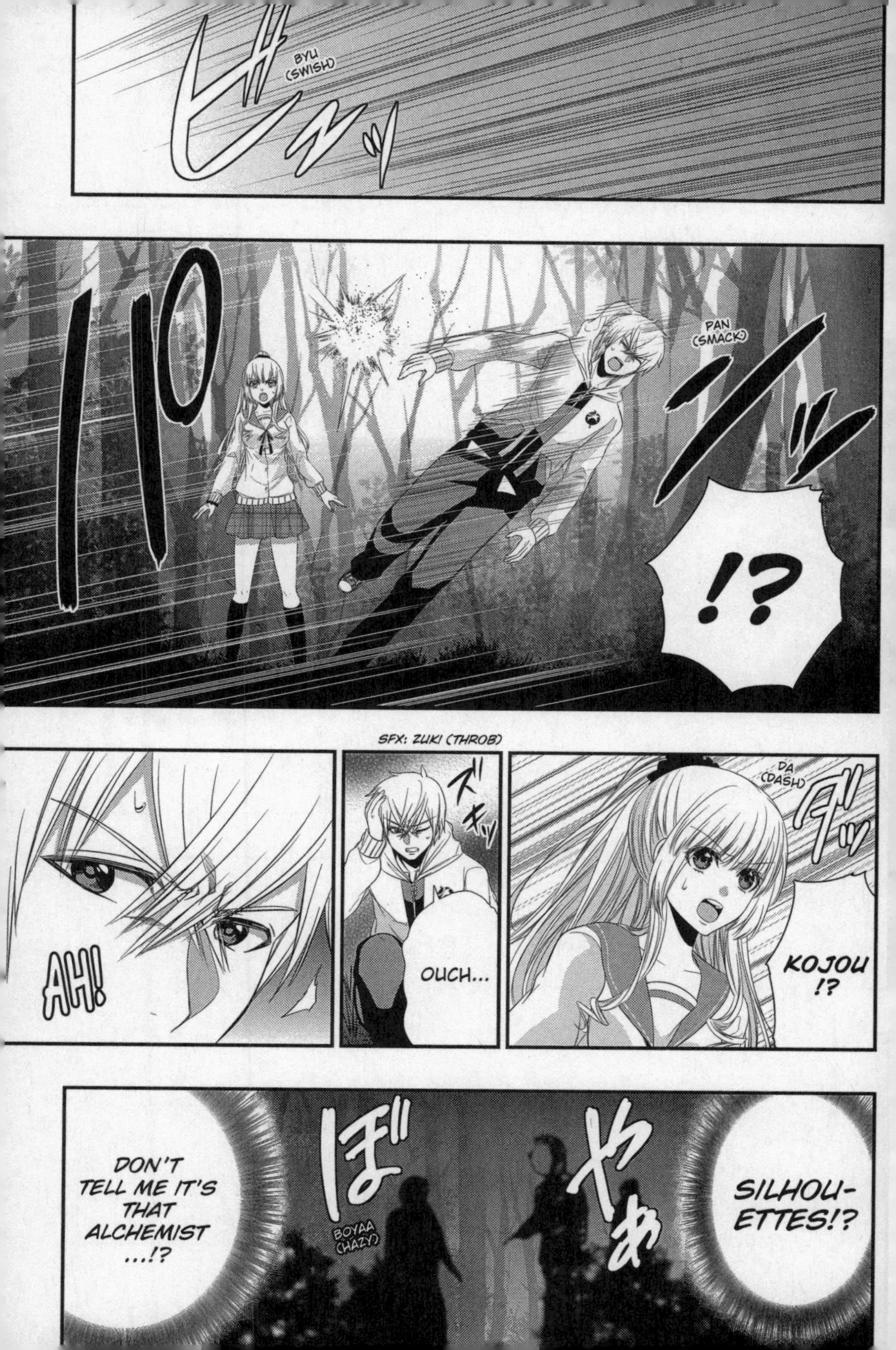
ビュッ
BYU (SWISH)
パンッ
PAN (SMACK)
!?
ダッ
DA (DASH)
KOJOU !?
ズキッ
SFX: ZUKI (THROB)
OUCH...
AH!
SILHOU-ETTES!?
ぼやぁ
BOYAA (HAZY)
DON'T TELL ME IT'S THAT ALCHEMIST ...!?

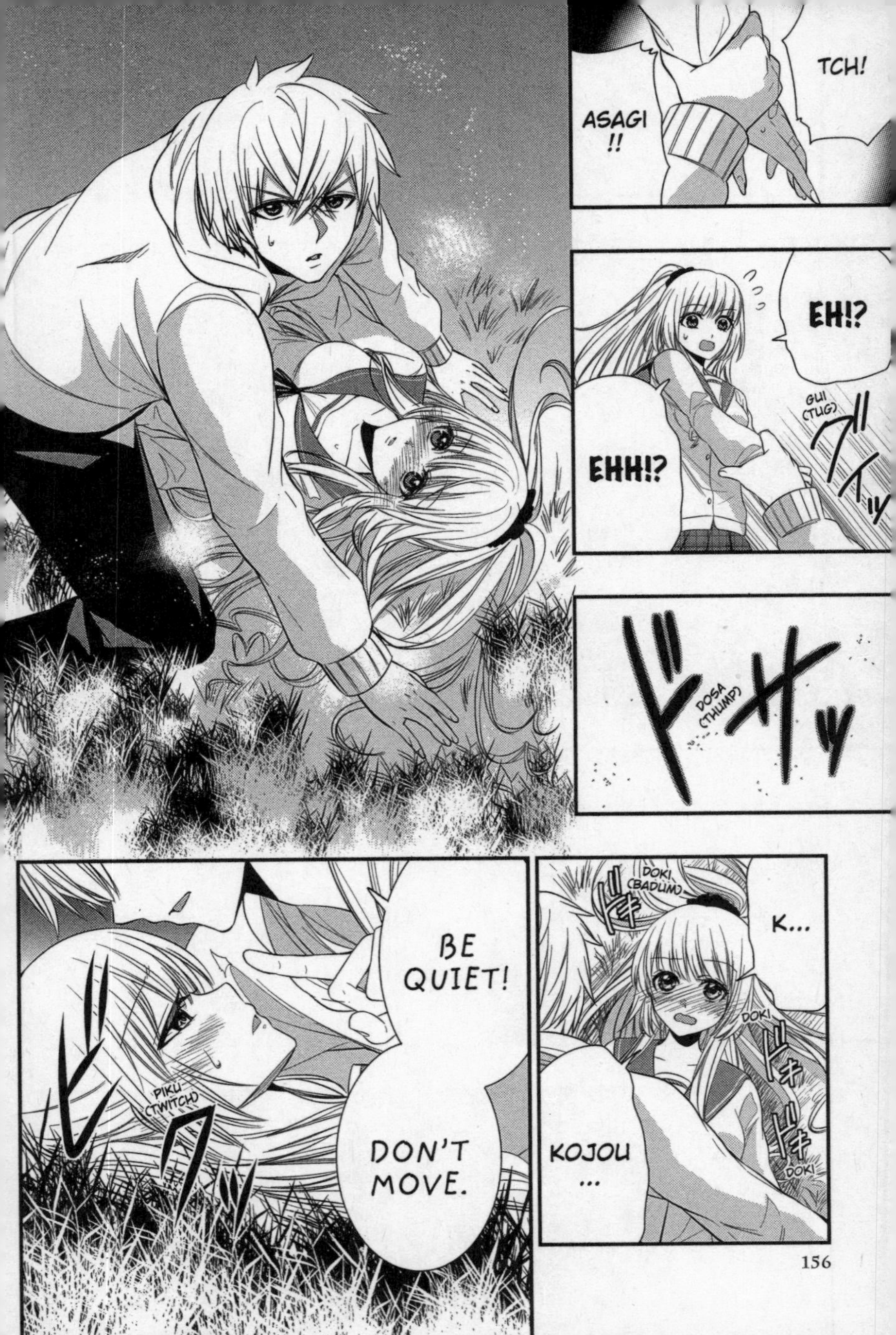
TCH!
ASAGI !!
EH!?
GUI (TUG)
EHH!?
DOSA (THUMP)
DOKI (BADUM)
K...
DOKI
DOKI
KOJOU ...
BE QUIET!
DON'T MOVE.
PIKU (TWITCH)

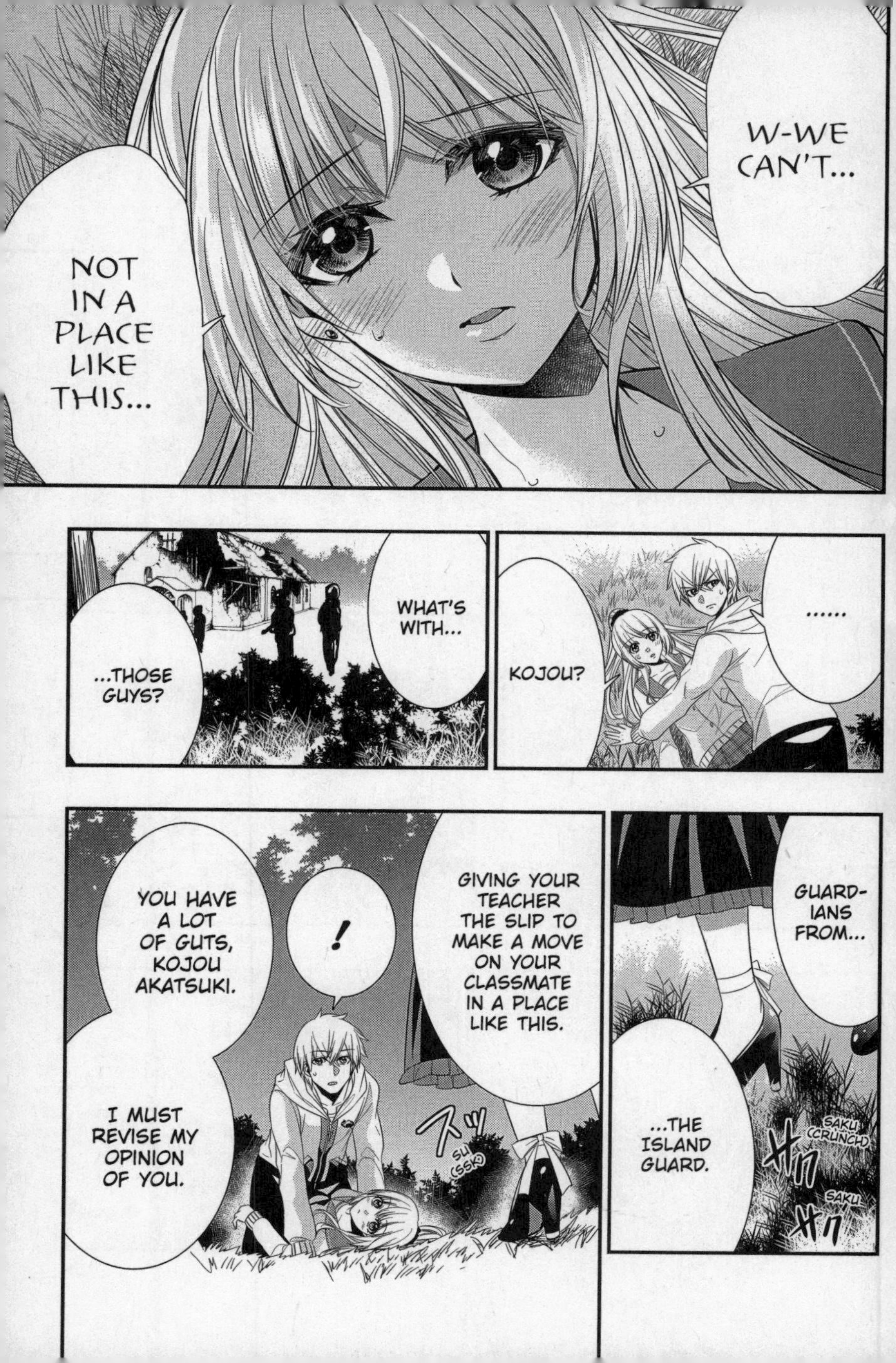
W-WE CAN'T...
NOT IN A PLACE LIKE THIS...
......
KOJOU?
WHAT'S WITH...
...THOSE GUYS?
GUARDIANS FROM...
...THE ISLAND GUARD.
サク SAKU (CRUNCH)
サク SAKU
GIVING YOUR TEACHER THE SLIP TO MAKE A MOVE ON YOUR CLASSMATE IN A PLACE LIKE THIS.
!
YOU HAVE A LOT OF GUTS, KOJOU AKATSUKI.
I MUST REVISE MY OPINION OF YOU.
スッ SU (SSK)

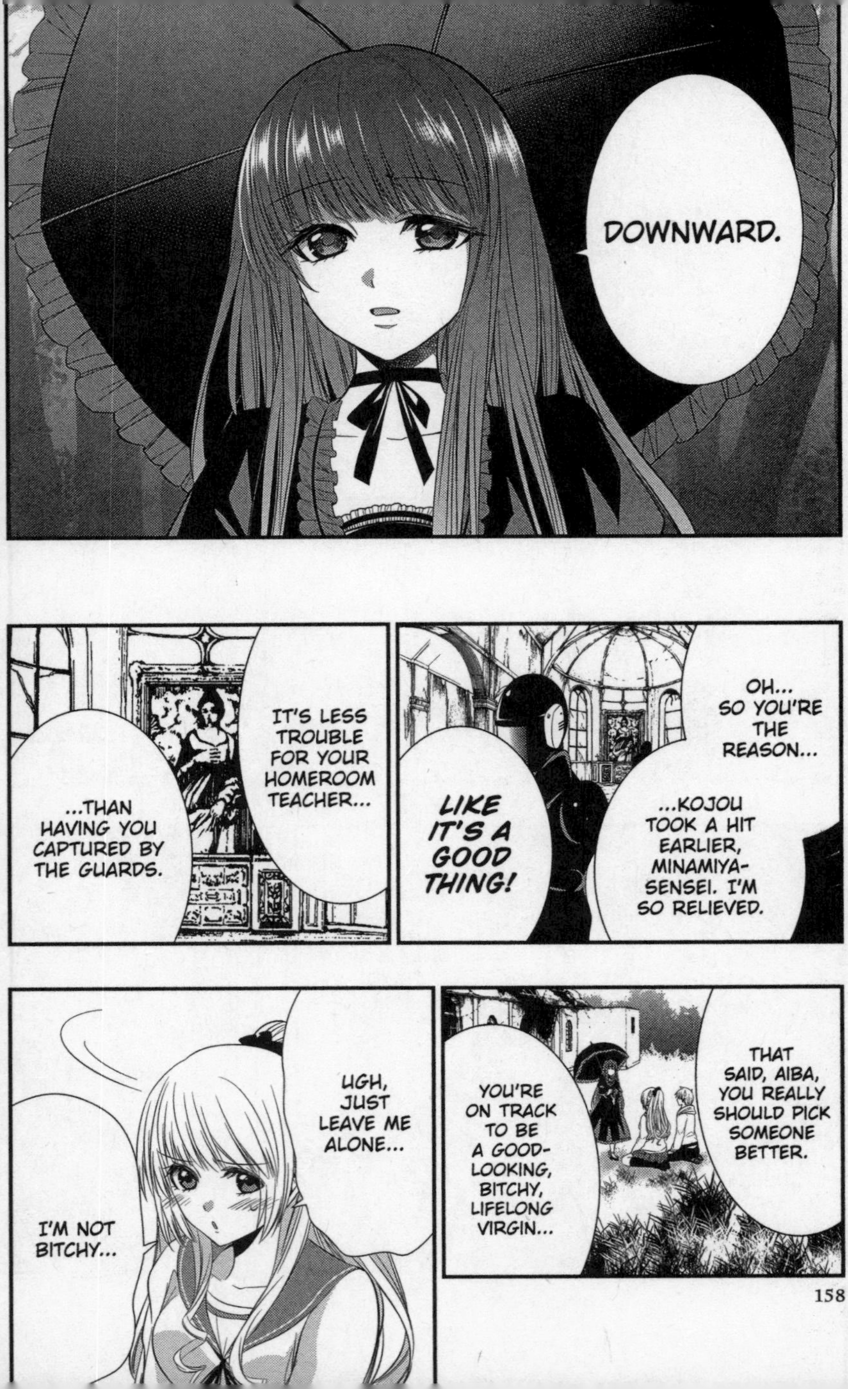
DOWNWARD.
OH... SO YOU'RE THE REASON...
...KOJOU TOOK A HIT EARLIER, MINAMIYA-SENSEI. I'M SO RELIEVED.
LIKE IT'S A GOOD THING!
IT'S LESS TROUBLE FOR YOUR HOMEROOM TEACHER...
...THAN HAVING YOU CAPTURED BY THE GUARDS.
THAT SAID, AIBA, YOU REALLY SHOULD PICK SOMEONE BETTER.
YOU'RE ON TRACK TO BE A GOOD-LOOKING, BITCHY, LIFELONG VIRGIN...
UGH, JUST LEAVE ME ALONE...
I'M NOT BITCHY...

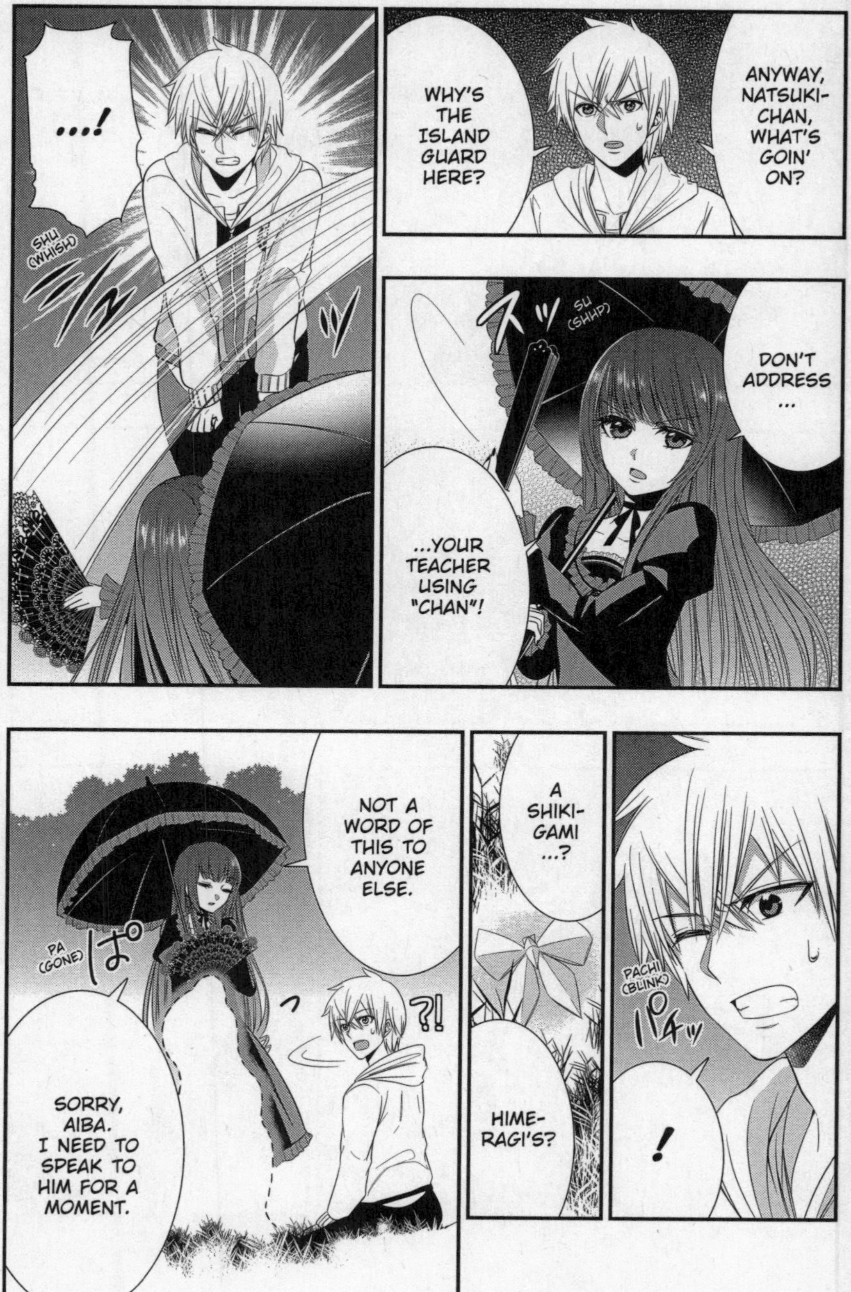
ANYWAY, NATSUKI-CHAN, WHAT'S GOIN' ON?
WHY'S THE ISLAND GUARD HERE?
SU (SHHP)
DON'T ADDRESS ...
...YOUR TEACHER USING "CHAN"!
...!
SHU (WHISH)
PACHI (BLINK)
!
A SHIKI-GAMI ...?
HIME-RAGI'S?
NOT A WORD OF THIS TO ANYONE ELSE.
PA (GONE)
?!
SORRY, AIBA. I NEED TO SPEAK TO HIM FOR A MOMENT.

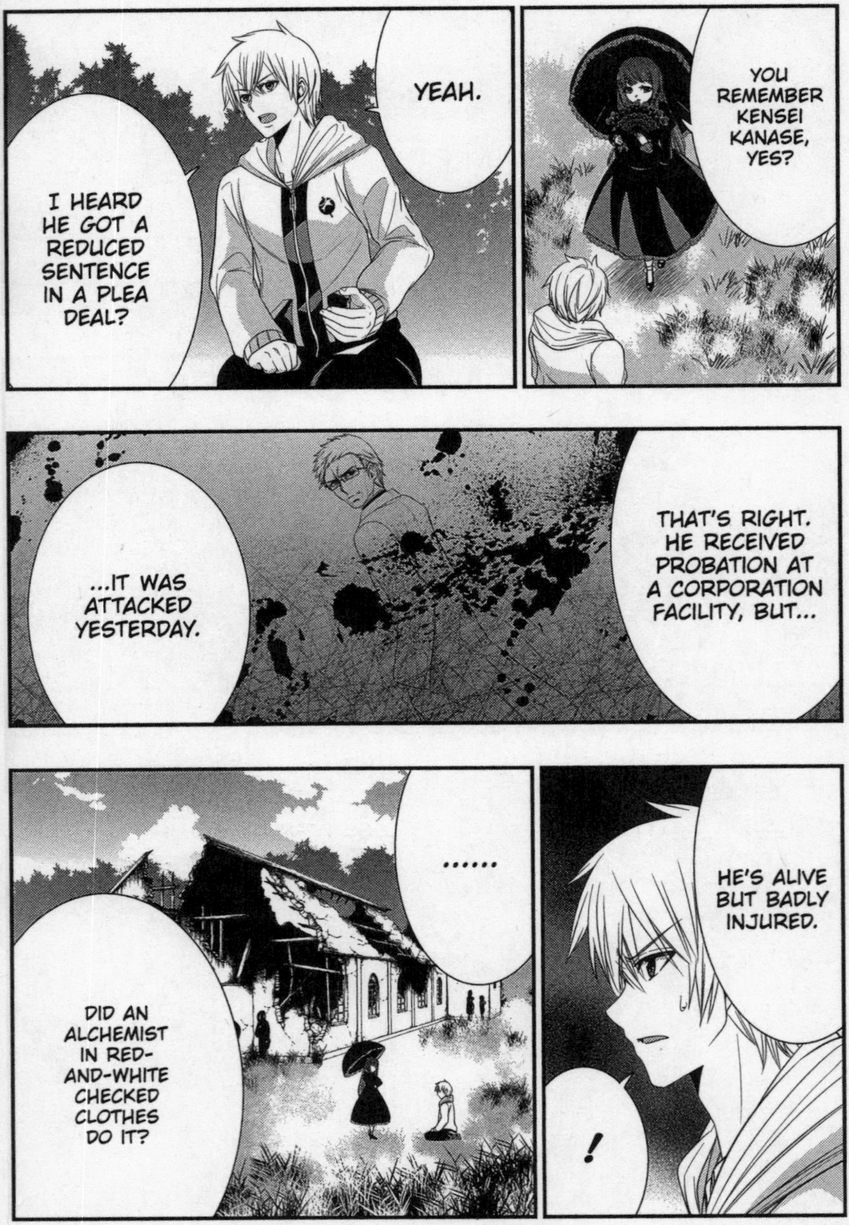
YOU REMEMBER KENSEI KANASE, YES?
YEAH.
I HEARD HE GOT A REDUCED SENTENCE IN A PLEA DEAL?
THAT'S RIGHT. HE RECEIVED PROBATION AT A CORPORATION FACILITY, BUT...
...IT WAS ATTACKED YESTERDAY.
HE'S ALIVE BUT BADLY INJURED.
!
......
DID AN ALCHEMIST IN RED-AND-WHITE CHECKED CLOTHES DO IT?

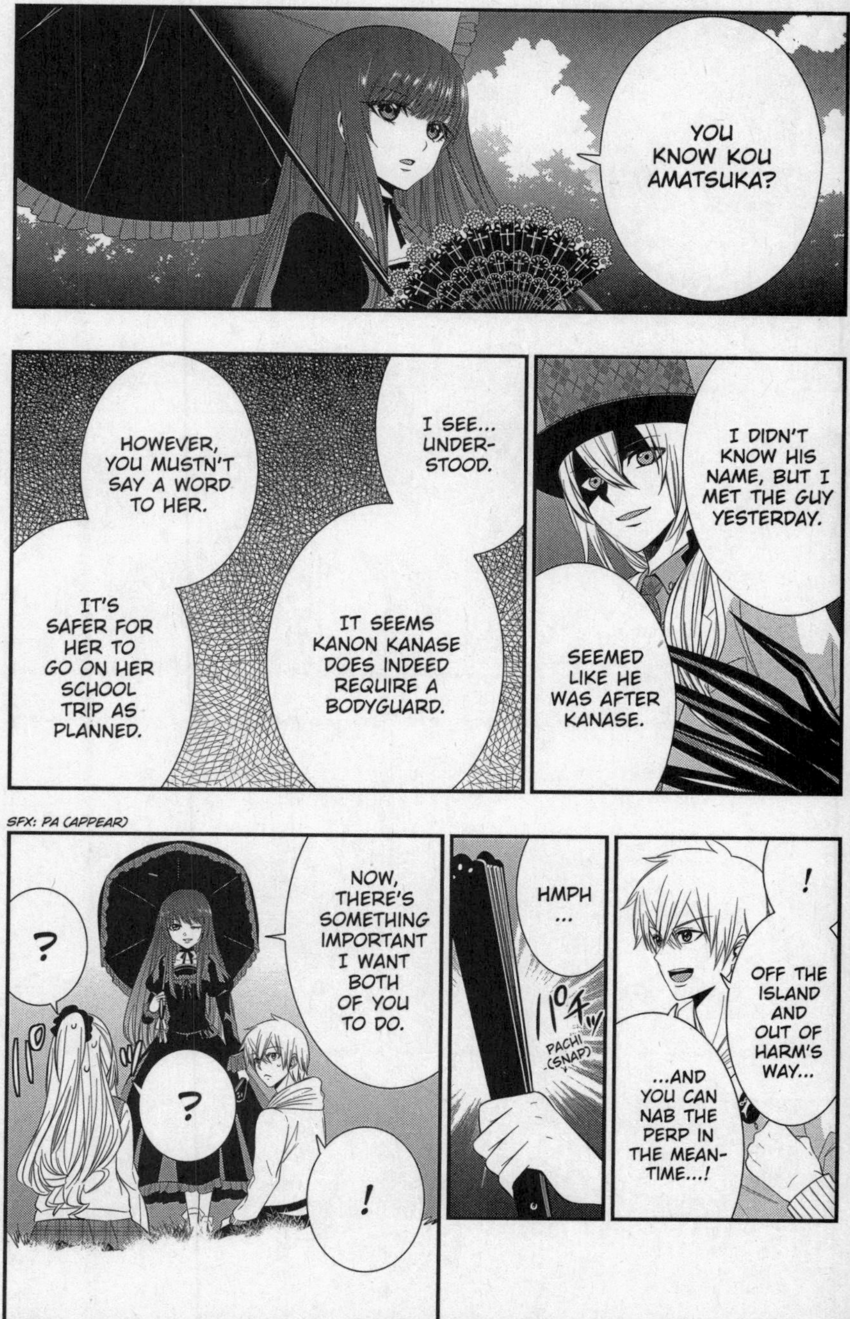
YOU KNOW KOU AMATSUKA?
I DIDN'T KNOW HIS NAME, BUT I MET THE GUY YESTERDAY.
SEEMED LIKE HE WAS AFTER KANASE.
I SEE... UNDER-STOOD.
IT SEEMS KANON KANASE DOES INDEED REQUIRE A BODYGUARD.
HOWEVER, YOU MUSTN'T SAY A WORD TO HER.
IT'S SAFER FOR HER TO GO ON HER SCHOOL TRIP AS PLANNED.
!
OFF THE ISLAND AND OUT OF HARM'S WAY...
...AND YOU CAN NAB THE PERP IN THE MEAN-TIME...!
HMPH...
PACHI (SNAP)
NOW, THERE'S SOMETHING IMPORTANT I WANT BOTH OF YOU TO DO.
?
?
!
SFX: PA (APPEAR)

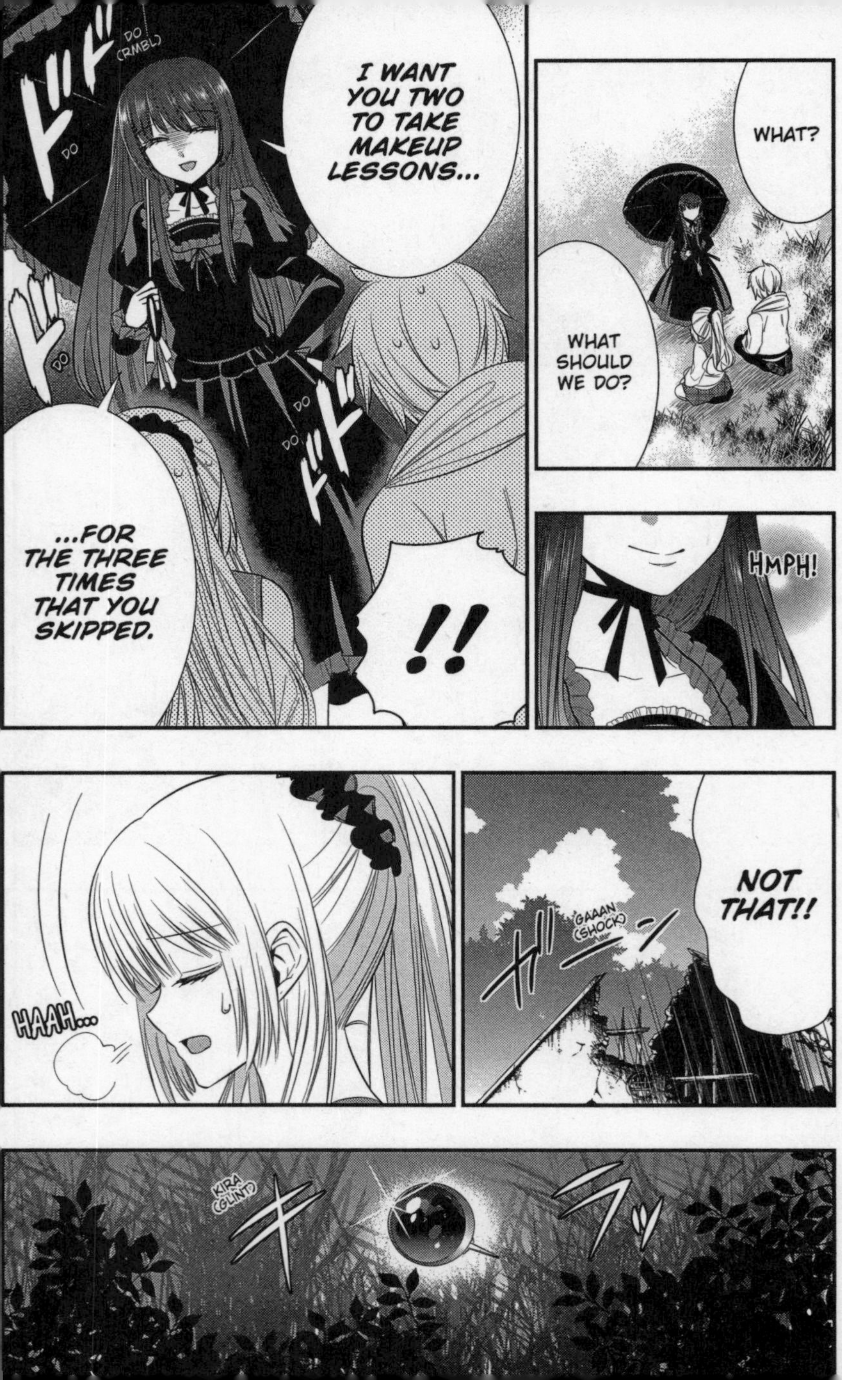

WHAT?
WHAT SHOULD WE DO?
HMPH!
I WANT YOU TWO TO TAKE MAKEUP LESSONS...
DO (RMBL)
DO
DO
DO
DO
...FOR THE THREE TIMES THAT YOU SKIPPED.
!!
NOT THAT!!
GAAAN (SHOCK)
HAAH...
KIRA (GLINT)

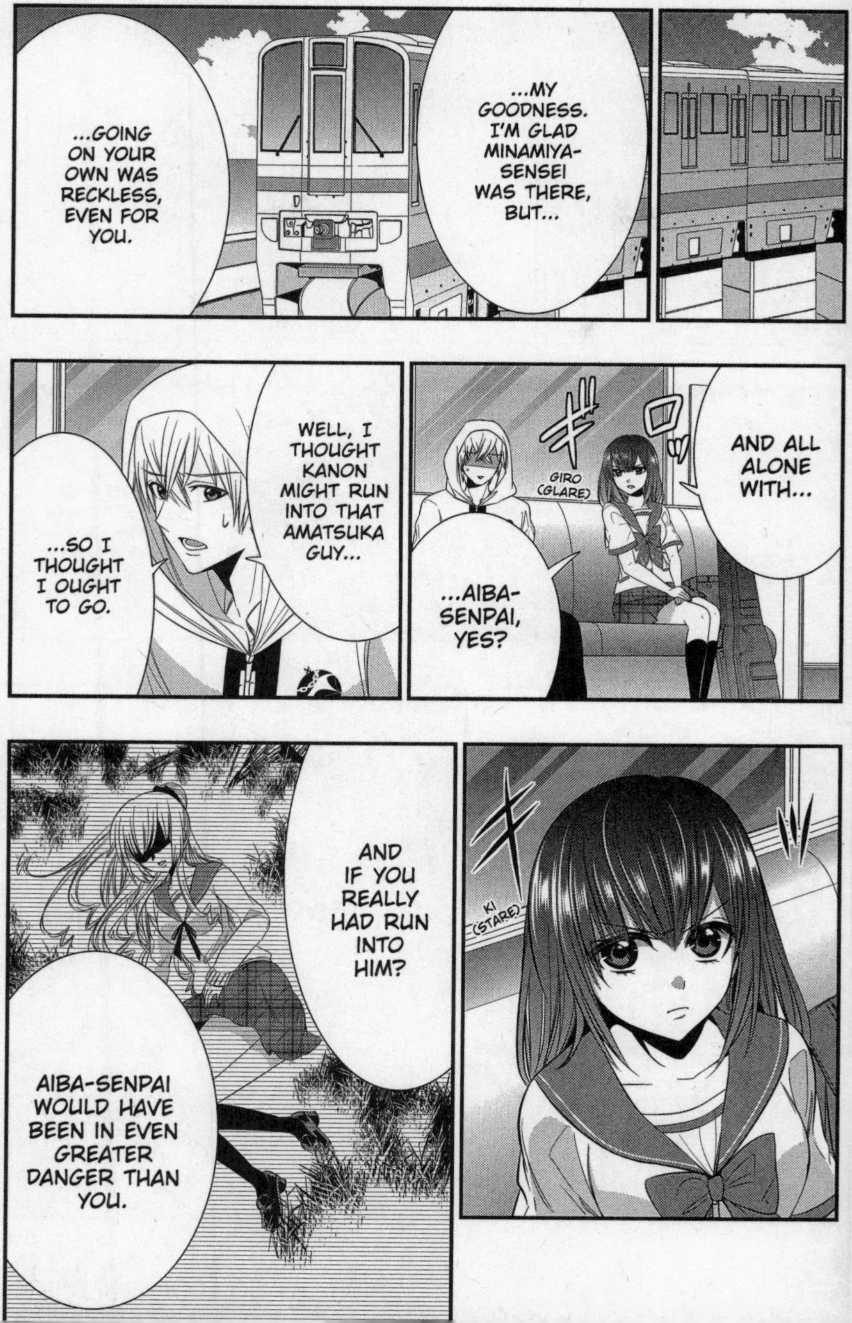
...MY GOODNESS. I'M GLAD MINAMIYA-SENSEI WAS THERE, BUT...
...GOING ON YOUR OWN WAS RECKLESS, EVEN FOR YOU.
AND ALL ALONE WITH...
GIRO (GLARE)
...AIBA-SENPAI, YES?
WELL, I THOUGHT KANON MIGHT RUN INTO THAT AMATSUKA GUY...
...SO I THOUGHT I OUGHT TO GO.
KI (STARE)
AND IF YOU REALLY HAD RUN INTO HIM?
AIBA-SENPAI WOULD HAVE BEEN IN EVEN GREATER DANGER THAN YOU.

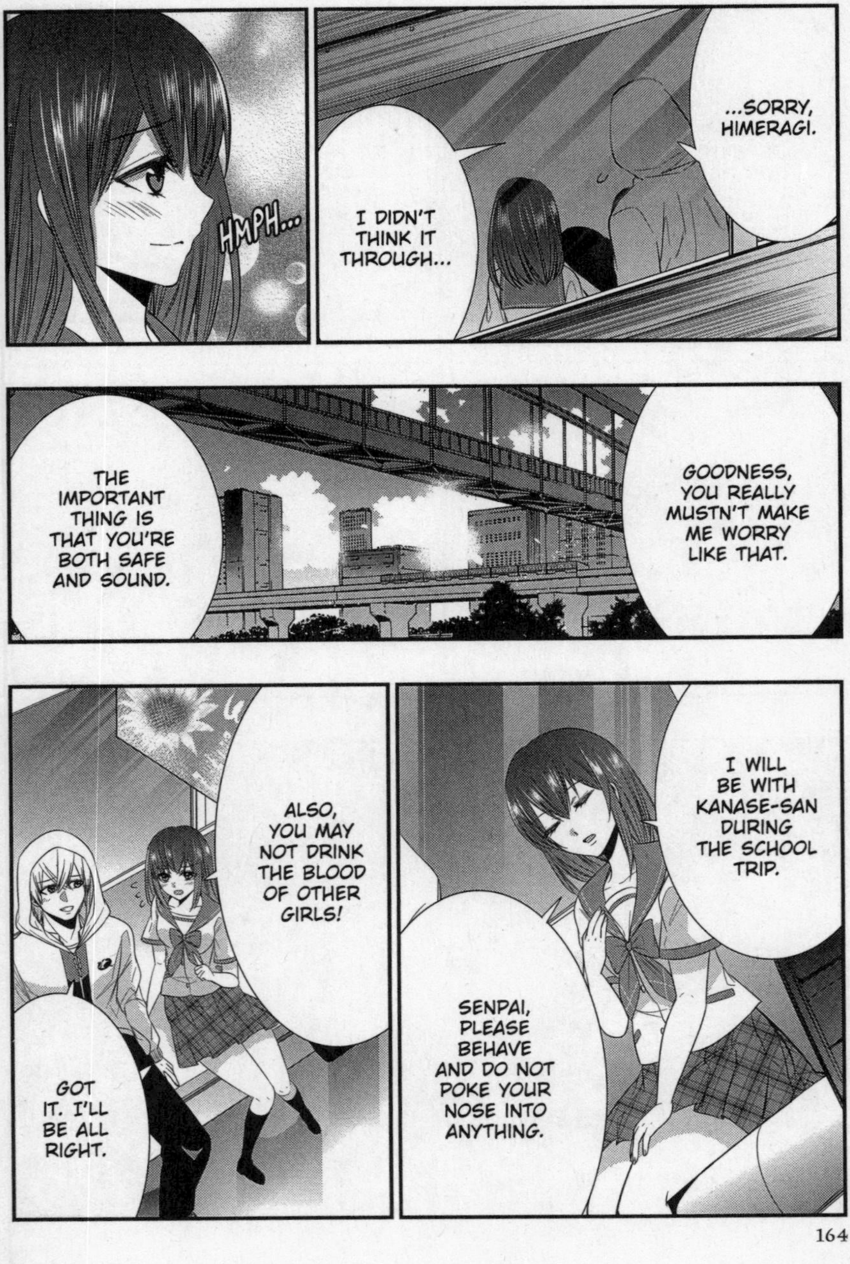
...SORRY, HIMERAGI.
I DIDN'T THINK IT THROUGH...
HMPH...
GOODNESS, YOU REALLY MUSTN'T MAKE ME WORRY LIKE THAT.
THE IMPORTANT THING IS THAT YOU'RE BOTH SAFE AND SOUND.
I WILL BE WITH KANASE-SAN DURING THE SCHOOL TRIP.
SENPAI, PLEASE BEHAVE AND DO NOT POKE YOUR NOSE INTO ANYTHING.
ALSO, YOU MAY NOT DRINK THE BLOOD OF OTHER GIRLS!
GOT IT. I'LL BE ALL RIGHT.

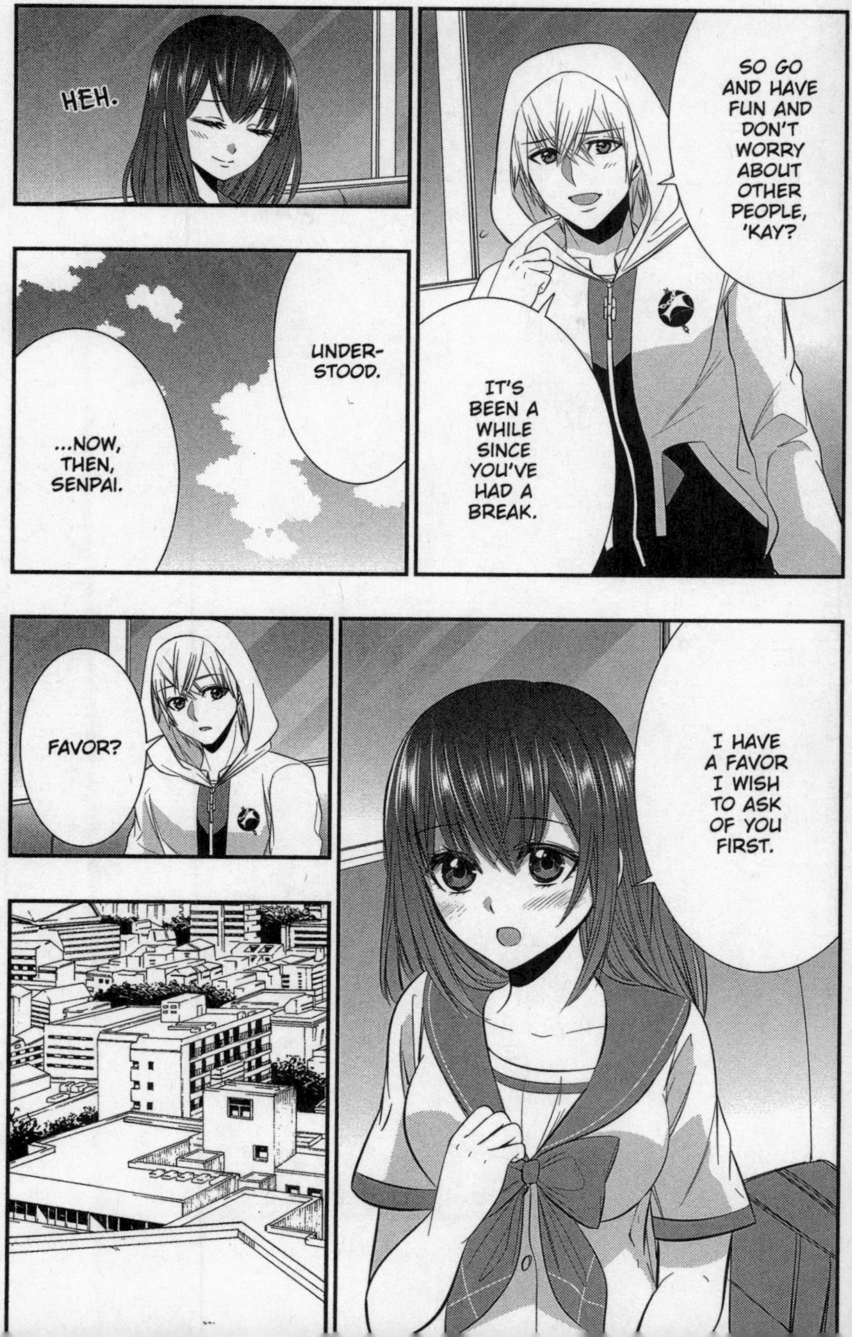
SO GO AND HAVE FUN AND DON'T WORRY ABOUT OTHER PEOPLE, 'KAY?
IT'S BEEN A WHILE SINCE YOU'VE HAD A BREAK.
HEH.
UNDER-STOOD.
...NOW, THEN, SENPAI.
I HAVE A FAVOR I WISH TO ASK OF YOU FIRST.
FAVOR?

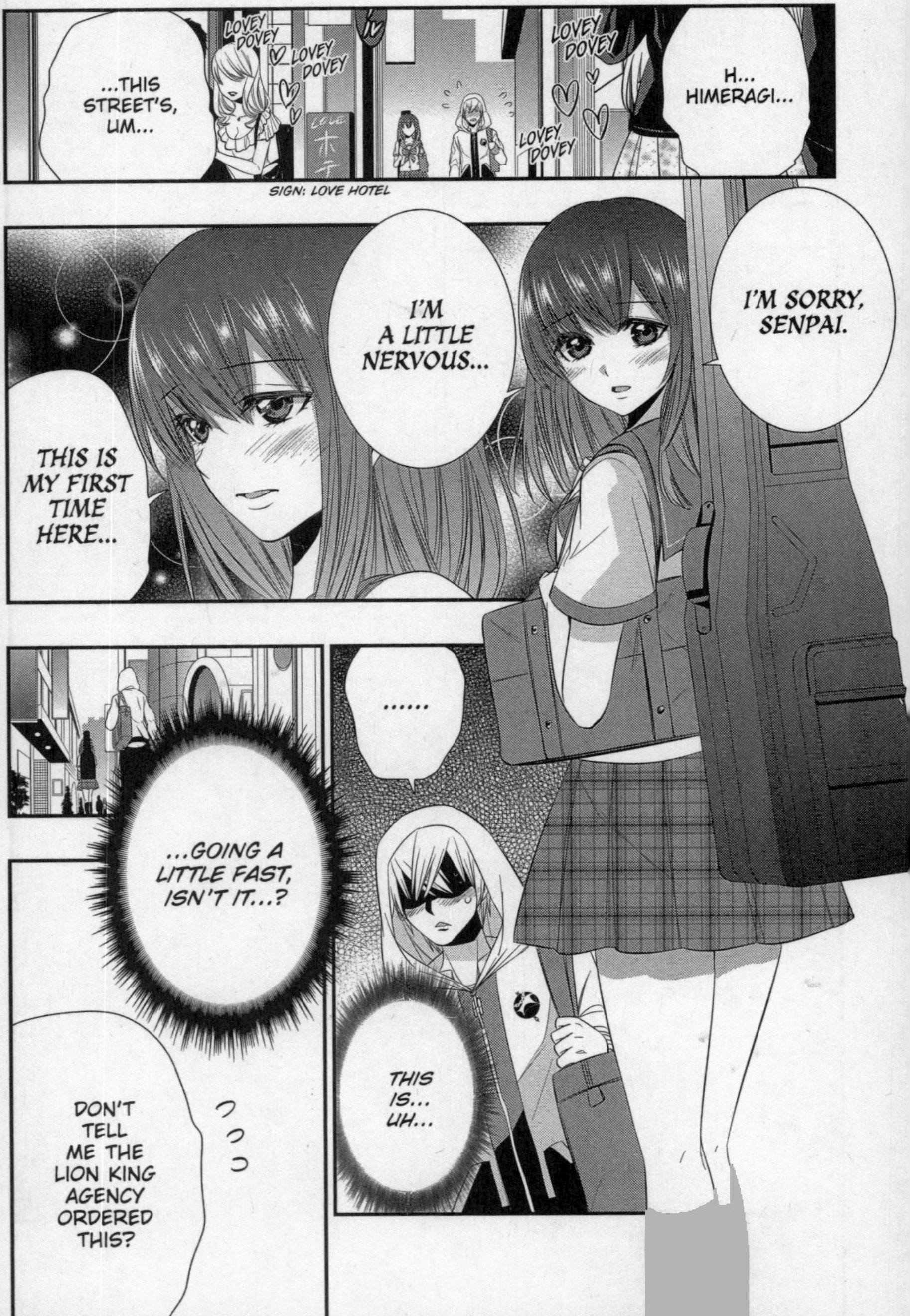
H... HIMERAGI...
LOVEY DOVEY
LOVEY DOVEY
LOVEY DOVEY
LOVEY DOVEY
LOVEY DOVEY
...THIS STREET'S, UM...
SIGN: LOVE HOTEL
I'M SORRY, SENPAI.
I'M A LITTLE NERVOUS...
THIS IS MY FIRST TIME HERE...
......
...GOING A LITTLE FAST, ISN'T IT...?
THIS IS... UH...
DON'T TELL ME THE LION KING AGENCY ORDERED THIS?

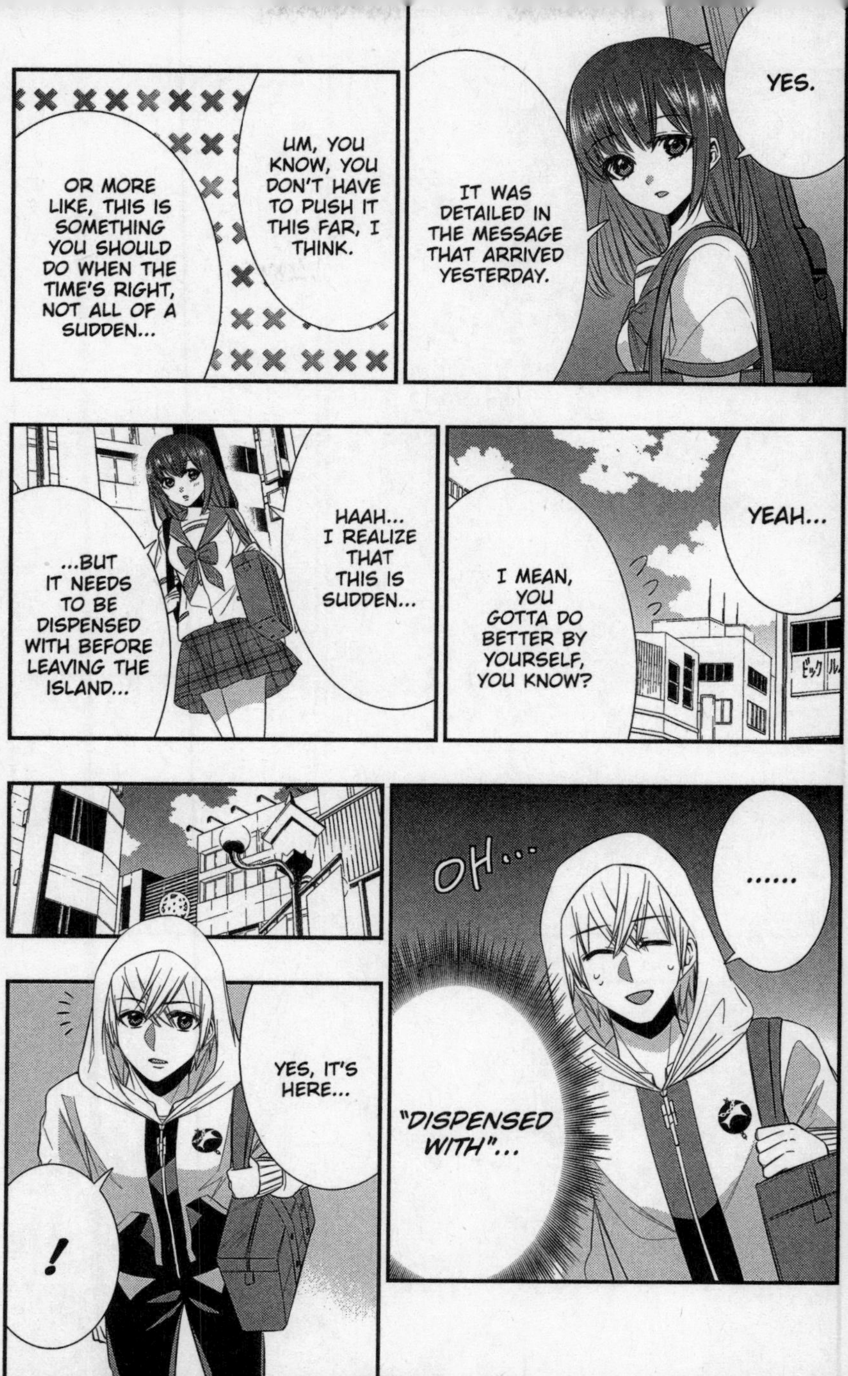
YES.
IT WAS DETAILED IN THE MESSAGE THAT ARRIVED YESTERDAY.
UM, YOU KNOW, YOU DON'T HAVE TO PUSH IT THIS FAR, I THINK.
OR MORE LIKE, THIS IS SOMETHING YOU SHOULD DO WHEN THE TIME'S RIGHT, NOT ALL OF A SUDDEN...
YEAH...
I MEAN, YOU GOTTA DO BETTER BY YOURSELF, YOU KNOW?
HAAH... I REALIZE THAT THIS IS SUDDEN...
...BUT IT NEEDS TO BE DISPENSED WITH BEFORE LEAVING THE ISLAND...
OH...
......
"DISPENSED WITH"...
YES, IT'S HERE...
!

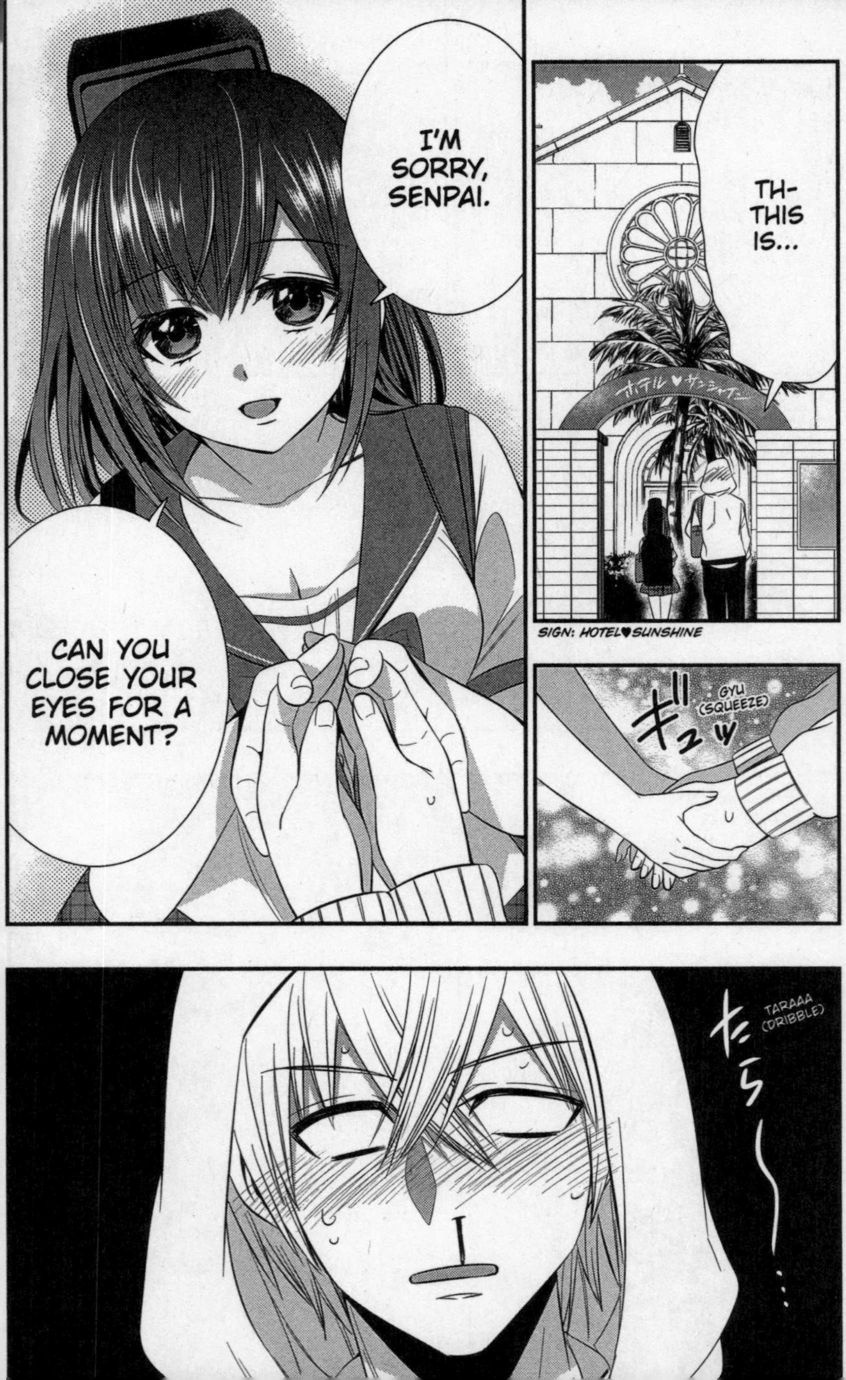
TH- THIS IS...
SIGN: HOTEL♥SUNSHINE
GYU (SQUEEZE)
I'M SORRY, SENPAI.
CAN YOU CLOSE YOUR EYES FOR A MOMENT?
TARAAA (DRIBBLE)

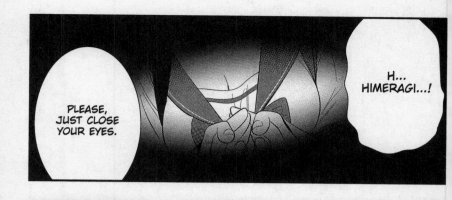

PLEASE, JUST CLOSE YOUR EYES.

H... HIMERAGI...!

YOU CAN OPEN YOUR EYES NOW, SENPAI.

KIN (TING)

......?

PACHI (BLINK)

WE HAVE ARRIVED.

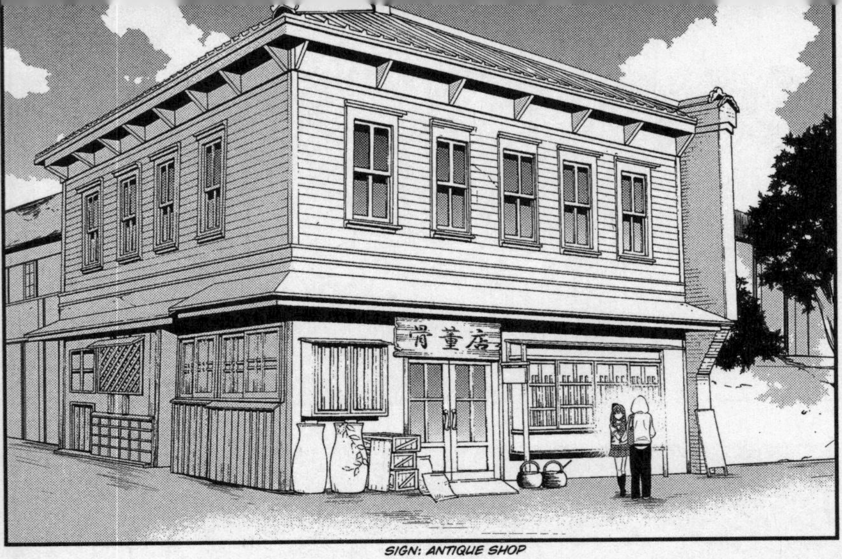
骨董店

SIGN: ANTIQUE SHOP

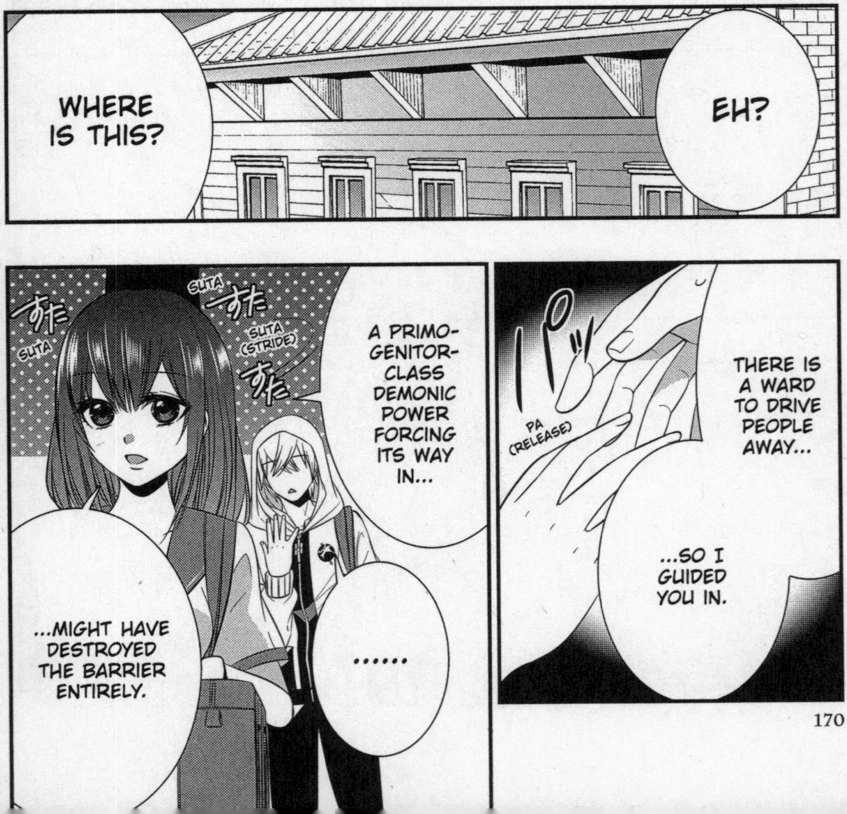
EH?
WHERE IS THIS?
THERE IS A WARD TO DRIVE PEOPLE AWAY...
PA (RELEASE)
...SO I GUIDED YOU IN.
A PRIMOGENITOR-CLASS DEMONIC POWER FORCING ITS WAY IN...
SUTA
SUTA (STRIDE)
SUTA
......
...MIGHT HAVE DESTROYED THE BARRIER ENTIRELY.

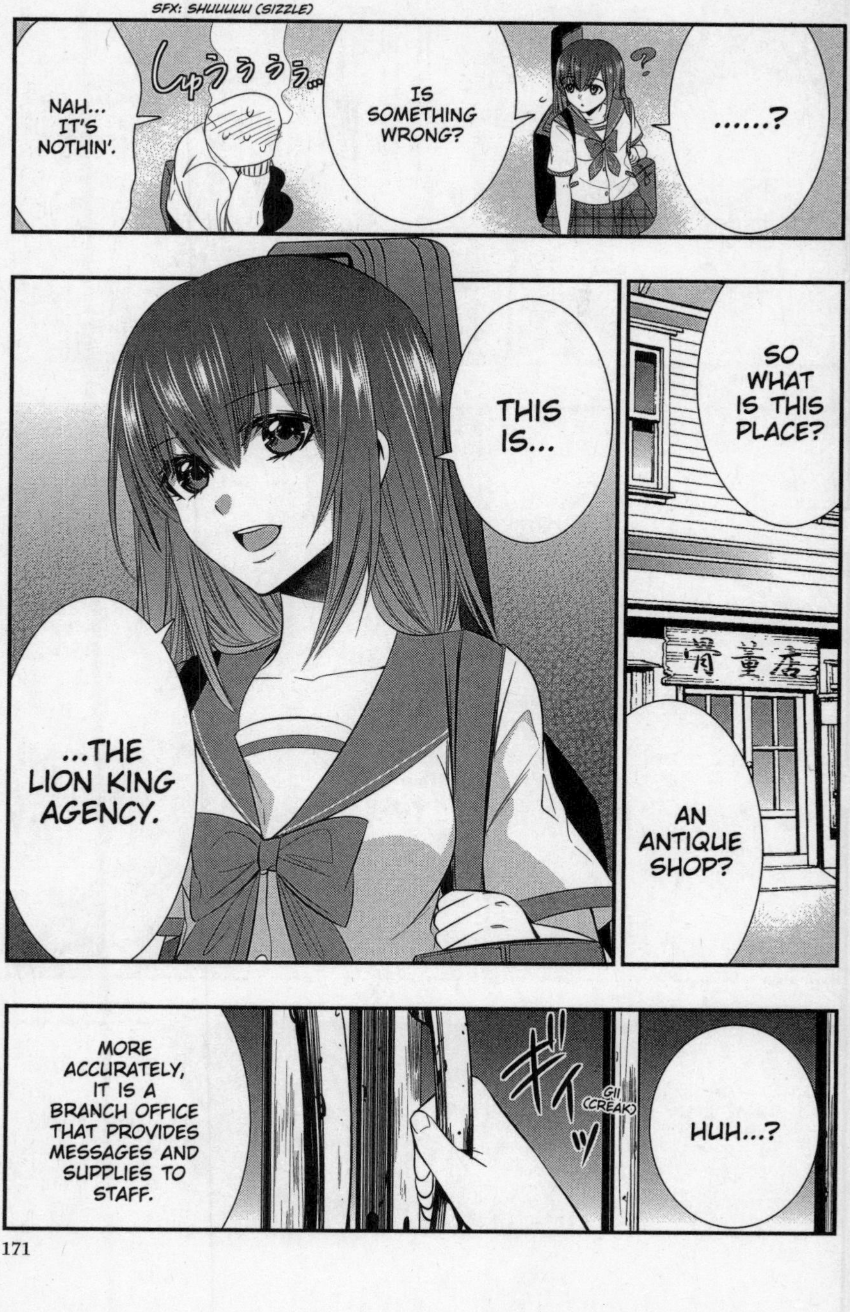
SFX: SHUUUUU (SIZZLE)
......?
IS SOMETHING WRONG?
しゅううううう
NAH... IT'S NOTHIN'.
SO WHAT IS THIS PLACE?
骨董店
AN ANTIQUE SHOP?
THIS IS...
...THE LION KING AGENCY.
HUH...?
ギィッ
GII (CREAK)
MORE ACCURATELY, IT IS A BRANCH OFFICE THAT PROVIDES MESSAGES AND SUPPLIES TO STAFF.

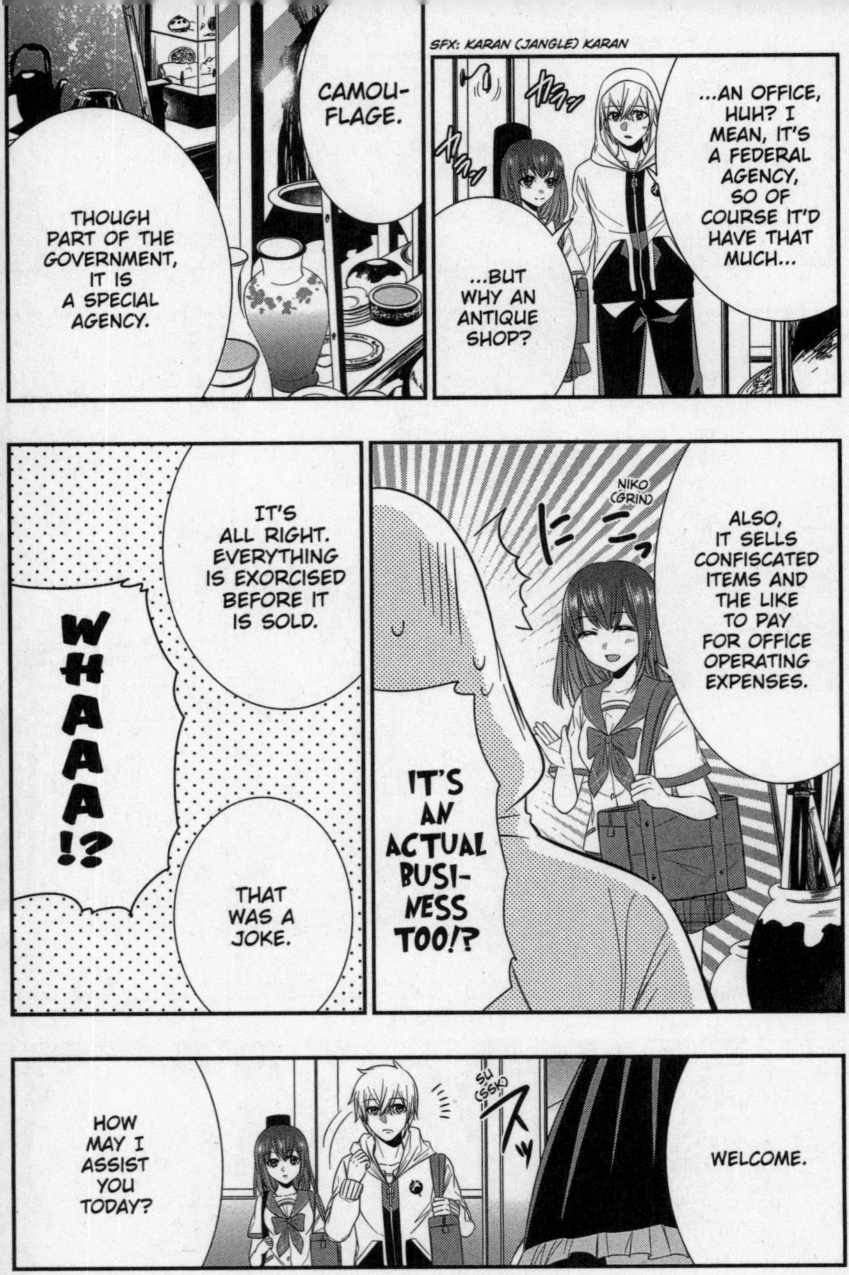
SFX: KARAN (JANGLE) KARAN
...AN OFFICE, HUH? I MEAN, IT'S A FEDERAL AGENCY, SO OF COURSE IT'D HAVE THAT MUCH...
...BUT WHY AN ANTIQUE SHOP?
CAMOU-FLAGE.
THOUGH PART OF THE GOVERNMENT, IT IS A SPECIAL AGENCY.
NIKO (GRIN)
ALSO, IT SELLS CONFISCATED ITEMS AND THE LIKE TO PAY FOR OFFICE OPERATING EXPENSES.
IT'S AN ACTUAL BUSI-NESS TOO!?
IT'S ALL RIGHT. EVERYTHING IS EXORCISED BEFORE IT IS SOLD.
WHAAAA!?
THAT WAS A JOKE.
WELCOME.
SU (SSK)
HOW MAY I ASSIST YOU TODAY?

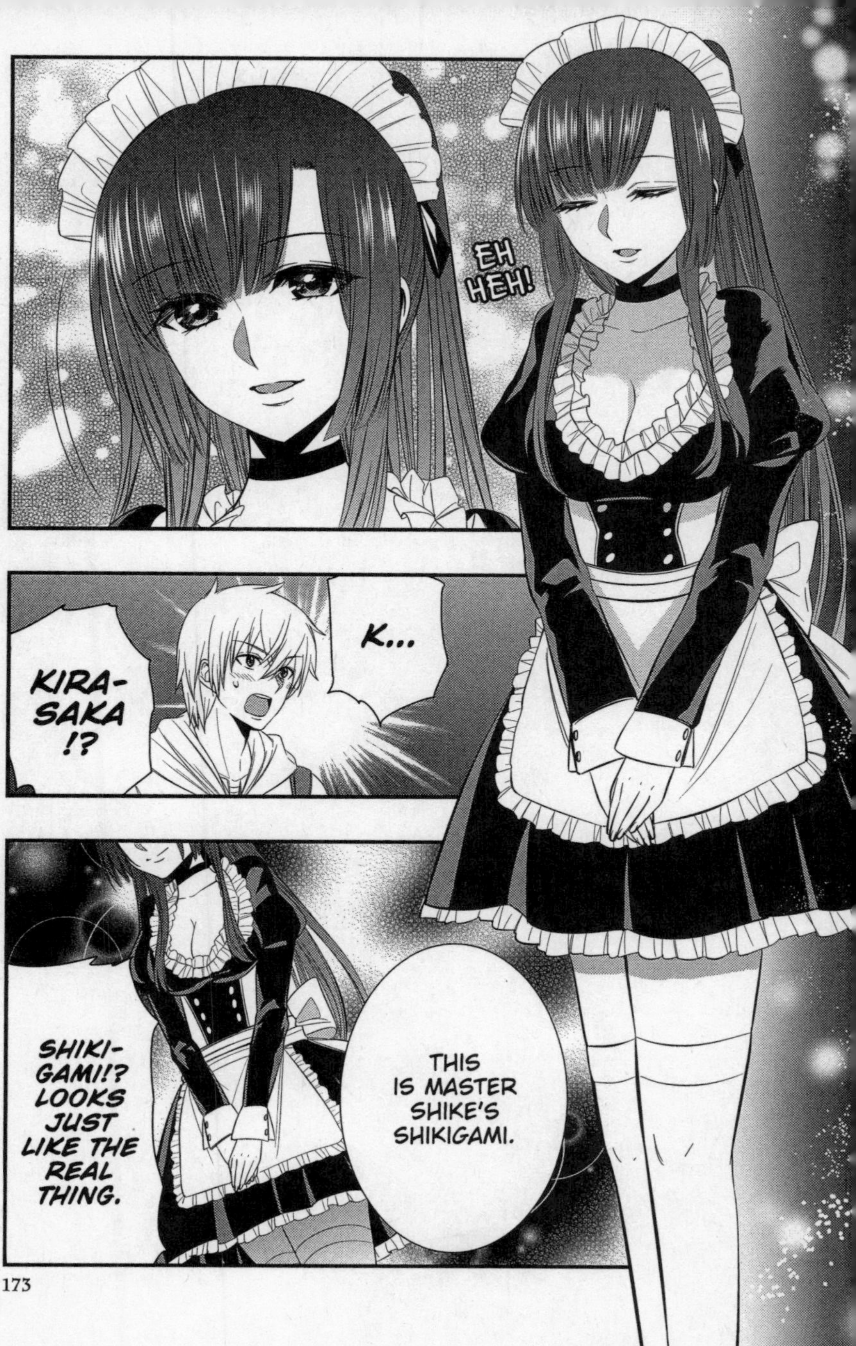
EH HEH!
K...
KIRA-SAKA!?
THIS IS MASTER SHIKE'S SHIKIGAMI.
SHIKI-GAMI!? LOOKS JUST LIKE THE REAL THING.

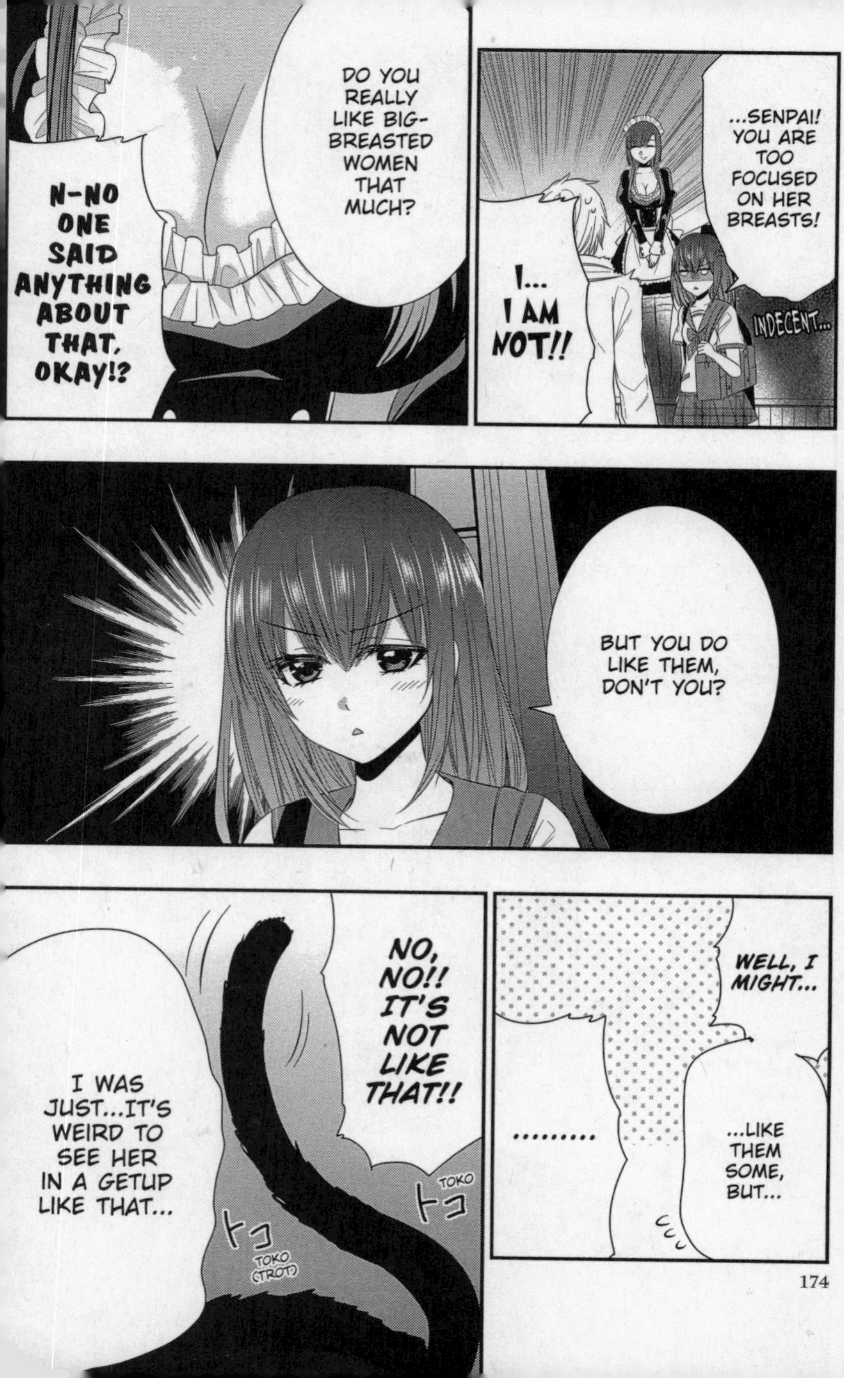
...SENPAI! YOU ARE TOO FOCUSED ON HER BREASTS!
I... I AM NOT!!
INDECENT...
DO YOU REALLY LIKE BIG-BREASTED WOMEN THAT MUCH?
N-NO ONE SAID ANYTHING ABOUT THAT, OKAY!?
BUT YOU DO LIKE THEM, DON'T YOU?
WELL, I MIGHT...
...LIKE THEM SOME, BUT...
....
NO, NO!! IT'S NOT LIKE THAT!!
トコ TOKO
I WAS JUST...IT'S WEIRD TO SEE HER IN A GETUP LIKE THAT...
トコ TOKO (TROT)

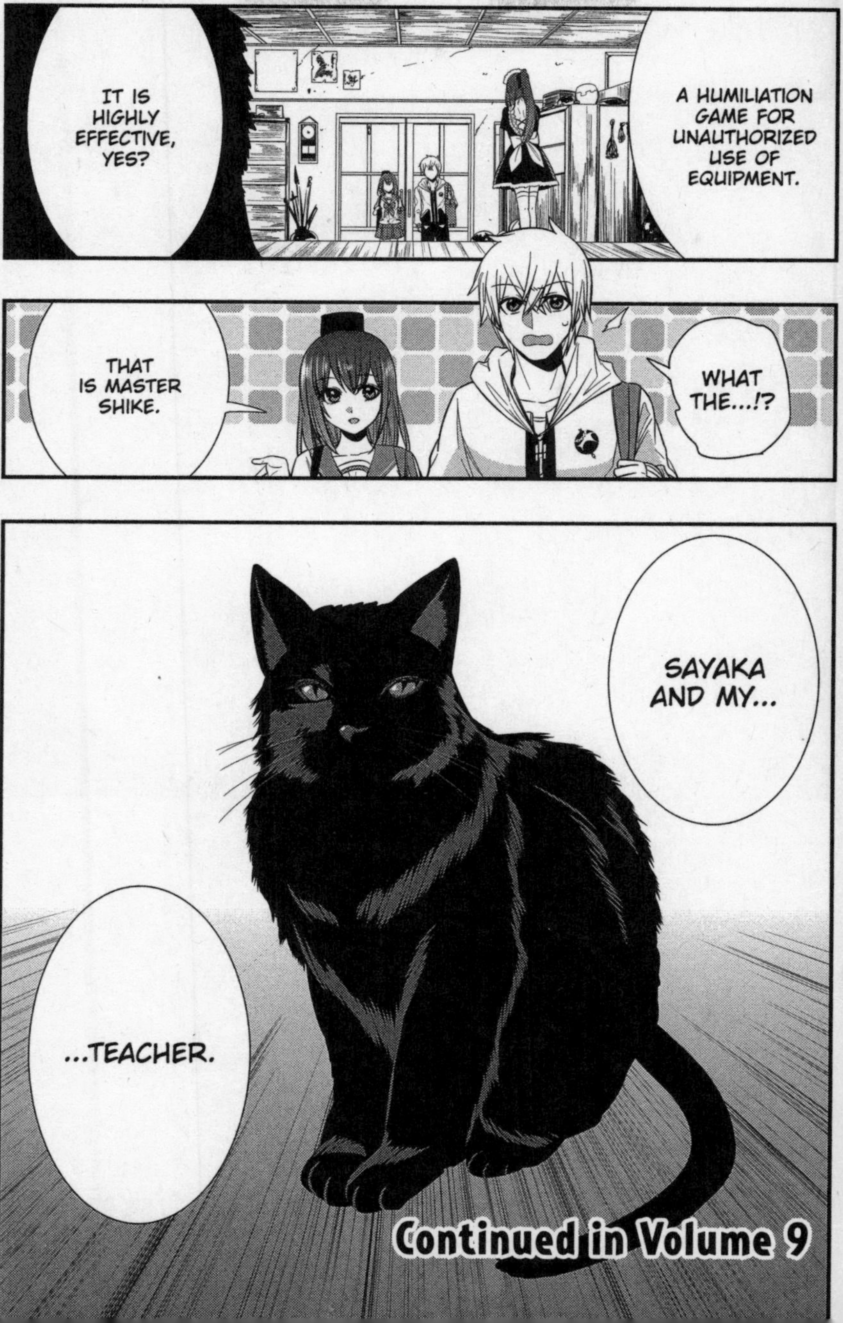
A HUMILIATION GAME FOR UNAUTHORIZED USE OF EQUIPMENT.
IT IS HIGHLY EFFECTIVE, YES?
WHAT THE...!?
THAT IS MASTER SHIKE.
SAYAKA AND MY...
...TEACHER.
Continued in Volume 9

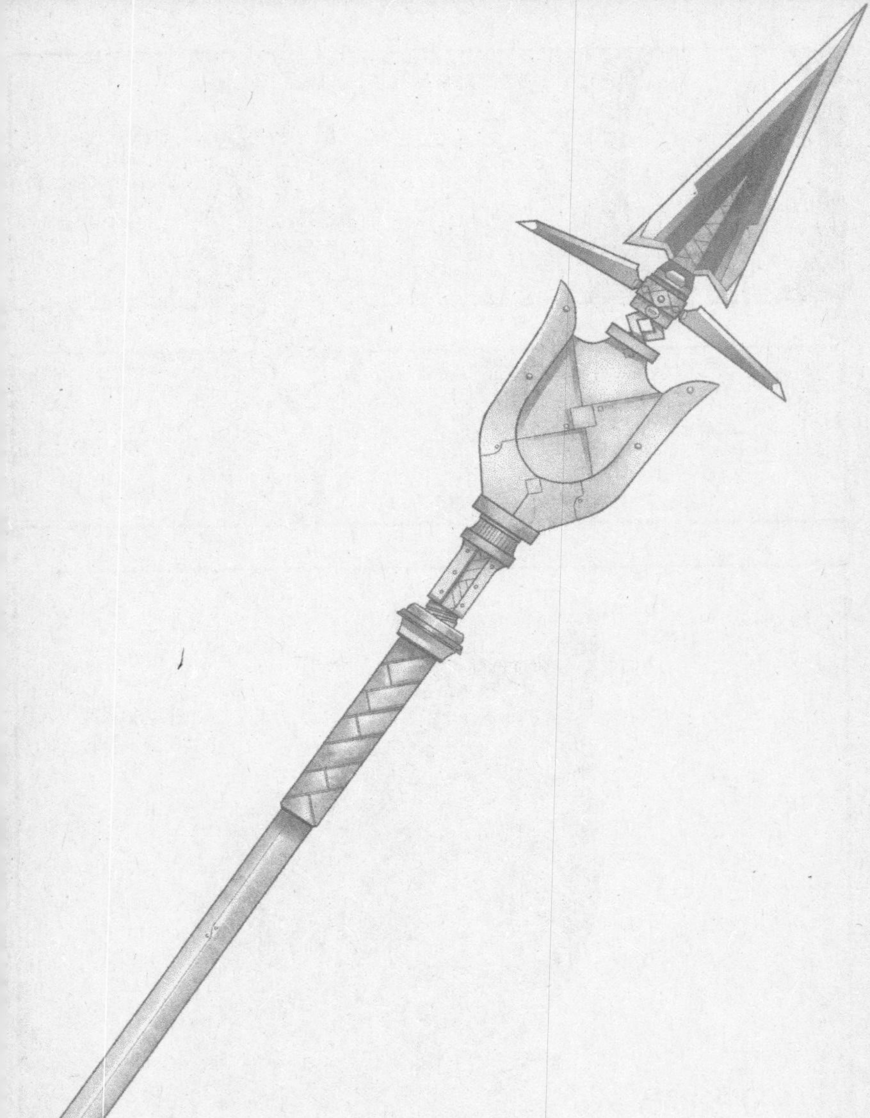

STRIKE THE BLOOD

The Fourth Primogenitor is immortal and indestructible. Rejecting his vampiric brethren, he does not desire domination, but only the service of the twelve Beast Vassals that are disaster incarnate, the sipping of blood, carnage, and destruction. The vampire is said to be ruthless and heartless, completely beyond the doctrines of the world, a monster who has laid waste to innumerable cities in the past.